ROUTLEDGE HANDBOOK OF PRIVATE SECURITY STUDIES

This Handbook offers a comprehensive overview of current research on private security and military companies, comprising essays by leading scholars from around the world.

The increasing privatization of security across the globe has been the subject of much debate and controversy, inciting fears of private warfare and even the collapse of the state. This volume provides the first comprehensive overview of the range of issues raised by contemporary security privatization, offering both a survey of the numerous roles performed by private actors and an analysis of their implications and effects. Ranging from the mundane to the spectacular, from secretive intelligence gathering and neighbourhood surveillance to piracy control and warfare, this Handbook shows how private actors are involved in both domestic and international security provision and governance. It places this involvement in historical perspective, and demonstrates how the impact of security privatization goes well beyond the security field to influence diverse social, economic and political relationships and institutions. Finally, this volume analyses the evolving regulation of the global private security sector. Seeking to overcome the disciplinary boundaries that have plagued the study of private security, the Handbook promotes an interdisciplinary approach and contains contributions from a range of disciplines, including international relations, politics, criminology, law, sociology, geography and anthropology.

This book will be of much interest to students of private security companies, global governance, military studies, security studies and IR in general.

Rita Abrahamsen is Professor in the Graduate School of Public and International Affairs at the University of Ottawa. She is author (with M. C. Williams) of *Security Beyond the State: Private Security in International Politics* (2011) and *Disciplining Democracy: Development Discourse and the Good Governance Agenda in Africa* (2000).

Anna Leander is Professor (MSO) at the Copenhagen Business School and Professor at the Institute of International Relations at PUC, Rio de Janeiro. She is editor of *Commercialising Security in Europe* (Routledge 2013), *Business and Global Governance* (Routledge 2010), and *Constructivism and International Relations* (Routledge 2006).

ROUTLEDGE HANDBOOK OF PRIVATE SECURITY STUDIES

Edited by Rita Abrahamsen and Anna Leander

LONDON AND NEW YORK

First published 2016
by Routledge
2 Park Square, Milton Park, Abingdon, Oxon OX14 4RN

and by Routledge
711 Third Avenue, New York, NY 10017

First issued in paperback 2017

Routledge is an imprint of the Taylor & Francis Group, an informa business

British Library Cataloguing-in-Publication Data
A catalogue record for this book is available from the British Library

Library of Congress Cataloging-in-Publication Data
Routledge handbook of private security studies / edited by Rita Abrahamsen and Anna Leander.
pages cm
Includes bibliographical references and index.
1. Private security services. 2. Privatization. 3. Contracting out. I. Abrahamsen, Rita, 1966- editor. II. Leander, Anna, editor.
HV8290.R68 2016
363.28'9—dc23
2015018623

ISBN 13: 978−0−8153−4756−9 (pbk)
ISBN 13: 978−0−415−72935−2 (hbk)

Typeset in Bembo
by FiSH Books Ltd, Enfield

CONTENTS

CONTRIBUTORS

Rita Abrahamsen is Professor in the Graduate School of Public and International Affairs. She is the author (with M. C. Williams) of *Security Beyond the State: Private Security in International Politics* (Cambridge University Press, 2011) and *Disciplining Democracy: Development Discourse and the Good Governance Agenda in Africa* (Zed Books, 2000). Her articles have appeared in leading journals, including *African Affairs, Alternatives, International Political Sociology, Journal of Modern African Studies, Political Studies, Third World Quarterly* and *Review of African Political Economy*. She was joint-editor of *African Affairs*, the highest-ranked journal in African studies, for six years from 2009 to 2014.

Hamilton Bean is Associate Professor in the Department of Communication at the University of Colorado Denver, where he specializes in the study of communication and security. From 2001 to 2005, he sold private information and analytical support services to US and international defence and intelligence agencies. Since 2005, he has been affiliated with the National Consortium for the Study of Terrorism and Responses to Terrorism (START) – a US Department of Homeland Security Center of Excellence based at the University of Maryland. His research has been published in *Homeland Security Affairs, Intelligence and National Security, International Communication Gazette, International Journal of Intelligence and Counter Intelligence, Journal of Homeland Security and Emergency Management, Rhetoric & Public Affairs*, and *Southern Communication Journal*.

Joakim Berndtsson is an Associate Professor at the School of Global Studies, University of Gothenburg. His primary research interest is the privatization of security, but also includes civil–military relations, public opinion of the armed forces in Sweden and the transformation of war. Additionally, he is involved in a research programme on information security, funded by the Swedish Civil Contingencies Agency. Recent work has been published in *Armed Forces and Society, International Journal*, and the *Journal of Ocean Development and International Law*.

Amanda Chisholm is a lecturer in International Relations at Newcastle University. Having recently finished an ethnographic research project on Gurkha security contractors in Afghanistan, she continues to be motivated by the ways in which everyday on-the-ground security practices are shaped and shaping global security markets. Amanda's research, rooted in feminist global political economy and security studies, contributes to the growing field of critical gender studies on private military and security companies (PMSCs). She remains interested by the ways in which race, class and gender intersect and make certain security subjectivities possible while foreclosing others. To this end, Amanda's current and future research plans continue to involve ethnographic methods to examine how PMSCs draw upon racial and gendered norms to naturalize and discipline global South migrant labourers but also how these global South men and women negotiate, challenge and resist these structural gendered and racial norms.

Benjamin de Carvalho is a Senior Research Fellow at the Norwegian Institute of International Affairs (NUPI). He holds his PhD from the University of Cambridge. His research interests lie in historical international relations broadly speaking and the formation of state, nation, and sovereignty during the reformations and the wars of religion more specifically. He has published in *The International History Review, Diplomacy and Statecraft* and *Millennium*. He has been co-editor of the Scandinavian-language journal *Internasjonal Politikk* (2007–11), and was central in establishing the Historical International Relations Section of the International Studies Association (ISA), for which he is currently serving as Program Chair (2015–17). He has also published extensively on UN peacekeeping in Africa. He is currently involved (with Halvard Leira) in a book project about privateering in historical perspective, and is working on a book about the emergence of the nation-state in Tudor England.

Renée de Nevers is an Associate Professor and Vice Chair in the Department of Public Administration and International Affairs at The Maxwell School at Syracuse University. Previously she taught at the University of Oklahoma, and was a Program Officer at the John D. and Catherine T. MacArthur Foundation. She has been a research fellow at the Belfer Center for Science and International Affairs, Stanford University's Center for International Security and Cooperation and the Hoover Institution, and the International Institute for Strategic Studies, and was a Fulbright Scholar in Russia in 2011. She received her PhD from Columbia University. Her current research focuses on the regulation and accountability of private military and security companies, and great power efforts to protect or manipulate sovereignty when confronted by new security challenges. She is the author of *Comrades No More: The Seeds of Change in Eastern Europe*, the co-author of *Combating Terrorism: Strategies and Approaches*, and numerous journal articles and book chapters.

Rebecca DeWinter-Schmitt is an expert in business and human rights, in particular pertaining to the private military and security industry. In various capacities, Rebecca has been involved in efforts to develop standards for private security providers. She is Co-Director of the Human Rights in Business Program housed at American University Washington College of Law's Center for Human Rights & Humanitarian Law. Rebecca is also Senior Managing Director at Human Analytics, a DC-based risk management consultancy specializing in helping public and private organizations address human rights risks associated with operating in complex environments. She serves on Amnesty International USA's (AIUSA) Business and Human Rights Group. Until 2012, Rebecca was an Assistant Professor at American University's School of International Service's Peace and Conflict Resolution Program. From 1998-2002, she was a staff member of AIUSA, first in its National Field Program and then as Program Associate to the Just Earth! Program on Human Rights and the Environment. Rebecca received her PhD from American University's School of International Service, her master's degree from the University of Marburg, Germany, and her undergraduate degree from Dickinson College, Carlisle, PA.

Roxanne Lynn Doty is Associate Professor in the School of Politics and Global Studies at Arizona State University. Her most recent book, *The Law into Their Own Hands: Immigration and the Politics of Exceptionalism*, was published by the University of Arizona Press in 2009 and awarded the Silver Book Award in 2010 by the Association of Borderland Studies. She is the author of *Anti-Immigrantism in Western Democracies: Statecraft, Desire, and the Politics of Exclusion* (Routledge, 2003) and *Imperial Encounters: The Politics of Representation in North-South Relations* (University of Minnesota Press, 1996). She has published in *International Studies Quarterly*, *Millennium*, *European Journal of International Relations*, *Review of International Studies*, *Alternatives*, and *International Political Sociology*. Doty teaches courses on ethics and human rights in global politics, global inequality, and critical international relations theory. She serves on the editorial boards of *International Political Sociology* and *Environment and Planning D: Society and Space* and the *Journal of Narrative Politics*.

Myriam Dunn Cavelty is a senior lecturer and Deputy Head of Research and Teaching at the Center for Security Studies (CSS), ETH Zurich. Her research focuses on the politics of risk and uncertainty in security politics and changing conceptions of (inter-)national security due to cyber issues (cyber-security, cyber-war, critical infrastructure protection) in specific. In addition to her teaching, research and publishing activities, she advises governments, international institutions and companies in the areas of cyber security, cyber warfare, critical infrastructure protection, risk analysis and strategic foresight.

Maya Eichler is Canada Research Chair in Social Innovation and Community Engagement and assistant professor in the Department of Political and Canadian Studies and the Department of Women's Studies at Mount Saint Vincent University (Halifax). Her research interests lie in feminist international relations theory, gender and the armed forces, the privatization of military security, and post-Soviet politics. She has published the book *Militarizing Men: Gender, Conscription, and War in Post-Soviet Russia* with Stanford University Press (2012) and recent articles in *Critical Studies on Security*, *Citizenship Studies*, and the *International Journal*. Her edited volume *Gender and Private Security in Global Politics* was published by Oxford University Press in 2015. Her current research focuses on the politics of veterans and the transition from military to civilian life in Canada. She serves as an Associate Editor for the *International Feminist Journal of Politics*.

Mark Erbel is a Senior Lecturer in Defence and International Affairs at the Royal Military Academy Sandhurst where he teaches Officer Cadets, Late Entry Officers, and Senior Captains in international relations. He wrote his doctoral dissertation in War Studies at King's College London on the causes, politics, process, and future of military outsourcing in the USA and the UK. His research interests include the sources and supply of US global power, military-to-military relationships between Western and Middle Eastern states, and the role of non-state actors in foreign, security, and defence policy and decision-making. Dr Erbel's publications have appeared in *The Ashgate Research Companion to Outsourcing Security* (forthcoming), *H-Diplo ISSF Forum* and *Journal of Contemporary European Research*.

Thomas Gammeltoft-Hansen is Research Director at the Danish Institute for Human Rights and Executive Chairman of the Association of Human Rights Institutes (AHRI). His research focuses on international refugee law, human rights, and the relationship between international law and politics. His books include *Access to Asylum: International Refugee Law and the Globalisation of Migration Control* (Cambridge University Press, 2011), which received the 2013

KG Idman Award for best publication in international law; *Protecting the Rights of Others* (DJØF, 2013); *The Migration Industry: The Commercialisation of International Migration* (Routledge, 2013); and *Sovereignty Games: Instrumentalizing State Sovereignty in Europe and Beyond* (Palgrave, 2008). In addition to his academic work, Thomas Gammeltoft-Hansen serves as member of the Danish Refugee Appeals Board.

Kevin D. Haggerty is a Killam Research Laureate and Editor of the Canadian Journal of Sociology. He is Professor of sociology and criminology at the University of Alberta and a member of the executive team for the New Transparency Major Collaborative Research Initiative. His work is in the area of surveillance, governance, policing and risk. He and his colleagues have just published the book *Transparent Lives: Surveillance in Canada* and he is the author or editor of an additional 8 books. He and his co-author (Aaron Doyle) have recently published the book *57 Ways to Screw Up in Graduate School* (University of Chicago Press).

Shannon Wheatley Hartman is a fellow of the Interactivity Foundation and fellow-in-residence of the Staley School of Leadership Studies at Kansas State University. Her work promotes exploratory, democratic discussion in and between communities on issues that press the global agenda. Her published research focuses on critical security studies, deliberative democracy, participatory action research, critical cosmopolitanism, and postcolonial studies.

Anton Katz, a member of the bars in Cape Town and New York, studied international law at the University of Cape Town (B.Sc and LLB degrees) and Columbia School of Law (LLM). His practice as a senior counsel (sylk) in Cape Town involves public law and human rights issues, principally concerning international law and constitutional law. He frequently appears in the Constitutional Court of South Africa, and has argued in the highest courts in Namibia, Botswana and Swaziland, the African Commission on Human and Peoples Rights in Banjul, the Gambia and the UN Human Rights Committee. He is currently a member (Chair Rapporteur, 2013) of the United Nations Working Group on the use of mercenaries as a means of violating human rights. He advises and represents clients on complex public law issues. His clients include international organizations, States, different spheres of government, non-governmental organizations and individuals. He has worked as a consultant to the UN Office on Drugs and Crime concerning the implementation of extradition and mutual legal assistance and the African Union, advising on the implementation of the OAU Convention on the Prevention and Combating of Terrorism. Anton Katz occasionally presides as a High Court judge in Cape Town.

Michael Kempa is a social scientist (PhD Law, Australian National University) with the spirit of an investigative journalist. He is Associate Professor in the Department of Criminology, University of Ottawa. His research draws on political science, international relations, and sociological theory to address the ways in which states and non-state organizations variously conceive of and attempt to institutionalize 'police power' in such domains as the economy, new forms of urban communal space, and international security. Trained in media through a Munk Fellowship in Global Journalism, University of Toronto, Dr Kempa tries to take the results of his research to the broadest possible audience. He contributes written, spoken and audiovisual materials to major news outlets (the Walrus Magazine, Canadian Broadcasting Corporation, National Post, and Global and Mail), as well as top-ranked social science journals, including the *British Journal of Criminology, Theoretical Criminology*, the *Akron Law Review*, and the *American Annals of Political and Social Science*. His first scholarly book, co-authored with Clifford Shearing and Julie Berg, and titled *Policing: Conceptualisations and Practices of Security*, is forthcoming with Routledge.

Christopher Kinsey is a Reader in Business and International Security with King's College London, Defence Studies Department at the Joint Services Command and Staff College, where he teaches military officers from around the world. His research examines the role of the market in conflict. Dr Kinsey has published books, book chapters and articles in leading academic journals on the subject. He has also presented papers to the UN Working Group on Mercenaries, NATO and the EU Sub-Committee on Human Rights. Dr Kinsey's present work looks at outsourcing of diplomatic security, regulation of private military and security companies, the impact of contracted logistical support to military expeditionary operations, and mercenary operations in Africa during the Cold War. His books include *Corporate Soldiers and International Security* (Routledge, 2006); *Private Contractors and the Reconstruction of Iraq: Transforming Military Logistics* (Routledge, 2009), and the edited volume, *Contractors and War: The Transformation of United States' Military and Stabilization Operations* (Stanford University Press, 2012).

Elke Krahmann is Professor of Security Studies at Brunel University London. She holds a PhD from the London School of Economics. Following a Post-doctoral Fellowship at Harvard University, she worked at the University of Bristol before moving to London. At the centre of her research is the theoretical and empirical analysis of new actors and new threats in contemporary security governance, including publications such as *States, Citizens and the Privatization of Security* (Cambridge University Press, 2010 – winner of the Ernst-Otto Czempiel award), *New Threats and New Actors in International Security* (Palgrave, 2005), and numerous articles in journals such as *European Journal of International Relations, Security Dialogue, Review of International Studies, Global Governance* and *International Studies Review*. She has been awarded major research grants from the Economic and Social Research Council (ESRC), the United States Institute of Peace and the Humboldt Foundation, and holds advisory board positions at the Institute for Peace Research and Security Policy Hamburg as well as the Development and Peace Foundation. Currently, she leads an international ESRC research project entitled Markets in the Making of Multilateral Military Interventions: International Organizations and Private Military and Security Companies.

Anna Leander is Professor (MSO) at the Copenhagen Business School and Professor at the Institute of International Relations (PUC, Rio de Janeiro). Her research focuses on the politics of security knowledge. She is particularly interested in commercial security knowledge. She has explored how commercial knowledge forms are re-produced and enacted through for example organizational practices, risk models, the marketing of commercial security, legal/regulatory arrangements, or the handling of big data and cyber security. She is currently engaged in four collaborative projects where her focus is on the role of commercial security knowledge. She has recently published articles in *International Political Sociology*, the *Leiden Journal of International Law*, the *Review of International Studies* and *Security Dialogue*, she has edited the volumes *Commercialising Security in Europe* (Routledge 2013) and *Business and Global Governance* (Routledge 2010) and she has also published numerous book chapters. For more information and a list of publications (see www.cbs.dk/en/staff/alempp).

Halvard Leira holds a PhD and a Cand. Polit. (MA) in Political Science from the University of Oslo, and an MSc (distinction) in International Relations from the London School of

Economics and Political Science (LSE). He is Senior Researcher at the Norwegian Institute of International Affairs (NUPI), where he leads the research group on diplomacy and foreign policy. Leira has published extensively in English and Norwegian on historical international relations, international political thought, historiography, foreign policy and diplomacy. His work has appeared in *Review of International Studies*, *Millennium*, *Leiden Journal of International Law*, *International Studies Perspectives*, *The Hague Journal of Diplomacy*, *Global Society* and *Cooperation and Conflict*. Leira was co-editor of the Scandinavian-language journal *Internasjonal Politikk* for five years (2007–11, 2013) and co-editor of the *Sage Library of International Relations sets International Diplomacy* (2013) and *Historical International Relations* (2015). He is currently section chair of the Historical International Relations Section of the International Studies Association.

Carolin Liss is a Research Fellow at the Peace Research Institute Frankfurt (PRIF), Germany. She holds a PhD from Murdoch University, Australia and an MA (Magister) degree in Politics and History from the University of Hannover, Germany. Before joining PRIF, Carolin worked at Griffith University, Australia. She is the author of articles on piracy, maritime security and the privatization of security and the book *Oceans of Crime, Maritime Piracy and Transnational Security in Southeast Asia and Bangladesh* (2011).

Margaret Maffai is the author of a number of articles on the subject of private military and security companies, including a model law for the regulation of PMSCs, co-authored with José Luis Gómez del Prado, former Chair-Rapporteur of the United Nations Working Group on the use of mercenaries. She has served as a consultant for the UN Working Group and the Office of the High Commissioner for Human Rights. She received her Bachelor of Arts degree at the University of Oregon and her law degree at the University of Wisconsin-Madison, and is admitted to practice law in Wisconsin and Oregon. She currently works as an attorney, consultant, and writer in Oregon in the United States.

Sean McFate is an Associate Professor at the National Defence University and an Adjunct Professor at Georgetown University's School of Foreign Service, both at Washington, DC. He is also a Senior Fellow at the Atlantic Council and a social scientist at the RAND Corporation. Prior to academia, McFate was an officer and paratrooper in the US Army, an advisor to Amnesty International on SSR issues, and manager for DynCorp International, a company that provides international security services, where he designed and implemented SSR programmes in Africa. He has written extensively on SSR and privatization, including his book *The Modern Mercenary: Private Armies and What They Mean for World Order* (Oxford University Press, 2015). McFate holds a BA from Brown University, an MPP from the Harvard Kennedy School of Government, and a PhD in International Relations from LSE.

Sarah Percy is Professor of International Relations at the University of Western Australia. Previously she was University Lecturer in International Relations and a Fellow of Merton College, Oxford. She has written extensively about mercenaries and the privatization of force. Her book *Mercenaries: The History of a Norm in International Relations* was published by Oxford University Press in 2007. She has further research interests in the areas of piracy and maritime security.

Andrew Phillips is an Associate Professor in International Relations and Strategy, and an Australian Research Council Discovery Early Career Research Award Fellow, in the School of Political Science and International Studies at the University of Queensland. His research focuses on the global state system's evolution from 1500 to the present, and on contemporary security challenges in East and South Asia, with a particular focus on Great Power rivalry and counter-terrorism. He is the author (with J.C. Sharman) of *International Order in Diversity: War, Trade and Rule in the Indian Ocean* (Cambridge University Press, 2015) and *War, Religion and Empire: The Transformation of International Orders* (Cambridge University Press, 2011, winner of the 2012 Crisp Prize from the Australian Political Science Association). He also has articles published or forthcoming in *European Journal of International Relations, International Studies Quarterly, Millennium, Review of International Studies, Pacific Review, Survival, Australian Journal of International Affairs, National Identities,* and *Security Challenges.* Prior to his post-graduate studies, Andrew worked for the Australian Government in the Department of Prime Minister and Cabinet.

Ajay Sandhu is a doctoral candidate in the sociology department at the University of Alberta and the primary instructor for courses discussing surveillance. His work focuses on the areas of surveillance, policing, and racial identity. His theoretical interests surround identity, self-presentation and the experience of surveillance. He has co-published (with Kevin Haggerty) an article that raises questions about policing's growing image management crises. His current ethnographic research examines how police officers experience camera surveillance in order to assess arguments about how cameras can be used to discipline police officers.

Clifford Shearing is a member of the Griffith Criminology Institute at Griffith University in Queensland, Australia. He also holds appointments in the Faculty of Law, University of Cape Town and the School of Criminology, University of Montreal. He was at the Centre of Criminology at the University of Toronto from the mid-1960s to early 2001, when he moved to the Australian National University as a foundational member of RegNet. He held the Chair of Criminology and the National Research Chair in Security and Justice at the University of Cape Town, where he directed its Centre of Criminology from 2006 to 2014. His research focuses on developments in the governance of security, most recently environmental security. In addition to his academic outputs, Clifford has made policy contributions to reshaping policing and security in Canada, Jamaica, Northern Ireland and South Africa.

Mirko Sossai is Assistant Professor of International Law at the Department of Law, University 'Roma Tre', Italy. Previously, he was research fellow at the LUISS Guido Carli University in Rome. He holds a PhD in international law from the University of Sienna (2005) and a degree cum laude from the University of Padua (2001). He published a monograph in Italian on the prevention of terrorism in international law, and co-edited (with Christine Bakker) the book *Multilevel Regulation of Military and Security Contractors: The Interplay between International, European, and Domestic Norms* (Hart, 2012).

Christopher Spearin is an Associate Professor in the Royal Military College of Canada's Department of Defence Studies located at the Canadian Forces College in Toronto. Dr Spearin's research concerns change in militaries, global security governance, non-state actors and conflict, mercenaries, the privatization of security, piracy, and Canadian foreign and defence policy. His work has been published in a number of edited books and in a variety of forums, including *Canadian Foreign Policy, Canadian Military Journal, Civil Wars, Contemporary Security Policy, Human Security Bulletin, International Peacekeeping, International Journal, International Politics, Journal of Conflict Studies, Journal of International Criminal Justice, Naval War College Review, Oxford Analytica, Parameters, Security Dialogue, Small Wars and Insurgencies* and *World Defence Systems.* He is the yearly contributor on Canadian foreign and defence policy in the longstanding *Canadian Annual Review of Politics and Public Affairs.*

Philip Stenning is a member of the Griffith Criminology Institute at Griffith University in Queensland, Australia. Prior to that he spent five years as Professor of Criminology at Keele University in the UK. He was Professor and Director of the Institute of Criminology at Victoria University of Wellington, New Zealand from 2003 to 2005. He was at the Centre of Criminology at the University of Toronto, Canada, from 1968 to 2002, progressing from Research Assistant to Associate Professor. In addition to his research on public and private policing during these years, Philip has more recently undertaken research on relationships between police and prosecutors and their governments, and on Aboriginal justice and policing issues. He has served as a consultant and adviser to a wide range of government departments and commissions of inquiry in a range of countries including Canada, New Zealand, Australia, South Africa, Venezuela and Brazil, as well as to the Council of Europe and the United Nations.

Maria Stern is Professor at the School of Global Studies, University of Gothenburg and associate editor at Security Dialogue. Her research interests span (feminist) critical security studies, feminist theory, post-colonial theory, international political sociology and research methodology. Her recent books include *Sexual Violence as a Weapon of War? Perceptions, Prescriptions, Problems in the Congo and Beyond* (co-authored with Maria Eriksson Baaz, Zed Books, 2013) and *Studying the Agency of Being Governed* (co-edited with Stina Hansson and Sofie Hellberg, Routledge, 2014).

Leila Stockmarr is a PhD fellow with the Department of Globalisation and Society at the University of Roskilde (RUC), Denmark. Recently she has been affiliated as a guest researcher with London School of Oriental and African Studies (SOAS). Her specialization is in security economy, critical security studies and Middle East politics. Stockmarr is especially interested in the role of security economies and arms production in the context of the Israel-Palestine conflict and the broader Middle Eastern region. Her work examines the relationship between high-tech economies and the production of security technologies and the broader role of security innovation in war and militarized economies. Her publications have examined the links between Israel's practices of war and control and the role of Israel's security industry in the global security economy.

Vron Ware is a Professor in sociology and gender studies at Kingston University London. She has published widely on issues of racism, feminism, national identity, Britishness and colonial history. Her study of Commonwealth soldiers in the contemporary British Army (*Military Migrants: Fighting for YOUR Country*) was first published by Palgrave Macmillan in 2012, and reissued in 2014.

Michael C. Williams is Professor in the Graduate School of Public and International Affairs at the University of Ottawa. His research interests are in international relations theory, security studies, and political thought. His most recent book (with Rita Abrahamsen) is *Security Beyond the State: Private Security in International Politics* (Cambridge University Press, 2011). His previous publications include *The Realist Tradition and the Limits of International Relations* (Cambridge University Press, 2005) and *Culture and Security: Symbolic Power and the Politics of International Security* (Routledge, 2007). He is the editor of several books, including most recently, *Realism Reconsidered: The Legacy of Hans J. Morgenthau in International Relations* (Oxford University Press, 2007). His articles have appeared in journals including the *European Journal of International Relations, International Organization, International Political Sociology, International Studies Quarterly, Millennium* and the *Review of International Studies*.

ACKNOWLEDGEMENTS

A big thank you is due to all our contributors for delivering their chapters on time and for their willingness to engage in multiple rounds of revisions. We would also like to thank Adam Sandor and Bo Christiansen for their timely and professional assistance with editing the Handbook. Finally, we are grateful to Andrew Humphrys and Hannah Ferguson at Routledge for their support, advice and guidance.

INTRODUCTION

Rita Abrahamsen and Anna Leander

The market for force has a long history and private security actors have throughout time shaped warfare, policing and state formation in various and important ways. In the late Middle Ages and the early modern period, for example, the *condotta* or contract system allowed business guilds, nobles and cities to hire private soldiers, while the Chartered Companies of the seventeenth and eighteenth centuries often wielded extensive military capacities and employed their own police. Private security companies like Wells Fargo, Pinkerton and ADT dates back to the 1850s' United States, and today it is easily forgotten that the first recognizable public police was founded in Britain as late as 1829. This long history aside, the contemporary market for force is of a different magnitude and arguably also of a different kind. Today, private security services are ubiquitous and the marketplace is truly global: private security companies guard shopping malls, residencies and public streets. They run prisons, detention centres, and even police receptions. They train armed forces and police, and perform intelligence assessments and risk analyses. They are engaged in cyber security, and develop, support and operate complex weapon systems. They escort convoys and ships, and provide personal security for diplomats, CEOs, NGO workers and journalists. The list could go on.

The traditional Weberian definition of the state as linked to the 'monopoly of the legitimate use of force' is thus increasingly out of sync with reality. Even as states continue to insist that they remain in charge of security and that some security functions are exclusive to the state and will not be outsourced, private security has become an intrinsic aspect of modern life. States may still have the ultimate say on what uses of force are legitimate and how such uses should be organized, but they increasingly exercise this ability by outsourcing and by collaborating with commercial companies. Therefore, even if private security occasionally causes great controversy and scandal, as when Blackwater shot and killed civilians in Iraq or when G4S failed to provide sufficient guards for the London Olympics, the underlying logics and benefits of privatization are not substantively questioned or altered. Instead, continual privatization seems to be hardwired into contemporary patterns and structures of governance.

This expansion of private security has been the focus of much debate, but spanning disciplines and often tackling very different concerns these discussions have often taken place in isolation from each other. This Handbook provides the first comprehensive overview of the range of issues raised by contemporary security privatization, offering both a survey of the numerous roles performed by private actors and an analysis of their implications and effects.

Seeking to overcome the disciplinary boundaries that have plagued the study of security privatization, the Handbook includes contributions from international relations (IR), politics, criminology, law, sociology, geography and anthropology. We thus seek to map the contours of what can be termed an emerging field of private security studies (PSS), although rather than defining the boundaries of this field we underscore its open and inter-disciplinary nature. We suggest that heterogeneous, and at times heterodox, approaches are required to capture the multiple dimensions and dynamics of security privatization. In order to make this case, we start with a review of explanations for the contemporary expansion of private security, demonstrating the wide range of factors and processes that need to be considered. We then outline the contours of PSS, before ending with a brief overview of the Handbook and its key sections.

The emergence of private security

The story of modern state formation is normally told as the story of the centralization of legitimate force in the hands of the state, leading to the formation of a uniformed police responsible for domestic law and order and a military dedicated to defence against external enemies. Much as this is the case, there is no doubt that the last few decades have seen a return and expansion of the importance of private security actors. There are a number of different, overlapping and sometimes contradictory ways of explaining this development, and these diverse accounts are worth reviewing in order to gain a better understanding of the multifaceted character of contemporary security privatization.

In the discipline of IR, explanations of the rise of private military security in the twentieth century almost inevitably start with the end of the Cold War. The military downsizing that resulted from the end of superpower rivalries is seen to have provided both 'push' and 'pull' factors. On the one hand, demobilized military personnel and decommissioned equipment provided a ready supply of capacity, while on the other, demand increased as rich countries became more reluctant to intervene in unstable parts of the globe and abandoned previous Cold War allies or clients to their own devices. This is the period that saw the rise of companies such as the South African Executive Outcomes and the British company Sandline, both hired by beleaguered governments in the South to fight insurgencies that erupted at the end of bipolarity. The immediate Cold War years also saw a growing market presence of former Soviet and Southern actors such as Ukrainian-run transport and logistics companies, whereas Nepalese Gurkhas, Ugandans and Colombians were among the many nationalities contracted to work in multinational companies.

On its own, this account of changing geopolitics downplays a range of other factors that also encouraged the expansion of the market. One of these is the reorganization of the economy and of production that followed the oil shocks of the 1970s. Often referred to as 'post-Fordism', companies were increasingly organizing their activities through networks rather than conventional markets and hierarchies. Strategic alliances, partnerships, outsourcing and licensing became core aspects of economic life that was increasingly project-focused and intent on reducing margins by facilitating just-in-time production. This also affected the market for force. Already in the early 1980s, the defence industry was pressuring governments to remove barriers to cross-country collaborations, and the industry developed such collaborations to a larger extent than governments expected. From this perspective, governments' politically motivated restrictions on markets and the continued attachment to public production models were hopelessly out of sync with the needs and realities in the industry.

Another key factor, the Revolution in Military Affairs (RMA), gave added force to the arguments in favour of markets. The RMA refers to the integration of innovations in information technology into the defence sector and the effects were revolutionary, as it required a profound transformation of the entire organization of the armed forces and their relationship to private companies and the market. The technologies at the heart of the RMA were often developed by private companies. Moreover, the presence of companies was often needed for maintenance and sometimes even for the operation of technological systems. 'Off-the-shelf' and 'dual-use' technologies gained importance, as did the outsourcing, privatization and 'private-public-partnerships' arrangements through which they were produced. Hence, cyber security, robotics, biometrics and other military-technological innovations have not only reshaped warfare, but also given private actors a far more central and indispensable role at the heart of military organizations. In this sense, the rise of the private military sector is intimately linked to the RMA and the increasing reliance on complex information technologies.

These developments went hand in hand with another set of factors, namely the increasing role of neoliberal forms of governance. Neither the RMA, nor the related reorganization of the relationships between the state and the private sector is conceivable without the growing dominance of neoliberal economic models and the neoliberal emphasis on privatization and outsourcing of previously public goods and services. Governing through markets or quasi-market mechanisms has increasingly become a value in and of itself, and in the same way as social services like health and education have been affected by demands to 'slim down the state', so public security institutions have felt the emphasis on fiscal discipline, value for money, and efficiency. More than simply reorganizing public provision, part and parcel of the neoliberal model is to encourage individuals, companies and public administrations to take responsibility for their own security; decide what is required and provide for it themselves. According to this logic, state planning will always be less desirable than decentralized choices. Increasingly therefore non-state actors find themselves having to decide what kind of security they want and need – and from what kind of provider. The result is the emergence of markets as core to the governance of security. In this market, it is not only the public sector that has become dependent on a rapidly growing private security. It is also private actors who contract private security for their own needs in ways that leave the public out of the equation.

Contemporary society has also been characterized as a 'risk society' (Beck 1992) in which markets and companies have a core role to play. Risk-based thinking entails a shift in the social technologies of security. Rather than being concerned with past offences, criminal justice and the actual 'catching of criminals', the logic of risk is primarily future-oriented. It is about responding to future threats independently of whether these threats are identified on the basis of statistical probabilities, big-data, faith, or imaginary game-based scenarios about the 'unknown unknowns', 'black swans' of security, or catastrophic emergencies. Security becomes first and foremost about resilience in the face of future threats, big or small, and the potentially unlimited scope for devising forms of resilience, combining different forms of risk thinking, in turn pave the way for a constantly expanding security market. Companies take an active role in designing places that foster security, in developing new surveillance technologies, in carrying out risk profiling, in ensuring spatial demarcations and especially in combining a wide range of heterogeneous risk management tools that they can sell to others or implement for themselves. The resulting extensive role for markets is enhanced by the replacement of a national security narrative by a myriad of small, unspectacular, local solutions. Security as risk management is no longer simply about national interests or about questions of justice or social and political reform but about technocratic solutions. The focus on risk is inscribed in and perpetuated through a host of regulatory arrangements that increasingly mix hard and soft, regulation of the national and the international, as well as the public and the private. Various audit requirements, procedures and reporting mechanisms, codes of conduct, benchmarks and best practices work to ensure both that risk is managed in a legitimate and accountable manner and that it is consolidated as a security technology in which private actors have a core role. We have ended up in an 'audit society' marked by the 'risk management of everything', as Michael Power (1999) puts it. Security is no exception.

These interrelated developments have generated a self-sustaining, self-perpetuating commodification of security, where security is a commodity to be bought and sold in a competitive marketplace rather than a public good provided by the state. The global private security market both reflects and reproduces this commodification; a marketplace where companies can offer their services in competition with states. In such a marketplace, the public is increasingly transformed into a consumer looking for the best quality service while the private acquires previously public responsibilities for deciding upon and ensuring security. Both do so by shopping around for the best service. At the level of the individual, consumers become increasingly 'responsibilized' and come to accept that it is both their right and their responsibility actively to engage in their own security provision. If the security provided by states in the Gulf of Aden, Stockholm, Rio de Janeiro, Ottawa or Afghanistan is not good enough, private security companies can be used to enhance it or to replace it. Consumer satisfaction, combined with the emphasis on cost-efficiency and state minimalism, thus provide a powerful dynamic favouring the growth of private security as well as its continual expansion in a global marketplace.

A comprehensive account of the emergence and growth of private security actors thus requires attention to a series of inter-connected transformations, some at the level of state and inter-state relations, some at the level of society and the individual. While these transformations can be observed globally, their impact and specific articulation vary from place to place. Thus, while the growth of private security can be observed in most parts of the world and is related, in one way or another, to the set of explanations outlined above, there are always important local factors and dynamics. In other words, the rise of private security requires attention both to local specificity and its interaction with global dynamics.

The emergence of private security studies

As private security has expanded, so too has the study of security privatization. Publications began to appear in the mid-1990s, but the study of private security really took off in the early 2000s and is showing no sign of slowing. On the contrary, the number of books and articles grows by the day, making the study of private security an unruly, rapidly expanding and vibrant area of research with constantly shifting boundaries. An important change is also underway; whereas to date most investigations and discussions have been confined to their own individual discipline, approaching the topic from a distinct disciplinary perspective and utilizing specific analytical and methodological tools, there is a trend towards research that spans the conventional boundaries between academic disciplines. It might thus be possible to speak of PSS as something more than simply an area of study belonging equally to different disciplines, but instead as an emerging field of study that enlists researchers, approaches, and methodologies from a range of disciplines and backgrounds in an effort to make sense of various aspects of private security. In this sense, PSS is a novelty; still tentatively emerging, expanding and consolidating. We nevertheless suggest that as a label, PSS is instructive in pointing to a common set of concerns and a shared realization that an understanding of the multifaceted phenomena of security privatization requires a willingness to cross disciplinary divides to embrace a range of tools and approaches. As such, PSS does not exist as a unified field of study, with clear boundaries between insiders and outsiders, but is instead defined by its diversity and heterogeneity. The aim of this Handbook is to showcase this creative and open vibrancy, while at the same time pointing to some of the characteristics, contours and shared concerns of PSS.

A notable feature of PSS is its relationship to practice. Even as studies focus on the theoretical implications, or investigate the ethics of security privatization, this is a research area that has evolved in close dialogue with practice and the real-world problematics arising from the increasing role of companies and markets in security provision. In this sense, PSS has largely been 'problem-driven' and practice-oriented, and its origins mirror the way these problems were viewed from within the various academic fields that began analysing the issue. In international politics, for example, the focus was originally on the ways in which the emergence of companies such as Executive Outcomes, KBR or MPRI changed the relations among states and the nature of conflict. In development and area studies the debate was about how processes of political and economic development were changing as a consequence of increasing security privatization. In criminology, early studies documented the re-emergence of private policing and pointed to its relationship to neoliberal restructuring and risk-based thinking. In military sociology, questions were raised about how marketization shifted the organization, ethics and identities of soldiers. In law, scholars focused on how law ensured (or could be reformed to ensure) adequate accountability and regulation of the flourishing markets. In geography, scholars took an interest in how the private security markets redesigned space. Scholars of ethics and normative theory raised questions about the underlying philosophical assumptions on which the widespread embrace of markets was based, whereas economists investigated its efficiency in different contexts. Gender studies scholars wondered about its impact on the reproduction of gendered roles across contexts, and anthropologists were keen to know how cultures were being redefined by commercialization. Media studies analysed the ways in which commercial security was mediated and transforming both media and its links to society in the process. Much as this list of disciplinary concerns could be expanded, it serves to illustrate that as private security has become ubiquitous, its study has become integrated into a wide range of academic fields – as is clearly evident from this Handbook.

The orientation towards practice is also reflected in the prominent contributions that para-academic research has made to PSS. Think tanks, activist organizations and journalists have played a key role in putting private security on the agenda, in collecting information about it and in pushing it into different academic disciplines. For example, in the early 1990 journalists reporting on international conflict, prisons, ministries of defence, extractive industries or the development of new surveillance technologies were increasingly finding themselves reporting on the activities of companies and markets. The *Washington Post*'s 'Top Secret America' (2010) database that collected information about the 'national security enterprise' of intelligence contracting thus belongs to a venerable tradition of work designed to document and raise questions about private security. Second, NGOs such as Human Rights First, International Alert, StateWatch, Amnesty International, DCAF, the International Consortium of Investigative Journalists and War on Want have played a similar role documenting issues, raising questions and pushing them onto the public and hence also the academic agenda. Third, private companies, the armed forces and governments have actively engaged in efforts to research and spread information about the growing role of private security. Sandline, for example, ran one of the first websites collecting information about what was then called private military companies, including academic articles from all disciplines. Industry organizations such as the Association of Private Military Companies (now renamed the International Peace and Stability Operations Association) launched an academically influential e-mail discussion list, as well as a collection of online information. In many countries, the armed forces and governments have been financing and encouraging research, not only in the context of military academies but also through research councils, consultancies and projects undertaken with universities aimed at improving the management of the rapidly expanding markets. Activists, companies, organizations and government agencies have thus played a core role in producing private security knowledge, and by implication, in the development of PSS.

The study of private security has come to inhabit a range of academic disciplines and involve a range of heterogeneous forms of knowledge production, both inside and outside the academe. In this sense, the emerging field of PSS shares a core characteristic of much contemporary knowledge production: it is inherently 'transgressive'. It transgresses not only the boundaries of disciplines and topics, but also the frontier separating scientific and practical knowledge. This fundamental feature of PSS as a field of study has two implications for this volume and its organization. First and foremost, it means that what we refer to as PSS lacks a simple, unified story of academic origin and therefore also a natural disciplinary home. In this volume we have decided to embrace this fact and treat it as a something valuable to be cherished. We therefore do our best to capture the multiple research agendas that flourish in this field. We wish to encourage a vision of a PSS united by a common focus of study but not by a singular question, a unified approach, a disciplinary perspective or a grand theoretical ambition. The Handbook therefore provides a view of the real-existing diversity of PSS, with the main proviso that this diversity could be even greater. Rather than seeking to draw strict boundaries and to 'discipline' PSS, we hope to provide a sense that diverse engagements are not only welcomed in the present but also to be encouraged in the future. It can also be seen as a sign that the field is maturing and becoming increasingly capable of providing competent expertise.

Second, much as speaking, reading and working across the conventional boundaries between academic disciplines and between theory and practice may sound attractive, it is also demanding. The academic disciplines and non-academic perspectives brought into the debate each have their own vocabularies, priorities, hierarchies, and taken for granted understanding of what is 'relevant' and 'interesting', what everyone should know, which authorities should be listened to, and how the validity of any argument made in relation to security privatization should be assessed. They have different analytical strategies and ways of evaluating arguments and claims. Therefore what works and counts as legitimate and interesting in one context may be dismissed as irrelevant, bogus, and missing the core debate and authorities in another. If the transgression of boundaries in PSS is to result in a conversation rather than in cacophony of diverse voices, or worse mutual condescending condemnations, it requires more than simply granting space to multiple, heterogeneous expressions. It requires that this space be used with the intention to communicate in spite of the inherent obstacles to communication. This has implications for how this volume should be read. It presupposes that readers engage the chapters with an open and interested mind; with the intention of learning from them. It has also had a bearing on the way the chapters have been written. The Handbook is intended to 'bring together' knowledge in a way that makes debate and dialogue possible, and hence facilitate the consolidation of the field of PSS as an area of debate. We of course hope that our picture of PSS will entice others to engage the discussion to take the field further and develop it in new and exciting directions.

Outline of the Handbook

As discussed above, PSS is a vibrant and expanding field, spanning disciplines, themes and continents. Organizing and structuring such diversity is almost inevitably arbitrary and also fraught with pitfalls. We have opted for an open and flexible organization of the Handbook, so as to allow for the inclusion of multiple perspectives and interpretations. The book starts with a historical section (Part I), designed both to show the shifting historical relations between the public and the private and historical continuities of contemporary security privatization. This part analyses the role of private force in European state building and in the development of the international system of states. It shows how what we today call the public police originated from within the private sector, and also how private companies and private force were central to European imperial expansion. Rich in historical depth and breadth, the section grounds the Handbook in an understanding that private force stands in an evolving and dynamics relationship to the public.

Part II turns to the roles and functions performed by contemporary security companies, and illustrates the extent to which private security around the globe is embedded in almost every aspect of modern life. Ranging from the mundane to the spectacular, from secretive intelligence gathering and surveillance to piracy control and warfare, this section shows how private actors play key roles in security provision and governance. It also documents the manner in which the private has become embedded in the public, and how multiple forms of cooperation and competition between the public and the private now characterize the provision of security in diverse fields, ranging from security sector reform to the surveillance of neighbourhoods.

This broad involvement of private actors has not been without controversy, and debates regarding the acceptability, desirability and efficacy of private actors abound in both academic and policy circles. Part III of the Handbook is dedicated to some of these debates, and seeks to capture the extent to which the impact of security privatization goes well beyond the security field to influence diverse social, economic and political relationships. It thus shows how security privatization can be seen to reconfigure the public and private into new global security assemblages, and how the expansion of private security poses new challenges for democracy. It also draws attention to the gender and race implications of security privatization, as well as to the growing role of private security actors in punishment and migration control.

The final section of the Handbook (Part IV) discusses the crucial issue of regulation, focusing on both soft and hard law. This is an area of rapid and continual change, and the section discusses the evolution of the norm against mercenaries as well as recent efforts to develop various non-binding codes of conduct. It also analyses the shortcoming of the existing international legal framework, and the extent to which procurement policies can act as an effective form of regulation.

Taken together, the 26 chapters of the Handbook offer a rich and multi-faceted perspective on contemporary private security, its roles and attending controversies. They do not add up to the final word on security privatization, nor do they all sing to the same tune. Instead, the Handbook seeks to offer a comprehensive, inclusive and open platform whence future conversations about PSS can continue and expand.

Bibliography

Beck, U. (1992) *Risk Society: Towards a New Modernity*, London: Sage.
Power, M. (1999) *The Audit Society. Rituals of Verification*, Oxford: Oxford University Press.

PART I

Historical perspectives on private security

1

PRIVATE FORCE AND THE MAKING OF STATES, *c.* 1100–1500

Benjamin de Carvalho

Understanding the role of private force in the making of states poses quite a conundrum. The current use of the term 'private force' is irremediably associated with the state, and when we refer to private force, we do not mean the use of force in the private sphere – private violence, so to speak, as opposed to violence in public display. Instead the term describes force wielded by private actors as non-state actors. The concept of private force is therefore unthinkable without the concept of the state, as it is precisely the emergence of the state that is the condition of possibility of private force. To be sure, we may find examples of force used by 'non-rulers' before the emergence of the state. Yet, that force is not similar to private force after the emergence of states as autonomous moral universes covering the entirety of the globe. In this world, force wielded by private actors is by definition non-state, and if not condoned by it, a *de facto* and *de jure* challenge to the authority of the state.

This chapter shows how the distinction between the public and the private emerges with respect to the use of force in conjunction with the long rise of the state in Europe. As Patricia Owens has convincingly argued, there is no a priori public or private violence, as violence 'is made public or private through political struggle and definition' (Owens 2010: 32). Through a conceptual historical account of the organization of warfare through the five centuries of consolidation and centralization of power which crystallized in the sovereign state, I show that '[s]ome forms of violence are *made* public and others are *made* private through historically varying ways of organizing and justifying force' (ibid.: 32). Echoing Peter W. Singer (2008), Owens draws attention to the fact that the distinction between private and public violence has never been 'solidly fixed' (Owens 2010: 18). In drawing a historical conceptual analysis of the changing organization of military power in the making of states, I show why we need to take an empirical rather than an ideological approach to the distinction between different types of force, as only then can we hope to understand why and for what purposed power was organized in specific ways, and the consequences of that organization.

The chapter takes as its starting point the late eleventh century, a period when public authorities had been decimated throughout Christendom and when kings no longer had the aura of public authority, but were (private) contestants for public authority on equal footing with their competitors. Both public and private force was private, so to speak. I proceed in five sections. The first addresses the relationship between war-making and state-making, a relationship which is central to much of the literature on state formation and to our further discussion.

The next three sections address the chronology of changes in the organization of force, and move from warfare as a knightly (largely) private enterprise to the wars of mercenaries, culminating in the early attempts at holding standing permanent armies around the late fifteenth century. The claim is not that this process was linear or inevitable, and, as demonstrated in the last section, the centralization of the legitimate means of warfare in the hands of public authorities did not mean the end of private enterprise in a world of states. Rather, private enterprise continued alongside public force, albeit in a different character.

Force in the making of states

The link between states and war is well established, and there is little doubt that wars have had an important impact on state formation in Europe (see Davis and Pereira 2008; Pereira 2008). Charles Tilly's *Coercion, Capital and European States* (1992), for example, has shown how the requirements of warfare forced states to consolidate their administrative and economic apparatus, and institutionalize the practice of war as an intrinsic part of the state. But the link between violence and the state is not just empirical. Violence is central to the state also at the conceptual level. As Max Weber put it:

> If no social institutions existed which knew the use of violence, then the concept of 'state' would be eliminated ... Force is a means specific to the state. Today the relation between the state and violence is an especially intimate one ... We have to say that a state is a human community that (successfully) claims the monopoly of the legitimate use of physical force within a given territory.
>
> *(Weber 1963: 78)*

This monopoly of legitimate violence in turn rests on a specific distinction between private and public property, a separation that first emerged during the Middle Ages. It is important to keep in mind, though, that although we can trace this distinction back to the Middle Ages, private and public force operate, and have operated, differently at different times and places.

What is central to Weber's ideal type of the state, is that its central characteristic is the legitimate monopoly of the use of force. The key impetus behind this monopolization came during the Middle Ages, which saw an increasing tendency of states to monitor, control, and monopolize the effective means of violence in (what was to become) their territory. Illustrating this process is the fact that nobles lost their right to wage private war (Tilly 1992: 68–9). In fact, as Norbert Elias has noted:

> The society of what we call the modern age is characterized, above all in the West, by a certain degree of monopolization. Free use of military weapons is denied the individual and reserved to a central authority of whatever kind ... The financial means thus flowing into this central authority maintain its monopoly of military force, while this in turns maintains the monopoly of taxation.
>
> *(Elias 1996: 345–6)*

While this is a fairly obvious state of affairs to the contemporary commentator, this was not the case in early medieval Europe. In fact, at the beginning of the twelfth century, the disintegration of the Roman Empire had resulted in a mosaic of fragments counting 'hundreds of principalities, bishoprics, city-states, and other authorities [exercising] overlapping control in the small hinterlands of their capitals' (Tilly 1992: 40). The story of the formation of the modern state is the story of how this process was reverted; how the pieces of the European mosaic increased in size and decreased in number.

By the end of the eleventh century, this transformation was far from completed. Great autonomy was exerted by the feudal lords, and 'each castle in the country had become a center of rule independent of the [ruler's] castle' (Poggi 1978: 26). The kings of twelfth-century Europe were *primus inter pares*; they were the most powerful of the princes, but not strong enough to hold all their rivals in check. In twelfth-century Europe, heavily armoured knights were exercising direct lordship over nucleated peasant villages, and, final authority lay not with the king, but with the feudal lord, duke, count or baron (Stacey 1994: 29; Strayer 1973: 49–50). The inherent trend of feudalism towards fragmentation of power to the advantage of the vassal fief holders had led to the erosion of the landed patrimony of the kings, who by the twelfth century 'had learned to conceive of the territories they ruled as their own [family] patrimonies' (Poggi 1978: 35). In short, the starting point for the political centralization of the state was the private estates of rulers, in fierce competition with feudal rivals.

Thus, in order to maintain their fragile position as primus inter pares, the king engaged in 'private wars' against the other *seigneurs* of the country. The resulting trend towards the creation of a criss-crossing pattern of competing power networks, where rival lords and kings claimed sovereignty over the same territories had created a situation often referred to as 'feudal anarchy' (ibid.: 27, 31), where even the smallest knights 'retained the rights and functions of rule within their estates; here they continued to hold sway like little kings' (Elias 1996: 317). In these early times of state-building, the basis for the king's power, as well as the resources he could draw on in order to fight the neighbouring barons or princes and assert his power, were his private family possessions (ibid.: 281).

I will concentrate on the period between approximately 1100 and 1500, as this period marks the beginning of the era of the supremacy in combat of the mounted knight, while 1477 saw the collapse of the duchy of Burgundy, the last feudal alternative to the state. The end of the fifteenth century also witnessed a change in the political atmosphere in Europe: the economic situation was improving after the end of the Hundred Years War (1337–1453), and the frequency of warfare was declining. In so doing, I will account from how war changed from being a largely private matter to increasingly becoming the sole prerogative of the ruler. By successfully reforming the ways wars were fought, centralizing rulers were able to win the power contest against their feudal rivals, and reform a conduct that counteracted political centralization (see Avant 2000).

Social order and the medieval knight, *c.* 1100–1300

While the early medieval period saw attempts at political centralization frustrated by private war making, it simultaneously marks the beginning of a number of processes that came to curtail the war-making rights of private knights. In fact, the early Middle Ages experienced important changes in the ideas about war. Between the year 1000 and the beginning of the twelfth century, Europe witnessed what amounted to a large-scale 'peace programme': repression of pillage, the birth of chivalry, the formation of the idea of the crusade and modification of the relationship between the powerful and the poor. In large part, the drivers behind these reforms were a ruling class, which now identified more closely with the need for order than their rights to wage war. Ecclesiastical efforts also ran in parallel with this, leading to the emerging chivalric code of conduct. Where knighthood had appeared from the early 1100s as an amalgam of military profession and social rank prescribing the behaviour of its adherents in both peace and war, the bearing of arms was increasingly 'seen as a noble dignity connected with a code of conduct, the violation of which might cost a man his status as a warrior' (Stacey 1994: 29–30).

Moreover, knighthood, with all its prescriptions of conduct, became a way of life for the medieval warriors. War in the Middle Ages was thus waged between members of the same class, who regarded each other as equals. This entitled them to certain privileges, for example the right to be ransomed – and not killed – if captured in war, but also bound them by obligations towards humane conduct towards prisoners of similar social rank. During war, these warriors gained honour and reputation on the battlefields, and during peaceful times tournaments gave them the opportunity to show their prowess in combat. But although the norms and ideals of chivalry emerged in the early Middle Ages, few attempts were made to record them systematically before the end of the thirteenth century. At this time, didactic treatises on warfare, military discipline and the organization of armies began to appear (Contamine 1984: 119). Examples of these are *Enseignements et ordenances pour un seigneur qui a des guerres et grans gouvernements a faire* (1327) by Theodore Paleologus, *L'arbre des batailles* (c. 1387) by Honoré Bovet, *Le livre des fais d'armes et de chevalerie* (1410) by Christine de Pisan and *Le Jouvencel* (c. 1470) by Jean de Bueil. Advocating honourable and virtuous conduct, these treatises also set forth to reform the role of the knight, turning the emphasis away from virtuous conduct in battle per se, to the virtuous qualities of 'public service'. In *Book of Order and Chivalry* (c. 1310) Raymon Lull makes the case that force must be put in public service: 'To a knyght appereyneth that he be lover of the comyn wele. For by the comynalte of the people was the chyvalrye founded and establysshed. And the comyn wele is gretter and more necessary than propre good and specyall' (cited in Vale 1981: 22–3). These treaties, in turn, were closely linked to the emerging state rulers. In fact, many were initiated by the rulers themselves, as their authors were either at the service of the kings, or eager to receive or retain their protection.

In addition an emergent body of military regulations and ordinances sought to regulate the relationship between private force and public service. Based on the treatises, ordinances were sent to the captains of most armies throughout Europe. *Estatuz, ordenances et cusutmes a tenir en l'ost* was issued by Richard II in 1385, and *Statutes and Ordinaunces to be keped in time of Werre* was published by Henry V in 1419; in Italy Orso degli Orsini drew up the *Governo et exercitio de la militia* for Alfonso I the Magnanimous of Aragon in 1447 (Contamine 1984: 119–21), and towards the mid-fifteenth century, the tract on *The Way Soldiers Dress in the Kingdom of France Both on Foot and on Horseback* was issued. During the same period, it also became common to issue a general edict announcing the disciplinary orders to each army at the moment it assembled. In these ways, private force was increasingly tied to public loyalty and institutionalized in uniforms and insignia borne in battle, symbolizing loyalty to the king. By the same token, private force was legitimized through its public utility. As Strayer (1973: 56) put it, 'loyalty to the state became more than a necessity and a convenience; it was now a virtue'.

Institutionalizing these new rules and regulations was not a straightforward process, and attempts at reforming the ideals of chivalry were often met with resistance from a warring class which had the *chevalier errant* (or roving knight), whose vocation was the pursuit of just quarrels, as its ideal. However, this aspect should not be overemphasized, as a large part of it is a fiction cast upon it by later writers. In fact, one should not leave from sight the fact that throughout the medieval period, money was the almost obligatory link between soldiers and authority, and that this is precisely what plunged Europe into a vicious circle of violence. From about 1250 to 1450, private armies of mercenaries, who made a living by plunder when they were not employed, ravaged most of Europe. The Great Companies spread terror in France and Spain, the Free Companies pillaged Italy and the Ecorcheurs ('skinners') ravaged France and the Western part of Germany. As one medieval commentator complained: 'I see all Holy

Christendom so tormented by wars and divisions, robberies and dissensions that one can scarcely name a petty province, be it a duchy or county, which enjoys peace' (Contamine 1984: 90, 123–5).

The wars of the mercenaries, *c.* 1250–1450

The two last centuries of the Middle Ages saw little peace, as the professional soldier of the period was far from responsive to arguments concerned with public duty and common good. No matter if they fought because of feudal duty or wages, ransom and booty provided a major incentive for the medieval knight to wage war. The emphasis on private economic gain in warfare can be traced back to the law of arms, as knightly customs revolved around two fundamental propositions. Firstly, as Maurice Keen underlines, 'soldiering in the age of chivalry was regarded as a Christian profession, not a public service. Though he took up arms in a public quarrel, a soldier still fought as an individual, and rights were acquired by and against him personally, and not against the side for which he fought' (cited in Stacey 1994: 31). Every knight participated in wars with his own horse and equipment at his own risk. Thus, the medieval knight fought on his own, and not as a servant of the state. Secondly, the law of arms was of a contractual character, stipulating that serving in a war gave a right to a share of its profit. This right was legally enforceable and was judged by special courts, such as the Court of Chivalry in England and the Parliament of Paris in France. These profits were gained chiefly through pillaging, plunder and ransom.

The effectiveness and discipline of force depended largely on how well paid the soldiers were. Without reasonable wages, soldiers would use their power in their own private interest, even when under service of the prince. In the treatise on warfare *Le Jouvencel*, Jean de Brueil complained about the perfect lack of discipline in the armies, and the ease with these armies could dissolve into hordes of brigands and pillagers (Vale 1981: 164). In a system where 'public' force consisted of hired private individuals and groups on an ad hoc basis, the end of warfare often resulted in a surplus of large companies of men trained to fight and armed to the teeth. These soldiers 'either dissolved or formed a small and dangerous private army under the captain who had recruited them. Such "free companies" were completely uncontrolled by any governmental agency' (Strayer 1973: 85). During the thirteenth and fourteenth centuries, Europe was constantly either at war, or threatened by these armies of uprooted mercenaries who had turned to brigandage and private wars, and whose loyalty lay with private captains rather than with public authorities (Vale 1981: 155).

Private force was a widespread threat to the public peace, and also frustrated the attempts at centralization of power. Efforts to eliminate private wars, and the introduction of the idea of waging war on behalf of the public good were intended to limit pillage and banditry during war, but also to generate peace. Thus, the popularity of treatises such as *L'Arbre des Batailles* or *Le Jouvencel* among military leaders who were seeking to create disciplined chivalries is easily understandable, especially when contrasted with the medieval knight 'engaging in spontaneous acts of individual prowess' (Allmand 1976: 18). These manuals not only emphasized that soldiers should go nowhere at all without the license of the military commander, but also introduced the idea that paid soldiers were entitled neither to booty nor to ransom, and that those who went to war to pillage, were not to receive wages. This idea was crucial to the later public monopolization of warfare, as it introduced the idea of the soldier as a public servant bound to obey his paymaster, rather than fighting his own private battles. Theretofore, feudal knights and smaller barons had profited of declared wars between kings to fight each other, with the result that it was often difficult to see on which side they were fighting.

Illustrative of this is Robert Stacey's summary of the Hundred Years War:

> in the extraordinary confusion … it was sometimes extremely difficult to tell who the prince was in whose name the various free companies, local lords, and wandering gangs of outright extortionists were in fact fighting. That they fought in the name of some prince mattered: without princely sanction their war was not a public one, and so by the law of arms they acquired no legally enforceable title to the ransoms and booty they captured.
>
> *(Stacey 1994: 32)*

The kings gradually claiming the profits of war for themselves, the knights and smaller barons were now losing what had been an important incentive to wage war.

While the medieval period witnessed a widespread *de jure* confusion in terms of who had the competent authority to wage war, there was increasingly a *de facto* monopolization of the means of war by greater lords and kings who controlled their territories in a quasi-sovereign manner. As such, while public authority did play a part in defining who had the right to wage war, and while there was an increasingly clear understanding of who was sovereign and who was not, there was still no 'absolute polarity between public and private warfare. The realities of power were simply too complex' (ibid.: 32). This is not to say that medieval warfare happened within a complete absence of rules, but rather to emphasize that the rules guiding warfare at the time were in place less to define the distinction between public and private than to 'protect the rights of the individual soldiers who joined in the fighting wherever they might choose to fight' (ibid.: 39). As individuals could no longer take part in looting wherever they wanted, a share in the plunder of war gradually came to depend on soldiers being duly enlisted on an army muster list and 'as the costs of war rose ever higher, only kings and a few other great lords could afford to maintain such a force' (ibid.: 32, 39).

By the fifteenth century, more or less successful attempts to restrict private war had been made by the kings of England, France, Castille and Aragon, whereas the German and Italian nobles still retained that right almost entirely to the extent that 'the feudal right of the noble to engage in private war whenever he considered justice to have been denied him existed [now] in direct proportion to the lack of central authority' (Allmand 1976: 27). Moreover, the introduction of permanent armies during the very end of the fifteenth century was not only the result of the evolution of institutions, a higher level of economic activity, or even improved systems of taxation. The standing armies were also a product of changes in the attitudes towards war. One of the conditions of possibility of their emergence were changes in the social function and role of the warring classes; from private feudal lords to servants of the public interest of the sovereign. In other words, the king's war had to become the kingdom's war, and rulers such as Charles VII of France were towards the mid-fifteenth century actively trying to break the privileged allegiance of the soldiers to certain princes or lords, and were now claiming for themselves alone the right to wage war (Contamine 1984: 168–9).

Towards permanent armies, *c.* 1450

A strong demand for soldiers led to an overflow of mercenaries, and the limited resources for wages at the ruler's disposal could only strengthen their dependence on pillaging. This changed somewhat as rulers started to maintain under arms a certain number of soldiers, even in times of peace. This increasingly shifted the power from private warring groups and feudal lords towards centralizing (state) rulers. As Norbert Elias (1996) noted, the kings of larger states such as France or England for a long time had internal rivals to their power; princes or barons that had some sort of claim to rule, and against whom they had to defend and strengthen themselves. This is echoed by Tilly, who argues that within 'any particular state ... local and regional powerholders have ordinarily had control of concentrated means of force that could, if combined, match or even overwhelm those of the state' (Tilly 1992: 69). It was this balance that was shifting at the end of the fifteenth century. Slowly the rulers of Europe were starting to gain terrain over their rival barons and dukes. Once the principle was generally accepted that only the king had the right to make war – and prevent others from doing so – it had to be admitted also that only soldiers in the king's service or under his license were permitted to bear arms. Thus, together with a build-up of the ruler's permanent armies, the disarmament of the nobility increased the power of the sovereign over his earlier rivals.

Yet one should not overemphasize the importance of this in practice, as the level of discipline of the fifteenth-century standing armies was initially not very different from their predecessors. A number of measures were therefore introduced which aimed to increase the discipline and corporate identity of these armies. In 1473, the Burgundian army was the first to be differentiated by insignia that had no connection with social status. The role of the individualistic knight was thus more and more downplayed in the armies of the fifteenth century.

As emphasized by Tilly (1992), the maintenance of a regular army required more resources and thus the introduction of new taxes. By the end of the fifteenth century, the *taille des gens de guerre*, a temporary tax levied in order to be able to pay mercenaries to stop them from plundering that had been introduced after the Hundred Years War, had become a permanent tax in France (Howard 1976: 18). As expenses related to the permanent maintenance of armed forces increased, only kings had resources to maintain standing armies. Warfare was now not only an activity reserved for the emerging states, but also an activity that was demanding increasingly higher resources. By maintaining larger standing armies, the business of war became the *de facto* and *de jure* monopoly of the state; noble knights and barons were losing both their right to engage in private warfare as well as the resources necessary to do so. The monopolization of warfare contributed to the centralization of power in the state. The fact that one now had to be enrolled on the official muster list of an army in order to get any share in plunder was a strong blow to the feudal knights and lords, for whom 'the only way [to] get hold of more than the produce of their own fields was by plundering the fields of others ... and ransoming prisoners of war' (Elias 1996: 317). Eliminating in part the economic rationality of war for the private competitors of the emerging states thus weakened their economic foundation and socio-political function. The king was now taking control of the checks and balances typical to feudalism. Unconditional loyalty to the kingdom – the last blow to the feudal independence of the nobility – was finally achieved by drawing the knights to the royal courts.

Conclusion

The state's claims to monopolize the legitimate means of violence did not emerge *ex nihilo*, but was rather the result of a long process through which private force was increasingly bound to public service. The claim of the monopoly of the armed forces was not effective as long as the territory was constantly pillaged by roving companies of bandits. For a long time, rulers' claim of the monopoly of the right to make war conflicted with the fact that large portions of the population were constantly under arms. By establishing regular standing armies the king could now put an end to the plundering of mercenaries in peacetime through fighting them, but also by eliminating their appearance at the end of wars – since the king's soldiers now kept their functions also in times of peace.

The nobility had now lost its economic incentives and possibilities to wage war, and was increasingly losing its function as warriors. The warrior nobles were also losing their rights to bear arms; a right now reserved to the soldiers of the state – mostly laymen by the end of the fifteenth century. Revolutions in the practices of war such as the increased use of artillery also tipped the balance in favour of large states, which were the only ones to possess the resources to maintain sizable standing armies. Warfare was becoming a public business; a business assumed by soldiers no longer recruited from the nobility.

Janice Thomson (1994) has argued that the rise of the sovereign state happened with the elimination of private violence. Her argument, in short, is that the emergence and enforcement of the idea of sovereignty as a new geo-spatial conception of politics led states, willingly or unwillingly, to address the 'problem' of private force, and in the end eliminate it. In her account, the state rose on the ashes of private violence, so to speak. It was the process of eliminating private force, by nationalizing armies on land and outlawing privateering at sea that led to the consolidation of a specific type of polity, the state. Yet, the fact that states increasingly became the only units able to legitimately wage wars does not mean that private force disappeared. Contrary to Thomson's argument, there is no necessary linearity to such long-term processes, and the public monopolization of the means of violence did not bring the demise of private force altogether.

As Tarak Barkawi (2010) has reminded us, even long after the age of nationalism, states came to draw upon foreigners for their armies. Moreover, as this chapter argues, and as shown throughout this Handbook, distinctions between public and private force vary across time and place, and we should avoid seeing the two in straightforward opposition, but rather as intertwined. Private force continued to play a role in international politics long after the consolidation of the state: states used privateers in a wide range of settings for centuries (Leira and de Carvalho 2010), states sponsored private military companies in the wars of religion (de Carvalho 2003; 2014), and private enterprise was, paradoxically enough, the central component of most (state) colonial ventures in the Atlantic (de Carvalho in press; Chapter 4, this volume). As such, the sovereign state did not emerge as private force was eliminated. Rather, it emerged as the role of private force changed, and as it was re-intertwined with public force in different ways.

Bibliography

Allmand, C. T. (ed.) (1976) *War, Literature, and Politics in the Late Middle Ages*, New York: Barnes & Noble Books.

Avant, D. (2000) 'From Mercenary to Citizen Armies: Explaining Change in the Practice of War', *International Organization* 54(1): 41–72.

Barkawi, T. (2010) 'State and Armed Force in International Context', in A. Colas and B. Mabee (eds), *Mercenaries, Pirates, Bandits and Empires*, New York: Columbia University Press, pp. 33–54.

Colas, A. and Mabee, B. (eds) (2010) *Mercenaries, Pirates, Bandits and Empires*, New York: Columbia University Press.

Contamine, P. (1984) *War in the Middle Ages*, New York: Basil Blackwell.

Davis, D. E. and Pereira, A. W. (eds) (2008) *Irregular Armed Forces and Their Role in Politics and State Formation*, Cambridge: Cambridge University Press.

de Carvalho, B. (2003) 'Keeping the State: Religious Toleration in Early Modern France and the Role of the State in Minority Conflicts', *European Yearbook of Minority Issues* 1: 5–27.

de Carvalho, B. (2014) 'The Confessional State in International Politics: Tudor England, Religion, and the Eclipse of Dynasticism', *Diplomacy and Statecraft* 25(3): 407–31.

de Carvalho, B. (2015) 'On the Modern Origins of Feudal Empires: The Donatary Captaincies and the Legacies of the Portuguese Empire in Brazil' in S. Halperin and R. Palan (eds), *Legacies of Empires: Imperial Roots of the Contemporary Global Order*, Cambridge: Cambridge University Press, pp. 128–148.

Elias, N. (1996) *The Civilizing Process*, Oxford: Blackwell Publishers.

Howard, M. (1976) *War in European History*, Oxford: Oxford University Press.

Leira, H. and de Carvalho, B. (2010) 'Privateers of the North Sea: At World's End', in A. Colas and B. Mabee (eds), *Mercenaries, Pirates, Bandits and Empires*, New York: Columbia University Press, pp. 55–82.

Owens, P. (2010) 'Distinctions, Distinctions: "Public" and "Private" Force?', in A. Colas and B. Mabee (eds), *Mercenaries, Pirates, Bandits and Empires*, New York: Columbia University Press, pp. 15–32.

Pereira, A. W. (2008) 'Armed Forces, Coercive Monopolies, and Changing Patterns of State Formation and Violence', in D. E. Davis and A. W. Pereira (eds), *Irregular Armed Forces and Their Role in Politics and State Formation*, Cambridge: Cambridge University Press, pp. 387–407.

Poggi, G. (1978) *The Development of the Modern State*, Stanford, CA: Stanford University Press.

Singer, P. W. (2008) *Corporate Warriors*, Ithaca, NY: Cornell University Press.

Stacey, R. C. (1994) 'The Age of Chivalry', in M. Howard *et al.* (eds), *The Laws of War*, New Haven, CT: Yale University Press, pp. 27–39.

Strayer, J. R. (1973) *On the Medieval Origins of the Modern State*, Princeton, NJ: Princeton University Press.

Thomson, J. E. (1994) *Mercenaries, Pirates and Sovereigns*, Princeton, NJ: Princeton University Press.

Tilly, C. (1992) *Coercion, Capital, and European States*, Cambridge: Blackwell Publishers.

Vale, M. (1981) *War and Chivalry*, London: Duckworth.

Weber, M. (1963) *From Max Weber: Essays in Sociology*, New York: Oxford University Press.

2

THE 'PRIVATE' ORIGIN OF MODERN 'PUBLIC' POLICING

Michael Kempa

The history of the development of modern, Western public police power traces directly back to the 'non-state' sector. Long before professional, salaried and uniformed public police officers monopolized the use of legitimate force and the business of disciplinary surveillance, this work was done first by networks of community volunteers who were obligated to the Crown, and, later, by private actors working for money.

As Robert Reiner (2010) has authoritatively shown, early and uncritical academic reviews of the development of the modern public police portray the rise of men and women in blue as a reflection of social and political progress – a move driven by enlightened public reformers who pushed policing beyond the customary and voluntary systems for community patrol and crime prevention that had dominated Europe from the Middle Ages through the feudal order (Critchley 1967). However, these Whiggish histories provide too narrow an understanding of the depth of the shifts that occurred in Western policing over roughly a millennium. An historical review of the shift from volunteer community security to salaried public policing will of course uncover a cast of famous politicians, justice and safety practitioners and moral entrepreneurs jockeying within and around the legislative process to promote their preferred reforms. The 'Great White Men' of eighteenth and early nineteenth century history – in this case, personages such as the Fielding (half)brothers, Adam Smith, Patrick Colquhoun and Robert Peel – are undoubtedly important in the development of modern policing, but the public police are not the straightforward invention of any of these powerful public actors.

This chapter draws on critical political economy (Dubber and Valverde 2006; Neocleous 1998) to trace the history of 'policing as a grand intellectual project linked to state formation, prosperity and security in Enlightenment thought' (Rigakos *et al.* 2009: 2). The objective is to untangle how profound redefinitions of the entire concept of policing are tied to shifting systems of political economy. This approach rejects the structuralist, Durkheimian position that new ideas drive innovation on the ground and instead follows the more Foucauldian pathway of identifying how new ways of acting, relating and so thinking are opened up and diffused through the spread of new institutional technologies. Simply stated, new ways of setting up – institutionalizing – policing literally embody entirely new ways of thinking about the functions and responsibilities of states, citizens and markets, along with the proper form of relationships between them.

This form of blending grounded historical genealogy with critical political economy studies reveals that the modern public police is the curious, historically unique creation of the emerging merchant/capitalist class of the mid-eighteenth century. The influence of this capitalist class bridged the widening divide between the public and private sectors associated with the transition from mercantilist to liberal capitalist political economy. On the back of experiments in the private sector over the second half of the 1700s, the same sets of influential reformers then sought to 'publicize' what had mostly developed as a 'private' enterprise.

One reason why ideas about modern policing reform gained stronger influence in the private rather than public sector was the uniqueness of the proposed innovations. The idea that the problem of collective order could be solved by salaried, full-time agents of the law charged with the monopoly over the legitimate use of sovereign force and maintaining an 'unremitting watch over collective goings-on' (while typically being kitted out in blue pants) is very strange in historical terms. It comes as no surprise, therefore, that these proposals were met with a great deal of resistance in established public circles: the traditional (non-capitalist) elites clung to far broader ideas of policing that had dominated Western thinking for roughly a millennium, and succeeded in heading off the emerging capitalist class' charge for public-policing reform until 1829.

To trace this genealogy, the chapter begins by contrasting medieval and feudal conceptions and institutionalizations of policing – noting how little they have in common with the very narrow, public policing model that we recognize today. It then outlines the development and incubation of this strange, but contemporarily familiar institutional technology for policing, which germinated principally in the private sector throughout the second half of the eighteenth century and was finally enfolded within the public sector in the early nineteenth century. Finally, the chapter traces the particular instrumental, structural, and conceptual 'conditions of possibility' that had to align in space and time to enable politicians, legal practitioners, and moral entrepreneurs to publicize the new private policing technologies. Throughout, what I consider to be some of the most important gaps in our knowledge that form the basis of important directions for research are highlighted.

Western policing: from sovereignty to mercantilism

Public policing – defined as the exercise of state power to promote peace and collective order – was once a very broad enterprise. This is true at both the level of ideas (how we thought about and defined policing and its goals) and of the institutions charged with these broad functions (how we set up to accomplish these objectives).

Throughout the sovereign period from the Middle Ages to feudal times (*c.* 600–1500), the exercise of state power was not undertaken to advance any detailed set of public interests, such as reductions in crime rates, advances in public perceptions of safety, or confidence in the administration of justice. Rather, monarchs exercised their authority for the purpose of demonstrating and furthering their own sovereign authority – and not only in the terms of naked self-interest. Under the conditions of Thomas Hobbes's imagined 'social contract', it was believed that a rational human being (i.e., a propertied male, at this stage of history) would agree to submit to the power of the sovereign in exchange for the broader security that a powerful sovereign would be able to provide. Any sign of weakness, therefore, could spell the undoing not only of the sovereign himself but of the broader social contract, as rational subjects would opt out to seek their security elsewhere.

As Michel Foucault ([1979] 1991) has pointed out, texts that address the question of public order at that stage of history therefore provided programmatic advice to the sovereign on how best to exercise his power to maintain his position of authority and hence peace throughout the realm. Machiavelli's *The Prince* is of course the gold standard. This advice for how to 'police' the population is not limited to the actual exercise of sovereign authority – much of it has to do with establishing the symbolic representations of the awesome capacity for repressive power. Key examples here are the design of great castles and estates, along with the strategic intention to place the capital as near to the centre of the polity as possible in order to telegraph the idea that the sovereign's power is evenly distributed across the entirety of the territory.

This sovereign system for 'police' was designed to appeal to the rationality of the landed gentry and slowly urbanizing elites, such as heads of parishes. By having society's powerful buy in to the social contract, commoners could be kept under the control of local feudal lords and nobility who would coordinate volunteer systems for patrol and emergency response. Variations on the 'hue-and-cry', frankpledge and parish constable systems served as forms of non-state, but not quite 'private', policing throughout the territories of the fledgling great states of Western modernity. These systems mobilized volunteers to survey and assist their fellow community members on the fundamental principle of duties owed to the Crown: a contribution to collective order that was incumbent on all citizens, under the direction and supervision of greater citizens (Rawlings 2003: 41).

The sovereign policing model – involving the exercise and public spectacle of repressive authority for the maintenance of sovereignty and matched with local, voluntary order maintenance – began to shift in nature with the gathering pace of industrialization and the consequent rise of the merchant classes as powerful political actors over the course of the sixteenth and seventeenth centuries. The new merchants, who owned the means of goods production and distribution, began to rival the state revenue generation power of the old feudal lords by paying greater taxes on their prototypical industrial profits. As such, they were able to offer monarchs even greater means to expand their sovereign power to keep order throughout the realm and telegraph strength internationally.

With this critical shift, the wealth of the merchants became the concern of the sovereign: the very source of peace, order, and good government came to be understood within mercantilist political economy as the continued expansion of the wealth of the merchant class, and, with it, their capacity to pay taxes to the powerful sovereign. At this moment, therefore, we saw a tremendous expansion in Western, mercantilist notions of the proper role for the state in exercising police power in market space and foreign diplomacy in service of peace, order, and good government (Dubber and Valverde 2006; Neocleous 2008). Simply stated, the mercantilist system for political economy holds that markets exist to serve the sovereign, and through him, the polity, and thus governing markets and ensuring the rate-paying capacity of the merchant class is an important field for the exercise of public police power.

Within this political economy framework, the concept of 'police' came to be conflated with 'policy' generally, with a special eye on economic policy. Everything that the state did – every tool that it mobilized – towards ensuring the constant expansion of the emerging free market came to be understood and defined as an 'act of police'. Something as broad ranging as an effort to keep Dutch cucumbers out of the domestic English market to shore up prosperity in the farming sector would be, in this schema, understood as 'an act of police'.

In the shadow of this broad exercise of police power, the voluntary system for local order maintenance and crime control would continue its centuries-long march towards increasing formalization and centralization. The Crown undertook to formalize the roles and duties of the volunteer system with an eye not only to enhance its crime-control and order-maintenance effectiveness, but also to enforce laws against idleness, vagrancy and other forms of immorality that undermined the performance and profitability of the economy. Furthermore, establishing standards by which to judge the performance of local volunteers also became an important means for generating revenue for the sovereign through the imposition of fines upon nobles who were not living up to their listed duties. The historic record shows that the shire reeves and constables of the feudal to mercantilist eras devoted greater attention to discouraging idleness, drunkenness and other non-productive behaviours than to thief-taking and active patrol to deter crime (Rawlings 2003). A formalized system of volunteers was part-and-parcel of the broader mercantilist effort to aid in the policing of markets: the ground-level, 'flipside' of broader economic policy.

Until the highpoint of the mercantilist era (the late seventeenth century) therefore, any formalization of the voluntary system for policing had little to do with enhancing crime control or rendering a modern, professionalized service. Those ideas and institutional technologies would require a very different institutional context that embodied a radically different political economy: that of liberal capitalism.

Modern policing: the cross-pollination of public and private ideas and institutions

The early mercantilist industrial system began to gather sufficient steam to take on the form of a more advanced, capitalist industrial system throughout the eighteenth century. Specifically, the great privatization of feudal lands provided the resources and speculative wealth necessary to further expand the engines of production and more deeply empower the early merchants as the new capitalist class.

The resulting explosion in the size and complexity of private enterprise, and the widening of access to such burgeoning markets, began to shift thinking about the purposes and role for the state. Adam Smith's macroeconomic principle that excessive state intervention within complex markets could bring about negative 'unintended consequences' by upsetting the 'invisible hand' that guides them (i.e., their internal communicative, ordering and distributional mechanisms) began to push the concept of policing out of the market space. Private enterprise, in other words, began in the middle decades of the eighteenth century to be conceptually excluded from the domain of the state exercise of police power. This constricted, essentially liberal capitalist notion of policing was literally rendered 'thinkable' once the science of statistics had become sufficiently sophisticated to make it possible for observers to chart the cyclical regularities of market behaviour and the characteristics and behaviour of the population. In this context of the explosion of data – and the knowable and manageable market and population – public police power began to be more completely refocused on the social and political spheres surrounding private enterprise than in the previous mercantilist period. Police power, therefore, was focused nearly completely upon clearing any surrounding impediments to healthy market functioning.

Here, a fundamental difference between mercantilism and capitalism is key: whereas mercantilist markets were grown with the view to enhancing the wealth, power and capacity of the sovereign to maintain collective order, capitalist markets are grown to distribute wealth and rewards to well-behaved citizens – to govern, in the first instance, through (market) 'consensus'. Within the liberal capitalist scheme, therefore, sovereign control is usurped by disciplinary control as the primary means of policing the population at large. Within capitalism, repression is reserved for those who either cannot or will not be governed through the disciplinary, 'consensual' mechanisms of market reward. These residual categories – those who are understood to be 'feckless' (incapable or unwilling to assuming rational responsibility in the market order) – became the constricted and concentrated focus of the system for public police.

Distinct in this Foucault-tinted political economy, is the idea that new technologies and economic relationships enabled new ways of thinking about and doing policing – literally rendered them possible. In order to explain why these new approaches to policing took hold and spread, structural critical interpretations are helpful. As Durkheim and Marx have both concluded (albeit through different pathways of analysis), the massive social and economic disruption of the exploding industrial revolution produced far too many feckless actors for the traditional voluntary systems of community patrol to easily handle. As a result, centralization, formalization and public remuneration became the reformatory orders on the minds of a greater number of safety minded capitalists and legislators.

These reformatory ideas did not, however, take off in practical terms at the moment of their inception – at least not in the public sphere, and particularly not among the elite, landed gentry who continued to adhere to older, sovereignist or mercantilist notions of policing. This transitory tension and ambivalence in the minds of public thinkers and legislators is embodied in the writing of Adam Smith, for example, who shifts his concept of police from broad mercantilist notions to narrower law enforcement matters over the time of publishing early treatises on police through to his magnum opus, *The Wealth of Nations* (Neocleous 1998, 2008).

The Fielding half-brothers, a particularly influential duo of local British magistrates and police reformers, found themselves and their ideas for the formalization of the voluntary system for local crime control and morality enforcement caught up and frustrated in this early liberal capitalist ambivalence. The push made by John Fielding in the mid-1700s to unify community watch programmes into a single, professionalized police service, was a damp squib, receiving little Parliamentary or local support from the Parish leaders. The portion of their vision that was a more limited success – the Bow Street Runners – managed to bring together a regulated network of private thief-takers who would compile and share information to professionalize the investigation of crime in the service of both public prosecution and the recovery of losses for victims. Within this model, crimes would be solved in service of both public and private interests through a 'mixed model' of funding: some monies for the salaried Bow Street policing professionals would come directly from government subsidy, with the balance being raised through private sponsorship.

While the Fielding brothers' ideas did hit the public consciousness through their media engagement, they nevertheless failed to inspire complete legislative confidence. During the latter half of the eighteenth century, proposals for expanded public funding of the Bow Street Runners were only modestly and sporadically supported, and they never evolved to become the dominant public agency for professionalized criminal investigation that the Fielding brothers had envisioned (Rawlings 2003: 47). Their hybridized innovations focused on the public sector were, however, being matched, and even exceeded, by parallel initiatives that were more firmly rooted in the private sector. New professional policing technologies would take hold and germinate to a greater degree in the private sphere, for it was here that the new capitalist class was unencumbered by elite resistance, and so free to define policing far more narrowly and in the terms of their immediate interests: loss-prevention and the disciplinary logic of maximizing the productive capacity of all units.

Champions of industry built up formalized police institutions that directly met these needs, in both urban and rural settings. In urban centres, factory security and the conduits linking them and the marketplace became the business of private enterprise. A key example comes from Patrick Colquhoun, a powerful Scottish industrialist turned East London magistrate, who persuaded shipping merchants that an end to their massive financial losses to local piracy and employee complicity lay in their direct funding of a local, fully preventive private police service. In 1797, Colquhoun teamed with local mariners and the philosopher Jeremy Bentham to develop a plan for local, preventive disciplinary surveillance undertaken by uniformed professionals. Relying on statistical data, Colquhoun was able to persuade the West India Planters Committees and the West India Merchants to fund the new force for a one year trial period under his supervision.

In economic terms, the resulting Thames Valley Police was a runaway success. With the initial investment of £4,200, the new force began with about 50 men charged with policing 33,000 river shipping workers. Colquhoun argued that they had saved their masters over a hundred thousand pounds in the prevention of losses and preservation of life. By developing an argument for professional policing in straightforward economic terms – preventing loss was good for the performance of markets and kept the functioning of their internal distribution mechanisms honest – a sceptical British Parliament was persuaded to bring the Thames Valley Police under public auspices. With the passage of the Marine Police Bill on 28 July 1800, a private innovation for uniformed, preventive policing was for the first time fully folded into the public sphere.

The Thames Valley Police thus proved to be a beacon: under its light, the institutional technology of private, uniformed, professional policing took off in major urban centres, surging in the opening years of the nineteenth century. Advice on crime prevention, the establishment of hundreds of societies for the prosecution of offenders, the private employment of guards and watchmen to patrol business grounds and neighbourhoods, and the locksmith industries proliferated throughout this period (Rawlings 2003: 61).

It is here that a particularly rich avenue for future research can be found: much more needs to be known about the myriad of private security actors that sprang up in the early nineteenth century. A detailed review of their operational manuals and industry documents would investigate whether these agencies were as sophisticated in their disciplinary police science as Colquhoun's Thames Valley Police: did significant reliance upon coercive techniques continue to be evidenced in their manual and reports? Additionally, an investigation into these outfits' efforts to secure government subsidy on the basis that their activities produced a broader public 'security dividend' in the form of reduced crime or enhanced market performance would add texture to our understandings of the conflicts and cooperation between public and private interests that doubtless occurred in this period.

Away from the exploding urban centres, resource extraction industries set up nearly entirely private 'company towns', where worker (and sometimes family) housing, religious practice, and basic education and health services were sponsored directly by the new capitalist employers (Spitzer and Scull 1977). These spaces were also nearly entirely policed by private agencies. Intriguingly, this early institutional technology for modern, uniformed policing controlled worker populations by combining modern, disciplinary power with the maintenance of traditional, agrarian values of the new factory worker class. Applying capitalist technologies to the enforcement of feudal and mercantilist norms illustrates yet another point of similarity and continuity between the newly professionalized private institutions for policing and the volunteer sectors of public order maintenance that dominated the Middle Ages and the feudal system.

At this stage, therefore, modern policing went well beyond the sovereign enforcement of codified rules, to focus on the elicitation of desired behaviours in bodies rendered docile through repetitive micro correction through control of access to reward. This had long been done in the public sector – going back to the earliest sovereign and mercantilist systems of frankpledge and parish constables – but it was in the private sector that specialized policing institutions were developed to fully realize these liberal, capitalist policing ambitions in the manner of a precisely calibrated 'police science'.

The slow and difficult 'publicization' of specialized, modern policing

After 70-odd years of abortive policing reform legislation, Sir Robert Peel would finally succeed in his role as moral entrepreneur where others, such as the Fielding brothers, had mostly failed. Peel was simply the right person at the right time, speaking to a receptive audience as a product of shifting technologies, institutions, structures and mentalities. In short, the context was ready for the long-running ideas for public policing for which Robert Peel was then custodian.

At the outset of the nineteenth century, classic liberalism and its faith in the principles of open market capitalism held full sway. The feckless rabble classes were perceived to pose a pressing threat to keeping the ultimate source of order and security – the market – spinning on its delicate axis. In addition, the structural demands and strains placed upon collective order at the turn of the nineteenth century were extraordinary. Rebellion throughout the colonies threatened the stability of the market system in the metropole, as the interruption of raw materials and cheap labour to fuel the industrial engines of production, coupled with the destabilizing of friendly foreign markets for the exportation of metropolitan goods, threatened market stability and thereby social order at home.

In this context, an enterprising Sir Robert Peel found the right moment to sell the institutional technology of public policing to a sceptical British parliament and broader population. The brash and enterprising young politician had set off to Ireland to quell rebellion and make a name for himself. Upon arrival, he remained steadfast in the traditional belief that order could best be restored through motivating or forcing the landed gentry to take on their responsibilities as the coordinators of local volunteer patrols and surveillance. However, confronted by what Peel interpreted as the terrible quality of Irish nobility, he warmed to the idea of uniformed public officers. Back home in the Metropolitan Parliament, the introduction of this extraordinary technology was rendered an easier sell through appeals to British xenophobia and chauvinism: in Peel's appraisal, the Irish were simply incapable of being governed in the indirect, disciplinary manner of 'rational', free Englishmen, and so would require the extraordinary technology of a public police force.

In 1814, Ireland thereby became the 'hard edge of the wedge' for the normalization of an extraordinary constabulary technology that was brought within the fold of public governance. This took the form of a domestic armed cavalry that had more in common with what we would now consider to be domestic national security agencies than local policing agencies. On the back of the success of these agencies in suppressing revolutionary activity in Ireland, the Irish Constabulary was expanded and rolled out across the island of Ireland with subsequent legislation in 1822.

While the hard edge of modern policing were gathering pace in Ireland, the 'thin edge of the wedge' – that of the Thames Valley Police, the Bow Street Runners and other forms of private or hybridized local security that did ordinary patrols and kept up an unremitting disciplinary watch over collective goings-on – continued to develop and receive greater public subsidy on 'mainland' Britain. Foucault reminds us that ways of thinking are built into institutional technologies and repetitive practices: we think the way we are capable of behaving given the options made available through the institutional varieties around us. Simply stated, one can think as one is able to behave given the institutional options that exist. Thus, ways of thinking and behaving evolve and are subsequently reinforced through the institutional technologies that we create. Further, these ways of thinking and doing render possible particular forms of relationships, which denote modalities of power. The disciplinary society that grew first in the institutions of the private sector took hold and spread, propagating these forms of relationships, ways of acting, and so ways of thinking throughout society. As Foucault ([1979] 1991) points out, if the eighteenth century was the period for disciplining society, the nineteenth century would see the disciplining of government, which is to say, the public enfolding and institutionalization of the disciplinary technologies, institutions, practices, and relationships that were first typical to the private sector.

In this context, Robert Peel found parliament at last receptive to ideas for public policing reform. But the political pitch that worked for the policing of rational Englishmen was the 'thin edge' of uniformed policing, modelled on the example of the Thames Valley Police and Bow Street Runners. Specifically, Peel was able to present his proposal in the terms of a continuation of what was already familiar: simply the publicization of a preventive, consensual (persuasive), neutral agency that would maintain an unremitting watch over collective goings on. Peel's new police would rely on the light touch of disciplinary governance in the first instance, reserving sovereign repression for the last instance of those who demonstrated themselves to be feckless. In this sense, for Peel, the modern police were nothing more than the formalization of the voluntary policing and security duties that were incumbent on every citizen – and the sensible publicization of an institutional technology that had already been well developed in the private sector. For Peel and his converts, there was to be nothing 'political' about the new police; but, by our critical political economy, we see this set of beliefs to be profoundly grounded in liberal capitalist mentalities and technologies.

According to Peel, the police would have no special powers. They would be 'ordinary citizens in uniform', maintaining order through surveillance and persuasion, with coercion being the instrument of last instance. They would maintain patrols and work with citizens to prevent crime in the social and political sphere before it even happened. As such, security and justice could be achieved through this extraordinary technology, independent of what transpired in market and economic space. In this fashion, the core of private, disciplinary security, premised on surveillance, the internalization of the gaze, the threat of negative punishment (in the sense of removal of access to reward) came to reflect the core of Peel's famous nine principles for public policing.

These claims would not have struck Parliament and the public as plausible, were it not for the fact that society had grown accustomed to these extraordinary technologies in the contexts of Ireland, the private sector, and, to a lesser extent, civil society. A historically unique and rather unusual institutional technology for realizing particularly narrow 'policing' objectives had germinated in the private sector, and was publicized only gradually through an extraordinary alignment of factors. While the historical record of Robert Peel's techniques for shepherding his preferred policing reforms through Parliament is well developed, as are the arguments against such agencies presented by opposing political figures, much less is known about the forms of support and pressure provided by the emerging capitalist class over the period. What forms of lobbying, public opinion-leading, and other means of political persuasion and resistance did champions of the private security industry exert over this period? Without this important empirical work, we do not know whether or to what degree capitalists were keen to publicize policing at this stage of history (perhaps to relieve themselves of some of the burden of cost), or, may have preferred to jealously guard their direct control over the enterprise of security.

An additional significant research priority is to expand our knowledge beyond the British experience and develop similar understandings of the linkages between shifts in political economic ideas and structural pressures in other centres of modern European policing reform. As Emsley (2003) points out, there are greater similarities in the development of policing systems across Europe than is commonly assumed. Tracing the historical record of challenges in the imperial project and the relative health of emergent industrial, capitalist systems as it relates to shifts in policing models outside of Britain remains an important gap in the literature.

Conclusion

There is a lot of discussion in contemporary policing and security studies as to whether public and private policing are 'converging' – becoming more like one another in mentalities and purposes (Reiner 2010). This chapter has shown that it is not a question of simple recent convergence. Rather, policing has come full circle, to return an early liberal capitalist norm of common mentalities, institutions and practices of security across the public and private sectors. The original technology of salaried men and women in uniform maintaining collective order and seeking to prevent crime was largely the creation of the private sector. What is more, this extraordinarily narrow way of defining policing was itself only conceptually possible in the context of liberal capitalist political economy, which holds that markets are delicate machines best left to run according to their own internal dynamics. The point is driven home that the sharp divide drawn between the public and private sectors in modern capitalism has, historically at least, been blurred on the ground if not on paper.

Continuing to blend Foucault-inspired historical genealogies with critical political economic inquiry of the history of modern Western policing – moving well outside of the Anglophone context presented in this chapter – will help to untangle the ways in which policing systems both reflect and reinforce dominant ways of thinking about and doing the business of politics and economics. If liberal capitalism lives and breathes within its ways of thinking about and doing policing, it follows that historical, contemporary, domestic and global contests over policing forms are deeply tied to differing views and visions for political economy. Conversely, systems of policing that are alien to Western sensibilities are likely revealing of options for political economy that are fundamentally different to liberal capitalism. Studying the diversity of policing systems in historical and global context is part and parcel of broadening an understanding of options for political economy. How have ways of thinking about and defining policing broadened and narrowed with shifting views about what markets are and what they can and ought to do for us? Who has pushed for different concepts of policing – and what kinds of political economic arguments have they mobilized to achieve their aims? What types of alliances between the public, private and civil spheres have we seen on behalf of competing policing systems? Unearthing policing policy papers and procedural manuals in capitalist, communist, autocratic, democratic, theistic and blended societies will illuminate the ways in which policing institutions reflect and reify different ways of thinking about the problem of social order and its relationship to state, market, citizen and creator.

Bibliography

Critchley, T. A. (1967) *A History of Police in England and Wales, 900–1966*, London: Constable.

Dubber, M. D. and Valverde, M. (2006) 'Perspectives on the Power and Science of Police', in M. D. Dubber and M. Valverde (eds), *The New Police Science*, Stanford, CA: Stanford University Press, pp. 1–16.

Emsley, C. (2003) 'The Birth and Development of the Police', in T. Newburn and D. Collompton (eds), *The Handbook of Policing*, Cullompton: Willan, pp. 66–83.

Foucault, M. ([1979] 1991) 'On Governmentality', in G. Burchell, C. Gordon and P. Miller (eds), *The Foucault Effect: Studies in Governmentality*, Chicago, IL: University of Chicago Press, pp. 87–104.

Foucault, M. (2007) *Security, Territory, Population: Lectures at the Collège de France, 1977–1978* (ed. M. Senellart, trans. G. Burchell), New York: Palgrave.

Neocleous, M. (1998) 'Policing and Pin Making: Adam Smith, Police and the State of Prosperity', *Policing and Society* 8(4): 425–49.

Neocleous, M. (2008) *Critique of Security*, Montréal: McGill and Queen's University Press.

Rawlings, P. (2003) 'Policing before the Police', in T. Newburn and D. Collompton (eds), *The Handbook of Policing*, Cullompton: Willan, pp. 41–64.

Reiner, R. (2010) *The Politics of the Police* (4th edn), Oxford: Oxford University Press.

Rigakos, G., McMullan, J. L., Johnson, J. and Ozcan, G. (2009) *A General Police System: Political Economy and Security in the Age of Enlightenment*, Ottawa: Red Quill Books.

Spitzer, S. and Scull, A. (1977) 'Privatization and Capitalist Development: The Case of the Private Police', *Social Problems* 25(1): 18–29.

3

PRIVATE FORCE AND THE EMERGENCE OF THE INTERNATIONAL SYSTEM

Halvard Leira

In a scene from 'Two Swords', the first episode in the fourth season of the TV series *Game of Thrones*, Prince Oberyn Martell asks the sellsword (i.e. the mercenary) Bronn whether he is a hired killer. Replying that he started out that way, Bronn points out that he is now a knight. When asked how that came to pass, he replies: 'Killed the right people, I suppose.' Much like the system of the European Middle Ages, on which it is based, the TV series depicts a system of various polities where different forms of private force are prevalent, where different forms of force shade into one another and where private force matters greatly for the trajectory of the system. As is often the case, fiction highlights phenomena that are overlooked in other accounts, in this instance the overall systemic importance of private force.

The main argument of this chapter is that private force has played an important, but often overlooked role in the emergence and development of the current international system; our world would have looked different, if not for the continuous presence of different forms of force not tied directly to the modern states. This goes for the character of the basic units of the system, as well as for the modes of interaction and the gradual spread of the system. In the literature on historical forms of private force, states have tended to be the focal point. Taking the Weberian definition of the state as its starting point, and drawing extensively on Tilly and other historical sociologists, the argument has been that the abolishment of private force is a key part of modern statebuilding (Thomson 1994; Chapter 1, this volume). The tendency to focus on the state has been reinforced by the nationalist character of much historiography – the use of private force and its gradual banishment has traditionally been studied with the state as the container. There are two obvious problems with such an approach. First, studying the interplay between private force and state force (or control) solely through the lenses of the state, leads not only to a teleological reading of history, but also by necessity privileges the latter over the former, obscuring the possibility of private force undermining the very notion of stable states. Second, privileging the state also ignores what have become staple insights of historical sociology and constructivism over the last decades, namely that states and the state system should be understood as co-constitutive and that they thus emerged simultaneously. It follows logically from this that private force matters not only to the emergence of modern states, but also to the modern international system of states.

In the following pages, the relationship of private force to the emergence of the international system will be discussed in four steps, proceeding thematically rather than chronologically. Before turning to the empirics, it is nevertheless necessary to establish the understanding of some key terms and to say a few words about existing literature. This is followed by the first substantive section, which deals with the importance of private force to the early emergence and spread of the international system. The second section discusses how varieties of non-traditional forms of force helped maintain what was in many ways an international system of empires. The third section turns to the rules, norms and values of the system, and how the gradual abolishment (or forgetting) of private force has helped foster ideational cohesion in the international system. Finally, in the fourth section, focus is on modes of interaction, and on how an unintended consequence of the use of private force has been a functionalist push for a tighter integrated system. The chapter concludes that private force should be understood as one of the central productive forces in the gradual emergence of the modern international system.

Private force, international system

Two brief points must be made regarding the key terms of the chapter. First, as discussed by several authors (e.g. Owens 2010), the distinction between public and private (or state force and private force) is problematic, and even more so when the object of study stretches back more than five centuries. In this chapter, 'private force' will be used to designate force that is not under the full legal, political or otherwise control of the recognized head of the polity that commands them and even this distinction will be problematized when looking at empires. Second, when discussing the emergence of the modern international system of states, reference will be to a long development which might be said to have started just before 1500. Different dates are suggested as an end-point for this process, and some might argue that it is yet to finish, but the bulk of this chapter is concerned with processes taking place between 1492 and 1919 – we are thus dealing with a very protracted emergence. As the ensuing sections will make clear, this delimitation is only Eurocentric to the extent that the emergence of the international system itself was a process forcibly driven by European powers and private force working against and alongside that process. Most historical literature on private force has had a statist bias. This has two important implications for our study of the international system. The first regards the importance of the oceans. Unless established on previously uninhabited land, terrestrial force has had to deal with someone claiming some sort of right to the land. Although the early European overseas empires tried to establish similar rights to the ocean, these were never enforceable. The sea thus introduces a qualitatively different variable into the statist accounts. While one might rightfully argue that ocean-going force was typically launched from some specific piece of land, it was nevertheless typically utilized in a space above and beyond state control, in a space where there would be inter-polity governance, hegemonic governance or no governance at all. It follows from this that whereas terrestrial private force mattered as much as, or more than, maritime private force for the emergence of states, maritime private force is of particular importance for the emergence and character of the international system. This is illustrated masterfully in Glete's (2000) discussion of the transformation in naval warfare between 1500 and 1650, and how it related to not only state-building, but to systemic interaction within and outside of Europe.

The second implication of the statist bias concerns the availability of existing research. Insights into the importance of private force for the international system must typically be sought indirectly, in accounts dealing with states and their relations with different providers of private force. Overall, there is a dearth of general literature, and an overabundance of detailed case studies. Furthermore, the literature on piracy vastly outnumbers the literature on all other forms of private force taken together. With the intention of providing a broad overview, although it draws on a number of more specialized works, this chapter primarily references general secondary sources. Brevity also necessitates focus, and the chapter deals primarily with mercenarism, privateering and piracy, the most important forms of private force for the emergence of the international system.

Early emergence and spread of the international system

Many of the forms of violence that we now call private predate the first emergence of something resembling modern states. Piracy and mercenarism can be traced back to antiquity, while privateering emerged in the late Middle Ages (Percy 2007; Starkey 2011). Depending on one's definition of feudal warfare, it could well be argued that some form of mercenarism dominated warfare in the Middle Ages, and increasingly so in the later Middle Ages, while privateering and piracy obviously correlated with ebbs and flows in maritime trade. With the emergence of somewhat more centralized monarchies in Europe, increasing interaction across further distances within Europe and European expansion to other continents in the fifteenth century, these modes of violence would in important ways influence both how something like a system emerged and how it spread outwards from Europe.

Within Europe, mercenary forces continued to play an important role in wars well into the nineteenth century (Percy 2007), although changing greatly in character over the centuries. In particular during the religious wars, mercenaries were crucial to the very ability to fight war. Continuous warfare was one of the factors tying the polities of the continent into a system, largely completed in geographical terms by the first half of the eighteenth century, and the reliance on mercenaries for war fighting implied that they, at least indirectly, made the emergence of systemic interaction within Europe possible. The same goes for naval warfare, where the growth of national navies was slow and fitful (Bromley 1987). By way of example, both the Spanish Armada and its English counterpart in 1588 consisted of large numbers of private vessels, fighting alongside the royal ships and the Dutch rebellion against Spanish rule would have been squashed without the actions of the 'Watergeuzen' privateers. Mass mobilization of populations was difficult in this era, and the elaborate industrial complexes associated with a large navy were unsustainable for most political entities. Thus, private force was a necessary component of most large-scale war-fighting.

Moving further away from state sanction, in the Mediterranean (and spilling into the Atlantic), force was wielded, from the middle of the sixteenth century to the end of the eighteenth century, by a mixture of private and semi-private actors (Earle 2003). Here private force served as its own multiplier. Muslim corsairs were operating from 'Barbary', that is the principalities of northern Africa, from the start of the sixteenth century. When there was a lull in war fighting between Spain and England/the Netherlands (from 1604 and 1609 respectively), they were joined by former privateers wanting to continue their lucrative careers. Teaching the North Africans the use of square-rigged vessels, as well as manning and captaining ships, these mariners wielded private force from the Newfoundland banks, via Iceland, Ireland and the English southwest, and deep into the Christian parts of the Mediterranean. Although frequently referred to as pirates, their basis of legitimacy in existing principalities and the possibility of curtailing their activity through treaty of payoff, implies that they should rather be understood as privateers. The results of this use of force was a forcible tying together of the different political entities into an embryonic system, and an expansion of the same system, as slave-raiding, alliance-building, treaty-making and protection money implied continuous interaction. This reading differs somewhat from Löwenheim's (2007) perceptive analysis. He focuses on the corsairs as parasitical on the emerging international system, whereas I stress how there was also a productive element to their use of force. However, actions at sea were even more important for establishing and perpetuating systemic interaction outside of the European core.

Following rapidly from the great voyages of discovery, the Portuguese and Spanish tried to set up a duopoly controlling the interaction with the world outside of Europe, sanctioned by the pope through the treaty of Tordesillas (1494). The treaty effectively divided the globe into two spheres of interest. Political aspirations as well as religious difference following from the reformation, led other European polities to challenge this ordering of the globe. Dutch, English and French mariners would challenge the duopoly in the sixteenth and seventeenth centuries, in the Caribbean as well as in the East Indies. They were labelled pirates by the Spanish and Portuguese, and often sailed with deliberately unclear understandings with their principals, that is the political leaders to whom they owed allegiance – allowing for plausible deniability if need be, or simply because the principals had little possibility of enforcing a ban. In our current categorization, they can best be understood as privateers. Regardless of label, these privateers broke the duopoly, and made interaction outside of Europe systemic, in a political as well as in an economic sense. Politically, private force demonstrated the impossibility of fully controlling the oceans, thus forcing the early empires to recon with the other polities. Economically, privateering and the capture of booty led to a truly system-wide spread of goods; around the year 1600 sugar from the Americas actually cost less in London than in Lisbon or the Indies. The capture of booty in turn increased the speed of system-wide market integration.

Private violence was thus crucial in making a system out of the ever more global interventions of the European powers. Of further importance to the spread of this system were the many trading companies (see Chapter 4, this volume). The Dutch East India Company (VOC) was at its heyday the world's largest company, and in its initial phases it was an instrument of war, much more than an instrument of trade. The profits made from privateering were in turn essential for setting up the economic and military infrastructure that allowed for further territorial expansion. Acting as privateers in their own right, and hiring privateers and mercenaries when needed for consolidating power and fighting against other European powers or local opposition, the trading companies of the core European powers were productive of the global international political as well as economic systems.

Maintaining an imperial system

Private force was central to the emergence of a European system of polities, as well as to the establishment of global systemic interaction between empires, and it remained important for the further maintenance, spread and integration of this system. At home, armies would continue to contain significant numbers of foreigners, and should logically be categorized as some sort of private force; during the eighteenth century somewhere between one-third and two-thirds of the infantry forces of France, Prussia and Britain were recruited from outside of the borders of the polity (Percy 2007). The pattern was even clearer overseas. Even as some of the powers of western Europe gradually became more state-like, empires were dominating eastern and central Europe, and the major western European powers were all engaged in overseas imperial ventures. The pattern of rule, at least in Asia, followed the pattern of expansion. The companies, like the VOC and its British counterpart the East India Company (EIC) were private entities although often more or less entangled with the states, and they ruled in state-like fashion in their areas of control until 1799 and 1858 respectively. In particular the EIC relied on hired local forces for the maintenance of internal order and the occupation of new land. The British percentage of the EIC armed forces never exceeded 20, and was just above

10 per cent at the outbreak of the Indian Rebellion in 1857. In North America, even though there were trading companies like the Hudson Bay Company, political and military authority was never as hybridized as in Asia. Lack of available manpower at the outbreak of the revolution in 1776 thus necessitated the hiring of German mercenaries (collectively known as 'Hessians') to help make up the shortfall. Mercenaries accounted for up to half of the British forces in the different campaigns of the Revolutionary War.

Furthermore, private force was part and parcel of imperial interaction at sea. No practice illustrates this better than the success of the armed merchantmen – ships sailing primarily with the intent of trade, but with privateer commissions allowing them to capture prizes if opportunity arose. Particularly for long-distance voyages, such ships might carry flags, papers and commissions from a number of polities, allowing for a play of ambiguity in their interaction with representatives of other polities in distant seas. More generally, after having successfully challenged the Iberian duopoly in the sixteenth century, privateering continued to play an important part in the wars between European empires until the Napoleonic Wars. The French deliberately chose a naval strategy of privateer warfare in the wars around 1700, with extensive intermingling of private and public aspects of force. Ministers of state were investing in privateers, while the navy lent ships and even crews to privateers, in the process giving the privateering captains officer's rank. Privateering also provided, in France and elsewhere, an opening for money and manpower that was denied regular outlets during wartime, thus also partaking in the circulation of manpower and goods central to the functioning of markets. The consequences of this drive for investment could be challenging to political aims, as when citizens of the rebel Dutch provinces were partly financing privateers from the Spanish Netherlands in an effort to gain access to desired goods and markets, and to make a larger profit. Likewise, French merchants would be investing in Barbary corsairs, at the same time as the French government was negotiating to end their raids. When wars ended, piracy often increased, as a surplus of sailors found yet new outlets for their force. Privateering, sometimes shading into piracy also provided an important opportunity for investment in the colonies, particularly relevant for the British North American and Caribbean colonies, where money would be raised and commissions issued with little regard to the nationality of the captain and crew. Thus, when the American colonies rebelled in 1776, they could draw on a long tradition for privateering. Without a regular navy, they were forced to rely on privateering, and the dislike of standing forces implied that even during the war of 1812, the commissioned privateering vessels of the United States outnumbered the ships of the regular navy seven to one.

Private force also continued to influence the relationship between European empires and local rulers, and between other empires than the western European ones. When William Kidd stood trial for piracy in London, his major problem was that he had taken a ship in the Indian Ocean that was leased to a high official of the Mughal court. His use of private force thus threatened the interests of private investors in the EIC, another wielder of private force. The naval success of the English and Dutch, in particular, implied that sailors and captains from these countries would be hired by other political entities as well, as during the Cretan war between Venice and the Ottoman Empire (1645–69), when sailors and captains from these countries provided a kind of force that the galley fleets of the Mediterranean could not provide.

The numerically most important form of private force was the kind raised in the overseas possessions. However, the categorization of such force is not obvious. One could argue that imperial possession makes this kind of force public and that at least with increasing central control over the colonies, such as happened with the end of company rule in India in 1858, the force changes character from private to public. This would fit well with the argument that the nineteenth century in general saw a move from mercenarism towards citizen armies (Avant

2000). On the other hand, the continued participation and importance of colonial force in ordering colonies of origin, ordering other colonies and in fighting the wars of the imperial core, also implies that such force undermines any notion of 'national' armed forces. Whatever they were, they were not citizen armies (Barkawi 2010), and these forces were crucial to the fighting of both world wars. Even today, French and British armed forces employ significant numbers of foreigners, such as the Foreign Legion and the Ghurkas, as does the US armed forces.

The rules, norms and values of the system

The centrality of private force to the international system of empires did not imply a private morality or lack of public rules and norms in the wielding and valuations of such force. On the contrary, the systemic existence of private force provided some of the earliest examples of joint action based on common interests as well as values, in efforts to control, and eventually suppress, private force. Put briefly, private force mattered for the spread and development of international law (and/or varieties of communal imperial law), as well as for the gradual codification of regulations of force and the normative prerogative of the allegedly sovereign states. Private force helped spread rules and norms, but also became the focus of normative judgment.

Starting with the spread of norms and rules, the early development of norms against the use of mercenaries (Percy 2007) constitute the first kind of widespread reaction against one form of private force. Starting in the late Medieval Age, mercenaries became more and more unpopular, for a number of reasons. Their association with plunder and sheer banditry obviously played a part, as did the desire of princes and nobles to control their territory, but just as important (sometimes more so) was the notion that one should only fight for a right cause. Making money was not considered to be such a cause. Thus, a lot of the arguments against mercenarism were made in religious terms. However, what was deemed problematic was not private force as such, but uncontrolled private force. Mercenaries could be accepted, indeed embraced, if placed under appropriate authority. While the practice of hiring individual mercenaries was largely abandoned during the sixteenth century and completely after the Thirty Years' War, mercenary companies (more often than not organized geographically) were integral parts of armies for centuries after.

Moving out to sea, Benton (2009) stresses how the growing empires would try to project sovereignty across vectors of naval space. After the possibility of dominion, that is actual ownership of the sea, had been rejected, polities (and lawyers) still insisted on the possibility of claiming jurisdiction. Jurisdiction followed the ships, and concerned both activities onboard the ships and interactions with other entities. As an illustration of this, in closely connected ways, privateering and piracy spread notions of legality and rule-bound behaviour across the oceans.

With privateering followed a need for legitimate authorities that could issue commissions, that is legitimize privateering, for practices which would allow for effective privateering far from home-ports as well as for prize courts where captured ships could be condemned and the surplus divided. Imperial expansion and captures overseas thus led to three distinct developments in international maritime juridical interaction. First, governors were given the right to issue commissions. Second, established practices of ransom and parole, were perpetuated in colonial waters. These practices were building on medieval traditions that allowed for the release of prizes with their original crew and with promises of future retributions or the cessation of fighting, making privateering more effective and efficient by doing away with the need for a return with the prize to a friendly port. Third, a system of prize courts was established in the colonies. There were clearly a lot of shenanigans going on with the issuing of commissions and in and around these courts. Furthermore, ransom and parole were often used to avoid paying the state its share of the prize, and it was common practice to have different commissions (with different specified targets) from different issuers. The key point is nevertheless that there was a mutual expectation that commissions did matter, that ransom and parole were to be respected and that prizes were to be condemned in an official way, even if that official way might involve bribery and swindling of investors and the state. The high number of protracted cases involving the condemnation of prizes suggests that these concerns were real, and that complaints had a chance of being heard.

International law was also developed through such processes; among early founders of international law, Gentili worked as a prize lawyer, while Grotius wrote *De iure praedae* as part of the legitimation for Dutch privateering and the expansion of the VOC. What emerged was less a new form of the law of nations than attempts at universalizing the law of the powerful empires, as the polities had different regulations and different court systems. Nevertheless, there was a common expectation of the proceedings being rule-bound, with translatability across systems. As Benton (2009: 160) argues, prize law was fashioned into 'a loose international regulatory framework – an early example of global administrative law' around 1750.

Turning from privateering to piracy, the importance of notions of legality becomes even clearer. The classical image of pirates rejecting all authority and embracing the role of 'villains of all nations' does not really fit well with piratical practice (see Chapter 6, this volume). Most pirates were working on the margins of the system, rather than rejecting it outright. The stress on legal forms underscores this point, even during the 'golden age' of piracy (1715–25), pirates would typically try to obtain some kind of papers legitimating their venture. These papers might be stolen, outdated or forged, but were carried as some sort of insurance in case of capture. Again, the stress on a veneer of legality suggests that legal norms mattered.

Even if emerging international laws and regulations helped regulate the use of private force in the international system, the growing power of states and the increasing importance of global trade gradually increased pressure for doing away with such force all together. Not surprisingly, piracy was the first form to be challenged on a system-wide level. Although piracy has been condemned for millennia, the political character of most definitions of piracy implied that system-wide norms against piracy did not develop until the seventeenth century. Until then, local piracy, often committed by mariners and fishermen in collusion with local notables, would be tacitly accepted. By way of example, whereas 'local' piracy had traditionally been seen as condonable in northwestern Europe, by the 1620s and 1630s, this was no longer the case. One reason could well be the perceived threat from Barbary corsairs. Faced with the effects of long-range naval raiding, it became less possible to condone the local varieties (Earle 2003). International wielding of private force helped create a normative reaction against such force.

The Barbary Corsairs also provide an illuminating example both of the systemic importance of values and norms, and the limits to their effectiveness. There was no doubt that all the Christian powers abhorred the slave-raiding practices of the north African principalities, and some of them were at times able to co-ordinate action against them, but at no time were all the major navies working together to curb the threat. The possibilities of 'using' the principalities to gain political and mercantile advantages were greater than the desire to be rid of them once and for all (ibid.). The fight against the typical pirates, in particular the Caribbean and Atlantic ones, faced fewer such hurdles. From Gentili, pirates were defined as the enemies of all mankind, and with increasing world trade and increasing British naval force from around 1700 followed a push to eradicate piracy. Although the British navy was quite clearly the leading one in the fight, French, Spanish, Dutch and Portuguese forces were often also involved, and even if outright co-operation in battle was not common, there would typically be exchange of information and news. The joint condemnation of pirates as being the enemies of mankind gave a joint normative purpose to the hunt for them. By 1725, the classical pirates were all but eradicated in the Atlantic, even though a new outbreak in the aftermath of the Latin American wars of independence also had to be handled, and gradually piracy was combatted in other oceans as well.

While privateering faced less normative condemnation than piracy, the growing power of the norms of sovereign control and the many complaints against unchecked privateering implied a growing normative pressure for its abolishment. The Treaty of Paris (1856), outlawed privateering, and even non-signatories (like the US) adhered to it. If at first providing a field for the growth and spread of legal thinking about relations between entities, and what comes close to an international regime regulating privateering, with the rise of the territorial national states, the regulatory regime lost out to prohibition.

Apart from the imperial forces, mercenaries fell victim to the same kinds of pressure. Building on the existing distrust of mercenaries, states in the aftermath of the American and French revolutions gradually moved towards citizen armies. As discussed by Percy (2007) this move has been explained by material changes, the ideational preference (bolstered by nationalism) for citizen armies and by domestic politics; her compelling argument is that in addition to these factors, the further development of a wider norm against mercenarism was crucial to the system-wide adoption of citizen armies. The movement was twofold – states on the one hand reduced, and later stopped, recruiting foreign nationals, on the other hand they also enacted laws prohibiting their own citizens to enlist in foreign armed forces. Although there have been obvious exceptions to the rule, the norm of non-use of mercenaries and the ideology of citizen soldiers persisted through most of the twentieth century.

Forms of systemic interaction

The systemic application of private force was couched in a normative and legal framework, and upheld by specialized institutions (like prize courts). However, private force also influenced more general forms of systemic interaction, in effect fuelling the tighter integration of the system. Interestingly, these consequences were largely unintended.

Of particular interest in this respect is the wider system of interaction set up around privateering. As noted above, the increase and spread of privateering necessitated the establishment of prize courts in colonial outposts. However, if far from their home base, privateers would also regularly seek neutral ports. This in turn necessitated some sort of representation in these ports, both for polities outfitting privateers and for polities having their ships captured (Leira and de Carvalho 2010). These representatives, typically consuls, would protect the interests of their sending polity in local court proceedings, support privateers, ransom captured sailors, arrange for prisoner exchanges and in general facilitate interaction. Typically, such consuls would remain after the cessation of hostilities, continuing to protect the interests of their sending polity. Likewise, in the north African principalities, the constant influx of slaves and the need to provide constant gifts for the maintenance of peace led to a permanent diplomatic presence. Thus, privateering led to a gradual increase in the density of networks of information and interaction, functionally tying the system closer together.

Conclusion

This chapter has presented the case for the importance of private force to the gradual emergence of the international system which we live in today. Private force – and the reaction to it

– was central to the emergence of the system as a system, it helped spread the system from Europe to the rest of the world, it underpinned the system as a system of empires, it played a central part in the development of norms and rules of interaction and it spawned further systemic institutional developments.

However, the argument is not that private force somehow made the modern international system. Rather, I have stressed how private force has tended to be ignored in accounts of the international system; private force has been viewed as something negative, and primarily something to be eradicated through processes of state-building. In contrast, I suggest that private force, as a boundary-crossing or boundary-challenging phenomenon, must necessarily be studied in a systemic perspective. Likewise, the system can profitably be studied through the lenses of private violence. What thus emerges is a picture of a system where private violence played an integral and productive part to the gradual systemic development. Our accounts of both the system and of private violence become better through studying them together, rather than separately. There seems to be little doubt that this is also the case for current affairs, and the historical record should thus provide ample inspiration for studying both the systemic effects of the current growth of private force and the systemic character of this private force. It obviously also helps that the historical record provides for a fascinating read; raise the black flag!

Bibliography

Avant, D. (2000) 'From Mercenary to Citizen Armies: Explaining Change in the Practice of War', *International Organization* 54(1): 41–72.

Barkawi, T. (2010) 'State and Armed Force in International Context', in A. Colas and B. Mabee (eds), *Mercenaries, Pirates, Bandits and Empires*, London: Hurst & Company, pp. 33–53.

Benton, L. (2009) *A Search for Sovereignty. Law and Geography in European Empires 1400–1900*, Cambridge: Cambridge University Press.

Earle, P. (2003) *The Pirate Wars*, New York: Thomas Dunne Books.

Glete, J. (2000) *Warfare at Sea, 1500–1650: Maritime Conflicts and the Transformation of Europe*, Abingdon: Routledge.

Leira, H. and de Carvalho, B. (2010) 'Privateers of the North Sea: At Worlds End – French Privateers in Norwegian Waters', in A. Colas and B. Mabee (eds), *Mercenaries, Pirates, Bandits and Empires*, London: Hurst & Company, pp. 55–82.

Löwenheim, O. (2007) *Predators and Parasites: Persistent Agents of Transnational Harm and Great Power Authority*, Ann Arbor, MI: University of Michigan Press.

Owens, P. (2010) 'Distinctions, Distinctions: "Public" and "Private" Force?', in A. Colas and B. Mabee (eds), *Mercenaries, Pirates, Bandits and Empires*, London: Hurst & Company, pp. 15–32.

Percy, S. (2007) *Mercenaries: The History of a Norm in International Relations*, Oxford: Oxford University Press.

Starkey, D. J. (2011) 'Voluntaries and Sea Robbers: A Review of the Academic Literature on Privateering, Corsairing, Buccaneering and Piracy', *The Mariner's Mirror* 97(1): 127–47.

Thomson, J. (1994) *Mercenaries, Pirates, and Sovereigns: State Building and Extraterritorial Violence in Early Modern Europe*, Princeton, NJ: Princeton University Press.

4

COMPANY SOVEREIGNS, PRIVATE VIOLENCE AND COLONIALISM

Andrew Phillips

This chapter analyses the central role company sovereigns – the most important practitioners of non-state violence during the colonial era – played in driving Western colonial expansion. The chapter begins with a conceptual overview that problematizes the dichotomy between public and private violence, introduces company sovereigns, and distinguishes them from other forms of state and non-state colonial violence. I then define company sovereigns more comprehensively, and trace their evolution from the seventeenth through the twentieth centuries. This encompasses their initial role as pioneers of European imperialism in Africa, Asia and the Americas; their revival during the 'new imperialism' of the late nineteenth century; and their delegitimation and abolition in the twentieth century. The final section argues not only that international relations scholars should acknowledge company sovereigns as much as sovereign states as the true vanguards of the spread of a European-dominated global colonial order, but also that their role is crucial to contextualize and comprehend the contemporary re-emergence of private international violence.

Non-state violence: an essential feature of European colonialism

In situating private violence within the context of European colonial expansion, three framing observations are required. First, the contemporary distinction between public and private violence is socially constructed, and emerged only recently in historical terms (Owens 2008). Before the late eighteenth century, when Europeans began to imagine the economy as a discrete sphere of interaction distinct from other forms of social activity, they generally did not see violence as the sovereign state's exclusive preserve. Instead, rulers typically shared quintessentially sovereign prerogatives, including the rights to wage war and violently enforce laws, with numerous non-state actors. Before the 1800s, rulers generally lacked the desire or the capacity to pursue a monopoly over legitimate violence. Instead, they authorized non-state actors to use force for various purposes, from tax collection through to law enforcement and – most importantly for present purposes – overseas territorial expansion (Allen 2011: 191–2).

Second, what little coercive power European sovereigns did enjoy dissipated rapidly over distance (Roper and van Ruymbeke 2007: 4). This ensured that non-state violence featured especially prominently in European efforts to project power into the Americas, Asia and Africa. Before the annihilation of distance that nineteenth century advances in transportation and communication wrought, Europeans faced formidable logistical challenges advancing their overseas colonial ambitions (Headrick 2012: 8). In part, they overcame the tyranny of distance by delegating sovereign powers to wage war, make laws and pursue diplomacy to non-state actors. Thus, '[t]he exercise of sovereignty was extended by dividing it' (Halliday 2013: 269). Entities such as the English and Dutch East India Companies enabled Europeans to pursue wealth and power at trans-continental distances by investing quasi-autonomous corporations with extensive powers of government overseas. Not all European states expanded through the use of company sovereigns. But the practice was sufficiently conspicuous among leading colonial powers to warrant foregrounding company sovereigns as central actors.

Third, the violence – both state and non-state – that attended European colonial expansion took a bewildering variety of forms. To make this discussion manageable, I classify forms of colonial violence within a 2 × 2 taxonomy that builds on Stephen Krasner's distinction between authority and control as aspects of sovereign power (Krasner 1999: 4–6). At one end of the continuum, we find sovereign statist forms of violence, where sovereign states both authorized violence and directly controlled the means through it was exercised. An example would be the Portuguese Estado da India's use of naval violence to establish the king of Portugal's claims to maritime hegemony in the early modern Indian Ocean. At the other end of the continuum, we find forms of violence that sovereign states neither authorized nor controlled, but that also attended Western expansion, including pirates, bandits and adventurers, who used violence for purely private gain, or to pressure Western governments to extend their authority into new territories.

At the mid-point of the continuum, we find two further forms of violence – non-state authorized and state controlled, and state-authorized and non-state controlled. Non-state-authorized but state-controlled forms of violence were extremely rare – perhaps the only notable example would be the English East India Company's co-opting of royal naval resources to fend off French predation in the Indian Ocean in the mid-eighteenth century (Marshall 1980: 25). Conversely, state authorized but non-state controlled violence was a central feature of European expansion. Indeed, this chapter's central claim is that company sovereigns from the 1600s to the 1900s served as one of the principal vanguards of European conquest in the Americas, Africa and Asia. Accordingly, the following discussion first defines company sovereigns, before tracking their historical evolution and reflecting on their contemporary legacies for world politics.

Company sovereigns as vanguard agents of European imperialism

Company sovereigns constituted hybrid polity forms, which combined governance functions characteristic of the sovereign state with the profit-maximizing motivations of the private corporation:

> [Company sovereigns] did what early modern governments did: erect and administer law; collect taxes; provide protection; inflict punishment; perform stateliness; regulate economic, religious, and civil life; conduct diplomacy and wage war; make claims to jurisdiction over land and sea; cultivate authority over and obedience from those people subject to [their] command.
>
> *(Stern 2011: 3–4)*

They derived their power from revocable charters granted to them either by kings or parliaments, and so theoretically remained subordinate to their home states. But in practice, they operated so far from Europe as to enjoy virtually free rein in their colonizing efforts. Likewise, company sovereigns retained international legal personalities distinct from their home states, being able to conclude treaties with foreign powers without the imprimatur of rulers back in Europe.

Their governmental prerogatives notwithstanding, it was profit – not power – that primarily motivated the company sovereigns' creation and expansion. Thus, the English East India Company (hereafter the EIC) was set up in 1600 to maximize merchants' profits from trade with Asia. It did so by pooling their capital in a single organization, and then investing this organization with a royally guaranteed monopoly to manage England's Asian trade (Stern 2011: 10). Likewise, company sovereigns and 'private' proprietors led European expansion in the Americas, with profit-seeking proprietors charged with recruiting settlers, purchasing and transporting slaves, and establishing and managing plantations to produce commodities (especially sugar and cotton) for sale in Europe (Hsueh 2010: 1).

The enormous distances separating Europe from the rest of the world in the pre-industrial era made colonialism extremely expensive and risky. For cash-strapped European governments still struggling to consolidate power at home, company sovereigns provided a cheap means of mobilizing the money and initiative of powerful subjects to advance imperial ends. The global expansion of trade after 1500, following the European 'discovery' of the Americas and the opening of a direct maritime trading route to Asia, made trans-continental imperialism potentially extremely profitable. Medieval European traditions of delegating governmental powers to local elites to subdue Europe's 'internal frontiers' meanwhile provided a precedent for outsourcing early modern imperialism to company sovereigns (Lloyd and Metzer 2013: 13). The resulting intersection of opportunity with precedent provided the context for company sovereigns' emergence as imperialism's violent vanguards from the seventeenth century onwards.

Company sovereigns in the Americas, Africa and Asia from 1500 to 1750

European colonial violence in the early modern period centred primarily on three onslaughts respectively directed at the Americas, Africa and Asia. In the Americas, Europeans dispossessed and exterminated large sections of the indigenous population, and laid claim to the New World's vast reserves of land and precious metals. In Africa, they established the transatlantic slave trade, which saw close to ten million African slaves forcibly transported to the Americas and other parts of the Atlantic basin from 1450 to 1867 (Lovejoy 1982: 477). In the Indian Ocean and East Asia, they gate-crashed vast trading networks stretching from Zanzibar to Nagasaki. Company sovereigns were integrally involved in spearheading each prong of this triple assault on the non-European world.

European colonialism in the Americas assumed various forms, consonant with the different traditions and resources of the primary colonial powers, the English, Dutch, French, Spanish and Portuguese. These variations notwithstanding, most of these powers resorted to forms of proprietary colonization, involving company sovereigns and other forms of chartered authority (Tomlins 2001: 316). For the Atlantic powers, distance was the problem and delegation the solution in conquering the New World:

> Encomenderos in New Spain, patroons in New Netherland, Brazilian donatory captains, and various seigneurs and companies in the French Empire … exercised local authority by virtue of grants, customarily of lands, that incorporated responsibility for maintaining order at some level just as aristocrats and lower landholding orders did in Western Europe.
>
> *(Roper and van Ruymbeke 2007: 7)*

Admittedly, the Iberian powers tried to keep sub-rulers in the Americas tightly reined under the yoke of royal authority. Conversely, both the English and the Dutch relied extensively on company sovereigns to spearhead American colonization. The Hudson Bay Company (the HBC) and the Dutch West India Company (WIC) both played crucial roles in advancing these polities' interests in the Americas. At one time the largest landowner in the world, governing a territory encompassing 'nearly three million square miles – ten times the size of the Holy Roman Empire at its height' (Newman 2000: 4), the HBC also effectively controlled the highly lucrative fur trade throughout much of British North America from the seventeenth though nineteenth centuries. Less successful in the scale of its conquests, the WIC critically aided Dutch settlement of the Americas. The WIC was also heavily involved in facilitating the trade of another key commodity of the Atlantic plantation economy – African slaves (Postma 1990: 16–17).

Having ravaged and reduced the indigenous Amerindian population, European invaders turned to African slaves to feed labour-intensive agricultural industries, most notably sugar and cotton production. Company sovereigns again played key roles in sustaining this process. Company sovereigns initiated diplomatic relations with African rulers, established fortified trading networks along the African coast, and maintained vast merchant fleets to transport slaves to New World plantations. Prior to the nineteenth century, a combination of diseases and indigenous martial prowess generally kept Europeans confined to the African coast (Cooney 1980: 158). Consequently, company sovereigns relied on African rulers as 'wholesalers' to supply the slaves that company agents then exported. In the long term, the costs of maintaining fortress networks in Africa helped bankrupt the WIC and its English counterpart, the Royal African Company, and more improvised and nimble private consortia emerged to fill the resulting vacuum (Carlos and Kruse 1996: 294). This caveat aside, in the seventeenth century in particular, company sovereigns played a pioneering role in forging the transatlantic slave economy.

Finally, company sovereigns were central players in opening up Asian markets to European commerce in the seventeenth through to the nineteenth centuries. Preceded by the more classically statist Portuguese Estado da India, company sovereigns such as the Dutch and English East India Companies helped facilitate a twenty-five-fold increase in maritime trade between Europe and Asia from 1500 to 1800 (de Vries 2010: 718). Company sovereigns at times inflicted near-genocidal levels of violence on local populations to secure their commercial objectives. Thus, the Dutch East India Company (VOC) exterminated the native population of the Spice Islands (located in what is now Indonesia) in the 1620s and repopulated them with slaves in an effort to monopolize global production of cloves, mace and nutmeg, spices worth more than their weight in gold (Adams 1996: 18). More commonly, though, company sovereigns were supplicants rather than suzerains in Asia. From Mughal India to Qing China and Japan, the company sovereigns typically maintained networks of trading 'factories' under local rulers' sufferance, and from a position of military inferiority. This changed only from the mid-eighteenth century, when the English East India Company abandoned its earlier aversion to territorial aggrandizement, and embarked on a haphazard series of conquests that had by 1849 won it near-total hegemony on the Indian sub-continent. By this time, however, Europeans were beginning to question the legitimacy and utility of company sovereigns, potentially condemning them to terminal decline (Stern 2008: 283).

The decline, revival and abolition of company sovereigns, 1750–1950

Whether aiding in the conquest of the Americas, mediating the transatlantic slave trade or elbowing their way into Asian palaces and bazaars, company sovereigns played a crucial role in leading early modern Western colonial expansion. From the mid-eighteenth century, however, intellectual shifts in Europe and accelerating global military competition together seemed set to condemn company sovereigns to oblivion. Intellectually, Europeans increasingly reconceived the economy as a realm separate and distinct from other spheres of social life. In the English-speaking world in particular, this shift saw liberals such as Adam Smith challenge company sovereigns' monopolistic privileges as antithetical to the merits of free-market economics (Jones and Ville 1996: 898). Conservatives meanwhile attacked company sovereigns from a different vantage point. Scandalized by the East India Company's conquest of Bengal in the 1760s, Edmund Burke bemoaned the threat to both English and Indian liberty that the Company's unprecedented accumulation of power in the sub-continent supposedly represented (Dirks 2009). Reflecting different ideological standpoints, these critiques converged in their hostility to company sovereigns' retention of governmental prerogatives.

This shifting intellectual climate corresponded with a global acceleration of military competition, which also augured ill for the company sovereigns. From the Seven Years' War onwards (1756–63), European inter-state rivalries intensified and globalized. For the company sovereigns, this exacerbated an inner tension between their driving motives of profit and power, which they had long struggled to reconcile. In Asia in particular, company sovereigns had generally avoided large-scale conquest, for fear that the overheads of governing large indigenous populations would corrode any profits they might otherwise yield from their trading operations. The heightened competition of the late eighteenth century nevertheless pushed company sovereigns towards ever-greater reliance on territorial expansion and the taxation of local populations. These expedients, frequently driven by the rapacity of local company agents, proved financially ruinous in the long run. They also began to change the company sovereigns' very nature, as conquest and government eclipsed trade and profit as their primary purposes.

By the end of the Napoleonic Wars (1815), most of the company sovereigns were either bankrupt or subject to much tighter state supervision, consistent with their newly dominant function as governors rather than traders (Stern 2008: 283). This trend continued over the nineteenth century, as the sovereign state's dominance over alternative polity forms grew apace. In 1857, the 'Indian mutiny' saw the British Raj nearly toppled. Following this near-fatal crisis, the British Crown assumed direct responsibility from the EIC for governing its vast Asian empire. In North America, meanwhile, the Deed of Surrender saw the HBC yield the vast bulk of its territory to the British Crown (which in turn transferred it to the newly formed Canadian Confederacy) in 1869–70 (Newman 2000: 575).

From the Hudson Bay to south Asia, company sovereigns appeared fated to extinction by the mid-nineteenth century. Had this proved to be the case, they could perhaps be written off as an exotic footnote to the story of European imperial expansion, institutional hybrids that were dismantled once sovereign states marshalled the capacity to directly fund and administer trans-continental colonization. But company sovereigns proved far more resilient and adaptive than such a linear narrative would suggest.

The last third of the nineteenth century saw a surge in global interconnectedness, propelled by revolutionary advances in communication and transportation technologies, most notably the telegraph, the steamship and the railway. This growth in interconnectedness coincided after 1873 with a prolonged global economic depression, and a further intensification of imperial rivalries. This competition was particularly pronounced in sub-Saharan Africa, mainland south-east Asia and the Pacific, and it was in these regions that company sovereigns re-emerged to assert their home states' colonial interests.

Company sovereigns revived after the 1870s as a familiar means for countries to extend imperial influence while supposedly deflecting the costs and risks of colonial expansion to private actors. In practice, the rebooted chartered companies were more tethered to home governments than their early modern antecedents. Moreover, hopes that they would relieve governments of the financial risks and costs of imperialism proved forlorn, with taxpayers typically having to bail out ill-conceived and profit-less colonial adventures (Reno 2004: 613). Nevertheless, nineteenth-century company sovereigns proved at least as rapacious and no less violent than their forebears. This is most evident in the depredations of the Congo Free State, perhaps history's most notorious expression of private colonial violence.

The Congo Free State (today's Democratic Republic of the Congo) encompassed a territory in Central Africa approximately the size of western Europe, which Belgian King Leopold II ruled as his private fiefdom from 1885 to 1908. Exports of rubber and ivory, harvested by an enslaved local workforce, formed the foundation of the Congo Free State's economy. Notorious for its brutality, the Congo Free State presided over the death of up to ten million Africans (Weisbord 2003: 6). The regime's violence ultimately sparked an international campaign, provoking such popular outrage that Leopold was eventually forced to transfer sovereignty over the Congo Free State to the Belgian government (ibid.: 35).

Beyond its singular savagery, the Congo Free State merits attention to illustrate how unremarkable private colonialism was well into the twentieth century.[1] Besides the Congo Free State, the German East Africa Company and the British South Africa Company respectively spearheaded German and British imperialism throughout much of sub-Saharan Africa, the latter administering what is now Zimbabwe until 1924. Likewise, Portugal's Mozambique Company (established in 1892) ruled much of Mozambique until 1942, when Lisbon asserted direct authority over the territories it had formerly ruled. Elsewhere, the British North Borneo Company administered North Borneo (now the Malaysian state of Sabah) until 1946, when the territory briefly became a Crown colony prior to Malaysian independence in 1957.

Private colonial violence thus formed a common feature of international politics until the mid-twentieth century. No single international scandal matching the revelation of the Congo Free State's atrocities ever emerged to delegitimize the chartered companies wholesale as a model of political and economic organization. Instead, they died a slow death, being incrementally liquidated for both functional and normative reasons.

Functionally, chartered companies proved brutal and ineffectual as colonial administrators. Low levels of capitalization meant that most lacked the resources to invest in the infrastructure needed to effectively administer their territories. Instead, they relied on short-term coercive measures (most notably corvee labour systems) to exploit their colonies' natural resources. This set a pattern of weak and predatory governance that would persist into the post-colonial era (Vail 1976: 389). Likewise, the chartered companies failed to contain European colonial rivalries. Advocates conceived chartered companies as a cheap means of asserting metropolitan governments' strategic and commercial interests without directly investing governments' interests or prestige (Reno 2004: 608). In practice, however, they rarely contained diplomatic or military rivalries, but instead often required political, financial and even military rescue from their government patrons (Vail 1976: 416).

Normatively, it would be anachronistic to credit the chartered companies' demise to the decolonization movement, which gained global momentum after 1945, as the last company sovereigns were being wound up. Even before then, Western governments were increasingly tying the legitimacy of colonial rule to notions of trusteeship and economic development (Bain 2003: 113). In this light, chartered companies' well-publicized failures to advance their subjects' welfare contributed significantly to their delegitimation. As Western governments embraced more expansive programmes of social reform, both at home but also in the colonies, the idea of delegating rule to profit-driven companies correspondingly lost favour. By the mid-twentieth century, chartered companies' past governance failures, combined with their increasing incongruence with established norms of development and nascent norms of decolonization, at last condemned them to oblivion.

The company sovereigns: theoretical relevance and contemporary legacies

The above survey demonstrates company sovereigns' centrality as agents of European colonialism. The sheer scale of the company sovereigns' violence merits greater attention within international relations (IR), a discipline that aims to understand, address (and, ideally, redress) the problem of violence in global politics. Beyond this broad exhortation, a greater focus on the company sovereigns promises three more concrete pay-offs.

First, a greater focus on company sovereigns promises to yield a better understanding of the international system's origins and expansion. Writing of western Europe's transition from medieval heteronomy to sovereign anarchy, Ruggie has observed: 'The chief characteristic of the modern system of territorial rule is the consolidation of all parcelized and personalized authority into one public realm. This consolidation entailed two fundamental spatial demarcations: between public and private realms and between internal and external realms' (Ruggie 1993: 151). Although Ruggie stresses the protracted nature of this dual demarcation, his analysis supports a conventional Westphalian narrative of the modern international system's origins. Through this narrative, various 'monopoly mechanisms' (Stinchcombe 1998: 267) squeezed out competitors to the sovereign state, first within Europe, and then throughout the wider world. Key to this process was the state's monopolization of coercion within tightly delimited territorial boundaries, and its concomitant disarmament of non-state actors. Violence through this process became a prerogative of public power, increasingly invested exclusively in the sovereign state.

Conversely, if we bring the company-state back into our analyses of the international system's evolution, we can discern a more crooked and elongated path to sovereign-territorial modernity. Rather than seeing the medieval-to-modern transition as an ever-narrowing funnel, in which competitive pressures weeded out alternatives to the sovereign state, we see instead the reconfiguration of medieval forms and practices, and their adaptation to the post-1500 challenges of trans-continental colonization. Far from being peculiar to medieval Europe, heteronomous (i.e. territorially non-exclusive) non-state polity forms thrived over the course of early modern Western colonial expansion. Indeed, at the very moment that some non-state polity forms (e.g. city-states and city-leagues) were vanishing from Europe, others (pre-eminently the company sovereigns) were emerging to take the lead in projecting Western power into the non-European world (Curtin 1984: 4).

Acknowledging this reality reinforces and enriches an established revisionism, which has challenged the Peace of Westphalia as signifying an epochal rupture demarcating the medieval from the modern eras (Teschke 2003; Osiander 2007; Nexon 2009). More fundamentally, it also helps destabilize the dual demarcations (inside/outside, public/private) that are routinely seen as underpinning modern political life. While drawing on medieval precedents of chartered authority, company sovereigns were emphatically modern institutions, combining features of the sovereign state and the limited liability corporation. But their very hybridity also meant that they transgressed the inside/outside and public/private dichotomies we conventionally associate with modernity. Especially in pre-colonial Asia, company sovereigns won locals' grudging acceptance precisely because of their willingness to share sovereign prerogatives with host communities within limited commercial enclaves (Phillips and Sharman 2015). Likewise, though dedicated mainly to profit (a quintessentially 'private' motive), company sovereigns were also public entities, exercising powers of war and law-making commonly identified with sovereign states. In their very constitution, they confounded notions of territorial exclusivity and the compartmentalization of power into distinct public and private spheres. Recognition of this reality promises to expand our awareness of the diverse polity forms that populated the early modern world, and remind us of the prevalence of heterogeneity over sovereign-territorial homogeneity as a hallmark of the age of European expansion.

Second, a greater focus on the company sovereigns compels us to acknowledge their pioneering role alongside sovereign states as agents of European expansion. Too often, our conception of the dynamics of European conquest remains hostage to a state-centric 'vanguardist' vision of history (Buzan 2010: 2). Through this optic, the sovereign state – the supposed exemplar of European modernity – formed the primary agent through which Westerners forced themselves on non-European societies. Many scholars adhering to this narrative have attributed the 'rise of the West' to the centripetal consequences of the early modern 'military revolution' (McNeill 1982; Parker 1996). Through this reading, a combination of military-technological innovation and bureaucratic-administrative centralization yielded precociously powerful 'national states' (Tilly 1992: 5–6). These national states equipped Europeans with the institutional wherewithal to then conquer large sections of the non-European world.

This narrative struggles to accommodate the pivotal role company sovereigns, as relatively decentralized networked polities, played in driving European expansion. Far from developing as a contrivance of kings, the early company sovereigns more often emerged at the initiative of powerful subjects, who sought rulers' imprimatur to pursue profit-oriented colonial enterprises. The 'empire of civil society' (Rosenberg 1994), rather than rulers themselves, frequently took the lead in planting colonies overseas. Likewise, as successors to medieval forms of chartered authority, company sovereigns embodied not the Hobbesian centralism of the ideal-typical sovereign state, but testified to the immense power of dispersed and delegated forms of authority as instruments of imperial expansion.

Finally, a greater understanding of the company sovereigns' nature and history helps us to better comprehend the contemporary resurgence of 'private' international violence. The operations of private security actors in Africa, particularly with regard to securing resource enclaves in weak states, have led some to draw parallels between this practice and the activities of nineteenth century chartered company sovereigns (Reno 2004). Such parallels are useful to the extent that they rescue us from the historical amnesia that characterizes state-centric studies of global politics. But they can be dangerous to the extent that they foster the 'back to the future' fallacy, that today's private security actors somehow form linear descendants to yesterday's company sovereigns.

The early modern company sovereigns, their nineteenth and twentieth century successors, and today's private security actors undeniably share important features. All combine profit seeking with either possession of direct coercive power, the execution of security prerogatives traditionally associated with sovereign states, or some combination of the two. Nevertheless, each emerged at distinct historical junctures, distinguished by contingent conceptions of sovereignty and equally idiosyncratic conceptions of the public/private divide. Emerging at a time when Europe was still shedding its heteronomous medieval inheritance, early company sovereigns embodied a conception of sovereignty as divisible and capable of delegation to actors that only later generations would conceive as 'private' in character. Conversely, the chartered companies arose during the age of the 'new imperialism', when modern ideas of sovereignty were more clearly formed and public/private distinctions more sharply delineated. The existence of a highly stratified international order, that abridged or withheld sovereign rights from many non-European societies, nevertheless left space for the resurgence and re-articulation of forms of company sovereignty to stabilize the international system's 'turbulent frontiers' (Reno 2004: 613). Finally, today's private security actors operate within partially de-territorialized 'global security assemblages' (Abrahamsen and Williams 2011: 3), where norms of sovereign statehood have been universalized, and the arrogation of sovereign powers to corporate actors has been correspondingly limited. At the same time, a combination of neoliberal economic ideals, state weakness in the developing world, and a growing enthusiasm for public-private partnerships has created a niche for private actors to supplement rather than supplant indigenous sovereign power in the provision of security services.

My point is not to suggest that a neat institutional genealogy can be traced linking the English East India Company to today's global private security providers. Rather, I have sought to demonstrate the historic centrality of company sovereigns to the colonial experience, and to illustrate how foregrounding company sovereigns more prominently in our analyses allows us to lay bare the historically varied and contested constitutive divisions – between inside and outside and between public and private – that help make up international systems. Pursuing such an enterprise not only enables us to better understand the modern international system's evolution; it also helps us to better contextualize and comprehend the significance of private international violence as an enduring feature of contemporary global politics.

Note

1   I classify the Congo Free State as an example of private colonialism because King Leopold II ruled it as his own private property, separate and distinct from his position as the public sovereign and head of state. In this respect, it was comparable to other forms of proprietary colonialism.

Bibliography

Abrahamsen, R. and Williams, M. C. (2011) *Security Beyond the State: Private Security in International Politics*, Cambridge: Cambridge University Press.

Adams, J. (1996) 'Principals and Agents, Colonials and Company Men: The Decay of Colonial Control in the Dutch East Indies', *American Sociological Review* 61(1): 12–28.

Allen, D. W. (2011) *The Institutional Revolution: Measurement and the Economic Emergence of the Modern World*, Chicago, IL: University of Chicago Press.

Bain, W. (2003) *Between Anarchy and Society: Trusteeship and the Obligations of Power*, Oxford: Oxford University Press.

Buzan, B. (2010) 'Culture and International Society', *International Affairs* 86(1): 1–25.

Carlos, A. M. and Kruse, J. B. (1996) 'The Decline of the Royal African Company: Fringe Firms and the Role of the Charter 1', *Economic History Review* 49(2): 291–313.

Clulow, A. (2013) *The Company and the Shogun: The Dutch Encounter With Tokugawa Japan*, New York: Columbia University Press.

Cooney, S. (1980) 'Overseas Companies as Transnational Actors during the European Conquest of Africa', *Review of International Studies* 6(2): 154–79.

Curtin, P. D. (1984) *Cross-Cultural Trade in World History*, Cambridge: Cambridge University Press.

De Vries, J. (2010) 'The Limits of Globalization in the Early Modern World', *Economic History Review* 63(3): 710–33.

Dirks, N. B. (2009) *The Scandal of Empire: India and the Creation of Imperial Britain*, Cambridge, MA: Harvard University Press.

Erikson, E. (2014) *Between Monopoly and Free Trade: The English East India Company, 1600–1757*, Princeton, NJ: Princeton University Press.

Halliday, P. (2013) 'Laws' Histories: Pluralisms, Pluralities, Diversity', in L. Benton and R. J. Ross (eds), *Legal Pluralism and Empire, 1500–1850*, New York: New York University Press, pp. 261–77.

Headrick, D. R. (2012) *Power over Peoples: Technology, Environments, and Western Imperialism, 1400 to the Present*, Princeton, NJ: Princeton University Press.

Hsueh, V. (2010) *Hybrid Constitutions – Challenging Legacies of Law, Privilege, and Culture in Colonial America*, Durham, NC: Duke University Press.

Jones, S. R. H. and Ville, S. P. (1996) 'Efficient Transactors or Rent-Seeking Monopolists? The Rationale for Early Chartered Trading Companies', *Journal of Economic History* 56(4): 898–915.

Krasner, S. D. (1999) *Sovereignty: Organized Hypocrisy*, Princeton, NJ: Princeton University Press.

Lloyd, C. and Metzer, J. (2013) 'Settler Colonization and Societies in World History: Patterns and Concepts', in C. Lloyd and J. Metzer (eds), *Settler Economies in World History*, Leiden: Brill, pp. 1–34.

Lovejoy, P. E. (1982) 'The Volume of the Atlantic Slave Trade: A Synthesis', *Journal of African History* 23(4): 473–501.

Marshall, P. J. (1980) 'Western Arms in Maritime Asia in the Early Phases of Expansion', *Modern Asian Studies* 14(1): 13–28.

McNeill, W. H. (1982) *The Pursuit of Power: Technology, Armed Force, and Society since AD 1000*, Chicago, IL: University of Chicago Press.

Newman, P. C. (2000) *Empire of the Bay: The Company of Adventurers that Seized a Continent*, London: Penguin.

Nexon, D. H. (2009) *The Struggle for Power in Early Modern Europe: Religious Conflict, Dynastic Empires, and International Change*, Princeton, NJ: Princeton University Press.

Osiander, A. (2007) *Before the State: Systemic Political Change in the West from the Greeks to the French Revolution*, Oxford: Oxford University Press.

Owens, P. (2008) 'Distinctions, Distinctions: "Public" and "Private" Force?', *International Affairs* 84(5): 977–90.

Parker, G. (1996) *The Military Revolution: Military Innovation and the Rise of the West, 1500–1800*, Cambridge: Cambridge University Press.

Phillips, A. and Sharman, J. C. (2015) *International Order in Diversity: War, Trade and Rule in the Indian Ocean*, Cambridge: Cambridge University Press.

Postma, J. M. (1990) *The Dutch in the Atlantic Slave Trade, 1600–1815*, Cambridge: Cambridge University Press.

Reno, W. (2004) 'Order and Commerce in Turbulent Areas: 19th Century Lessons, 21st Century Practice', *Third World Quarterly* 25(4): 607–25.

Roper, L.H. and Van Ruymbeke, B. (Eds.) (2007) *Constructing Early Modern Empires: Proprietary Ventures in the Atlantic World, 1500–1750*, Leiden: Brill.

Rosenberg, J. (1994) *The Empire of Civil Society: A Critique of the Realist Theory of International Relations*, London: Verso.

Ruggie, J. G. (1993) 'Territoriality and Beyond: Problematizing Modernity in International Relations', *International Organization* 47(1): 139–74.

Stern, P. J. (2008) '"A Politie of Civill & Military Power": Political Thought and the Late Seventeenth Century Foundations of the East India Company State', *Journal of British Studies* 47(2): 253–83.

Stern, P. J. (2011) *The Company-State: Corporate Sovereignty and the Early Modern Foundations of the British Empire in India*, Oxford: Oxford University Press.

Stinchcombe, A. (1998) 'Monopolistic Competition as a Mechanism', in P. Hedstrom and R. Swedberg (eds), *Social Mechanisms: An Analytic Approach to Social Theory*, Cambridge: Cambridge University Press, pp. 268–305.

Teschke, B. (2003) *The Myth of 1648: Class, Geopolitics, and the Making of Modern International Relations*, London: Verso Books.

Thomson, J. (1994) *Mercenaries, Pirates and Sovereigns: State-Building and Extra-Territorial Violence in Early Modern Europe*, Princeton, NJ: Princeton University Press.

Tilly, C. (1992) *Coercion, Capital, and European States, AD 990–1992*, Oxford: Basil Blackwell.

Tomlins, C. (2001) 'The Legal Cartography of Colonization, the Legal Polyphony of Settlement: English Intrusions on the American Mainland in the Seventeenth Century', *Law and Social Inquiry* 26(2): 315–72.

Vail, L. (1976) 'Mozambique's Chartered Companies: The Rule of the Feeble', *Journal of African History* 17(3): 389–416.

Weisbord, R. G. (2003) 'The King, the Cardinal and the Pope: Leopold II's Genocide in the Congo and the Vatican', *Journal of Genocide Research* 5(1): 35–45.

PART II

The place of the private in contemporary security

5

PRIVATE SECURITY GUARDS

Authority, control and governance?

Joakim Berndtsson and Maria Stern

Who guards life and property in our societies? And who guards the guardians? To an increasing degree, the answer to these questions is: commercial security actors. In this chapter, we explore more fully these vexing questions, as well as what might be at stake in their answers. In particular, we query the ways in which public–private distinctions are being drawn and unsettled, spheres of authority and governance coincide and clash, and how control and oversight are determined in the practice and governance of contemporary security guarding.

The ubiquitous use of private security guarding is part of a widespread and quickly accelerating global trend of increasing commercialization of security actors and governance. The market for private security services is vast and expanding; in many countries, private security guards outnumber the police and sometimes even the military. In the US, more than 1 million people work as security guards (US Department of Labor 2013). By comparison, the EU-27 market is home to 54,000 security companies, employing around 1.3 million, while in India there are over 7 million guards (Eurostat 2013; Gooptu 2013: 14). This development has also given rise to large private security companies (PSCs) such as G4S, employing over 618,000 people in 120 countries, and Securitas, with around 300,000 employees in 52 countries, according to these companies' own websites. Importantly, the trend towards security privatization is not confined to liberal democracies in the 'global North', nor is it concentrated to developing states in the 'global South'. Private security is a *global* phenomenon, associated with developments in peaceful societies as well as in armed conflicts and military operations in the post-Cold War era.

The increasing privatization of security guarding figures centrally in changing patterns of global security governance. The forms of security privatization in guarding are many and varied, as are the activities and roles taken on by commercial actors. For instance, private security companies supply both armed and unarmed guards to state and non-state clients operating in a variety of different settings, ranging from conflict zones to stable and peaceful societies. Security guarding, as it occurs in different sites across the globe, involves particular and highly contextual public–private, local–national–global security constellations, as well as seemingly incongruous political and juridical arrangements for their enactment and oversight. Indeed, some authors have also observed a 'close association between state security and corporate security', both being 'party to a fluid and largely informal relationship' (O'Reilly 2010: 184). In the context of globalization, this has created a 'sovereignty/capitalism nexus' and a 'hybrid transnational policing marketplace' (ibid.: 198, 203).

Nonetheless, in the literature on private security, there has been a tendency to focus on the more 'spectacular' use of armed security contractors in the wars in Afghanistan and Iraq. While this focus is understandable, it also is important to acknowledge the profound impact of the more 'routine' and 'commonplace' activities of private security more generally, and guarding, in particular; the 'full significance and impact of contemporary processes of privatization cannot be grasped through a focus on the military sector alone' (Abrahamsen and Williams 2011: 2). Hence, while dramatic developments have spurred significant research interest in security privatization in the context of armed conflict, less effort has so far been made to connect these complex and vital questions about authority, control and governance with concerns related to private guarding in non-conflict settings. However, questions of authority and governance, control and oversight, as well as who/what can do what and how under the name of security guarding in settings that span (and unsettle) the 'peace–war' spectrum have implications for the both the practice and politics of guarding, as well as for security governance and politics more generally.

In the remainder of this chapter, therefore, we address the privatization of guarding by focusing our lines of inquiry around the following interrelated questions:

- Who guards in what context?
- What are the implications of privatization for the practice and politics of guarding?
- What are the implications for security governance and politics more generally?

A comprehensive overview of security guarding across the globe is clearly beyond the scope of this chapter. Instead, we draw upon our (and others') analyses of guarding in peace and war, aiming to identify recurrent themes and significant differences that can be gleaned from specific sites. These themes include: firstly, public–private distinctions and, secondly, spheres of authority and governance and attending questions of control and oversight. Additionally, by exploring guarding in sites that span both 'mundane' and 'exceptional' security practices, the chapter highlights the interrelated dynamics of divergent security guarding contexts and practices and unsettles any tidy topographies of 'peace' and 'war', 'exceptional' and 'mundane', or even a spectrum between them.

The chapter begins by offering a conceptual discussion of guarding, as well as brief snapshots of three different security guarding contexts to provide a backdrop for our discussion of the themes raised. Next we explore the central themes of public–private distinctions and authority and governance in relation to our threefold question.

Setting the scene: loss prevention and the guarding of life and property

As many of the contributions in this Handbook show, the commercial security industry covers a very wide and disparate range of activities, technologies and actors. Still, there is no commonly agreed upon definition of what constitutes a private security (or military) company, nor is there any exhaustive list of activities or services that should be included under such rubrics as commercial 'security', 'protection' or 'policing'. Similarly, there are many different ideas of what characterizes a private security guard or the activity of guarding itself. A definitive distinction between policing and guarding, for instance, remains elusive. Both the police and the military are charged with demarking (public) order from disorder, as well as guarding and protecting that which society values, such as human life, property, particular freedoms, etc. While conceptual development and discussion remain highly important, our endeavour here is not to remedy this situation. Rather, we argue that the lack of clear-cut definitions and delineations is magnified through security privatization, and that one important task for research is to explore the ways in which private security guarding helps shape ideas, practices and policies linked to 'public' and 'private' security provision and governance. Before proceeding, we dwell a bit longer on the concept of private security guards and what they do.

On a very general level, we can say that private security guards are individuals who work for commercial entities that seek to provide 'loss prevention' and 'protection of life and assets' (South 1988: 38; Abrahamsen and Williams 2011: 39). This means that private security guards are involved in preventing (deadly) harm to persons (e.g. when working as bodyguards) or assets such as (private or public) property and information. Performing typical duties and functions such as 'patrolling, transit and guarding,' private security guards are also, in many contexts, 'the public face of the security industry' (Zedner 2009: 103). These guards police 'privately defined orders'; however, they also increasingly police public order – a remit that is often seen as the ultimate purview of the state (Shearing and Stenning 1987: 13–14). The distinctions between public and private orders (as well as who/what defines such distinctions) accordingly transform and blur. The ways in which these duties are performed, by whom, for whom and under what circumstances differ widely between cases, giving rise to a variety of concerns linked to the lines of distinction between public and private actors and responsibilities, spheres of authority and governance, as well as issues of control, regulation and oversight. To illustrate the very different practices that make up guarding in varied contexts, we offer some brief snapshots drawn from three seemingly very different contexts: the Democratic Republic of Congo (DRC), Sweden, and the wars in Iraq and Afghanistan.

In the DRC – a war-torn country where a plethora of armed groups continue to engage in combat in the Eastern territory over, among other things, access to lucrative minerals – private guarding is becoming widespread (Schouten 2014). The market has expanded from a handful of companies in the late 1980s and early 1990s to between 35 and 45 companies in 2008, employing an estimated 25,000 people (de Goede 2008: 42). Some international security companies such as G4S provide guarding services to government bodies, transnational companies (including mining companies), international humanitarian agencies, international organizations, as well as to private individuals. Moreover, one section of the national police – the Brigade de Garde – is, in effect, run partly as a commercial security outfit. For a fee, armed police can be hired to protect private property and individuals, and while the Brigade police are often less well equipped than other private security outfits in terms of vehicles and communications, they have two distinct advantages; they are generally cheaper and, perhaps even more importantly, they are armed (ibid.; Schouten 2014: 144). Such outsourcing occurs both formally and under specific regulation, and informally through personal contacts. Additionally, and particularly in volatile and more militarized areas, guards from the national armed forces are for hire through informal channels to protect both individuals, and companies.

In Sweden, known as a strong democratic state, the domestic security industry consists of over 500 companies, employing around 20,000 people. The use of private security companies to provide protection and investigation services for individuals and other private companies is by no means a novel phenomenon. However, over the past decades, the sight of uniformed private guards patrolling public and semi-public places (such as shopping malls, airports, sports arenas and high streets) has become increasingly common. In addition, since 2006, Swedish state authorities have contracted with private companies such as Saladin, Control Risks and Vesper Group to provide armed and unarmed protection as well as risk assessments and intelligence services to overseas diplomatic and development cooperation missions in Pakistan, Afghanistan and Iraq (Berndtsson 2012; Berndtsson and Stern 2013). Finally, under a new law that entered into force on 1 July 2013, it is possible for shipping companies with ships sailing under Swedish flag to employ armed guards to protect against piracy on certain voyages. The tasks of the vetting and controlling the private guards are mainly in the hands of the shipping companies (Berndtsson and Østensen 2015).

In Iraq and Afghanistan – two war-torn countries where violent conflict is still very much a reality – tens of thousands of armed and unarmed guards from private security companies continue to protect local politicians and businesspeople, foreign diplomatic staff, convoys, embassies, and military bases (Avant 2005). In these situations of violent conflict, guards have formed a vital part of the military, diplomatic and aid missions of Western countries that are incapable of meeting and/or unwilling to meet perceived security needs with state-based solutions (Kinsey 2006). Indeed, these guards and other private security services have been indispensable for both military and civilian efforts during these wars (Dunigan 2011). At the same time, the substantial number of violent incidents where guards have been involved, along with several cases of fraud and breaches of contract, coupled with a general lack of state oversight and control of their activities, has raised serious questions about the ethics and legitimacy of security privatization in violent conflict (Pattison 2014).

These three seemingly disparate cases provide examples of the very different contexts in which commercial security guards are hired to protect life and property. In addition, they hint at the importance of questions about who the guards are: Are they employed and trained by a public body under democratic control and oversight? Are they hired by a private profit-driven company and trained under sketchy circumstances? The three cases also suggest the very different impact that the increase in commercialized guarding might have on the practices, politics, and governance of security and protection. Finally, they underscore the importance of addressing questions surrounding ideas about public–private distinctions, spheres of authority and security governance, as well as issues of control and oversight in relation to the ethico-politics of the commercialization of guarding. Below, we probe these themes further by drawing on the cases introduced above, as well as pointing to other cases where these themes emerge.

Public–private distinctions

The task of guarding life and property has often been seen as one of, if not the primary, merit of the modern liberal state. Indeed, according to the logics of modern state sovereignty, the state is often seen as ultimately responsible and accountable for ensuring the protection of its citizens and their goods, private industries well as, of course, the public bodies and infrastructures that make up the state apparatus (see Introduction, this volume). Security, broadly understood, is frequently seen as a 'public good' and the modern state the locus of the public. While such notions are deeply imbedded in the modern political imaginary, it is also clear that the public–private distinction constructed through this storyline, as well as the notions of the state as a distinct (and primary?) locus of politics poorly reflect the complex webs, networks or assemblages of security actors, logics, practices, and technologies that make up security guarding today. As many authors have shown, these lines of distinctions are 'fuzzy' at best (e.g Johnston 1992: 205; Leander 2006: 28). Although clear-cut and static distinctions between the private and the public clearly exist only in theory, they remain firmly etched into common (and shared) public political imaginaries (Owens 2008).

Consider once more the brief introduction to the case of the DRC above. The issue of the Brigade de Garde – a public entity tasked mainly with police work on part of the state – being formally rented out to private enterprises. This is clearly a striking example of how our notions of public and private are being confounded. Lines of distinction are being (re)drawn and unsettled, and our notions of what constitutes a police officer or a private security guard are being called into question. In the DRC, a public, violence-wielding institution 'doubles' as a commercial entity, providing (armed) protection to clients, which in many cases are made up of international companies. The result is very different to the idea(l) of security as a public or collective good, with the state providing publicly funded protection through institutions such as the police or the military. Such crisscrossing of public–private divides calls into question the prevalence of sovereign security logics in relation to commercial ones (Leander 2006), and begs the question of whether or not the 'right' to security and protection must be bought from 'public' forces. This question, in turn, raises further and thorny questions about the way in which different lives and assets are valued.

Additionally, and importantly, the Congolese state often falls far short in its remit of providing security for all of its citizens; this 'doubling' is therefore further problematic. That those who are supposed to protect the population, yet do so poorly, are for hire (both the Brigade through formal and informal channels, and the national armed forces through informal channels) to and in competition with various 'private' actors, including foreign commercial companies, calls into question the legitimacy and loyalties of the state security institutions, and ultimately, the Congolese nation-state project. It also severely unsettles familiar distinctions between public and private guarding activities that are borne out of the primacy of the sovereign state's role as ultimate guarantor of the life of the population.

Again, this is not an issue particular to the context of 'weak' or 'developing' states struggling with the effects of violent conflict. Similar logics and processes are also at work in Sweden, where conditions are vastly different. Since 2007, security guards from Securitas have performed the majority of security work at Stockholm's Arlanda airport, the most trafficked airport in Sweden. In effect, these guards also help 'secure' the Swedish state, European territory, the safety of passengers from all over the globe, global airspace, as well as the economic interests of a host of companies (Berndtsson and Stern 2011). However, the guards are not the sole providers of protection at the airport. Beside the private guards, security staff from Swedavia (a state owned company), as well as members of the Swedish Border Police, Swedish Customs, and the Swedish Security Service also work to prevent the loss of life and assets. The (re)drawing of lines of distinction between public and private spheres at the airport frames much of the terms of, and the struggles over, power, knowledge and authority in relation to the use of private security guards. For instance, Swedish national police have ultimate authority and accountability over security at Arlanda, yet this remit is rendered practically impossible as their presence at the airport is limited. Contention surrounding who has adequate training and knowledge to guard the airport properly, as well as how the division of labour should occur, figure centrally in discussions over demarcations between the public and private spheres.

There are many other examples of how security privatization raises questions about public–private distinctions. For instance, several authors have pointed to the 'hybrid' or 'protean' character of private security companies and their employees (Carmola 2010: 10–12, 27–39; Abrahamsen and Williams 2011: 59). In zones of armed conflict such as Afghanistan and Iraq, private security guards – often with a military or police background – work for private companies but frequently perform duties closely associated with the military, such as interrogation of prisoners, intelligence gathering or armed convoy escorts (Singer 2003). Higate (2012), for example, explores how prospective private security guards (who are ex-military British and US soldiers) retrain to perform such 'private' guarding duties; yet their embodied (masculine) subjectivities as soldiers (who have been produced as particular masculine soldier-selves) render it difficult for them to inhabit a private security guard-self. While private guards and soldiers often perform very similar acts, the remit of protecting a client in contradistinction to fulfilling a military aim requires different forms of restraint – restraint that the ex-soldiers struggle to employ.

In other cases, employees of private security companies are explicitly described as more or less 'public'. One example of this is the employment of 'security coordinators' by the Swedish Ministry for Foreign Affairs to manage security and provide bodyguards to the Swedish embassies in Iraq, Afghanistan and Pakistan. Not only are these coordinators deeply involved in organizing and governing security at the embassies, they are also listed as 'diplomatic staff' and described by state officials as 'the extended arm of the ambassador' and essentially as 'public servants from the private sector' (Berndtsson 2012: 318; Berndtsson and Stern 2013). Surprisingly, given the sensitive and precarious theatre of operation, the hiring of a security company to play such a vital role was seen as unproblematic by the Swedish government. As many of the private security personnel are former police or military officers, the Ministry's Security Secretariat in Stockholm implied that the difference between 'private' and 'public' security actors was essentially non-existent; the contracting of private actors, even as they were granted diplomatic status, was therefore rendered without controversy in their accounts. Nonetheless, a representative of the Swedish International Development Cooperation Agency (Sida), whose work is dependent on security clearance by the Embassy in Kabul, for instance, lamented this state of affairs and queried the commercialization of the logics of risk assessment (Berndtsson and Stern 2013).

As we shall see below, the impetus to contest and (re)inscribe lines between public and private security provision and governance follows from the very indistinctness of these lines. The discomfort with such indistinctness is coupled with the notion that they should somehow be clearly defined; public and private orders should be distinguishable and the public order should trump the private ones, even though it is clear from the workings of guarding and security provision more generally that the public and the private are indeed quite blurred. Furthermore, a routine focus on this binary allows us to turn a blind eye to what might be at stake in the practice of guarding. However, this does not mean that these distinctions are unimportant. On the contrary, security actors from the individual guard at the airport or at the embassy, to company management and state security and police officials, frequently use (their interpretations of) these lines of distinction to rationalize their own and each other's roles, behaviour and responsibilities. Vitally, contestations and practices over lines of distinction between (and 'within') the public and private spheres raise important questions about spheres of authority and governance. Who guards in what contexts matters in terms of how such guarding is governed and who can be held accountable.

Spheres of authority and governance

As noted above, the lexicon of modern state sovereignty provides a familiar and tenacious framework for allotting accountability and defining the parameters of security governance. The Weberian edict of state monopoly over the legitimate use of force continues to hold sway in terms of the underlying logic for the ultimate role of the state as provider of security and the maintenance of public order. However, this logic is often overridden in practice, and through the complex webs of (globalized) governance arrangements at play in different security assemblages (see Chapter 13, this volume). Overlapping spheres of authority and parallel, crisscrossing, and/or discontinuous lines of accountability render the governing of security guarding precarious and incoherent in many contexts, further raising questions about the ethico-politics of security practices that poorly resonate with the political and juridical structures available for their governance.

Furthermore, the question of democratic control and oversight sheds light on basic assumptions that cast the commercialization of security as a site of considerable controversy. The publicly recognized slip of private interests and activity into what many concur should be a democratically controlled public realm (security) is most obvious in the context of armed conflicts, such as those in Iraq and Afghanistan. The much-publicized shootings in Baghdad's Nisour Square in 2007 serves now as a cautionary example of the problems associated with uncontrolled and unregulated private companies engaging in military-like activities (Dunigan 2011: 71–2). The Nisour Square shootings and the absence of functioning systems of state control and oversight led to public outrage, calls for more regulation and accountability, as well pertinent questions about who can do what, where, in the name security or protection (Leander 2010). While the highly charged dilemmas posed by PSCs in conflict zones continue to attract attention, less violent but certainly not less important crisscrossing of what is commonly understood to be public–private spheres and activities occur in security practices across the globe. While most go unnoticed in the everyday security landscape of modern life, such crisscrossing cause alarm when they clearly challenge dearly held notions of who can use force when, where, how, against whom, and for what purposes. Witness for example the uproar that ensues when private security guards in different contexts act in violent ways that fall outside the legitimate use of force by the police – force that is (ideally) subject to democratic oversight and strict regulation. One example is the storm of protest that followed upon recent reports of severe violence and abuse by private security guards against refugees and asylum-seekers in Burbach, Germany (Kirschbaum 2014).

What might such outrage be about? If a state no longer maintains control (so the logics goes) over the means of the use of force; over the security knowledge and technology that allows for the detection of threat and the management of risk; over the practice of protecting its citizens and their assets; and if accountability, and regulation of guarding are not subject to democratic oversight, then the basic workings of security governance and modern liberal democracy require critical scrutiny. The fact that these rules never correlated with the actual workings of politics is not the point. What is at stake is the sense that democratic oversight allows for a system of control, and importantly, enforcement so that the (legitimate) use of force is not unwittingly wrested from the state – as a democratically appointed guarantor of security for the population and upholder of public order. Yet security practices often resonate poorly with the political and juridical structures available for their governance.

For instance, as explained above, a mix of public and private actors guard Arlanda airport in close proximity. However, the different 'public' and 'private' actors enjoy different mandates and authority, and must navigate an intricate web of instructions and regulations, supervision, and evaluation from authorities on the local, national, regional, and global levels. In this particular context, struggles over public–private demarcations, roles and responsibilities among security actors help create and shape a number of 'public–private', 'private-private' and 'public-public' contestations linked to problems associated with the ways in which the contracted security guards performed their duties (Berndtsson and Stern 2011). Such contestations reveal how the inaccurate, yet obdurate binary of public–private poorly reflects the dividing lines where vital political questions about the governance of security are posed, debated and settled.

Another example is found in the increasing use of private guards on board commercial vessels to protect against piracy. Like many other countries, the three Scandinavian countries (Denmark, Norway and Sweden) have recently put regulations in place that permits the use of armed guards on certain voyages. While there are some differences between the countries' legal procedures, rules for the carrying and use of arms, and the applications procedures that precede licensing, there are also similarities in terms of how security onboard ships is being governed.

To a considerable degree, tasks such as conducting risk assessments, vetting personnel, making decisions on rules for the use of weapons, as well as reporting and oversight measures, are left in the hands of shipping companies, ship captains, and the PSCs themselves. A very blunt description of the indirect role of the state was offered by a representative of the Swedish Transport Agency, the organization tasked with overseeing the use of private guards on board Swedish ships: 'We work with risk-based systems oversight. That means that we normally do not make on-sight inspections; instead, we review the systems and procedures that the shipping company and the security company have' (Swedish Transport Agency, e-mail conversation, 11 October 2013).

In essence, what has been created in the three Scandinavian countries cases is a regulatory 'façade' and a way of governing security at a distance and through the market (Berndtsson and Østensen 2015).

In the DRC, security governance is notoriously precarious. While the Congolese state is ultimately responsible for and dictates the remit and actions of the state security agents (the police and the military), in practice many informal arrangements and (globalized) public–private constellations govern security provision and guarding in the Congo (Hönke 2013; Schouten 2014). The distinction between public and multiple private orders become further blurred when state security agents act simultaneously as public servants and as individual actors who utilize their public position in a parallel informal economy and politics (Eriksson Baaz and Verweijen 2014). Furthermore, a plethora of international actors are involved in reforming the state security sector (Boshoff *et al.* 2010); and many competing armed groups continuously unsettle state sovereign control over public order. In such a context, the question of authority over guarding practices becomes even more salient – and slippery. Although the head of police is officially responsible for the activities of the Brigade de Garde, informalized arrangements often accompany formalized ones, and authority and accountability remain blurry at best. When members of the national armed forces are for hire through informal political economies, notions of accountability and sovereign control, not to mention democratic oversight, abide as theoretical fantasies of security sector reform that have little to do with what occurs on the ground.

Conclusions

In this chapter, we have endeavoured to connect issues of authority, control and governance raised in the context of armed conflict with concerns related to private guarding in non-conflict settings. The three seemingly disparate cases from where we have drawn most of our examples provide insight into the very different contexts in which commercial security guards are hired to protect 'life and property'. As we have shown, questions about who provides the guards, and who these guards are, matter for both the practice and politics of guarding, as well as for security governance and politics more generally. Indeed, pertinacious notions of who can use force when, where, how, against whom, and for what purposes in the name of security and protection bang against the realities of complex and shifting practices, identities, and spheres of authority involved in guarding. Paying attention to the contestations involved in practicing and governing security guarding also unsettle other lines of distinction, such as that between peace and war, or the mundane and the exceptional. The cases discussed above reveal important similarities across the 'peace–war spectrum'; the unsettling of lines of distinction, for instance, between public and private actors, responsibilities, control and spheres of authority figure centrally in debates about, and the practice of, guarding in sites as disparate as the DRC, Sweden and Afghanistan. Hence, our analysis ultimately underscores the importance of addressing questions about private guarding across cases and contexts to better understand the impact of private security guards on issues of governance and the politics of security more generally.

Bibliography

Abrahamsen, R. and Williams, M. C. (2011) *Security Beyond the State: Private Security in International Politics*, Cambridge: Cambridge University Press.

Avant, D. D. (2005) *The Market for Force: The Consequences of Privatizing Security*, Cambridge: Cambridge University Press.

Berndtsson, J. (2012) 'Security Professionals for Hire: Exploring the Many Faces of Private Security Expertise', *Millennium-Journal of International Studies* 40(2): 303–20.

Berndtsson, J. and Østensen, Å. G. (2015) 'The Scandinavian Approach to Private Maritime Security – A regulatory façade?', *Journal of Ocean Development and International Law* 41(2): 138–52.

Berndtsson, J., and Stern, M. (2011) 'Private Security and the Public–Private Divide: Contested Lines of Distinction and Modes of Governance in the Stockholm-Arlanda Security Assemblage', *International Political Sociology* 5(4): 408–25.

Berndtsson, J, and Stern, M. (2013) 'Sweden: Public Servants from the Private Sector', in A. Leander (ed.), *Commercialising Security in Europe: Political Consequences for Peace Operations*, London: Routledge, pp. 58–78.

Boshoff, H. *et al.* (2010) *Supporting SSR in the DRC: Between a Rock and a Hard Place*, Clingendael: Netherlands Institute of International Relations.

Carmola, K. (2010) *Private Security Contractors and New Wars: Risk, Law, and Ethics. Contemporary Security Studies*, Abingdon: Routledge.

de Goede, M. (2008) 'Private and Public Security in Post-War Democratic Republic of Congo', in S. Gumedze (ed.), *The Private Security Sector in Africa: Country Series*, Pretoria: Institute for Security Studies, pp. 35–68.

Dunigan, M. (2011) *Victory for Hire: Private Security Companies' Impact on Military Effectiveness*, Stanford, CA: Stanford Security Studies.

Eriksson Baaz, M. and Verweijen, J. (2014) 'Arbiters with Guns: The Ambiguity of Military Involvement in Civilian Disputes in the DR Congo', *Third World Quarterly* 36(5): 803–20.

Eurostat (2013) 'Security and Investigation Services Statistics', April, http://epp.eurostat.ec.europa.eu/statistics_explained/index.php/Security_and_investigation_services_statistics_-_NACE_Rev._2.

Gooptu, N. (2013) 'Servile Sentinels of the City: Private Security Guards, Organized Informality and Labour in Interactive Services in Globalized India', *International Review of Social History* 58(1): 9–38.

Higate, P. (2012) 'The Private Militarized and Security Contractor As Geocorporeal Actor', *International Political Sociology* 6(4): 355–72.

Hönke, J. (2013) *Transnational Companies and Security Governance: Hybrid Practices in a Postcolonial World*, Abingdon: Routledge.

Johnston, L (1992) *The Rebirth of Private Policing*, London: Routledge.

Kinsey, C. (2006) *Corporate Soldiers and International Security: The Rise of Private Military Companies*, New York: Routledge.

Kirschbaum, E. (2014) 'German Government Condemns Pictures Showing Refugees Abused' Reuters, 29 September, www.reuters.com/article/2014/09/29/us-germany-refugees-abuse-idUSKCN0HO1G0 20140929.

Leander, A. (2006) 'Privatizing the Politics of Protection', in J. Huysmans, A. Dobson and R. Prokhovnik (eds), *The Politics of Protection: Sites of Insecurity and Political Agency*, Abingdon: Routledge, pp. 19–34.

Leander, A. (2010) 'The Paradoxical Impunity of Private Military Companies: Authority and the Limits to Legal Accountability', *Security Dialogue* 41(5): 467–90.

O'Reilly, C. (2010) 'The Transnational Security Consultancy Industry', *Theoretical Criminology* 14(2): 183–210.

Owens, P. (2008) 'Distinctions, Distinctions: "Public" and "Private" Force?', *International Affairs* 84(5): 977–90.

Pattison, J (2014) *The Morality of Private War: The Challenge of Private Military and Security Companies*, Oxford: Oxford University Press.

Schouten, P. (2014) Private Security Companies and Political Order in Congo: A History of Extraversion, PhD thesis, School of Global Studies, University of Gothenburg, Sweden.

Shearing, C. D. and Stenning P. C. (eds) (1987) *Private Policing*, London: Sage Publications.

Singer, P. W. (2003) *Corporate Warriors: The Rise of the Privatized Military Industry*, Ithaca, NY: Cornell University Press.

South, N. (1988) *Policing for Profit: The Private Security Sector*, London: Sage.

US Department of Labor (2013) 'Occupational Employment Statistics: 33-9032: Security Guards', May, www.bls.gov/OES/current/oes339032.htm.

Zedner, L. (2009) *Security*, Abingdon: Routledge.

6

PMSCS IN MARITIME SECURITY AND ANTI-PIRACY CONTROL

Carolin Liss

The use of privately contracted armed security personnel (PCASP) onboard merchant vessels is today a widely accepted measure to protect ships from attacks by Somali pirates. The large-scale employment of private military and security companies (PMSCs)[1] to provide armed guards is a new phenomenon, given that the armament of merchant ships was until recently rejected by the shipping industry, governments, and international (maritime) organizations. This chapter traces the short history of the employment of PMSCs at sea, with particular attention being paid to armed anti-piracy services – the most prominent services provided by PMSCs in the maritime sphere at present. It will be argued that even though these companies play an increasingly important role in security governance, the maritime environment poses specific challenges for regulators, resulting in some PMSC's activities being left unmonitored. The specific challenges PMSCs and regulators face when private security providers operate at sea will be highlighted in the discussion of anti-piracy services conducted by PCASP.

The first part of this chapter provides an overview of the rise of PMSCs in maritime security governance and describes the different kinds of services offered by these companies. The second part focuses on anti-piracy services provided by PMSCs. It discusses the emergence of anti-piracy PMSCs, which began to operate in the Malacca Strait in the early 2000s, and the recent boom of the industry fuelled by the large number of serious attacks conducted by Somali pirates between 2007 and 2012. The third part discusses the specific challenges that the maritime sphere poses for PMSCs and those trying to control these companies and their activities. Special attention is paid to the regulation of anti-piracy PMSCs and the persistent problems associated with the working practices of these companies. The conclusion presents the finding that PMSCs have today become an integral part of maritime security governance, even though some serious concerns remain over the working practices of PMSCs and their employees.

PMSCs in maritime security

In the past, a range of non-state actors was involved in different aspects of maritime warfare, including the disruption of enemy trade. The most prominent of these actors were privateers: private persons (or vessels) authorized by a government through a 'letter of marque' to attack enemy ships in time of war. However, with the establishment of permanent navies and the development and enforcement of the idea of a state monopoly on violence (at sea), such armed non-state actors all but disappeared from the oceans. Privateering, for example, began to be delegitimized and was abolished with the 1856 Declaration of Paris (Thomson 1994: 70–71).

Since the end of the Cold War the notion of the state as the sole provider of (maritime) security has increasingly been challenged and 'new' actors such as non-governmental organizations (NGOs) and private businesses have played ever more important roles in security governance. PMSCs active in the maritime sphere are among these new actors. They are private businesses and are part of the wider private security industry. Indeed, some of the well-known companies such as Academi (formerly Blackwater) and AEGIS that operate on land also offer maritime services.

The rise of PMSCs active on land and in the maritime sphere has been facilitated by similar, interconnected factors that include:

- the broader process of privatization of public services and state sector enterprises, such as education and healthcare on land and the privatization of ports in the maritime sphere;
- the global downsizing of major militaries; and
- the changing nature of conflict after 1989.

(Singer 2003; Avant 2005)

In the maritime sphere, this has resulted in an increased focus on non-traditional security threats such as piracy, illegal fishing and maritime terrorism. Government agencies such as navies have adapted their operations and today focus much more of their activities on addressing such 'soft' maritime security threats (Till 2013: 31–8, 282–305). Additionally, new regulations, including the International Ship and Port Facility Security (ISPS) Code, were introduced in response to threats such as terrorism that required increased security measures from states and the shipping industry. Complying with the new security regulations and responding to the broadened range of security threats require additional manpower and often task-specific resources and can overstretch capacities of government agencies – especially in developing countries where resources are particularly sparse. This lack of capacity and the new requirements necessary through regulations such as the ISPS Code are reasons why PMSCs have become increasingly involved in addressing (non-traditional) maritime security threats.

Compared with services provided on land, PMSC business in the maritime sphere took longer to become established, and the major focus and expertise of these companies have concentrated mainly on a small range of services. PMSCs offer passive maritime services such as risk assessments, as well as active services that focus mostly on the armed and unarmed protection of maritime assets and installations. Indeed, in contrast to the activities of privateers and other for-profit actors in the past, PMSCs primarily provide defensive maritime services at sea or on land. In relation to the landward portions of maritime operations, PMSCs are primarily hired to provide port security, including access control, the screening of containers, and emergency responses. These land-based maritime activities resemble other PMSC operations on land and are not the focus of this chapter.

PMSCs also offer maritime services that are predominantly conducted at sea. The most prominent of these are the protection of offshore energy installations; operations against illegal fishing;[2] and the protection of vessels such as merchant ships, fishing boats, yachts, and cruise ships. Protection of these assets is needed against attacks from a range of perpetrators, including pirates, terrorists, insurgents, and radical civil protest groups. Offshore oil and gas installations, for instance, have been targeted by environmental activists and insurgents. Greenpeace activists' attempt to climb onto a Gazprom oil platform in September 2013 to protest drilling in the Arctic and attacks against offshore oil and gas installations by the Movement for the Emancipation of the Niger Delta are but two examples (Kashubsky 2013). At a time when rising demand for oil and gas is leading to an increase in offshore energy exploitation, and more countries are changing their laws to allow not only state but also private forces to protect oil and gas installations, it is believed that business for PMSCs will continue to increase.

The services offered for the oil and gas industry also include the protection of vessels travelling to and from offshore energy installations such as oil platforms, which overlaps with other vessel protection services advertised by PMSCs. These include the armed protection of a range of different vessels, including the guarding of fishing boats against attacks from other fishers or insurgents. PMSCs have, for example been employed to provide armed guards to protect Japanese-owned fishing boats and Philippine tuna fleets (author's interviews). However, the most prominent and lucrative vessel protection services offered by PMSCs are anti-piracy services.

PMSC anti-piracy services

PMSCs offer a range of anti-piracy services, including risk assessment and consulting, training of crews, provision of armed guards onboard vessels, the use of armed escort vessels to protect a client's ship, and the recovery of hijacked ships and cargoes. The most prominent and controversial of these services is the use of armed guards onboard the client's vessel to protect merchant ships, fishing boats, and pleasure craft against pirate attacks. Anti-piracy PMSCs are employed by ship or cargo owners and are only hired when government agencies cannot ensure the safety of shipping, and the client believes that the threat is significant enough to justify the additional costs. Indeed, hiring a PMSC is costly, and in the highly competitive shipping industry any additional expenses are generally avoided. The employment of anti-piracy PMSCs started with the increase in pirate attacks in the Malacca Strait area in the early 2000s, but it was the more recent spate of serious attacks conducted by Somali pirates that caused the boom of the industry.

Anti-piracy PMSCs were first employed in southeast Asia. Between the 1990s and the mid-2000s, this region was the global hot spot of pirate attacks on commercial vessels and fishing boats. In southeast Asia, pirates were particularly active in the waters of Indonesia, Malaysia and the Philippines. While most attacks at the time were simple hit-and-run robberies by opportunistic pirates, more serious incidents such as hijackings also occurred. Organized pirate gangs or syndicates were responsible for these more serious attacks in which vessels and their crew were held hostage for a limited time and the cargo stolen. In other cases, the entire vessel was seized, given a new identity, and used for trade as a so-called 'phantom ship' (Liss 2011).

At the turn of the century, pirate attacks in the Malacca Strait started to cause concern. The number of reported incidents jumped from two reported actual and attempted attacks in the waterway in 1999 to 75 the following year. In 2001, the number dropped to 17 and declined again in the following year with 16 reported incidents. In 2003, 28 incidents were reported, and there were 37 in 2004, 12 in 2005 and 11 in 2006 (ICC 2007). The attacks in this area caused international concern because of the Malacca Strait's strategic importance. The strait connects the Indian Ocean with the South China Sea and the Pacific Ocean, and more than 60,000 vessels weighing over 300 gross tons passed through the strait each year at the time. These included a large number of tankers carrying oil from the Middle East to destinations such as China and Japan. The Malacca Strait is a favoured location for pirate attacks because ships have to slow down to safely manoeuvre through the narrow waterway, allowing pirates to approach and board targeted vessels more easily. Following the September 11 terrorist attacks, unfounded speculation that terrorists would collude with pirates in the Malacca Strait caused additional concern, as did accusations that the politically motivated Free Aceh Movement (Gerakan Aceh Merdeka, or GAM) which fought for independence from Indonesia, or rogue members of the group, were responsible for some attacks in the strait (Liss 2011).

In response to this increase in pirate attacks, some ship owners hired PMSCs to protect their vessels. In most cases, PCASP was hired to secure the client's ship, but as demand increased, a few companies also acquired escort vessels that accompanied the client's ship through the strait. The Singapore-based (and Hong Kong-based) PMSC Background Asia, for example, used escort vessels to guard tankers in the strait, and the Australian-based company Counter Terrorism International (CTI) provided protection for a tug in the strait and for a vessel that departed from an oil rig and passed through the waterway (author's interviews). Even though the protection primarily aimed to deter pirates, many PMSCs at the time advertised to provide anti-piracy and anti-terrorism protection for vessels because of the suspected terrorist activities in this area. The majority of PMSCs that were active in the Malacca Strait had their head-quarters in Singapore or outside the Asian region, in countries such as the UK and Australia. Most were very small companies (often consisting of only 2–5 permanent employees), founded and staffed by ex-military or ex-law enforcement personnel. However, the employment of anti-piracy PMSCs remained limited and restricted to the Malacca Strait because pirate attacks in other southeast Asian waters were mainly hit-and-run robberies that did not warrant the cost of hiring a PMSC. As the number of attacks in the Malacca Strait continued to decline, with only one or two incidents reported each year since 2008, the employment of anti-piracy PMSCs in the Malacca Strait also dropped.

As the use of anti-piracy PMSCs began to decline in the Malacca Strait, the industry began to flourish and then boom in the wider Gulf of Aden area. Since 2008, attacks by Somali pirates in the Gulf of Aden, the Red and Arabian Seas, the Indian Ocean, and Omani waters have caused international concern. The number of actual and attempted attacks in these waters rose from 51 in 2007 to 111 in 2008, 218 in 2009, 219 in 2010, and peaked at 237 attacks in 2011 (ICC 2012). The attacks in this area differ significantly from incidents in southeast Asia because Somali pirates are mainly interested in ransom payments. The perpetrators usually board a targeted vessel, take control of the ship, and hold it and the crew hostage for a prolonged period of time until a ransom is paid. A World Bank study estimates that between April 2005 and December 2012, 179 ships were hijacked by Somali pirates, and they collected between US\$339 million and US\$413 million in ransom during this time (World Bank 2013). Somali pirates have targeted ships of all types, sizes, and nationality, including merchant ships, yachts, fishing boats, UN supply ships, and supertankers.

Somali piracy has triggered international responses. Like the Malacca Strait, the wider Gulf of Aden area is important for international shipping and therefore the world economy, which depends on the timely, safe, and cost-effective transport of goods by sea. To combat Somali piracy, governments from around the world have sent naval vessels to protect international ship-ping, often as part of missions sanctioned or organized by multilateral organizations, such as NATO and the EU (Ehrhart *et al.* 2010). For additional protection, some countries, including France and the Netherlands, have also used military personnel as armed guards on merchant and fishing boats under their flags.

As government efforts initially showed little effect, ship owners turned to PMSCs to protect their vessels. Like in the Malacca Strait, most ship owners would pay for PCASP to travel onboard their ships in high-risk areas, but some companies also began to offer the use of armed escort vessels. Between two to six guards are usually employed to protect a merchant ship, but because Somali pirates also target other vessels, PMSCs are also hired to protect fishing boats, yachts, and cruise ships, and the number of guards and their responsibilities change accordingly. In the Gulf of Aden area, PMSC guards have to stay onboard the client's vessel longer than in the Malacca Strait because the pirates operate in a larger area. Guards usually board ships that travel from Europe towards Asia after the Suez Canal and debark after the high-risk area in places such as the Seychelles or Sri Lanka. Like the Somali pirates, PCASP do also carry (heavy or war) weapons, which need to be taken onboard the client's ship and then removed upon debarkation of PMSC personnel.

With the large number of successful hijackings and the payment of millions of US dollars in ransom, demand for private protection skyrocketed. Since private maritime security was previously a niche business, more and more maritime PMSCs were established to meet demand, and some already established PMSCs that offered services on land began to advertise maritime services as well. At the peak, an estimated 300 companies were believed to offer anti-piracy services, though not all of these enterprises were actually active. Many of these companies have their headquarters in the UK and the USA, but PMSCs also emerged in countries such as Germany, Singapore, Spain, India and Australia. This mushrooming of anti-piracy PMSCs was possible because many of these enterprises are small businesses, with a small number of permanent staff; some companies even operate without a fixed office. The companies are often run by ex-military personnel who hire the guards to protect vessels on short-term contacts when needed. Preference is usually given to guards with a military background. However, a few companies are successful enough to offer guards more permanent contracts of six to twelve months. In recent years, the number of companies has declined because some companies have failed to win customers, did not become profitable enough, or did not have sufficient funds or skills to organize armed international operations (author's interviews; Berube 2014).

Due to the combination of government efforts and the employment of PCASP, the number of Somali pirate attacks began to decline drastically in 2012. That year, 'only' 75 attempted and actual attacks were reported, and in the following year the number dropped further to 15 incidents. Of these 15, only two were successful hijackings, and both vessels were released within a day (ICC 2014: 20). As Somali piracy declined, pirates in southeast Asia and the Gulf of Guinea began to increase their activities. Indeed, in 2013, southeast Asia was once again the region with the most reported pirate attacks in the world. Most attacks in southeast Asia remain simple hit-and-run robberies that do not warrant the employment of PMSCs. However, a few ship owners who have hired PCASP to protect their ships in the wider Gulf of Aden area pay for the guards to stay onboard longer if the vessel will be passing through the Malacca Strait (author's interviews). The employment of PMSCs off Somalia, therefore, has a spillover effect into southeast Asia. This differs from practices in the Gulf of Guinea, where shipowners have to pay local forces or local(ized) security companies for protection.

The maritime sphere: special challenges

The drop in successful hijackings by Somali pirates has in part been attributed to the employment of PMSCs. Indeed, the use of PCASP on ships is now regarded as an accepted and successful method to deter pirates. This acceptance indicates a re-evaluation of the use of PCASP onboard ships, which until the spate of Somali pirate attacks was firmly rejected by the maritime industry, policy makers, and international organizations. However, the employment of PCASP has also raised concerns and created challenges for governments and international regulatory bodies. The working practices of PMSCs at sea, the companies' lack of transparency, and the dearth of public oversight of their activities are of particular concern (see, for example,

Liss 2011; UN Security Council 2012; Liss with Schneider 2015). Government oversight and control of PMSC operations is particularly challenging in the maritime sphere because:

- government control at sea is often weak;
- operations at sea are conducted far from the eyes of impartial observers;
- PCASP works across borders within a single operation; and
- PMSCs often operate in environments with overlapping jurisdictions.

To illustrate, Somali pirates attack vessels far off the coast, where the presence of government forces or any other observers is low. Usually only the crew of the target vessel, the PCASP on board, and the pirates can provide information about incidents. Also, on a voyage a vessel that trades internationally typically passes through international waters and the waters under the jurisdiction of coastal states, and the ship itself has the nationality of the country of registration and is bound to the flag state's laws. Jurisdiction over water areas and vessels is largely determined by the United Nations Convention on the Law of the Sea (UNCLOS).[3] The convention loosely defined four maritime zones, namely the territorial sea (with a maximum width of 12 nautical miles from the shore), contiguous zone (24 nm), Exclusive Economic Zone (EEZ; up to 200 miles) and high seas. The high seas are all waters beyond the EEZs and are outside the jurisdiction of individual states. Coastal states have limited rights to enforce national laws on specific issues in the other three zones. For example, coastal states have the exclusive right to exploit natural resources, including fish stocks, in these zones. However, ships do enjoy the right of innocent passage (Stopford 2009: 663–6). UNCLOS also endorsed the right of any state to register ships, provided a 'genuine link' between the state and the vessel exists (Article 91), and stipulates that the flag state is responsible for the protection of vessels flying its colours.

With the increasing employment of armed private guards on merchant and fishing vessels, efforts have been made to control the activities of maritime PMSCs. On the international level, the International Maritime Organization (IMO) began to publish guidelines in 2008 that recommended that flag states in cooperation with ship owners should generate policies to regulate the use of armed PMSC personnel on ships. Even though later versions were more detailed, the general tenor did not change, and the publications remained only guidelines (IMO 2011: 31). In fact, no binding international regulations exist that specifically address the use of private armed guards in the maritime sphere. The governance of anti-piracy PMSCs has therefore largely been left to flag states.[4]

In the past, only a very small number of ships that, for example, carried particularly valuable or dangerous cargo, were protected by private armed guards. Flag states therefore generally did not have comprehensive regulations that governed the use of armed PMSC guards on ships and only a few countries, including Greece and Japan, proscribed the arming of merchant ships. Flag states approached the regulation of maritime PMSCs differently. Some states, including many flag of convenience (FOC) countries, did not establish clear rules and do not carry out active regulatory measures. Unlike national registers, which only accept vessels from their own country, FOC states have open registers that offer registration to any vessel without significant restrictions. Open registers are often 'convenient' for shipowners because of their lax regulations in regard to tax and company laws, crew origin, and vessel safety and security standards (Stopford 2009: 666–75). While they do not prohibit the employment of armed guards, they have delegated the responsibility to ship owners and masters of protected vessels. The Bahamas, as well as Antigua and Barbuda, for example, declared that they will not accept liability for any difficulties caused by the employment of PCASP on vessels under their flags.

Other states have introduced new regulations and are actively exercising control over

PMSCs and their maritime activities. These countries include Greece, Japan, Germany, Norway, Denmark, Sweden and the UK (International Chamber of Shipping and European Community Shipowners Associations 2012). Some countries, such as Spain, have applied the regulations that govern land-based PMSCs to maritime operations, but most flag states have introduced specific regulations for the maritime sphere. However, because every flag state generates its own regulations, major variations in regulatory frameworks exist. Differences can be found, for example, in the licensing of PMSCs and individual guards, the types of weapons allowed, requirements regarding compliance with international voluntary initiatives such as the International Code of Conduct for Private Security Services Providers, and the regulation of the export, transport and storage of weapons (see Liss with Schneider 2015).

Despite the introduction of regulations, many problems and concerns persist. As mentioned above, some flag states do not make serious efforts to regulate anti-piracy PMSCs. A further fundamental problem is that ship owners can change the flag, and therefore the set of laws they have to comply with, easily. Flag states that introduce regulations that are too stringent therefore face the risk that ship owners will change the registration of their vessels to another flag. Furthermore, it remains difficult for flag states to control the activities of anti-piracy PMSCs, even when they introduce new regulations. To begin with, many regulations only address certain aspects of PMSC anti-piracy operations. For example, while Denmark, Sweden, and Norway have introduced regulations, they place the responsibility for vetting PMSCs and the control over the use of weapons and their storage onboard the ship largely in the hands of the client and the master of the protected vessel (Berndtsson and Østensen 2015). Other regulations do not consider the international transportation of weapons or their storage between anti-piracy operations. Also critical is that flag states do not provide oversight of the actual PMSC operations and rely on reports from PMSC clients or the companies themselves for information (Liss with Schneider 2015).

These shortcomings have resulted in problematic working practices of anti-piracy PMSCs and a general lack of government control over their activities. Concerns are the unsupervised use of weapons that can lead to the killing of fishermen or other seafarers mistakenly identified as pirates. The acquisition, transport, and storage of weapons are also worrisome. PMSCs either legally or illegally purchase their weapons or rent them from private businesses or governments. Government control over these weapons is difficult, even when they are acquired legally. For instance, hundreds of Sri Lankan government-owned weapons that had been hired by PMSCs reportedly went missing (UN Security Council 2012: 278–81), and the large number of weapons approved for export to be used by British security firms raised concerns that the weapons could 'have ended up in the hands of pirates themselves' (Leftly 2014).

Furthermore, at the end of an operation, the weapons are either thrown overboard or stored for the next operation. Storage is available in certain ports, some of which are located in countries facing political unrest, or on so-called floating armouries. The latter are mostly old vessels located in international waters that store weapons, ammunition, and equipment (such as body armour and night vision goggles) for different companies. Around 18–20 such armouries are believed to be in operation. Many of them are privately owned, but some are at least in part run by government agencies, such as the Sri-Lankan navy (UN Security Council 2012: 278–81). While these floating armouries are convenient for PMSCs because they do not have to go through the time consuming and expensive procedures to get permits for their employees to enter or exit ports with weapons, they often operate beyond the control of authorities.

Summarizing these concerns about the private anti-piracy business, a UN Security Council report states:

[T]his highly profitable business has expanded beyond the provision of armed escorts to the leasing of arms, ammunition, and security equipment, and the establishment of 'floating armouries' that operate in international waters beyond the remit of any effective international regulatory authority. ... The absence of control and inspection of armed activities inevitably creates opportunities for illegality and abuse, and increases the risk that the maritime security industry will be exploited by unscrupulous and criminal actors, eventually coming to represent a threat to regional peace and security, rather than part of the solution.

(UN Security Council 2012: 24)

Conclusion

PMSCs are increasingly active in the maritime sphere, where they are engaged in the protection of maritime installations such as offshore oil and gas platforms and in addressing maritime security threats such as piracy. The explosion in the employment of anti-piracy PMSCs in the Gulf of Aden and the introduction of new laws and regulations that allow the use of PCASP on ships indicates that PMSCs have become accepted players in maritime security governance. These new regulations will also further facilitate the employment of PCASP in the future. Not only has a precedent been set, but some of the new regulations do not restrict the use of armed guards to anti-piracy services. Furthermore, in some cases water areas now merely have to be defined as 'high-risk areas' to allow the use of PCASP on ships and possibly oil and gas installations, which are also registered under flags. In this context, it is, however, important to remember that PMSCs only address the symptoms, but not the root causes of threats such as piracy – which include instability and conflict on land, poverty and environmental destruction.

Moreover, the activities of PMSCs justifiably still cause concern, which centres mostly on the companies' working practices and the lack of government oversight of PMSCs and their activities. As discussed above, oversight of PMSCs is especially difficult when they operate at sea and in environments with overlapping jurisdictions. PMSC operations at sea are not restricted to anti-piracy services, and other services such as the protection of offshore oil and gas installations and operations against illegal fishing cause similar problems. More efforts are therefore needed to effectively monitor and regulate PMSCs and hold them accountable for their actions in order to protect civilians and avoid the uncontrolled use and circulation of weapons. Last but not least, given the difficulties flag states encounter in controlling maritime PMSCs and the reluctance of some flag states to craft regulations, alternative approaches to regulate PMSCs and monitor their operations on the international level should be given more consideration.

Notes

1   Some authors prefer to use the term private *maritime* security companies for enterprises that offer anti-piracy services. Here, however private military and security companies will be used because a wider range of maritime services is discussed and the companies involved do not all offer only maritime services, as will be discussed later.
2   However, the advertisements for protection of fishing grounds or EEZs against illegal fishers seem to have declined (or disappeared) in recent years.
3   See www.un.org/depts/los/convention_agreements/texts/unclos/closindx.htm for the text of UNCLOS.
4   Regulatory efforts have also been made within the industry. These will not be discussed here.

Bibliography

Avant, D. (2005) *The Market for Force: The Consequences of Privatizing Security*, Cambridge: Cambridge University Press.

Berndtsson, J. and Østensen, Å. G. (2015) 'The Scandinavian Approach to Private Maritime Security – A Regulatory Façade?', *Journal of Ocean Development and International Law* 46(2): 138–52.

Berube, C. (2014) 'PMCS: The End or the Beginning', Center for International Maritime Security, 17 April, http://cimsec.org/pmcs-end-beginning/10926.

Berube, C. and Cullen, P. (eds) (2012) *Maritime Private Security: Market Responses to Piracy, Terrorism and Waterborne Security Risks in the 21st Century*, Abingdon: Routledge.

Chapsos, I. and Holtom, P. (2015) 'Stockpiles at Sea: Floating Armouries in the Indian Ocean', in *Small Arms Survey 2015*, Cambridge: Cambridge University Press, pp. 216–41.

Ehrhart, H.-G., Petretto, K. and Schneider, P. (2010) *Security Governance als Rahmenkonzept für die Analyse von Piraterie und Maritimem Terrorismus. Konzeptionelle und Empirische Grundlagen*, Working Paper no. 1, Hamburg: PiraT.

ICC (2007) *Piracy and Armed Robbery against Ships: Report for the Period 1 January–31 December 2006*, London: International Maritime Bureau.

ICC (2012) *Piracy and Armed Robbery against Ships: Report for the Period 1 January–31 December 2011*, London: International Maritime Bureau.

ICC (2014) *Piracy and Armed Robbery against Ships: Report for the Period 1 January–31 December 2013*, London: International Maritime Bureau.

IMO (2011) 'Guidance on Armed Security Personnel on Ships Agreed, International Maritime Organization', *IMO News*, no. 3.

International Chamber of Shipping and European Community Shipowners Associations (2012) 'Comparison of Flag State Laws on Armed Guards and Arms on Board', www.ics-shipping.org/docs/default-source/Piracy-Docs/comparison-of-flag-state-laws-on-armed-guards-and-arms-on-board3F9814DED68F.pdf.

Kashubsky, M. (2013) 'Protecting Offshore Oil and Gas Installations: Security Threats and Countervailing Measures', *Journal of Energy Security* 13 August, http://ensec.org/index.php?option=com_content&view=article&id=453:protecting-offshore-oil-and-gas-installations-security-threats-and-countervailing-measures&catid=137:issue-content&Itemid=422.

Leftly, M. (2014) 'British Weapons Could Be Arming Somali Pirates', *Independent* 5 January, www.independent.co.uk/news/uk/politics/british-weapons-could-be-arming-somali-pirates-9039176.html.

Liss, C. (2011) *Oceans of Crime: Maritime Piracy and Transnational Security in Southeast Asia and Bangladesh*, Singapore: Institute of Southeast Asian Studies and International Institute for Asian Studies.

Liss, C. with Schneider, P. (eds) (2015) 'Special Issue: Regulating Private Maritime Security Providers', *Ocean Development and International Law* 46(2).

Singer, P. W. (2003) *Corporate Warriors: The Rise of the Privatized Military Industry*, Ithaca, NY: Cornell University Press.

Stopford, M. (2009) *Maritime Economics* (3rd edition), London: Routledge.

Thomson, J. E. (1994) *Mercenaries, Pirates and Sovereigns: State Building and Extraterritorial Violence in Early Modern Europe*, Princeton, NJ: Princeton University Press.

Till, G. (2013) *Seapower: A Guide for the Twenty-First Century* (3rd edition), New York: Routledge.

UN Security Council (2012) *Somalia Report of the Monitoring Group on Somalia and Eritrea Submitted in Accordance with Resolution 2002 (2011)*, 13 July, New York: United Nations.

World Bank (2013) *Pirate Trails: Tracking the Illicit Financial Flows from Piracy off the Horn of Africa*, Washington, DC: World Bank.

7

PRIVATIZING MILITARY LOGISTICS

Mark Erbel[1] and Christopher Kinsey

This chapter sets out to explain why governments are privatizing military logistics, and what implications such a trend has for the supply of war into the future. It takes a broad approach, examining a variety of drivers behind military outsourcing and the problems that outsourcing creates politically and for military commanders who are responsible for utilizing force. Our main objective is to show that logistics outsourcing is possibly the most representative and important (yet neglected) aspect of the wider phenomenon of military outsourcing. It most comprehensively encapsulates the drivers of contracting in general, involves the largest number of the contractor workforce and expenditure, and is exemplary of the future of military outsourcing. Moreover, not only is it highly relevant to foreign and defence policy, but governments have also become heavily dependent on logistics contractors for the long term whereas they could – political will provided – always replace private security contractors with regular troops. This should cause us to reconsider the overwhelming focus the literature places on the outsourcing of various security functions to armed contractors.

This chapter first defines logistics and underscores its relevance to foreign and defence policy. Next, after a brief historical account of logistics outsourcing, it gives a comprehensive explanation of why states today have chosen to outsource military logistics instead of doing it themselves. It then introduces three key debates around military outsourcing – whether it saves money, how decision-makers are affected by contractors, and the problem of the 'revolving door'. The chapter concludes by considering the future of the outsourcing of military logistics, finding that outsourcing is not only here to stay because its driving forces persist, but that it is likely to accelerate and lead to the integration of public and private workforces in the defence enterprise. The chapter draws primarily on evidence from the USA and the UK, the two countries that have gone the furthest in outsourcing military logistics and have historically set standards that other countries eventually follow.

What is military logistics and why does it matter?

We should first explain what we mean by military logistics. Military logistics is 'the science of planning and carrying out the movement and maintenance of [air, sea, and land] forces' (NATO 1997: 1). Martin van Creveld gave equal importance to logistics and strategy in his seminal work *Supplying War*:

> Strategy, like politics, is said to be the art of the possible; but surely what is possible is determined not merely by numerical strengths, doctrine, intelligence, arms and tactics, but in the first place, by the hardest facts of all: those concerning requirements, supplies available and expected, organization and administration, transportation and arteries of communication.
>
> *(Van Creveld 1977: 1)*

This makes logistics a critical element of fighting power because it alone 'determines what military forces can be delivered to an operational theatre, the time it will take to deliver that force, the scale and scope of forces that can be supported once there and the tempo (speed) of operations' (Uttley and Kinsey 2012: 401). But logistics is more than just the deployment and sustainment of military forces in wartime. Military logistics also includes the defence industrial and civilian supply base and must address the question of whether they are able to meet the needs of potential future military operations. Without a sound appreciation of logistics, scholars and practitioners alike run the risk of misunderstanding and – in the case of the latter – making grave errors in the application of the armed forces. Unfortunately, logistics is often neglected in favour of strategy and tactics; scholars would rather know about the ways of war (tactics, the disposal of force) and the ends (strategy), but not the means (logistics) by which strategy and tactics are achieved.

Military logistics is thus central to the formulation of policy, strategy, and tactics as well as the conduct and outcome of war. This is why this chapter matters. Students of strategic studies, security studies, and international politics alike all need an appreciation of how governments generate military capability, including by and with contractors. This should also be at the centre of any policy or academic discussion about the use of military force today. After all, it is the military logistician who in the end is equipped to turn political objectives into reality, and is tasked with enabling each and every military deployment more generally.

Why, where and how is military logistics outsourced?

Before examining its contemporary drivers, it is worth pointing out that outsourcing military logistics is not a new phenomenon. As Shouesmith points out, 'civilian suppliers have featured on operations throughout history, often in the form of in-country agents' (Shouesmith 2010: 28). A temporary change from this practice occurred with the rise of nationalism at the end of the eighteenth century and the introduction of conscription through which governments became able to internalize functions that had previously been performed by contractors and thereby achieve greater military self-sufficiency. This internalization was seen as a military necessity as total war became more common in international politics. With contractors – unlike regular soldiers – under no moral or legal obligation to stay on the battlefield, European governments found that their survival in a total war depended on mobilising the male adult population to avoid the risk of being abandoned on the battlefield during an existential conflict (McNeill 1984). Nevertheless, the military still relied on contractors to undertake certain logistical and engineering tasks such as aircraft and helicopter maintenance, and this situation continued throughout the world wars and the Cold War. For instance, the ratio of contractors to regular US military personnel was 1 : 20 in World War I, 1 : 7 in World War II and 1 : 6 in Vietnam (US Department of Defense 2014). It was, however, only with the introduction of neoliberal economics by Prime Minister Margaret Thatcher in the UK and President Ronald Reagan in the US at the start of the 1980s that outsourcing and core competency, not self-sufficiency, once more became the officially preferred way to supply military operations for some Western governments.

Today there are as many, and often more contractors working overseas supporting the military than there are soldiers. Most of these contractors provide logistics services. For instance, in Iraq, Afghanistan, and the Central Command (CENTCOM) area the number of contractors working for the US Department of Defense in recent years matched and often exceeded those of regular US military personnel, in the most extreme case standing at more than double the number of US troops in Afghanistan in late 2008 (71,755 and 32,500, respectively; Schwartz and Swain 2011: 2, 7, 10, 13, 26). The services these contractors provide range from more menial tasks such as basic life, facilities, and logistics support (for instance cooking, cleaning, barracks maintenance, or logistics planning, most famously the US Army's LOGCAP contract) and transportation services (for instance of military equipment, regular mail, or food, water, and petrol) to hi-tech equipment maintenance, infrastructure support, or air-to-air refuelling. These support services represented 93.8 per cent of contracted services provided in Iraq and Afghanistan at the time, compared to only 6.2 per cent security contractors (US Department of Defense 2008: 1–3). More generally, operations and support contract spending alone in the US exceeded procurement spending by 2012, being $150 billion and $100 billion, respectively, while support in the UK will represent 54 per cent of the total costs of new equipment purchases from 2012 to 2022, standing at £86 billion and £73 billion, respectively (Erwin 2012; UK National Audit Office 2013: 5).

Why was the decision taken to outsource military logistics far beyond the levels seen during the Cold War? First, ideas are hugely relevant for determining the propensity to outsource. Countries espousing a liberal approach to civil–military relations (as the US and the UK) rather than a republican vision (as for example Germany) have shown a greater willingness to outsource military responsibilities (Krahmann 2010: ch. 2, 7). The drive to outsource the military supply chain is partly a consequence of the view of the market as more efficient than the military in providing services (Singer 2003: 66–70). States that generally support the private provision of public services and buy into the notion of 'core competency' (i.e. the idea that organizations have only few unique capabilities and responsibilities that set them apart from competitors and that they must perform themselves) are more likely to outsource (Taylor 2004: 185–90).

There are also functionalist explanations that focus on broad social structures that shape the military as an organization. The increasing use of contractors in military operations is in part the consequence of the technological sophistication of modern weapons systems (Kinsey 2009: 19, 69–70). This had two quite distinct impacts on military force structure; first, at the individual level, soldiers become more specialized in the use of technically sophisticated weapon systems and are less likely to want to perform the type of mundane functions their predecessors once did; second, at the organizational level, militaries transforming into smaller core-competency armies focused on generating maximum firepower do not retain the manpower to perform many support functions. Moreover, the more quickly technological sophistication advances, the more likely it is that states will outsource support services in order to be able to maintain and operate new equipment (Taylor 2004: 191–3).

It is also vital to consider how central a country's defence industry is to its wider security architecture, as this can affect a government's willingness to support or even subsidize domestic companies, for example by letting contracts for goods and services. This is especially important in the US (Erbel 2014), where the defence industry is considered to be 'democracy's arsenal' (Gansler 2011). Militaries thus now follow a similar trend as the private sector. Since the 1980s many armies decided to 'concentrate on their 'core competencies' and outsource their other needs from other specialists' (Taylor 2004: 187; see also Kinsey 2014a: 186–8). The outcome is a core-competency force structure where the military undertakes only a handful of the tasks a military operation entails, mostly those which one might call 'inherently govern-mental' in that the task is so intimately related to the public interest that it must be performed by a government employee. The most obvious of these tasks is high-intensity war fighting, while in logistics this also includes those required in the early, 'hot' phase of military operations.

Political cost calculations also affect the outsourcing of military logistics. Often governments outsource because it is more politically feasible than using regular troops. For example, some governments now cap the number of soldiers that can be deployed on an operation, to mini-mize the profile of the operation, to put as few uniformed troops in harm's way as possible, or to avoid sensitive geopolitical situations. This is done to maintain public support for the oper-ation (Shouesmith 2010: 28) and may explain why the UK and US militaries have outsourced their supply chain in Pakistan to local contractors – they know that deploying foreign troops to the country is politically impossible (Kinsey 2014b: 8).

A highly relevant yet mostly ignored driver of logistics outsourcing is the gap between defence posture, hi-tech warfare, and the level of available resources. Differently expansive defence postures create different demands for deployability, equipment, and sustainability. Since the 1950s the US and the UK in particular faced a persistent gap between their expansive global defence political commitments, their demands for hi-tech weapon systems and military superiority, and the level of available resources. Both states turned to the market – first for inspi-ration, then for service provision – to bridge that gap (Erbel 2014: ch. 2 and 3). Today it appears unrealistic for a government to be able to achieve even a minimum military global presence without the support of contractors (Taylor 2004: 193–6). Consequently, the gap between commitments, requirements, and resources appears to be widening in favour of the market. Militaries continue to lose critical skill sets to contractors, particularly in technological fields, as the armed forces continue to push for technological advances (the 'Revolution in Military Affairs') that mostly originate in the private sector. Not least because the companies retain the relevant intellectual property rights and thus the technological data for these new systems (from computers, to drones, to the newest fighter jets), new systems generally come with a sizeable contractor workforce 'attached' for the training of soldiers in their use, their maintenance, and sometimes their operation. For instance, contractors conduct the take-off and landing of drones as well as repairs and upgrades to the systems for several Western militaries, which can involve 160 to 180 personnel to complete a 24-hour mission of a Predator or Reaper drone (Clanahan 2012). A less expansive defence posture and/or an acceptance of less than the most sophisti-cated equipment could therefore have alleviated some of the pressures that led to and sustained outsourcing.

Finally, it makes a significant difference how governments pay for war (Erbel 2014: ch. 3). In essence, if war-related expenses are covered by supplementary budgets (e.g. in the US) or by the Treasury (the UK), states are funding defence on the assumption of 'peacetime', regardless of how elusive 'peacetime' may be. In these cases, governments are incentivized to reduce the standing army and outsource capability as much as possible to show that their 'base budget' or peacetime budget is low. As pure combat functions are not outsourced even in an ideal-typical 'core compe-tency' army, this dynamic means that logistics is usually the first to be contracted out.

The preceding paragraphs underscore that logistics outsourcing is perhaps the most repre-sentative of the history, drivers, and trajectory of contemporary military outsourcing. Most discussions about security contracting begin at the end of the Cold War, while – as we showed above – contemporary military outsourcing in the logistics sphere stretches back at least to the 1950s. Moreover, governments do not ultimately depend on the capabilities provided by armed contractors as even an ideal-typical 'core-competency' army will always retain the knowledge of how to use force. They could thus use soldiers for these tasks, whereas they can no longer operate without technical support contractors (who also represent a much larger share of the industry). Moreover, it is reasonable to assume that security contracting may not have happened so swiftly (or at all) had governments not had decades of experience in drawing on the market for logistics support (Erbel 2014: ch. 6).

Debating the outsourcing of military logistics

This section introduces three of the main debates about the outsourcing of logistics: whether outsourcing saves money, whether the dependency on contractors influences decision-makers, and the potentially negative influence of outsourcing on political decision-makers' behaviour. While these are not the only debates on the topic, they are among the most important because they impact on the more general controversies relating to outsourcing, namely those surrounding one of the main arguments put forward in favour of outsourcing, the relationship between outsourcing, the national interest, ethics and the accountability and transparency of defence policy and military operations.

The debate around whether outsourcing costs or saves money is as old as outsourcing itself. There is no straightforward answer to this question and opinions are often sharply polarized. Usually both sides rely on the studies that have been conducted to test the assumption that outsourcing saves money. These studies come up with diametrically opposed results (US General Accounting Office 1997: 4; Uttley 2005: 37; Krahmann 2010: 112). Agreement therefore only exists on the fact that there is insufficient data and no agreed-on cost comparison criterion to determine whether outsourcing generally has saved money or not, leaving us unable to make generalizations about the cost-efficiency of contracting against performing tasks in-house. To engage in this debate, there are several factors to consider, key among them being which function is being outsourced, where, and for how long.

The Project on Government Oversight (POGO), one of the main US watchdog NGOs, conducted one of the most detailed and systematic studies of the costs of contracting out military responsibilities (POGO 2012). They examined 35 different tasks in order to make a like-for-like comparison between contractor and federal government employee costs. In 33 of the tasks examined, government employees cost less than contractor sources, with the two remaining ones being groundskeepers and medical record technicians (ibid.: 17–18). Not only does the report highlight the importance of separating different tasks in order to make an informed estimate of whether outsourcing saves money, it also cites official reports that show that government agencies won 83 per cent of competitions against private sector companies. Projected cost savings from opening up certain tasks to the market are therefore not necessarily a function of business efficiencies but of competition more generally and often produced 'in-house' (ibid.: 8). It is also important to ask whether an activity being outsourced is being performed at home or on a deployed operation overseas, and by whom. On the one hand, the short-term provision of menial services by local nationals can be much cheaper than deploying Western government employees. On the other, hiring Western contractors for technologically sophisticated or security-related tasks overseas is often much more expensive than using Western government employees (ibid.: 1; Commission on Wartime Contracting 2011). Sometimes, however, these are moot points. When the knowhow or intellectual property that is key to a contract is owned by private companies, outsourcing is not just an option, but a necessity if the government cannot or does not want to do without the capability. This is the case for example for operating, maintaining, and upgrading drones and other aircraft. Situations such as these are becoming more frequent as industry increasingly owns technologies and intellectual property rights upon which governments depend (Erbel 2014).

Even in those instances in which industry providers are doubtlessly cheaper, we should not neglect the fact that companies are by their nature profit-seeking organizations. Savings could thus come from using poorly paid labourers or providing a low quality of service (Smith 2012). The industry also claims to be able to 'hire and fire' employees more easily than the public sector and thus operate more cheaply. On one hand, this is another ethically questionable 'advantage' as it relies on job insecurity of employees. On the other, questions arise whether this supposed advantage materializes, especially in hi-tech domains. A former manager of one of the largest logistics contracts in the US, the Logistics Civil Augmentation Program (LOGCAP), the late Mr Charles Smith cast doubt on the 'hire and fire' argument. While ships were in dock at a facility in South Carolina, contractors conducted maintenance on its equipment before the ship was sent out again for another year. As the company was unable to find qualified personnel for the short timeframe during which ships were in dock and 'firing' them for the year the ships were at sea, the government ultimately had to find new work for the company so that the company could keep the contract and its employees (C. M. Smith, telephone interview by Erbel, 25 April 2013). Falsely relying on the hire-and-fire argument can in fact make outsourcing more expensive because companies have to pay their employees even when there is no government work available. A final point to be made here is that some cost savings can actually be the result of shifts in budgets. When a responsibility is outsourced (medical care costs for contractors for instance) and taken off the military budget and shifted to another budget (from military health to general health in this case), the cost saving for the military is matched by a cost increase elsewhere. Ultimately the cost has to be paid for (by the taxpayer, or perhaps by the contractor) and the cost saving is thus merely a matter of reshuffling.

At the end of the day, therefore, more reliable and detailed data and especially agreed-upon cost-comparison criteria are needed in order to answer the central question about whether or not contracting is cost-effective. This is challenging because, by turning to private finance initiative programmes governments have made it generally more difficult for the public and parliamentarians to access the true cost of defence, not least because of the very long time span of support contracts (Krahmann 2010: 112). Former US Under Secretary of Defense for Acquisition Jacques Gansler, a respected expert and practitioner in this field, is leading an effort to develop valid cost comparison models that all stakeholders can agree to (Gansler *et al.* 2012).

Second, concerns also arise from governments' increasing dependence on contractors, especially regarding operational security and the degree to which contractors may influence and shape governments' decision-making processes. Operational security concerns the disclosure of sensitive information before it was meant to become public knowledge. The high level of public distrust of contractors is generally seen to be behind this fear. Outsourcing so far has presented no problems to operational security, not least because information is circulated to everybody – not just contractors – on a need-to-know basis and is contingent on holding a security clearance (Erbel 2014: ch. 6). Nonetheless, governments' dependency on contractors raises questions about their autonomy in decision making. As Shouesmith notes, there is a 'should' and a 'could' aspect to decisions (D. Shouesmith, interview by the authors, Shrivenham, 13 June 2013). In defence, the 'should' asks, for instance, whether the government should embark on a military operation, while the 'could' inquires whether the ability and capacity to do so exist. Military logistics evidently goes to the essence of such decisions. Shouesmith and industry representatives in the US all agree that industry is not part of the 'should' decision, but can (and sometimes has to) come in immediately thereafter to determine the 'could' (ibid.). But can we really divorce the two aspects from one another? Do capabilities not inform what governments perceive as achievable, maybe even as desirable?

Consequently, when the industry points out that certain capabilities are at risk of being lost if government stops investing in them, does this not have the (possibly unintended) consequence of somehow forcing the government to continue to use or at least maintain certain capabilities even if they do not currently 'use' them but are hesitant about not having access to them in the future? In the UK, debates about whether and how to maintain a nuclear deterrent are perhaps the most extreme example of this conundrum. More generally, investments in new technologies for purely military use, such as autonomous surveillance and attack systems, cyber-warfare technologies, or new missile capabilities are made with an eye to future battlefields, often decades down the line. New technologies are also drawn mostly from privately owned corporations and – importantly for our purposes – entail decades-long logistics contracts that are becoming key components of the lifecycle of a defence system and central to the long-term investment strategies of defence companies. As a result, if governments wish to retain existing or develop new capabilities for the distant future, they have to invest in their maintenance and/or development today. According to a senior US defence official some budget requests are therefore 'motivated by industrial base considerations' (Weisgerber 2012). It is important to note here that this is not about industry conspiring to 'trick' governments to intervene in places just so they use their equipment or desire to buy new systems; governments should not be assumed to be naïve or fawning to industry in this way. It is rather about industry strongly affecting and informing the very structures of decision making in such a way that governments' strategic decisions become inseparable from the wellbeing of the defence industry. While governments therefore retain decision-making power and autonomy on high-strategic issues, certainly vis-à-vis their logistics contractors, we must remain cognisant of the fact that this is strongly circumscribed by parameters set by and/or dependent on industry (Erbel 2014).

Governments' dependence on industry can also affect the incentive structure of state employees, encouraging them to treat companies favourably. This can occur not only to ensure a successful career within government, where outsourcing has become standard procedure and a good relationship with industry a necessity, but being perceived as 'friendly' to industry can also facilitate passage through the 'revolving door' after retiring from government service. Given that logistics is particularly manpower and money-intensive, this issue takes on considerable relevance as it affects a high number of people across government and on all levels. While exchanging personnel between government and industry doubtlessly has positive implications, ranging from giving people more choice and mobility in employment to ensuring that the state has access to the newest technologies, skills, and knowhow, there are also potential downsides. The most important risk is that superiors may suppress dissent and criticism of industry and contractors within their ranks. The aforementioned Mr Smith, for instance, had worked as a LOGCAP manager in the US Army for decades but was eventually removed from his position (together with others) for confronting the company holding the contract over what he and some of his co-workers considered were unreasonable costs being charged to the army (Smith 2012).

Conclusion

This chapter has shown that logistics outsourcing, often put in second place in academic literature, is the most representative and possibly important domain that has undergone contractualization in the past decades in many armed forces, as it is particularly representative of the causes, process, and likely future of military outsourcing generally.

As far as the causes of the privatization of military logistics are concerned, they are likely to stay relevant well into the future. The shifting of manpower to the private sector to achieve core competency, the ownership and development of knowhow and technologies by the private sector, and the prevalence of market ideology have progressed to such an extent that many military forces will be unable to deploy without contractor support. Importantly, this is not the case with armed contractors providing security as they, unlike logisticians, do not offer the military capabilities that it does not have (no matter how narrow the 'core' becomes). The UK military in particular has both recognized this and seized upon it. The 'Total Support Force' (TSF) now blends public and private actors and organizations into a joint support force for the armed forces. This exemplifies how the merger of public and private in the military logistics sphere is not only here to stay but expanding and formalizing considerably. In the US there are similar plans, the 'Joint Logistics Enterprise', which is intended to use capabilities from military, civilian, and industry sources.

Even more fundamentally, the future will likely see continued outsourcing because the strategic outlook and budgeting assumptions are unlikely to change. As long as foreign and defence political objectives and commitments exceed the available resources, and as long as the US and UK militaries in particular wish to operate equipment that is the most sophisticated on the globe, these two governments are likely to continue to look to the market for solutions, at least for so long as the market provides the required services and capabilities. Only abject failure in one or more of these fundamental driving forces could lead to a radical reappraisal of the feasibility of drawing on contractors to enable military capability.

We hope that future research will therefore direct less attention to the, admittedly 'sexier', activities and exploits of armed security contractors and more to logistics. We think this is especially important when making arguments about the big picture of military contracting. In this chapter we hope to have outlined the long causal links that extend from high political objectives all the way down to who fulfils some of the most basic, menial tasks in the defence enterprise. Logistics is the backbone of military strategy, and its contractualization may just be the backbone of military outsourcing writ large.

Note

1   The views expressed in this chapter are those of the author alone and do not necessarily reflect those of the UK Ministry of Defence or the UK government.

Bibliography

Clanahan, K. D. (2012) 'Drone-Sourcing? United States Air Force Unmanned Aircraft Systems, Inherently Governmental Functions, and the Role of Contractors', *Federal Circuit Bar Journal* 22(1), http://papers.ssrn.com/sol3/papers.cfm?abstract_id=2051154.

Commission on Wartime Contracting (2011) *Transforming Wartime Contracting: Controlling Costs, Reducing Risks*, final report to Congress, Arlington, VA: Commission on Wartime Contracting in Iraq and Afghanistan.

Erbel, M. (2014) Contractors and Defence Policy-Making: Examining the Drivers, Process, and Future of Military Outsourcing, PhD dissertation, King's College, London.

Erwin, S. S. I. (2012), 'Defense Industry Targets $150B Weapons Maintenance Market', *National Defense Magazine* July, www.nationaldefensemagazine.org/archive/2012/July/Pages/DefenseIndustry Targets$150BWeaponsMaintenanceMarket.aspx.

Gansler, J. S. (2011) *Democracy's Arsenal: Creating a Twenty-First Century Defense Industry*, Cambridge, MA: MIT Press.

Gansler, J. S., Lucyshyn, W. and Rigilano, J. (2012) *Toward a Valid Cost Comparison of Contractor and Government Costs*, College Park, MD: Center for Public Policy and Private Enterprise, www.acquisitionresearch.net/files/FY2011/UMD-CE-11-209.pdf.

Kinsey, C. (2009) *Private Contractors and the Reconstruction of Iraq: Transforming Military Logistics*, New York: Routledge.

Kinsey, C. (2014a) 'The Rise of Contractors in 21st Century Warfare', in The Emirates Center for Strategic Studies and Research (ed.), *The Future of Warfare in the 21st Century*, United Arab Emirates: ECSSR, pp. 167–89.

Kinsey, C. (2014b) 'Transforming Supplying War: Considerations and Rationales behind Contractor Support to Future UK Overseas Military Operations in the 21st Century', *International Journal* 69(4): 1–16.

Krahmann, E. (2010) *States, Citizens and the Privatisation of Security*, Cambridge: Cambridge University Press.

McNeill, W. H. (1984) *The Pursuit of Power: Technology, Armed Forces, and Society Since AD 1000*, Chicago, IL: Chicago University Press.

NATO (1997) *NATO Logistics Handbook* (3rd edition), Brussels: NATO.

POGO (2012) *Bad Business: Billions of Taxpayer Dollars Wasted on Hiring Contractors*, Washington, DC: Project on Government Oversight.

Schwartz, M., and Swain, J. (2011) *Department of Defense Contractors in Afghanistan and Iraq: Background and Analysis*, report R40764, Washington, DC: Congressional Research Service.

Shouesmith, D. (2010) 'Contractorisation: Opportunity or Threat?', *Military Logistics International* 5(2): 28–30.

Singer, P. W. (2003) *Corporate Warriors: The Rise of the Privatised Military Industry*, Ithaca, NY: Cornell University Press.

Smith, C. M. (2012) *War for Profit: Army Contracting vs. Supporting the Troops*, New York: Algora Publishing.

Taylor, T. (2004) 'Contractors on Deployed Operations and Equipment Support', *Defence Studies* 4(2): 184–98.

UK National Audit Office (2013) *Equipment Plan 2012 to 2022*, report by the Comptroller and Auditor General, HC 886, session 2012–13, London: The Stationery Office.

US Department of Defense (2008) *CENTCOM Quarterly Contractor Census Report*, November, Washington, DC: Office of the Deputy Assistant Secretary of Defense (Program Support).

US Department of Defense (2014) Contingency Contracting throughout US History, Washington, DC: Office of the Under Secretary of Defense (Acquisition, Technology, and Logistics).

US General Accounting Office (1997) *Outsourcing DOD Logistics: Savings Achievable but Defense Science Board's Projections are Overstated*, GAO/NSIAD-98-48, Washington, DC: General Accounting Office.

Uttley, M. (2005) *Contractors on Deployed Military Operations: UK Policy and Doctrine*, Carlisle, PA: Strategic Studies Institute.

Uttley, M. and Kinsey, C. (2012) 'The Role of Logistics in War', in J. Lindley-French and Y. Boyer (eds), *The Oxford Handbook of War*, Oxford: Oxford University Press, pp. 401–16.

Van Creveld, M. (1977) *Supplying War: Logistics from Wallenstein to Patton*, Cambridge: Cambridge University Press.

Weisgerber, M. (2012) 'QDR Emphasizes Cyber, Science and Technology', *Defense News* (4 March), www.defensenews.com/article/20140304/DEFREG02/303040038/QDR-Emphasizes-Cyber-Science-Technology.

8

PRIVATIZING INTELLIGENCE

Hamilton Bean

This chapter describes why and how private sector corporations assist governments in intelligence collection, analysis, and operations. It explains the actual and potential benefits and risks associated with private intelligence, maps the terrain of private intelligence scholarship, and points to pathways for future investigations that draw upon developments in private security studies (PSS) research. The dramatic expansion of intelligence contracting and outsourcing – 'private intelligence' – has accompanied the rapid growth of private security. However, the study of private intelligence has received far less scholarly attention. Despite its growing significance, only a handful of academic monographs concerning private intelligence have appeared over the last decade, and intelligence educators have mostly avoided the topic. Investigations of private intelligence mainly focus on US developments, and similar to the early study of private security, the literature includes a considerable amount of non-academic work by journalists, think tanks, and security professionals and is still mostly concerned with identifying, denouncing, or defending its practices. Academic explanation and understanding of the drivers, forms, and outcomes of private intelligence is lacking. Nevertheless, recent analyses within the fields of political science, history, philosophy, law and communication have highlighted three inter-related focal points for discussion:

- the historical continuity or discontinuity of private intelligence structures and practices;
- individual morality versus institutional integrity; and
- the values of organizational efficiency and effectiveness on one hand, versus the values of transparency and accountability on the other.

This chapter engages those focal points by first describing the twenty-first century expansion of private intelligence. It concentrates on US developments due to dearth of examples from other countries (although this situation is changing). The chapter then summarizes and synthesizes scholarship that investigates why and how private sector actors assist governments in intelligence collection, analysis, and operations, as well as identifies the actual and potential benefits and risks associated with private intelligence using the case of the Pentagon's Capstone programme. The chapter argues that dissolving the public/private distinction in terms of the work that intelligence collectors, analysts, and operators perform may be appropriate, but equating the underlying drivers of business and government is not. The deepening enmeshment of the public and private sectors, and their associated logics, creates significant challenges for intelligence stakeholders in terms of understanding, oversight, and accountability. The conclusion describes pathways for future investigations of private intelligence that draw upon developments in PSS.

The contemporary expansion of privatized intelligence

This section charts the development of private intelligence and identifies two major waves of public debate concerning its practices. From one perspective, private intelligence is as old as private security. Advancing armies often paid outsiders to supplement their knowledge of the enemy or local conditions. In the United States, companies and individuals aided government officials long before the establishment of the modern US intelligence community in 1947, and private intelligence played a pivotal role in the Revolutionary War, Mexican–American War, Civil War, World Wars I and II, and Cold War conflicts (Cohen 2010). But in modern parlance, contracting refers to the process of integrating a company's employees into a government agency's existing staff, while outsourcing, by contrast, entails turning over entire business functions to an outside vendor. While paid sources provide raw information to intelligence agencies, contractors and vendors generally produce finished intelligence products (reports, analyses, briefings, etc.) or advise agencies on how to improve technological or organizational processes. While sometimes described as a new phenomenon, it is more accurate to view the rise of private intelligence as a logical expansion of the military–industrial complex into related domains.

The dramatic rise of private intelligence, and the associated public debate over its appropriateness, can be traced to the surge in US intelligence contracting and outsourcing in the wake of the 11 September 2001 (9/11) terrorist attacks. The simultaneous proliferation of new and diverse threats, the legacy of agency downsizing in the aftermath of the Cold War, the liberalization of the US defence sector under the Clinton administration, and numerous reports and recommendations of defence industry associations had left intelligence officials eager for outside expertise that could cost-effectively supplement and enhance their agencies' collection and analytical capabilities. With 9/11 serving as the catalyst for a massive expansion of private intelligence, by 2009, the US Office of the Director of National Intelligence acknowledged that private sector contractors constituted nearly one third of the US intelligence community's workforce. Within specific agencies, the percentage of contractors was much higher. At that time, contractors of all types consumed an estimated 70 per cent of the US intelligence community's overall budget for goods, services, and personnel (Shorrock 2008).

Executive orders, institutional memoranda, and the United States Code generally prohibit private contractors or vendors from conducting intelligence operations or governmental activities that affect the life, liberty, or property of private persons. High profile cases, including the prisoner abuse scandal at Abu Ghraib prison in Iraq, and NSA contractor Edward Snowden's monumental disclosures, have raised public concerns about whether this policy is routinely being violated. Commentators have questioned the activities and influence of core personnel contractors who work side-by-side their intelligence agency counterparts, as well as the specialized private intelligence firms that maintain their own staff and supply agencies with intelligence products or consulting services. Often led by former intelligence officials, private intelligence contractors include the subunits of major defence corporations such as Serco, General Dynamics, Boeing, BAE Systems, Sotera, Raytheon, Booz Allen Hamilton, Computer Sciences Corporation, CACI, Science Applications International Corporation, ManTech, Northrup Grumman, and Lockheed Martin. Smaller information brokers and specialized intelligence shops including Oxford Analytica, Economist Intelligence Unit, Jane's Information Group, Chesapeake Strategies Group, Control Risks, iJet, Eurasia Group, International Intelligence, Kroll, Stratfor, OSINT Group, Strategic Insight Group and SITE Intelligence Group, among many others, also participate in the private intelligence market.[1]

Figures concerning the size and scope of the private intelligence market are difficult to locate and vary depending on what kinds of activities are included. Most intelligence contracts are classified, and even non-classified contracts are often withheld from public disclosure. In 2008, the *Washington Post* put the number of US intelligence contractors at approximately 37,000 with a cost of roughly US$50 billion (O'Harrow 2008). A subsequent *Washington Post* investigation in 2010 by Dana Priest and William Arkin identified 1,931 private companies working on programmes related to counterterrorism, homeland security, and intelligence in roughly 10,000 locations across the United States. In 2014, the US Government Accountability Office (GAO) determined that the government had no reliable way of knowing exactly how many core personnel contractors worked within US intelligence agencies. There has been no public disclosure of agency expenditures on information brokers, and publicly available figures for private intelligence expenditures in other countries are either non-existent or extremely difficult to find.

Two waves of public debate

The initial wave of public debate concerning the post-9/11 private intelligence boom occurred during the 2006–8 period. In a 2006 article, US Army Major Glenn James Voelz argued that private intelligence was valuable for analysis, collection management, document exploitation, production, and linguistic support. However, Voelz stressed that more could be done to improve managerial effectiveness and oversight. In *Outsourced*, Hillhouse (2007) offered a fictionalized account of intelligence outsourcing, and her blog and commentary drew international media attention. With public concern growing, in 2007, the US House and Senate required the Director of National Intelligence to report on the activities performed by private contractors. These developments gained significant momentum following the publication of journalist Tim Shorrock's (2008) book-length investigation of the topic, *Spies for Hire*. Shorrock's well-researched account generated institutional defensiveness and bolstered lawmakers' calls for improved agency transparency and accountability. Investigative journalists including Joshua Foust, Mark Mazzetti and Jeremy Scahill, among others, continued to reveal details of the private intelligence industry from 2009 to 2011.

A second wave of public debate concerning private intelligence began to swell in 2012 following what has come to be known as the Stratfor hacking incident. Founded in 1996, Stratfor is a US company that provides numerous types of analytical products to government and corporate clients. In February 2012, Wikileaks began posting copies of nearly 5 million Stratfor emails that had been obtained by the hacker group Anonymous. The group had broken into Stratfor's computer network in 2011, and through its disclosures, it aimed to reveal Stratfor's web of informers, pay structure, and collection methods. However, public debate concerning Stratfor's activities was soon overshadowed by the extraordinary disclosures in 2013 of Booz Allen Hamilton contractor Edward Snowden. Snowden's leaks of the details of NSA collection programmes revealed the immense scope and scale of US intelligence activities, many conducted with the assistance of private corporations. The revelations indicated possible illegalities, as well as the dangers of allowing private contractors to access the government's most closely guarded secrets. Snowden's revelations belied claims of sufficient government oversight of private intelligence, generating renewed calls from lawmakers for improved transparency and accountability.

Defenders and critics

Defenders of private intelligence present it as an unproblematic public–private partnership and a mere shift in the way that government fulfils its intelligence responsibilities (Hansen 2014). Private intelligence contractors and firms help intelligence agencies obtain valuable expertise and improve their efficiency and effectiveness. Defenders also emphasize the similarities between intelligence agencies and large corporations, noting how both often need to rapidly secure specialized skills on a temporary basis. The private intelligence market also enables agencies to tap experts who, presumably, would otherwise abandon the intelligence sector. Thus, for defenders, the actual and potential benefits of private intelligence include flexibility, unique expertise, improved coverage of diverse topics, innovation, dexterity and knowledge retention. While defenders concede that a few cases of private intelligence mismanagement and abuse have occurred, these are in no greater proportion than those occurring within government agencies or other corporations. Most defenders also acknowledge the higher cost of private intelligence, as well as that institutional secrecy, the vagaries of contracting and outsourcing, and the scope and scale of private intelligence make third-party oversight problematic or ineffective.

The arguments of private intelligence critics centre upon the risks of private sector actors performing inherently governmental functions, as well as the wastefulness, lack of oversight, and lack of accountability of the industry (Keefe 2010). Critics presume (and insiders confirm) that the fragmented and compartmentalized structure of the US intelligence community leads to wasteful duplication of effort and a lack of coordination and intelligence sharing. Instead of viewing private intelligence firms as a valuable resource, critics worry that the privatization of intelligence siphons off the best collectors and analysts from government agencies. Critics also presume that contractors may place profits over patriotism, leading to an ill-considered or nefarious influence on national security policy and strategic decision-making. In 2010, the philosopher Christopher Caldwell argued that private intelligence violates the Just War tradition and is a serious moral wrong because firms collect and analyse information not as an end in itself or to protect national interests, but as a means to accrue revenue and profit. Caldwell surmised that because private intelligence activities mostly occur outside the gaze of public oversight, the possibility for wrongdoing was increased. Likewise, the philosopher James Roper argued that private intelligence was unethical because it conflated the differing social functions of business and government. Democratic governments are obliged to give citizens a voice, protect rights and liberties, provide societal functions (security, public health, social services), and balance competing priorities. Such obligations generally are not required of private corporations. Roper thus concluded that private intelligence changed the very nature of the state. Some critics have acknowledged that private firms provide agencies with technical strengths, managerial expertise, and workforce flexibility. These critics are concerned, however, that the vast number of private sector personnel, their cost, and regulatory vagaries complicate officials and lawmakers' ability to oversee and evaluate private intelligence. The next section uses the case of the Pentagon's Capstone programme to pinpoint three focal points of disagreement between private intelligence defenders and critics intimated in this overview.

Core disagreements

Similar to the early study of private security, scholarly work explaining and understanding private intelligence has emphasized disagreements far more than it has produced consensus knowledge. This is due, in part, to institutional secrecy and the absence of empirical examples of private intelligence practice. However, instances of private intelligence practice occasionally surface in the public domain, and using the case of the Pentagon's controversial Capstone programme, this section identifies three focal points that animate the private intelligence debate:

- historical continuity versus discontinuity;
- individual morality versus institutional integrity; and
- efficiency and effectiveness versus transparency and accountability.

Capstone was a human intelligence collection programme administered by the Pentagon from 2008 to 2010 that aimed to provide US military commanders in Afghanistan with descriptions of the social environment in which they operated. Details about Capstone first emerged in the *New York Times* in 2010 (Filkins and Mazzetti 2010). In 2008, Eason Jordan (a former news executive) and Robert Young Pelton (a writer) proposed creating a private subscription information service, AfPax, that would use company employees and informants to interview local Afghan officials, including militia leaders, and provide reports on the situation in the provinces. The bulk of the funding and subscribers, however, would come from the US military, which would also obtain exclusive access to a specialized database that would include tailored information based on the military's requirements. The incoming top US commander in Afghanistan at the time, General David McKiernan, endorsed Jordan and Pelton's proposal and introduced the two men to another US official, Michael Furlong, who arranged funding and contract management. General David Petraeus, then-Commander of US Central Command (CENT-COM), also wrote a January 2009 letter endorsing the proposed programme. However, while setting up AfPax, Furlong allegedly used some of the funding to hire other Capstone subcontractors, some of whom were former CIA or Special Forces operatives, to gather information about Afghan tribal structures and the workings of militant groups. In the process, these Capstone subcontractors occasionally gleaned detailed information about the location of suspected militants, and Furlong fed those reports directly into the military operations centre in Kabul for possible lethal military action. Some officials became concerned that Furlong was running an off-the-books spying operation, using private intelligence contractors for inherently governmental activities. The CIA alerted the Pentagon, which eventually ended Capstone and investigated Furlong.

Capstone is a good case for illustrating core points of debate concerning private intelligence. As already noted, the defenders of private intelligence assert that there is a lack of evidence that it contributes to waste, fraud, or abuse. Perhaps these defenders have ignored Capstone, let alone the 2004 Abu Ghraib prison debacle in Iraq, where private military intelligence contractors allegedly influenced members of the 372nd Military Police into committing acts that violated the Geneva Convention on the Treatment of Prisoners of War. Another example of the wastefulness of private intelligence is Trailblazer, a $280 million NSA information technology contract established in 2000 that involved SAIC, Boeing, Computer Sciences Corporation, and Booz Allen Hamilton. Trailblazer was cancelled in 2006 due to cost overruns and mismanagement. Some private intelligence defenders argue that cases such as Capstone, Abu Ghraib and Trailblazer are rare and stem from US policy failures rather than the nature of private intelligence per se. Defenders of private intelligence, however, sanction institutional and corporate secrecy – a condition that obscures the forms and influence of private intelligence – and then treat the lack of evidence of organizational waste, fraud, abuse as if it were not contingent on that condition. Secrecy aside, as an example of private intelligence practice, the Capstone case highlights three focal points that run throughout debates about private intelligence more generally.

Historical continuity versus discontinuity

The Capstone case underscores the question of whether contemporary private intelligence activities qualitatively differ from their historical antecedents. As Cohen (2010) has explained, private sector organizations have long assisted government clients. One is tempted to trace a straight line between the US government's contracts with the Pinkerton company during the American Civil War to the US intelligence community's use of private contractors today. Cohen and others have shown that public criticisms of private intelligence are nothing new either – charges of war profiteering characterize both current and historical debates. Likewise, Robert Newman noted 40 years ago, in his article 'Communication Pathologies of Intelligence Systems', that when an intelligence system is run by an organization whose mission is being evaluated, the organization endeavours to please its evaluator – its intelligence product will inevitably be self-serving (Newman 1975). In other words, private companies have an incentive to produce intelligence products that conform to the expectations of their client in the hopes of obtaining continued and expanded funding. Intelligence products that challenge, undermine, or contradict a client's preconceptions are risky.

Contemporary critics tend to assert historical discontinuity, arguing that the 1990s liberalization of defence and intelligence sectors broke with prior practices and created both unprecedented conditions and unforeseen consequences. Liberalization accelerated and intensified the shift of intelligence expertise from public to private actors in ways that have made transparency and accountability much more difficult to obtain. The sheer number of private intelligence contractors and firms aiding government agencies represents a unique historical situation. As Peter Gill noted:

> [P]ublic–private contracting and partnership are facts of any liberal capitalist economy, but the merging or symbiosis of interests in security and intelligence apparatus takes us into the realms of a corporatist state in which government takes place through private corporations. This raises profound issues about the nature of intelligence governance.
>
> *(Gill 2014: 14)*

Some stakeholders may reluctantly recognize, yet find it difficult to accept, that private sector forces and logics have *already* transformed intelligence structures and practices in enduring ways, reflecting and reinforcing the state as a thoroughly hybrid form (Leander 2014). Scholars have only begun to explore the actual and potential benefits, risks, and consequences of this condition.

Individual morality versus institutional integrity

The Capstone case also draws attention to the debate over individual morality versus institutional integrity. Some commentators have depicted Furlong as a rogue intelligence official using private contractors to do his unethical bidding, while others find fault in the larger intelligence system that permits (and tacitly encourages) private actors to press ethical and legal boundaries. Defenders of private intelligence tend to assert that critics presume that it is 'inherently evil' (Cohen 2010: 250) or that intelligence contractors are 'motivated primarily by their paychecks' (Hansen 2014: 59). However, declaring that critics believe that private intelligence is an innate evil or that contractors lack professional or patriotic duty directs attention away from structural conditions that encourage practices that undermine democratic values.

Defenders of private intelligence attempt to steer the debate towards the character, motives, or loyalties of individual intelligence analysts – private or public. Conversely, critics attempt to steer the debate towards the question of how permanently embedding the profit motive within the deepest structures of the nation's intelligence apparatus affects the entire communication system that constitutes the intelligence enterprise.

For example, Hansen (ibid.) rightly observes that the profit motive may or may not influence the psychological tendencies of various intelligence stakeholders. However, the profit motive demonstrably shapes who is able to speak to national security officials (legitimacy); what those speakers are encouraged, permitted, or forbidden to say in order to establish, protect, or develop relationships; and what channels speakers are able to use to exchange information (Bean 2011). Given commercial imperatives, it is difficult to imagine private intelligence providers down-playing the significance of threats, supporting national security budget reductions that endanger their revenue streams, or championing stricter oversight, control, and accountability. While these actions may be desirable for the citizens of democratic states, the enmeshment of corporate and public interests generates tensions that are not easily reconciled. The profit motive also discourages public assessment of the effectiveness of private intelligence because companies are usually unwilling to submit their work to public scrutiny in order to protect proprietary information or sources and methods. Scholars have only begun to explore the concrete and specific ways that institutional structures shape private intelligence's forms and outcomes.

Efficiency and effectiveness versus transparency and accountability

Capstone illustrates that private intelligence can indeed be efficient and effective. Several Capstone participants remarked that it was a cost-effective way of supporting intelligence operations and US policy. Others remarked that using private contractors also was an effective way to skirt the Pakistani government's prohibition on US military personnel operating in the country. That the programme initially received multiple endorsements from high-ranking US military officials speaks to its perceived usefulness and value. In one sense, problems arose because Capstone became too effective. Its ostensibly benign 'atmospheric protection reports' were eventually used for lethal targeting of militants – a clear crossing of the line into inherently governmental activities. Capstone was only halted after the CIA alerted the Pentagon that the programme was in possible violation of the law. Capstone thus illustrates defenders' claim that private intelligence can improve efficiency and effectiveness. It also illustrates, however, critics' claim that sometimes those benefits come at the expense of other important values, especially transparency and accountability.

Transparency regarding the number of private intelligence contractors is lacking. In 2014, the US Government Accountability Office (GAO) released a report, *Additional Actions Needed to Improve Reporting on and Planning for the Use of Contract Personnel*, that found that civilian US intelligence community elements used various methods to calculate the number of contract personnel. These calculations did not maintain documentation to validate the number of personnel reported for 37 per cent of records that GAO reviewed, and 40 per cent of the records did not contain evidence to support the reasons given for contractor use. These records also did not provide insight into the functions performed by contractors, especially those that could potentially influence the government's control over its operational or policy decisions. In other words, GAO underscored that there is currently no way of adequately assessing whether or how private intelligence activities influence government decision-making. This situation supports Leander's (2014) argument that a socially constructed public/private dualism has contributed to the elusiveness of intelligence personnel, expenditures, and practices.

In terms of accountability, Capstone demonstrates that what constitutes inherently governmental activity is ill-defined and contentious, and even when guidance is available, private intelligence providers have a financial incentive to explore ethical grey areas and press legal boundaries in order to maximize their usefulness and value to their clients. Jon Michaels (2008) argued that ethical and legal unaccountability was, in fact, part of what made private intelligence appealing to government agencies in the first place. Task orders, statements of work, and other contracting documents can permit a great deal interpretive flexibility. The ambiguities of public–private collaborations often shield both the agency and its private sector partner from effective congressional, regulatory, and judicial oversight. In a novel twist, Michaels suggested that private intelligence providers could help hold government agencies accountable. Specifically, providers could be held financially or legally responsible for obtaining from their government agency client the proper authorizations that permit certain kinds of intelligence work. In this scheme, private corporations would serve as the agents of disclosure, providing government oversight committees evidence of prior legal authorization and descriptive accounts of their work to which they could later be held accountable. However, scholars have only begun to explore ways to align the (sometimes competing or even incompatible) values of intelligence efficiency, effectiveness, transparency, and accountability.

In sum, the interrelated debates concerning historical processes, individual morality and institutional integrity, and competing organizational values constitute much of the terrain of private intelligence scholarship. These three themes are by no means a definitive list. Many additional issues are ripe for research, and the final section of this chapter indicates how PSS can inform future investigations.

Conclusion

A historical view of private intelligence suggests that in the modern era corporations and government agencies have always been linked in some way and will continue to be. However, the type and number of private actors participating in national intelligence have varied considerably. Some place the peak for private intelligence in the United States in the first decade of the twenty-first century. Others see only superficial abatement of the trend towards intelligence contracting and outsourcing in recent years. Despite the questions that these conditions pose for the way that intelligence is understood, organized, and conducted, private intelligence remains poorly researched (Hansen 2014). Indeed, this chapter has focused almost exclusively on US developments, but commentators have identified similar developments emerging in the United Kingdom (Ortiz 2013), South Africa (Butt 2010), and Australia (Palmer 2013). Comparative investigations are needed of private intelligence in other countries. Because of its overwhelming US focus, scholarship concerning private intelligence has also developed somewhat independently of the broader discourse of PSS.

For example, while private intelligence scholars have, to date, mostly focused on the role and ethics of intelligence contracting and outsourcing, PSS has expanded its inquiries to include the broader phenomena of commercialization, commodification, governance, and governmentality. PSS investigations also increasingly focus on the enmeshment or simultaneity of the public and private realms, which undermines the notion that a pristine domain of intelligence – one free of private influence – is even possible. As Leander writes, separating these domains is 'a formalistic exercise that hides more than it reveals and blinds itself to the hybrid and its implications' (Leander 2014: 201). Leander calls for the dissolution of the dualism and the development of a practice approach in order to capture elusive and powerful phenomena. Leander's (2011) related discussion of the paradox of accountability also has relevance for the study of private intelligence. Specifically, Leander demonstrates how attempting to politicize military markets is necessary for adequate public debate, yet doing so sparks reactionary legal and technocratic attempts to downplay, silence, or discredit such efforts. In the context of intelligence, politicization is often depicted as an affront to professionalism and objectivity. It is therefore worthwhile to consider how the politicization of the intelligence market might proceed similarly or differently from its military cousin.

As a gesture towards increased public understanding of intelligence, I have investigated how stakeholders manage competing ethical principles underlying private enterprise and national security. My analysis of the discourse surrounding Capstone (Bean 2013) revealed how advocates of market-based government used particular discursive resources to shield themselves from charges of immorality. I employed an ethics-as-practice perspective that may be useful for other PSS investigators who analyse organizational dilemmas that require moral agency. Actors strategically and opportunistically draw upon discursive resources to persuade themselves and others of the ethicality of their practices. Communication serves as the site where advocates of market-based government are able to manage, dismiss, or refute charges of immorality. Future private intelligence research ought to focus on comparative investigations, the broader role of commercialization, commodification, governance, and governmentality, the enmeshment of public and private realms, politicization of the intelligence market, and the interconnections among, discourse, ethics, and practice.

Finally, defenders of private intelligence rightly distinguish between the work of production-focused analysts and their sales-focused counterparts, but in emphasizing the similarities between analysts, defenders of private intelligence tend to elide the influence of the principle driver of private sector decision-making: organizational continuance and resource accumulation. While this driver is also present in public organizations, intelligence agencies cannot become insolvent in the traditional sense, and businesses and states do not 'fail' in the same way. Business and government also are not subject to equal measures of public scrutiny and accountably. Underlining these distinctions, however, risks reinforcing the public/private dualism that sustains the elusiveness and power of the intelligence sector. Therefore, there is much work for PSS scholars to do in examining why, how, and with what effect intelligence stakeholders assert or challenge the public/private distinction. As a trans-disciplinary and reflexive enterprise, PSS is well positioned to generate knowledge of the reciprocal influence of business imperatives and intelligence practice.

Note

1   This chapter does not examine the related topic of corporate espionage or the phenomenon of current and former intelligence agency personnel assisting private sector corporations in surveilling and influencing governmental and non-governmental organizations. On these topics, see Eamon Javers (2013), Gary Ruskin (2013) and Chapter 12 of the present volume.

Bibliography

Bean, H. (2011) *No More Secrets: Open Source Information and the Reshaping of US Intelligence*, Santa Barbara, CA: Praeger.

Bean, H. (2013) 'Outsourcing U.S. Intelligence', in S. May (ed.), *Case Studies in Organizational Communication*. Thousand Oaks, CA: Sage, pp. 247–59.

Butt, S. (2010) Outsourcing Intelligence: The Relationship Between the State and Private Intelligence in Post-Apartheid South Africa, Masters thesis, University of Cape Town, South Africa.

Caldwell, C. M. (2010) 'Privatized Information Gathering: Just War Theory and Morality', *International Journal of Intelligence Ethics* 1(2): 32–45.

Cohen, R. S. (2010) 'Putting a Human and Historical Face on Intelligence Contracting', *Orbis* 54(2): 232–51.

Filkins, D. and Mazzetti, M. (2010) 'Contractors Tied to Effort to Track and Kill Militants', *New York Times* March 14, www.nytimes.com/2010/03/15/world/asia/15contractors.html?pagewanted=all.

Gill, P. (2014) 'Thinking about Intelligence Within, Without, and Beyond the State', *All Azimuth* 3(2): 5–20.

Hansen, M. (2014) 'Intelligence Contracting: On the Motivations, Interests, and Capabilities of Core Personnel Contractors in the US Intelligence Community', *Intelligence and National Security* 29(1): 58–81.

Hillhouse, R. J. (2007) *Outsourced*, New York: Forge Books.

Javers, E. (2013) *Broker, Trader, Lawyer, Spy: The Secret World of Corporate Espionage*, New York: HarperBusiness.

Keefe, P. R. (2010) 'Privatized Spying: The Emerging Intelligence Industry', in L. K. Johnson (ed.), *The Oxford Handbook of National Security Intelligence*, Oxford: Oxford University Press, pp. 296–309.

Leander, A. (2011) 'Risk and the Fabrication of Apolitical, Unaccountable Military Markets: The Case of the CIA "Killing Program"', *Review of International Studies* 37(5): 2253–68.

Leander, A. (2014) 'Understanding US National Intelligence: Analyzing Practices to Capture the Chimera', in J. Best and A. Gheciu (eds), *The Return of the Public in Global Governance*, Cambridge: Cambridge University Press, pp. 197–220.

Michaels, J. (2008) 'All the President's Spies: Private–Public Intelligence Partnerships in the War on Terror', *California Law Review* 96(4): 901–66.

Newman, R. P. (1975) 'Communication Pathologies of Intelligence Systems', *Speech Monographs* 42(4): 2771–90.

O'Harrow Jr., R. (2008) 'Contractors Augment Intelligence Agencies', *Washington Post* August 28.

Ortiz, C. (2013) 'Security Partnerships, Intelligence and the Recasting of the UK Monopoly of Violence in the 21st Century', in C. Kaunert and S. Leonard (eds), *European Security, Terrorism and Intelligence: Tackling New Security Challenges in Europe*, Basingstoke: Palgrave Macmillan, pp. 215–28.

Palmer, M. (2013) 'Benefits, Challenges, and Pitfalls of Private Intelligence', *Salus Journal* 1(2): 3–7.

Priest, D. and Arkin, W. M. (2010) 'A Hidden World, Growing Beyond Control', *Washington Post* July 19, http://projects.washingtonpost.com/top-secret-america/articles/a-hidden-world-growing-beyond-control.

Roper, J. E. (2010) 'Using Private Corporations to Conduct Intelligence Activities for National Security Purposes: An Ethical Appraisal', *International Journal of Intelligence Ethics* 1(2): 46–73.

Ruskin, G. (2013) *Spooky Business: Corporate Espionage Against Nonprofit Organizations*, Washington, DC: Center for Corporate Policy.

Shorrock, T. (2008) *Spies for Hire: The Secret World of Intelligence Outsourcing*, New York: Simon & Schuster.

US Government Accountability Office (2014) *Additional Actions Needed to Improve Reporting on and Planning for the Use of Contract Personnel*, Washington, DC: US Government Accountability Office.

Voelz, G. J. (2009) 'Contractors and Intelligence: The Private Sector in the Intelligence Community', *International Journal of Intelligence and Counterintelligence* 22(4): 586–613.

9

CYBER-SECURITY AND PRIVATE ACTORS

Myriam Dunn Cavelty

In the last few years, cyber-security has received much attention internationally. Events and occurrences such as the cyber-attacks on Estonia in 2007; the discovery of Stuxnet, the industry-sabotaging super worm in 2010; numerous instances of cyber-espionage, culminating in the Snowden revelations in 2013; and the growing sophistication of cyber-criminals as evident by their impressive scams served to give the impression that cyber-attacks are becoming more frequent, more organized, more costly, and altogether more dangerous. As a result, cyber-fears have percolated upwards, from the expert level to executive decision-makers and politicians, and diffused horizontally, advancing from mainly being an issue of relevance to the US to one that is at the top of the threat list of more and more countries, resulting in a flurry of government-led and private-led cyber-security initiatives.

Cyber-security research has grown in parallel to this rising prominence (see Figure 9.1) – even if at a much slower pace than could be expected for such a fashionable topic, especially in international relations and security. This chapter will focus on the literature dealing with cyber-security issues of relevance to private security studies. The link between the two topics seems a given: due to privatization and deregulation of many parts of the public sector, almost all critical cyber-assets are in the hands of private enterprise nowadays. This means that the state is incapable of providing the public good of security on its own. To embed this discussion sufficiently, the chapter will show what the particularities of cyber-security as a (national) security issue are and how elusive the concept of cyber-security is, especially since it has different meanings for different stakeholders and over time.

In contrast to a focus on specific threat forms like cyber-crime, cyber-terrorism, or cyber-war (which is predominant in the literature), only a broad understanding of cyber-security as practice involving a multitude of actors inside and outside of government reveals the whole range of effects of cyber-security politics, since multiple actors use different threat representations employing differing political, private, societal, and corporate notions of security to mobilize (or de-mobilize) different audiences. Therefore, a broad definition of cyber-security is used. It understands cyber-security as a multifaceted set of technologies, processes and practices designed to protect networks, computers, programmes and data from attack, damage or unauthorized access, in accordance with the common information security goals: the protection of confidentiality, integrity and availability of information.

The chapter has four parts. It starts with a discussion of concepts, particularly focusing on

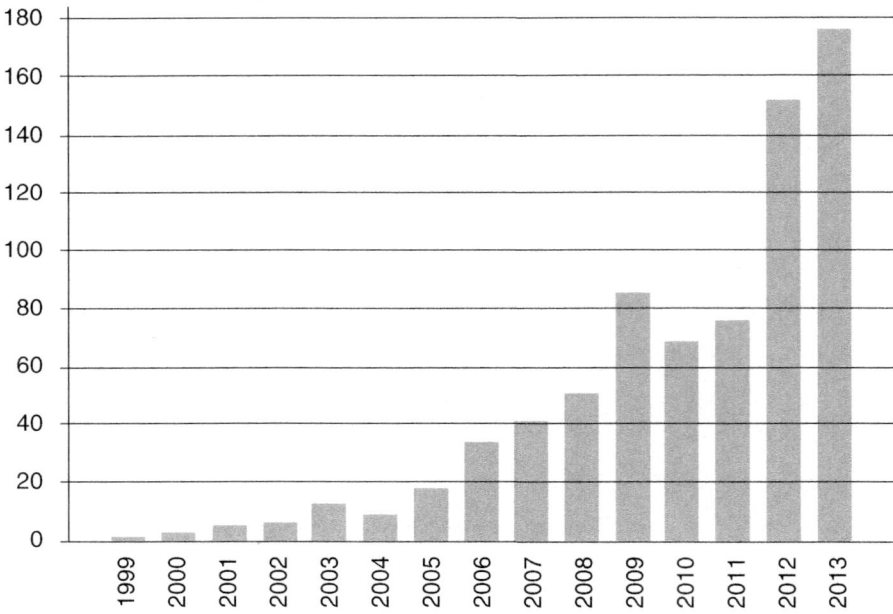

Figure 9.1 Published items in each year with topic cyber-security
Source: Web of Science.

the link between cyber-security and cyberspace. The second part shows how a national secu-rity connotation has been established and how and why it varies over time. The third and fourth parts discuss the cyber-security literature, with a focus on cyber-security research in 'traditional' and 'critical' security studies and a focus on research more directly dealing with private security issues is identified. In conclusion, it is established that the biggest difference between cyber-security and other private security topics is that the state is not giving away power and authority to private actors in traditional security matters but that the state is increas-ingly enforcing its authority in cyberspace, which has been almost exclusively dominated and shaped by private actors.

(In)security in/through cyberspace: concepts

In the process of building confidence measures in cyberspace, it has been acknowledged that implementing effective national and supra-national cyber-security policies requires both common knowledge and a shared understanding of what constitutes cyber-security, cyber-threats, or cyber-crises, among many other ubiquitous, but ambiguous terms (OSCE 2013). However, while finding common ground through shared definitions is helpful at the very least, it is also very challenging given the diverse and dynamic contextual factors that influence the development of national cyber-security strategies (Maurer and Morgus 2014). In fact, struggles over common definitions are symptomatic of an issue that mobilizes different stakeholders from different sectors with divergent interests and are an expression of the struggle over influence at the same time.

In the literature, two meanings of cyber-security can be identified: a technical (narrow/precise) one and a national security (broad/vague) one. In the technical sphere, cyber-security usually signifies a set of measures to protect networks, computers, programmes and data from attack, damage or unauthorized access, in accordance with the common information security goals such as the protection of confidentiality, integrity and availability of information (see May *et al.* 2004). In the national security setting, cyber-security can simply be described as the security one enjoys in and from cyberspace (Cornish *et al.* 2009).

A comparison of nationally existing definitions of cyber-security reveals that most states mix technical and national security elements (see Maurer and Morgus 2014). Overall, there seems to be a consensus that cyber-security is closely interlinked with the security of cyberspace. However, defining cyberspace precisely is a challenge, because it is a constantly changing and evolving non/space/place, both in terms of technology and of how the technology is used and how that use is governed. In fact, there is a good argument to be made that no such thing as one unique, singular cyber-space exists (Bingham 1996: 32). Still, at its most basic, cyberspace connotes the fusion of communication networks, databases, and sources of information into a vast, tangled, and diverse blanket of electronic interchange. Thus, a 'network ecosystem' is created, a place that is not part of the normal, physical world. It is virtual and immaterial, a 'bioelectronic environment that is literally universal: It exists everywhere there are telephone wires, coaxial cables, fiber-optic lines or electromagnetic waves' (Dyson *et al.* 1994). Importantly, cyberspace is also grounded in physical reality. As one observer argues, 'the channelling of information flows … occurs within the framework of a "real" geography' (Suteanu 2005: 130) made up of servers, cables, computers, satellites, and so on. Therefore, cyberspace is comprised of both material and virtual elements; it is a 'space of things and ideas, structure and content' (Deibert and Rohozinski 2010: 16).

By implication, cyber-security is as a type of security that works in and through cyberspace/s, and the making and practice of cyber-security is constrained and enabled by this environment and its geography. By implication, the cyber-security discourse has never been static, because the technical aspects and their use of the information infrastructure are constantly evolving and keep influencing various aspects of the debate. This is not to say that its material conditions are outside and above political decisions and discursive processes. But a close look at the cyber-security discourse reveals how material conditions, or rather, possibilities and impossibilities of threat and countermeasures, have been key to determining the shape of the danger discourse (Deibert 1997; Deibert *et al.* 2008). In particular, specifying whose security and what security is at stake becomes a key (political) question.

Linking 'cyber' to critical infrastructures

In a computing context, the term security implies a technical concept ('information security'). Arguably, this has little in common with the type of security concepts security scholars are interested in (Hansen and Nissenbaum 2009: 1160; Buzan and Hansen 2009: 15; Buzan *et al.* 1998: 25). However, specific security connotations are created in this realm through the connection of the cyber-prefix to other security-relevant issues like terror, espionage, war, weapons, or deterrence. To make such a link possible, an insecurity argument needs to be made first. This is easy in the case of cyberspace, since it is fundamentally insecure.

As is well known, today's version of cyberspace emerged out of the Advanced Research Projects Agency Network (ARPANET), which was funded by the Defense Advanced Research Projects Agency (DARPA) of the United States Department of Defense (DoD) from 1962 onwards, mainly for optimized information exchange between the universities and research laboratories involved in DoD research. When building the network, the designers emphasized robustness and survivability over security, simply because there was no apparent need for a focus on security at that time, given that information systems were being hosted on large proprietary machines that were connected to very few other computers. This turned into a legacy problem.

What makes systems so vulnerable today is the confluence of the following factors: the same basic packet-switching technology (not built with security in mind), the shift to smaller and far more open systems (not built with security in mind) and the rise of extensive networking at the same time (Libicki 2000), which resulted in a sprawling network with a very large numbers of insecure machines connected through insecure data distribution mechanisms. In addition, there are significant market-driven obstacles to IT-security, which came into play when the commercialization of the internet set in: There is no direct return on investment, time-to-market impedes extensive security measures, and security mechanisms often have a negative impact on usability so that security is often sacrificed for functionality (Anderson and Moore 2006).

Against this basic backdrop of technological insecurity, changes in the technical environment altered what was seen 'in need of protection' in the policy debate – the so-called referent object of security (Dunn Cavelty 2008). In the 1970s and 1980s, cyber-security (though not yet under that name) was mainly about those parts of the private sector that were becoming digitalized and also about government networks and the classified information residing in it. This relatively limited referent object was changed in crucial ways in the mid-1990s with the growth and spreading of computer networks into more and more aspects of life. In the early days (1970s and 1980s), mainly the hacking sub-culture, computer scientists, and later exponents of the anti-virus industry set the boundaries of the danger discourse (Dunn Cavelty 2013). In the mid-1990s, a diverse set of security professionals – mainly from law enforcement, the intelligence and the civil defence community as well as think tankers and military experts – built a more distinct national security connotation on top of this (Warner 2012).

In the contemporary political debate, some infrastructures are now regarded as 'critical' by the authorities because their prolonged unavailability could result in social instability and major crisis. The most frequently listed examples of critical infrastructures encompass banking and finance, government services, telecommunication and information and communication technologies, emergency and rescue services, energy and electricity, health services, transportation, logistics and distribution, and water supply (Abele-Wigert and Dunn 2006: 386–9). Today, these critical infrastructures mostly take the form of interconnected, complex, and increasingly virtual systems; in fact, the topic of cyber-security and critical infrastructure protection are often handled as one and the same. Because critical infrastructure systems combine symbolic and instrumental values, attacking them becomes integral to a modern logic of destruction that seeks maximum impact. In other words, cyberspace can become a force-multiplier by combining the risks to cyberspace with the possibility of risks through cyberspace (Deibert and Rohozinski 2010).

This combination has proven a key condition for promoting cyber-security to the forefront of current strategies for providing security. As a result, the link between national security and cyberspace has become an uncontested 'truth' with budgetary and political consequences. In this particular policy discourse, information technology is emerging as the common factor upon which all sectors of security converge, as most security issues and measures today have cyber (or computerized) components. The cyber-realm emerges as two things: it is an attack vector potentially threatening things of value for different actors (state, business, and individuals) and a dimension in which countermeasures against various sorts of threats – not only cyber-related – can be situated. This way, cyber-security is not just about the 'security of cyber', but is also 'security through cyber' (Betz and Stevens 2011).

Cyber-security in security studies

This section situates and classifies literature at the intersection of cyber-security and national security. Since this Handbook is interested in private security issues, I start by discussing literature in security studies, using the well-established differentiation between positivists/rationalists (or traditional security studies, with a strong nod towards non-academic research) on the one side and post-positivist or 'critical/reflexive' approaches on the other (Buzan and Hansen 2009; CASE Collective 2007: 561–5). Since private security aspects are not all too well developed in both, a third type of research that mainly uses economic models and explanations is discussed in the next section.

In traditional security studies, the majority of books, articles, and reports on cyber-security (and closely related issues) remains policy-oriented, centred on the US and does communicate little with more general international relations theory and research to this day. In other words, most of the work is not strictly academic. The two main questions that are being tackled are who (or what) is the biggest danger for an increasingly networked nation/society/military/business environment, and how to best counter the new and evolving threat (Gombert and Libicki 2014; Farwell and Rohozinski 2011). The threat-form that has triggered the biggest body of literature is cyberwar (exemplary, for a vast literature, see Arquilla and Ronfeldt 1993; Rid 2013). This is not surprising, given the potentially devastating impact of a full-fledged cyber-aggression and the long tradition in international law and military ethics to address new forms of warfare and weapons systems under legal and ethical viewpoints (Barrett 2013).

Apart from literature with an implicit or explicit problem-solving or purely conceptual orientation, theoretically guided or empirically sound academic research is still quite rare. Recently, however, a few cyber-security related articles have been published in high-ranking political science journals like *International Security* (Gartzke 2013; Kello 2013) or *Journal of Peace Research* (Valeriano and Maness 2014), which could indicate the beginning of a more sustained focus on cyber-conflict issues in the traditional security domain (see also Axelrod and Iliev 2013; Eun and Abmann in press). However, given the orientation of these journals, more or less aggressive forms of cyber-war and/or questions of international cooperation will likely remain at the centre of attention.

The importance and prominence of these publications notwithstanding, the growing body of literature on war in and through cyberspace falls short of capturing the diversity of cyber-security issues. Specifically, it fails to capture malicious cyber-activities that are not destructive and war-like but fall under the far more obscure domain of cyber-exploitation (but see Inkster 2013 on intelligence and Grabosky 2013 on crime), arguably the biggest problem in the cyber-domain nowadays. The difference between cyber-attack and cyber-exploitation is that cyber-exploitations do not seek to disturb the normal functioning of a computer system or network from the user's point of view like attacks do – quite the opposite: the best cyber-exploitation is such that the user never notices (Owens *et al.* 2009: 80ff.). How such an elusive phenomenon can be researched is another question altogether.

While private security actors play an important role in all forms of cyber-aggression and countermeasures, this topic is a non-issue in the emerging literature. This is not overly surprising, given the relative newness of the whole field, which has started to tackle the broad and seemingly more important issues first rather than sub-issues. Notable exceptions are publications on the cyber-(military–)industrial complex (Talbot 2011; Brito and Watkins 2011), which have included thoughts and data on the role of private business (mainly consultants) in the cyber-threat hype. Similarly, Bruce Schneier, a well-known cryptographer, has focused on power dynamics in cyber-security, including private actors (Schneier 2012, 2013). Furthermore, a few op-eds on the question of cyber-mercenaries or cyber-privateers exist (Ford 2010; Singer and Friedman 2014), which look at how private hacking groups are used for strategic purposes by states (i.e. Russia and China).

In critical security studies, three bodies of literature exist. The first focuses on 'postmodern war', a form technical-military interaction that centres on the centrality of information as the 'new metaphysics of power' (Dillon 2002; Hables Gray 2005). In general, this type of research has been interested in the larger shift in war fighting practices rather than specifics and/or focuses on aspects of information war more broadly. Practices of cyber-security are considered on the side, if at all. The second body of literature stems from the Munk School in Toronto, which has focused on issues like (electronic) surveillance and censorship for a considerable number of years and is concerned with the creation of more insecurity by (state) actors through cyber-means (Deibert 1997, 2013; Deibert and Rohozinski 2010). Private security actors and issues are not a particular focus in this literature. The third body of literature uses frameworks inspired by securitization theory (Buzan *et al.* 1998) and is mainly interested in how different actors in politics have tried to argue the link between the cyber-dimension and national security (Eriksson 2001; Dunn Cavelty 2008; Hansen and Nissenbaum 2009). In a similar vein, recent articles have focused on metaphors in the cyber-security discourse to explain political response (Barnard-Wills and Ashenden 2012; Stevens and Betz 2013; Dunn Cavelty 2013). Overall, the focus of this research is restricted in at least two ways. First, most of these studies focus on politically salient speech acts by 'visible' political figures that can be approved (or disproved) by general public. Such a focus reveals the constitutive effects the discursive practices of 'capable actors' have in (world) politics, but it is not sensitive towards how these discursive practices are facilitated or thwarted by preceding and preparatory linguistic and non-linguistic practices of actors that are not as easily visible, also outside of governments (Huysmans 2011: 371). Second, due to the focus on linguistic practices, this literature tends to ignore the technical and material factors important in cyber-security. Therefore, private security issues have sometimes been mentioned but they have not been at the centre of attention.

Cyber-security and economics

In both types of security studies, aspects of private security issues are dealt with on the margins, if at all. What about other types of literature? While it is impossible to speak about all cyber-security research with authority, there is research in other disciplines that focuses much more directly on private security actors and mechanisms. In this section, I briefly discuss two bodies of research with more or less direct bearing on the topic: research on the economics of information security and research on public-private partnerships, influenced by network governance literature.

Economics of information security research is mainly the brainchild of Ross Anderson, a security engineer and cryptographer at Cambridge University, who joined forces with Hal Varian, an economics professor (Anderson 2012). More recently, psychological research was brought in (i.e. Schneier 2008; Moore and Anderson 2011). The gist of this multifaceted research is that security failures are often due to perverse incentives or psychological factors such as heuristics and biases, but also emotions and culture rather than to the lack of suitable technical protection mechanisms. In his classic paper on the subject, Anderson (2001) shows how economic analysis explains many phenomena that security researchers had previously found perplexing, for example why mass-market software products contain so many security bugs, why their security mechanisms are so difficult to manage, why so many specialist security products are second rate, with bad ones driving good ones out of the market, and also, why government agencies concerned with information warfare concentrate on offence rather than defence.

In particular, Anderson and colleagues show convincingly that the reason for the continued existence and constant new creation of vulnerabilities in our information infrastructure is that security is constantly 'under-produced' in a market dominated by the so-called network effect, under which the benefits of a product increase when the number of users increases, and the 'winner takes it all', since large costs to users from switching technologies leads to lock-in quasi-monopolies and time pressures lead to a focus on fast delivery in commercial software development. Quality criteria, like security, therefore play only a minor role (Anderson and Moore 2006). In terms of strategic action, he explains the current insecurity conundrum through asymmetric information:

> Suppose that you head up a US agency with an economic intelligence mission, and a computer scientist working for you has just discovered a beautiful new exploit on Windows 2000. If you report this to Microsoft, you will protect 250 million Americans; if you keep quiet, you will be able to conduct operations against 400 million Europeans and 100 million Japanese.
>
> *(Anderson 2001: 5)*

In other words, intelligence services of this world are making cyberspace more insecure directly; in order to be able to have more access to data, and in order to prepare for future conflict (Greenwald and MacAskill 2013; Dunn Cavelty 2014). Since cyber-security is always also about technical insecurities, research that focuses on technical aspects of security can have considerable explanatory powers also for forms of national security.

Overall similar, but focused on a broader governance issue, is research on public private partnerships. As mentioned in the introduction, one of the key challenges for any cyber-security efforts from the view of the state arises from the privatization and deregulation of many parts of the public sector since the 1980s and the globalization processes of the 1990s, which have put almost all critical (information) infrastructure in the hands of private enterprise. This creates a situation in which market forces alone are not sufficient to provide security in critical sectors (also due to the perverse incentives described by Anderson *et al.*). At the same time, the state is incapable of providing the public good of security on its own, since an overly intrusive market intervention is considered a flawed and undesirable option, especially since the same infrastructures that the state aims to protect are also the foundation of the competitiveness and prosperity of a nation. Therefore, any policy trying to get more security in cyberspace must absorb the negative outcomes of liberalization, privatization, and globalization, without cancelling out the positive effects.

Public–private partnerships (PPP), a form of cooperation between the state and the private sector, are widely seen as a panacea for the problem of cyber-(in-)security. In specific, most existing PPPs serve the function of information-sharing. There are four different levels of information-sharing: information shared within the government, between different governments, between different companies, and between the government and the private sector (Prieto 2006; Dunn Cavelty and Suter 2009; Gal-Or and Ghose 2005). However, public-private information-sharing has proven to be difficult to establish: Companies are reluctant to share information on their vulnerabilities and security breaches, since public dissemination could result in new attempts by hackers to exploit the vulnerabilities, and above all, in a loss of reputation. Economic analyses have shown that the public announcement of security breaches is negatively correlated with the market value of the targeted firm (Campbell *et al.* 2003; Cavusoglu *et al.* 2004). Additionally, sharing information on incidents is risky, because public dissemination of secret information could also violate laws in the context of the protection of privacy (Branscomb and Michel-Kerjan 2006). For the government, releasing information on malicious actors is no less sensitive, as it is possible that the release of such material can seriously compromise intelligence activities and investigations (Moteff and Stevens 2003). Therefore, how incentives structures and costs can be adjusted to create more favourable conditions is the main focus of literature on public-private partnerships. This includes defining win–win situations for both public and private actors (Personick and Patterson 2003), how trust can be established and maintained (Branscomb and Michel-Kerjan 2006; Cukier *et al.* 2005; Aviram 2006), or the questions which conditions are conducive to an optimal involvement of the state in networks of cooperation (Suter 2007, 2012).

Conclusion

Cyber-security research is steadily growing, but in international relations and security studies, it is not a mature field yet. Apart from a few exceptions, research remains fragmented, is biased towards just one expression (cyber-war), and struggles to tap into existing funding resources. Given this relative weakness, many important issues remain under-researched. The importance of 'the private' in the establishment of the topic as national security issue is one of those issues. Following Leander (2010), research on this topic could be developed in three areas:

- discovering/denouncing/documenting private security;
- explaining and understanding private security; and
- debating the consequences of private security.

However, and importantly: cyber-security has always been a field of practice much defined by non-state (private) actors, as should have become obvious in this chapter. In contrast to many other security issues, private actors are not the ones that are increasingly pushing into in traditional (state) security fields in cyber-security – it is the state that is trying to (re)establish its authority in a space cultivated by innovative practices of companies and consumers on the one hand and criminal actors on the other. For research falling into the category of private security research, this is a challenge, because many of the assumptions about authority and necessary governance structures need to be questioned.

Bibliography

Abele-Wigert, I. and Dunn, M. (2006) *The International CIIP Handbook 2006: An Inventory of Protection Policies in 20 Countries and 6 International Organizations*, vol. I. Zurich: Center for Security Studies.

Anderson, R. (2001) 'Why Information Security is Hard – An Economic Perspective', in IEEE Computer Society (ed.), *Proceedings of the 17th Annual Computer Security Applications Conference*, Washington, DC: IEEE Computer Society, pp. 358–65.

Anderson, R. (2012) 'Security Economics: A Personal Perspective', paper presented at the Annual Computer Security Applications Conference (ACSAC) 2012, www.acsac.org/2012/openconf/modules/request.php?module=oc_program&action=view.php&a=&id=252&type=4.

Anderson, R. and Moore, T. (2006) 'The Economics of Information Security', *Science* 314(5799): 610–13.

Arquilla, J. and Ronfeldt, D. (1993) 'Cyberwar is Coming!', *Comparative Strategy* 12(2): 141–65.

Aviram, A. (2006) 'Network Responses to Network Threats: The Evolution into Private Cyber-Security Associations', in M. F. Grady and F. Parisi (eds), *The Law and Economics of Cybersecurity*, Cambridge: Cambridge University Press, pp. 143–92.

Axelrod, R. and Iliev, R. (2013) 'Timing of Cyber-Conflict', *Proceedings of the National Academy of Sciences* 111(4): 1298–1303.

Barnard-Wills, D. and Ashenden, D. (2012) 'Securing Virtual Space: Cyber War, Cyber Terror, and Risk', *Space and Culture* 15(2): 110–23.

Barrett, E. T. (2013) 'Warfare in a New Domain: The Ethics of Military Cyber-Operations', *Journal of Military Ethics* 12(1): 4–17.

Betz, D. and Stevens, T. (2011) *Cyberspace and the State: Toward a Strategy for Cyber-Power*, London: The International Institute for Strategic Studies.

Bingham, N. (1996) 'Object-ions: From Technological Determinism towards Geographies of Relations', *Environment and Planning D: Society and Space* 14(6): 635–57.

Branscomb, L. M and Michel-Kerjan, E. O. (2006) 'Public–Private Collaboration on a National and International Scale', in P. E. Auerswald, L. M. Branscomb, T. M. La Porte and E. O. Michel-Kerjan (eds), *Seeds of Disaster, Roots of Response: How Private Action Can Reduce Public Vulnerability*, Cambridge: Cambridge University Press, pp. 395–403.

Brito, J. and Watkins, T. (2011) *Loving the Cyber Bomb? The Dangers of Threat Inflation in Cybersecurity Policy*, working paper no. 11-24, April, Arlington, VA: Mercatus Center, George Mason University.

Buzan, B. and Hansen, L. (2009) *The Evolution of International Security Studies*, Cambridge: Cambridge University Press.

Buzan, B., Wæver, O. and de Wilde, J. (1998) *Security: A New Framework for Analysis*, Boulder, CO: Lynne Rienner.

Campbell, K., Gordon, A. L., Loeb, M. P. and Zhou, L. (2003) 'The Economic Cost of Publicly Announced Information Security Breaches: Empirical Evidence from the Stock Market', *Journal of Computer Security* 11: 431–48.

CASE Collective (2007) 'Europe, Knowledge, Politics Engaging with the Limits: The CASE Collective Responds', *Security Dialogue* 38(4): 559–76.

Cavusoglu, H., Birendra, M. and Raghunathan, S. (2004) 'The Effect of Internet Security Breach Announcements on Market Value: Capital Market Reactions for Breached Firms and Internet Security Developers', *International Journal of Electronic Commerce* 9: 69–104.

Cornish, P., Hughes, R. and Livingstone, D. (2009) *Cyberspace and the National Security of the United Kingdom. Threats and Responses*, London: Chatham House.

Cukier, K. N, Mayer-Schoenberger, V. and Branscomb, L. M. (2005). *Ensuring (and Insuring?) Critical Information Infrastructure Protection*, faculty research working paper RWP05-055, Cambridge, MA: John F. Kennedy School of Government.

Deibert, R. J. (1997) *Parchment, Printing, and Hypermedia: Communication in World Order Transformation*, New York: Columbia University Press.

Deibert, R. J. (2013) *Black Code: Inside the Battle for Cyberspace*, Toronto: McClelland & Stewart

Deibert, R. J. and Rohozinski, R. (2010) 'Risking Security: Policies and Paradoxes of Cyberspace Security', *International Political Sociology* 4(1): 15–32.

Deibert, R. J., Palfrey, J.G., Rohozinski, R. and Zittrain, J. (2008) *The Practice and Policy of Global Internet Filtering*, Cambridge, MA: MIT Press

Dillon, M. (2002) 'Network Society, Network-Centric Warfare and the State of Emergency', *Theory, Culture, and Society* 19(4): 71–9.

Dunn Cavelty, M. (2008) *Cyber-Security and Threat Politics: US Efforts to Secure the Information Age*, Abingdon: Routledge.

Dunn Cavelty, M. (2013) 'From Cyber-Bombs to Political Fallout: Threat Representations with an Impact in the Cyber-Security Discourse', *International Studies Review* 15(1): 105–22.

Dunn Cavelty, M. (2014) 'Breaking the Cyber-Security Dilemma: Aligning Security Needs and Removing Vulnerabilities', *Science and Engineering Ethics* 20(3): 701–15.

Dunn Cavelty, M. and Suter, M. (2009) 'Public-Private Partnerships Are No Silver Bullet: an Expanded Governance Model for Critical Infrastructure Protection', *International Journal of Critical Infrastructure Protection* 2(4): 179–87.

Dyson, E., Gilder, G., Keyworth, G. and Toffler, A. (1996) 'Cyberspace and the American Dream: A Magna Carta for the Knowledge Age', *The Information Society* 12(3): 295–308.

Eriksson, J. (2001) 'Cyberplagues, IT, and Security: Threat Politics in the Information Age', *Journal of Contingencies and Crisis Management* 9(4): 200–10.

Eun, Y.-S. and Abmann, J. S. (in press) 'Cyberwar: Taking Stock of Security and Warfare in the Digital Age', *International Studies Perspectives* doi:10.1111/insp.12073.

Farwell, J. P. and Rohozinski, R. (2011) 'Stuxnet and the Future of Cyber War', *Survival* 53(1): 23–40.

Ford, C. (2010) 'Here Come the Cyber-Privateers?', New Paradigms Forum, www.newparadigmsforum.com/NPFtestsite/?p=277.

Gal-Or, E. and Ghose, A. (2005) 'The Economic Incentives for Sharing Security Information', *Information Systems Research* 16(2): 186–208.

Gartzke, E. (2013) 'The Myth of Cyberwar: Bringing War in Cyberspace Back Down to Earth', *International Security* 38(2): 41–73.

Gombert, D. and Libicki, M. (2014) 'Cyber Warfare and Sino-American Crisis Instability', *Survival: Global Politics and Strategy* 56(4): 7–22.

Grabosky, P. (2013) 'Organized Crime and the Internet', *RUSI Journal* 158(5): 18–25.

Greenwald, G. and MacAskill, E. (2013) 'Obama Orders US to Draw Up Overseas Target List for Cyber-Attacks', *The Guardian* 7 June, www.theguardian.com/world/2013/jun/07/obama-china-targets-cyber-overseas.

Hables Gray, C. (2005) *Peace, War, and Computers*, Abingdon: Routledge.

Hansen, L. and Nissenbaum, H. (2009) 'Digital Disaster, Cyber Security, and the Copenhagen School', *International Studies Quarterly* 53(4): 1155–75.

Huysmans, J. (2011) 'What's in an Act? On Security Speech Acts and Little Security Nothings', *Security Dialogue* 42(4–5): 371–83.

Inkster, N. (2013) 'Chinese Intelligence in the Cyber Age', *Survival: Global Politics and Strategy* 55(1): 45–66.

Kello, L. (2013) 'The Meaning of the Cyber Revolution', *International Security* 38(2): 7–40.

Leander, A. (2010) 'The Privatization of International Security', in M. Dunn Cavelty and V. Mauer (eds), *The Routledge Handbook of Security Studies*, Abingdon: Routledge, pp. 200–10.

Libicki, M. C. (2000) *The Future of Information Security*, Washington, DC: Institute for National Strategic Studies.

Maurer, T. and Morgus, R. (2014) *Compilation of Existing Cybersecurity and Information Security Related Definitions*, October, Washington, DC: New America Foundation, www.newamerica.org/downloads/OTI_Compilation_of_Existing_Cybersecurity_and_Information_Security_Related_Definitions.pdf.

May, C. *et al.* (2004) *Advanced Information Assurance Handbook*, CMU/SEI-2004-HB-001, Pittsburgh, PA: CERT/CC Training and Education Center, Carnegie Mellon University.

Moore, T. and Anderson, R. (2011) *Economics and Internet Security: A Survey of Recent Analytical, Empirical and Behavioral Research*, Cambridge, MA: Computer Science Group, Harvard University, ftp://ftp.deas.harvard.edu/techreports/tr-03-11.pdf.

Moteff, J. D. and Stevens, D. D. (2003) *Critical Infrastructure Information Disclosure and Homeland Security*, report for Congress, RL31547, 29 January, Washington, DC: Congressional Research Service.

OSCE (2013) 'Permanent Council Decision No. 1106', OSCE Plenary, 3 December, www.osce.org/pc/109168.

Owens, W. A., Dam, K. W. and Lin, H. (eds) (2009) *Technology, Policy, Law, and Ethics Regarding US Acquisition and Use of Cyberattack Capabilities*, Washington, DC: National Academy Press.

Personick, S. D. and Patterson, C. A. (2003) *Critical Information Infrastructure Protection and the Law: An Overview of Key Issues*, Washington, DC: National Academy Press.

Prieto, D. B. (2006) 'Information Sharing with the Private Sector: History, Challenges, Innovation, and Prospects', in P. E. Auerswald, L. M. Branscomb, T. M. La Porte and E. O. Michel-Kerjan (eds), *Seeds of Disaster, Roots of Response: How Private Action Can Reduce Public Vulnerability*, Cambridge: Cambridge University Press, pp. 404–28.

Rid, T. (2013) *Cyber War Will Not Take Place*, London: Hurst & Company.

Schneier, B. (2008) 'The Psychology of Security (Part 1 and 2)', www.schneier.com/essays/archives/2008/01/the_psychology_of_se.html.

Schneier, B. (2012) 'When It Comes to Security, We're Back to Feudalism', *Wired*, www.wired.com/opinion/2012/11/feudal-security.

Schneier, B. (2013) 'The Battle for Power on the Internet', *The Atlantic*, www.theatlantic.com/technology/archive/2013/10/the-battle-for-power-on-the-internet/280824.

Singer, P. W. and Friedman A. (2014) *Cybersecurity and Cyberwar: What Everyone Needs to Know*, Oxford: Oxford University Press.

Stevens T. and Betz, D. J. (2013) 'Analogical Reasoning and Cyber Security', *Security Dialogue* 44(2): 147–64.

Suteanu, C. (2005) 'Complexity, Science and the Public: The Geography of a New Interpretation', *Theory, Culture and Society* 22(5): 113–40.

Suter, M. (2007) 'Improving Information Security in Companies: How to Meet the Need for Threat Information', in M. Dunn, V. Mauer and F. Krishna-Hensel (eds), *Power and Security in the Information Age: Investigating the Role of the State in Cyberspace*, Aldershot: Ashgate, pp. 129–50.

Suter, M. (2012) 'The Governance of Cyber Security: An Analysis of Public–Private Partnerships in a New Field of Security Policy', dissertation, ETH Zurich, Switzerland.

Talbot, D. (2011) 'The Cyber Security Industrial Complex', MIT Technology Review, www.technologyreview.com/news/426285/the-cyber-security-industrial-complex.

Valeriano, B. and Maness, R. C. (2014) 'The Dynamics of Cyber Conflict between Rival Antagonists, 2001–11', *Journal of Peace Research* 51(3): 347–60.

Warner, M. (2012) 'Cybersecurity: A Pre-History', *Intelligence and National Security* 27(5): 781–99.

10

PRIVATE EYES

Private policing and surveillance

Ajay Sandhu and Kevin D. Haggerty

Surveillance is a key attribute of contemporary life (Bennett *et al.* 2014). To appreciate the prevalence of surveillance we must recognize that it is not confined to draconian practices of social control, but entails any effort to collect information in order to further governmental ambitions. Here 'governmental' does not refer exclusively to state activities, but to public, private and individual efforts to advance different agendas. This is a necessarily broad definition, but one that usefully moves us beyond the usual focus on espionage and video cameras. Surveillance includes such things, but also extends to interpersonal scrutiny as well as to an expanding list of new technologies, including DNA databases, drones, metal detectors, satellites, biometrics, radio frequency identification (RFID) chips, online dataveillance, facial recognition, GPS tracking, identity cards, and the like. These varied devices and practices are changing how we raise our children, fight wars, deliver healthcare, educate students, socialize, conduct research, secure national borders, and conserve wildlife. Indeed, there are few realms of contemporary life that are not being transformed by new developments in surveillance (Ball *et al.* 2012).

This chapter focuses on the surveillance that is operative in private policing. In line with most researchers working in this field, we recognize that policing is accomplished through complex networks of private and public actors. These networks are composed of combinations of individuals and organizations that we might not immediately identify as 'the police,' but that nonetheless perform official and unofficial regulatory functions (Johnston and Shearing 2003). Readers should therefore bear in mind that while we single out some surveillance dynamics in private policing, surveillance on the ground typically involves heterogeneous interweavings of public/private organizations, individuals, texts, practices, and technologies (Haggerty and Ericson 2000).

In the following we emphasize both commonalities and differences in the dynamics of surveillance in private policing. In terms of the commonalities, the overriding point is that surveillance is central to the mandate and day-to-day operation of all policing. The second point is that such activities are remarkably diverse, and involve starkly different actors, technologies, and objectives.

To make these points we outline the relationships concerning surveillance among (a) private security officers who watch surveillance cameras, (b) private financial regulators responsible for monitoring financial markets and corporate activity for signs of fraud and other forms of manipulation, and (c) everyday citizens who are increasingly encouraged to be the police's 'eyes and ears'. We conclude with a brief discussion of the symbolic dimensions of such surveillance.

Camera operators

Not long ago citizens in democratic countries tended to see the prospect of surveillance cameras trained on the public streets as a characteristic feature of totalitarian societies. Today, however, many Western nations cannot seem to install cameras fast enough (Doyle *et al.* 2011). It has reached the point that surveillance cameras have become a banal aspect of urban life (Goold *et al.* 2013). The individuals watching all of these screens are often private security officers, tasked with deciding, on a moment-by-moment basis, exactly what to monitor. In North America and Europe this typically involves looking for crime or disorder, but in other contexts camera operators are attuned to signs of political unrest or lack of conformity to religious dictates (Alhadar and McCahill 2011).

When contemplating the surveillance conducted by the private police, most people probably immediately conjure up images of security guards scrutinizing camera screens. These individuals use increasingly sophisticated technologies. Even rudimentary cameras can now digitally record in colour, and can tilt, pan, and zoom. These systems are easily networked and integrated into wider communication systems, allowing camera operators in many jurisdictions to communicate with other security personnel in real time. Advanced systems can zoom in to read a text message on a smartphone from hundreds of meters away. The newest devices allow for audio recording and facial recognition.

An increasing percentage of the private security sector now spends their entire shift staring at the feeds from dozens of different cameras. In the United Kingdom the British Security Industry Authority suggests there might be as many as one camera for every 11 people (5.9 million cameras) (Barrett 2013), and this only represents one component of a global camera industry slated to grow from US$11.5 billion in 2008 to $37.5 billion in 2015 (Electronics Research Network 2011). This embrace of cameras has occurred in a neoliberal political environment where officials routinely proclaim that they are committed to 'evidence-based policy'. The reality, however, is that surveillance cameras are a clear example of how crime policy is, in fact, often developed in an empirical vacuum. In the United Kingdom, where cameras first made serious inroads, camera systems were initially introduced as part of the 'ring of steel' established around London's financial district to protect against IRA bombings. In the 1990s the Conservative government, eager to reinforce its 'law and order' agenda and develop high-profile ways to 'do something' about crime, established a Home Office programme to encourage local councils to install camera systems. These efforts gained added public support in the aftermath of a series of high profile horrific crimes, most notably the murder of the toddler James Bulger in 1993.

However, perhaps the greatest factor contributing to the appeal of cameras was the common-sense assumption that surveillance cameras trained on public areas would inevitably reduce crime. Notwithstanding this belief, it remains unclear whether the cameras fulfil that promise. While it can be hard to develop sound methodological studies to measure the effects of surveillance cameras (Farrington and Painter 2003), the existing research suggests that camera systems work best in highly controlled environments – such as car parks – but are not particularly good at deterring the more spontaneous forms of urban disorder fuelled by the combustible combination of alcohol and machismo. Dedicated criminals appear to simply move to other nearby locations, or develop sophisticated techniques to commit crimes even in plain view of the cameras. A prominent meta-analysis of the impact of surveillance cameras on crime commissioned by the British Home Office could therefore only conclude – after studying many years' worth of research – that it was too soon to come to a definitive conclusion as to the cameras' effectiveness (Gill and Spriggs 2005).

One of the most notable pragmatic problems camera operators face is that the cameras actually show too much. Any single camera shot will display far more than an individual could ever hope to scrutinize. Consequently, operators employ visual heuristics to help them identify what types of people and things are potentially 'out of order', and therefore deserving of greater scrutiny. The danger here is that these heuristics can be based upon deeply held prejudices and stereotypes. Research conducted in camera control rooms, for example, shows that in Western settings where the young black male has come to stand for criminal danger, camera operators typically use race as a primary discriminating category. The result is greater unwarranted camera attention being directed at black men (Norris and Armstrong 1999). Young people in general also tend to be monitored more closely, irrespective of their actions (or inaction). Daniel Neyland's (2006) study of surveillance camera operators captures a sense of how all-encompassing such suspicions can become in his chapter entitled 'Who are These Kids, and Why are They Standing Still?'. The cameras can also often reproduce a sexualized male gaze, with (predominantly) male camera operators objectifying women, but remaining oblivious to the types of harassment, intimidation, and dangers women face (Wright *et al.* 2014).

The fact that camera operators can have considerable discretion about who and what to watch can foster the impression that they are in positions of considerable power. In fact, these individuals tend to be among the most marginal actors in the criminal justice system. Gavin Smith's (2009) research on the occupational realities of camera operators shows them to be poorly paid, poorly trained, and have little job security. While watching the screens offers the occasional voyeuristic thrill, the reality is that most of the time the job is tremendously tedious. Being positioned near the bottom rung in the criminal justice division of labour also means that camera operators can find themselves bossed around and disrespected by the public police, who are their ostensible allies. Such occupational stresses can be compounded when monitoring becomes a psychological ordeal, as can happen when camera operators must helplessly watch people being beaten or committing suicide.

Financial surveillance

For decades we have seen the spectacle of corporate executives bilking taxpayers and investors of billions of dollars through a recurrent series of high profile economic crimes and misdeeds. Beyond the immediate financial losses, such activities are particularly hazardous to capitalist economies because they can undermine public trust in financial markets.

While the state has final authority to prosecute financial crimes, a complex network of public and private agencies is now responsible for investigating and regulating financial markets and business practices. These amount to quite different forms of surveillance conducted by private authorities. Such organizations sometimes conduct targeted surveillance, but also coordinate more rudimentary documentary and bureaucratic practices designed to make something as inscrutable as 'the market' into a phenomena that can be represented, analysed and managed (Ericson and Haggerty 1997). Private agencies provide forms of financial expertise that often cannot be found among the public police, including highly specialized auditors, lawyers, and forensic accountants.

As part of our dual emphasis on the centrality of surveillance in private policing – and the extreme diversity in what that surveillance entails in different contexts – we briefly identify some surveillance-related attributes of the private policing of economic crimes. Such efforts have created distinctive ways to visualize financial markets that, paradoxically, are also blinkered to certain varieties of economic wrongdoing.

Over the past two decades financial markets have become digitized. This allows massive amounts of financial instruments to be exchanged almost instantaneously, while also giving rise to new trading strategies designed to use the speed of these systems to capitalize on minute pricing differences (Lewis 2014). For regulators, computerization disconnected them from their previous personal relationships with traders who worked the stock market floors and who could offer clues about suspicious transactions (Thrift 2000). At the same time, digitization provided regulators with enormous amounts of data about market activity. Those data are the foundation of the distinctive contemporary financial surveillance modus operandi. Regulators now strive to create forms of computerized market legibility, whereby banks and other financial institutions must conform to 'know your customer regulations' and other standards for reporting and record keeping, all designed to make the movement of funds easier to trace using computers.

A prime example of this trend occurred in the aftermath of 9/11, when existing efforts to monitor financial activity for signs of money laundering by organized crime were quickly transformed into a heightened focus on trying to trace 'terrorist finances'. The upshot has been efforts to mandate that banks, international money transfer services, and other private financial institutions enhance the documentation of their customer's activities, and to routinely make that information available to the state (de Goede 2008). This amounts to a form of surveillance 'deputization' (Michaels 2010), whereby private agencies do the front-line collection of massive amounts of information which they share with the state, and which then serves as the informational backbone of state surveillance efforts. Edward Snowden's revelations make it clear that this type of surveillance deputization is now a key aspect of security efforts more widely, as communications service providers and internet service providers (ISPs) have been alternately enticed, threatened, or compelled to make their customer's data available to security agencies (Lyon 2014). Occasionally state security agents will simply hack into private corporate databases to obtain the desired information, without the corporation's (or client's) knowledge or consent (Gallagher 2014).

In the everyday operation of financial markets, traders are expected to buy and sell financial instruments according to a series of well-established trading rules and principles of market integrity. These are designed to prohibit such things as insider trading, wash trading, and other more complicated financial manipulations. Research conducted by James Williams (2009, 2013) in Canada stands out as some of the only criminological works that give us a sense of how surveillance operates in this world. As Williams demonstrates, the Toronto Stock Exchange contracts with the private organization Investment Industry Regulation Organization of Canada (IIROC) to identify forms of market manipulation, improper trade execution, and front-running. IIROC is then given access to the massive amounts of transactional data produced by the Toronto Stock Exchange.

Rather than making them omniscient, the volume of data available to regulators means that they face serious challenges in making sense of an almost unmanageable data glut. The solution has been for investigators to design computer algorithms to identify suspicious activities. These algorithms monitor the movement of funds between accounts, and the purchase and sale of stocks, bonds and other financial instruments, and automatically trigger an alert when they identify suspicious activity. That might happen, for example, when a trading rule has been violated – say a designated company 'insider' has traded some of his or her stocks. Alternatively, an alert might sound when trading occurs outside of established norms for a stock's price or for the volume of that stock traded in the recent past. In essence, these algorithms monitor for dramatic spikes in stock prices and trading volumes that occur outside of a statistically determined normal range. These statistical norms are themselves based on one month rolling averages. So, if a stock that last week traded at comparatively leisurely rate starts to sell rapidly, the computer produces an alert. Thousands of such alerts can sound in a single day, which the IIROC staff then try and decipher to determine whether they are explainable aberrations, or if they warrant further investigation.

While finance has become digitized, the actual understanding regulators have about the markets depends almost entirely on what data are scrutinized, and the design of the algorithms used to make sense of that information. The result is a series of notable regulatory blind spots. For example, the fact that the alert system only monitors a small number of market indicators, including volume, price, and volatility, provides a comparatively thin and rudimentary view of markets. Second, jurisdictional issues mean that the IIROC regulators only focus their attention on equities-based markets and cannot monitor activities on the bond, derivatives, and commodities markets. Consequently, they cannot detect the common practice of cross-market manipulation. Finally, the fact that the alert system is based on detecting statistical variations based on one-month averages means that financial actors involved in more long-term market manipulations are invisible to the regulations. All of this leads Williams to this conclusion:

> While it may be true that digitized financial markets are more transparent than ever, they are rendered surprisingly opaque by virtue of the superficiality of these representations and the surfeit of information relative to the paucity of 'true' market knowledge.
>
> *(Williams 2009: 481)*

Moreover, it is the established powerful actors who are best positioned to take advantages of these regulatory blind spots.

Citizens' eyes and ears

Security officials usually fear that vigilantes will violate a suspect's legal rights and safeguards. Nonetheless, in recent years, officials have championed new efforts to invigorate, direct, and coordinate everyday citizens as part of anti-crime and anti-terrorism efforts. The aim is for citizens to be the police's 'eyes and ears', as people are encouraged to scrutinize their local environment. These efforts represent instances of private policing surveillance in that they seek to integrate the primal human proclivity to watch one another (Locke 2010) into the state's security agenda.

Attempts to champion the surveillance potentials of everyday citizens find support in recent criminological research that advocates for extremely pragmatic strategies to make it more difficult, or even impossible, for potential offenders to commit crime. This is most apparent in Felson's (2002) routine activities theory, which sees crime as resulting from the combination of a potential offender, suitable target, and a lack of a competent guardian. It is also a component of Newman's (1973) early work advocating for the creation of 'defensible space' – an ambition embraced by advocates of crime prevention through environmental design (CPTED; Jeffery 1971).

All of these approaches assume that we can reduce crime by enhancing the public's ability to routinely monitor their environment, often referred to as 'natural surveillance'. Typically, the emphasis is on creating unencumbered sight lines in workplaces, neighbourhoods, and on city streets. One example might involve increasing the sight lines for a convenience store clerk by having him or her stand on an elevated platform while also reducing the height of merchandise shelves. Officials trained in CPTED encourage homeowners to install more lighting, cut down tall shrubs, and replace brick or wooden fences (that block people's views) with fences made of wrought iron bars that neighbours can see through. Planners now design entire subdivisions on these principles, populating suburbs with cul-de-sacs because of how they enhance the ability of neighbours to unconsciously monitor one another (Desyllas *et al.* 2003). All such initiatives enhance the public's surveillance abilities, often without people even knowing that this has happened, or that it is the result of explicit design decisions.

In the aftermath of the terrorist attacks of 9/11 the state turned to more direct attempts to empower and embolden citizens to actively scrutinize one another. Security officials from across the Western world nurtured a form of 'participatory surveillance' by urging citizens to watch out for suspicious individuals and activities. Many of these schemes were modelled on the longstanding Neighbourhood Watch programme (McConville and Shepherd 1992), which has homeowners mark their property for identification, conduct local street patrols, and display signage to announce their anti-crime vigilance. Comparable American terrorism-inspired developments include: 'If you see something, say something', TIPS, Marine Watch, Eagle Eyes, CAT Eyes, Talon, Real Estate Watch and Highway Watch (Stanley 2004). All such programmes exhort citizens to report suspicious activities to the authorities, and help them to do so through dedicated phone numbers and websites.

Similar ventures train citizens to search for and respond to terrorist threats. For example, the United States Department of Homeland Security supports the 'Citizen Corps' programme, which aims to 'harness the power of every individual through education, training, and volunteer service to make communities safer, stronger, and better prepared to respond to the threats of terrorism, crime, public health issues, and disasters of all kinds' (US Department of Homeland Security 2015). Citizen Corps teaches citizens how to look for threats, organize and create dedicated groups, and create defence strategies in case of a disaster or attack. It has a course specifically designed for children called 'youth preparedness' (FEMA undated) to teach kids how to be ready for emergencies by contributing to 'family disaster supply kits' and making escape plans.

The Texas Virtual Border Watch stands as one of the more fascinating of these recent 'watch' programmes. Now discontinued, this pilot initiative built upon an intriguing mix of computers, webcams, voyeurism, patriotism, and xenophobia to encourage citizens to use their home computers to remotely monitor cameras trained on the US border with Mexico in search of criminals or drug dealers illegally entering the US. People from anywhere in the world could register to become one of these virtual video vigilantes, and click on a button to alert the authorities if they saw anyone crossing the border illegally. While it did not meet its intended quotas for locating threats and making arrests (Koskela 2011), the virtual border watch provides an intriguing glimpse into how participatory surveillance can be technologically augmented.

All of these initiatives involve a form of 'reponsibilization', whereby the state's role in countering crime and terrorism is subtly transferred onto individual citizens who are encouraged to play a greater role in managing such risks. They are also examples of what Mathiesen (1997) refers to as 'synoptic' surveillance, which is characterized by 'the many' watching 'the few'. This is to be contrasted with forms of 'panoptic' surveillance famously identified by Foucault (1977), where 'the few' watch 'the many'.

Notwithstanding their official embrace, serious questions remain about the efficacy and desirability of such initiatives. Most basically, it is not clear that these programmes reduce crime. Typically introduced with a flourish in the aftermath of a high profile criminal or terrorist event, public enthusiasm for participatory surveillance tends to quickly wane, leaving behind only the signs proclaiming the existence of programmes that are effectively defunct. More problematically, empowering citizens to act on ill-defined notions of 'suspicious people' or 'suspicious activity' can encourage them to draw upon their own prejudices and unfounded anxieties as the basis for identifying who to watch. It is therefore not surprising that these programmes have been plagued with false reports and phony tips (Neumann 2008). Citizen watchers often target youths deemed to be in the wrong place at the wrong time, and individuals who conform to modern stereotypes of post-9/11 terrorism, which includes having brown skin or displaying markers of the Muslim faith (Chan 2008). For those being watched, such scrutiny can be a form of aggressive and stigmatizing exclusion that reminds them of their marginal status. So while these initiatives aim to protect citizens, there is also the danger that they can instead corrode the types of mutualism, respect, and trust that is intrinsic to the functioning of any healthy community.

Conclusion

The above three examples are so different that it might be hard to bear in mind that they are all instances of surveillance conducted by private policing. That, in part, is our point. Private policing is a remarkably varied enterprise, employing practices of surveillance and visualization that involve dramatically different actors, technologies, and routines. While such complexity can make it challenging to develop a comprehensive understanding of surveillance and private policing in all its different guises, it also presents valuable research opportunities. Studying surveillance provides a rewarding entrée for researchers seeking to understand the aims, objectives and practical strategies operative in private policing.

Much of the existing criminological research on surveillance concerns the question of whether it actually reduces crime and disorder. Such evaluative research is a well-established criminological enterprise (Sherman *et al.* 2006), although one with the tendency to produce frustratingly inconclusive results that prompt heated ideological debates about how to interpret those findings. Evaluative research, however, also risks making the mistake of accepting the stated aims of surveillance advocates at face value. Reducing crime is often only one of the ultimate aims or social consequences of surveillance – and sometimes not a particularly important ambition in comparison to surveillance's numerous other accomplishments. That is because surveillance, like policing itself (Manning 2012), is a highly symbolic activity that conveys a diverse set of meanings to quite different audiences.

Consider, for example, the participatory surveillance of citizens watching other citizens. While not particularly useful in identifying terrorists, this form of private policing involves rich drama whereby citizens literally perform a simulated police role. In the process, they align themselves with the state's security agenda while effecting an insider/outsider social cleavage – one where real or imagined enemies are positioned as external threats. Marginalized groups are stigmatized as 'outsiders', while 'insiders' are bonded together. Likewise, surveillance cameras perform important symbolic work irrespective of whether they actually reduce crime. For the private security sector, who often must struggle for official legitimacy, sophisticated cameras can signal their modernity and professionalism. By using cameras these organizations also convey to external agencies, such as the courts, that they are performing their anti-crime due diligence (Haggerty and Tokar 2012). For everyday citizens the cameras can themselves come to stand for safety, security, and urban renewal.

In terms of the surveillance of financial markets, regulatory efforts to fashion a bureaucratic and documentary field of visibility amenable to computerized scrutiny and other forms of representation actually help constitute the market itself (Williams 2009). In the process this surveillance conveys the reassuring – and perhaps completely false – impression that markets are amenable to meaningful understanding and regulation, and that such regulation is not capricious, but rooted in rational processes. In a charged political environment, financial surveillance by private actors also serves the basic but vital role of allowing politicians to appear to be addressing the persistent problem of corporate wrongdoing, again, irrespective of the efficacy of such financial oversight.

Bibliography

Alhadar, I. and McCahill, M. (2011) 'The Use of Surveillance Cameras in a Riyadh Shopping Mall: Protecting Profits or Protecting Morality', *Theoretical Criminology* 15(3): 315–30.

Ball, K., Haggerty, K. and Lyon, D. (2012) *The Routledge Handbook of Surveillance Studies*, Abingdon: Routledge.

Barrett, D. (2013) 'One Surveillance Camera for Every 11 People in Britain, Says CCTV Survey', *The Telegraph* 10 July, www.telegraph.co.uk/technology/10172298/One-surveillance-camera-for-every-11-people-in-Britain-says-CCTV-survey.html.

Bennett, C., Haggerty, K., Lyon, D. and Steeves, V. (2014) *Transparent Lives: Surveillance in Canada*, Athabasca: Athabasca University Press.

Chan, J. (2008) 'The New Lateral Surveillance and a Culture of Suspicion', in M. Deflem and T. Ulmer (eds), *Surveillance and Governance: Crime Control and Beyond*, Bingley: Emerald, pp. 223–39.

Coleman, R. and McCahill, M. (2011) *Surveillance and Crime*, London: Sage.

De Goede, M. (2008) 'Risk, Preemption and Exception in the War on Terrorist Financing', in L. Amoore and M. de Goede (eds), *Risk and the War on Terror*, Abingdon: Routledge, pp. 97–111.

Desyllas, J., Connoly, P., and Hebbert, F. (2003) 'Modelling Natural Surveillance', *Environment and Planning B* 30(5): 643–55.

Doyle, A., Lippert, R. and Lyon, D. (2011) *Eyes Everywhere: The Global Growth of Camera Surveillance*, Abingdon: Routledge.

Electronics Research Network (2011) 'Global Video Surveillance Market to reach US $37.7 Billion by 2015', *Semiconductor Research News*, www.marketresearchworld.net/content/view/3884/77.

Ericson, R. and Haggerty, K. (1997) *Policing the Risk Society*, Toronto: University of Toronto Press.

Farrington, D. and Painter, K. (2003) 'How to Evaluate the Impact of CCTV on Crime', in M. Gill (ed.), *CCTV*, Leicester: Perpetuity Press, pp. 67–79.

Felson, M. (2002) *Crime and Everyday Life* (3rd edn), Thousand Oaks, CA: Sage.

FEMA (undated) *Youth Preparedness: Implementing A Community-Based Program*, Washington, DC: Federal Emergency Management Agency, www.fema.gov/media-library-data/20130726-1903-25045-5654/youth_preparedness_implementing_a_community_basesd_program_v5_508.pdf.

Foucault, M. (1977) *Discipline and Punish: The Birth of the Prison* (trans. A. Sheridan), New York: Vintage.

Gallagher, R. (2014) 'Operation Socialist: The Inside Story of How British Spies Hacked Belgium's Largest Telco', https://firstlook.org/theintercept/2014/12/13/belgacom-hack-gchq-inside-story.

Gill, M. and Spriggs, A. (2005) *Assessing the Impact of CCTV*, London: Home Office Research, Development and Statistics Directorate.

Goold, B., Loader, I. and Thumala, A. (2013) 'The Banality of Security: The Curious Case of Security Cameras', *British Journal of Criminology* 53 (6): 977–96.

Haggerty, K. and Ericson. R. (2000) 'The Surveillant Assemblage', *British Journal of Sociology* 51(4): 605–22.

Haggerty, K. and Tokar, C. (2012) 'Signifying Security: On the Institutional Appeals of Nightclub ID scanning Systems', *Space and Culture* 15(2): 124–34.

Jeffery, R. (1971) *Crime Prevention Through Environmental Design*, Beverly Hills, CA: Sage.

Johnston, L., and Shearing C. (2003) *Governing Security: Explorations in Policing and Justice*, Abingdon: Routledge.

Koskela, H. (2011) 'Don't Mess With Texas: Texas' Virtual Border Watch Program and the (Botched) Politics of Responsibilization', *Crime, Media, Culture* 7(1): 49–65.

Lewis, M. (2014) *Flash Boys: A Wall Street Revolt*, New York: W. W. Norton.

Locke, J. (2010) *Eavesdropping: An Intimate History*, Oxford: Oxford University Press.

Lyon, D. (2014) 'Surveillance, Snowden, and Big Data: Capacities, Consequences, Critique', *Big Data and Society* 1(1): 1–13.

Manning, P. (2012) 'Drama, the Police and the Sacred in Policing', in T. Newburn and J. Peay (eds), *Policing: Politics, Culture, and Control,* Oxford: Hart, pp. 173–94.

Mathiesen, T. (1997) 'The Viewer Society: Michel Foucault's "Panopticon" Revisited', *Theoretical Criminology* 1(2): 215–34.

McConville, M. and Shepherd, D. (1992) *Watching Police Watching Communities*, London: Routledge.

Michaels, J. D. (2010) 'Deputizing Homeland Security', *Texas Law Review* 88: 1435–73.

Newman, O. (1973) *Defensible Space: Crime Prevention Through Urban Design*, New York: Collier.

Neuman, W. (2008) 'In Response to M.T.A.'s "Say Something'" Ads, a Glimpse of Modern Fears', *New York Times* 7 January, www.nytimes.com/2008/01/07/nyregion/07see.html?pagewanted=all&_r=0.

Neyland, D. (2006) *Privacy, Surveillance and Public Trust*, Basingstoke: Palgrave.

Norris, C. and Armstrong, G. (1999) *The Maximum Surveillance Society: The Rise of CCTV*, Oxford: Berg.

Sherman, L., Farrington, D. Welsh, B. and MacKenzie, D. L. (2006) *Evidence-Based Crime Prevention* (revised edition), Abingdon: Routledge.

Smith, G. J. D. (2009) 'Empowered Watchers or Disempowered Workers? The Ambiguities of Power Within Technologies of Security', in K. F. Aas, H. Oppen Gundhus and H. Mork Lomell (eds), *Technologies of (In)security*, Abingdon: Routledge, pp. 125–46.

Stanley, J. (2004) *The Surveillance Industrial Complex*, New York: American Civil Liberties Union.

Thrift, N. (2000) 'Pandora's Box: Cultural Geographies of Economies', in G. L. Clark, S. Gertler and M. P. Feldman (eds), *The Oxford Handbook of Economic Geography*, Oxford: Oxford University Press, pp. 689–704.

US Department of Homeland Security (2015) 'Citizen Corps', www.dhs.gov/citizen-corps.

Williams, J. (2009) 'Envisioning Financial Disorder: Financial Surveillance and the Securities Industry', *Economy and Society* 38 (3): 460–91.

Williams, J. (2013) 'Regulatory Technologies, Risky Subjects, and Financial Boundaries: Governing "Fraud" in the Financial Markets', *Accounting, Organizations and Society* 38(6–7): 544–58.

Wright, J., Glasbeek, A. and van der Meulen, E. (2014) 'Securing the Home: Gender, CCTV, and the Hybridized Space of Apartment Buildings', *Theoretical Criminology* 19(1): 95–117.

11

ENDURING CHALLENGES OF SECURITY PRIVATIZATION IN THE HUMANITARIAN SPACE

Christopher Spearin[1]

Back in the mid-1990s the United Nations Secretary-General Boutros Boutros-Ghali observed that securing the humanitarian space was 'one of the most significant challenges facing the humanitarian community' (Boutros-Ghali 1995: 172). In response to these challenges, CARE Canada and the University of Toronto's Program on Conflict Management and Negotiation in 1999 offered what was then regarded as a 'modest proposal': humanitarian non-governmental organizations (NGOs) might rely upon private security for their protection (Bryans *et al.* 1999: 31, 33–7). Today, NGOs routinely engage private military and security companies (PMSCs) as they operate in increasingly 'crowded' environments including states following whole-of-government (WOG) engagements. Certainly, the challenges involved in securing the humanitarian space have evolved in part because of the developed world's engagement in weak states following the events of 11 September 2001, and NGOs' interaction with PMSCs is arguably both a cause and a response to these still ongoing and morphing challenges.

With the passage of time and circumstance therefore, it is opportune to take stock of the rationales, debates, concerns, and ramifications regarding NGO/PMSC interaction and PMSC involvement in the larger humanitarian field. As a building block, this chapter first presents the characteristics of the humanitarian space as traditionally understood. It then turns to the contentious debates about how PMCS on their own or through NGO utilization might expand or limit this space. Here the chapter assesses PMSC services to NGOs and the changes regarding risk transference and the duty of care. The chapter then focuses on why PMSCs might wish to be involved in the humanitarian space. It recognizes the shift from seeking industry legitimacy to pursuing commercial opportunities and how this in turn reflects and exacerbates the continued flexibility of the term 'humanitarian'. This increased flexibility is also in keeping with the actions of many NGOs with more political bents. The chapter concludes by identifying issues for future consideration by policymakers and academics alike.

The humanitarian space

Given that Minear and Weiss (1995) describe humanitarian space as an accordion, it is clear that the concept is constituted in more than just a physically spatial sense. This space expands and contracts along three dimensions. The first concerns the ability to overcome distance or geographical barriers in order to conduct humanitarian deeds. The second deals with perceptions. This is the degree to which different groups, including conflicting parties, view the NGO presence as acceptable. The third relates to violence, or the threat thereof, which may either prevent NGOs from reaching those in need or be directed at them. Importantly, these dimensions are not walled or separated; matters pertaining to one dimension can easily overlap with another.

NGOs are not a passive audience vis-à-vis the humanitarian space; their relationships, decisions, and actions can impact upon its expansion and contraction. Regarding the security of NGO operations and their personnel then, the archetype is the acceptance approach. Instead of emphasizing reliance upon armed actors, acceptability rests in part on following the humanitarian ethic's three principles of neutrality, impartiality, and independence. Neutrality is meant to prevent advantage being conferred intentionally on an actor or group in a conflict zone. Impartiality ensures that humanitarian assistance is allocated on the basis of need, not on the basis of political necessity or favouritism. Independence allows for humanitarians to avoid linkage to the agendas of others that might somehow impact negatively upon the neutrality and impartiality of humanitarian activity (Spearin 2007). Acceptability also rests in part on developing trust and a sense of solidarity with those in need. This approach is no mean feat as it requires, and capitalizes upon, the time, experience, and ongoing dedication of NGO personnel.

Certainly, the acceptance approach is not the only security stance for NGOs. Van Brabant's (2000) pioneering work acknowledges two more points on the so-called humanitarian security triangle: protection and deterrence. The former is synonymous with hardening and the latter with presenting a counter-threat, including the reliance on armed actors of various sorts. To facilitate these approaches, NGO relationships with other actors that potentially operate under different ethical and moral frames are required. It follows, however, that security measures that physically and/or ideationally separate NGOs from affected populations risk closing the humanitarian space.

PMSC–NGO interaction

A common lament of NGOs is that other parties' actions have catalysed the contraction of the humanitarian space in different conflict environments over the past two decades. Previously, while humanitarian activities definitely had a political effect, it was unintended and the humanitarian presence was, more or less, respected by warring parties. But in the decade after the Cold War, NGO operations and their personnel were increasingly targeted for a variety of unsettling reasons:

- violent non-state actors did not feel bound to international humanitarian law developed by and for states;
- the perceived primordial nature of ethnic conflict prevented humanitarian work from being viewed in a benign light; and
- NGOs were soft targets possessing resources desirable for conflict continuation and/or personal and group enrichment.

With the so-called War on Terror, international NGOs became additionally vulnerable because they were frequently deemed infidels representative of Western values – despite the fact that they increasingly relied upon indigenous staff precisely because of security risks.

More and more in the twenty-first century, NGOs also accused other actors of limiting the humanitarian space through their instrumentalization of assistance – aid delivered for political benefit rather than on the basis of need. In Iraq and Afghanistan, militaries provided assistance as part of their larger counterinsurgency strategies. Civilian government organizations did too as part of the trend towards comprehensive or WOG solutions adopted by Western states. This intrusion, from the NGO perspective, has different actors working at cross-purposes and often relying upon the symbolism and characteristics of NGOs. Local beneficiaries and combatants alike increasingly became unsure as to who exactly were humanitarian NGOs or what the humanitarian endeavour actually was. It also heightened sensitivity to the fact that NGOs themselves were major recipients of government largesse and that outside forces wanted to coordinate with them. For NGOs, the humanitarian space shrunk, as they were confused with others, denied access, and/or subject to attack.

The NGO response to these challenges varied. On the one hand, some NGOs attempted to prevent others from closing the humanitarian space. Consider, for instance, the 2007 Guidelines for Relations between US Armed Forces and Non-Governmental Humanitarian Organizations in Hostile or Potentially Hostile Environments developed by NGOs and the US military. This document attempts to structure what militaries should and should not do vis-à-vis the humanitarian space. On the other hand, practitioners such as Ferreiro (2012) suggested that this was the new normal. NGOs would have to examine their own policies and at least be wary of the agendas of others in order to keep the humanitarian space open: 'The reality is that humanitarians are doomed to coexist with foreign troops in scenarios where donor governments pursue political agendas. Humanitarian agencies must be aware of the cost of this cohabitation, and learn to deal with it' (ibid.).

The presence of PMSCs in these complex conflict environments strikes at the heart of traditional NGO conceptions of how to keep the humanitarian space open. From one standpoint, PMSCs are yet another potentially armed actor in already dangerous milieus. As PMSCs do not wear state uniforms, parties on the ground can readily confuse their personnel with those of NGOs. From an alternative standpoint, PMSCs might be the best choice for NGOs wishing armed protection: 'the PSC [private security company] option may be the less sensitive one: rather than being associated with one party or side in the conflict, PSC protection could be seen as the enlisting of an "impartial" actor' (Holmqvist 2005: 21). Other analysts, however, have pushed back. They have noted several complications for NGO clients:

- PMSC activities may negatively influence local actors and NGO donors;
- indigenous security personnel may implicate NGOs with local conflict dynamics;
- NGOs may be viewed as yet another warring party; and
- PMSC contracts with other clients in, and out, of theatre could impact negatively upon both NGO reputations and their abilities to keep the humanitarian space open.

(Cockayne 2006; Speers-Mears 2009; Spearin 2005)

With a sense of understatement, the authors of an Overseas Development Institute (ODI) report concluded that reliance on PMSCs 'creates particular vulnerabilities for humanitarian organisations' (Stoddard *et al.* 2008: 27).

Furthermore, the nature and degree of PMSC utilization suggests that NGOs themselves are adopting the acceptance approach less and less. Certainly, the possibility of a 'Mad Max NGO' identified at the turn of the last century – an NGO that uses force independently in order to gain access – did not come about (Donini 1998: 89; Spearin 2007: 9). Regulatory developments taken by PMSCs and by states over the 2000s have established the industry's defensive, rather than offensive, credentials (e.g. the so-called Montreux Document; see Chapters 24 and 26, this volume). Nevertheless, many NGOs have engaged PMSCs and, as a result, adopted either protective or deterrent stances, which is not surprising given the military/police pedigree of many firms. These stances are both 'soft' and 'hard'. The former, which are arguably less problematic, include training, risk analysis, and security auditing. The latter include communications, the imposition of physical barriers, and armed and unarmed guards for static sites, convoys, and personnel (Glaser 2011; Spearin 2000). While statistics vary, they underscore a not insubstantial level of NGO reliance on PMSC services. Buchanan and Muggah (2005) estimate that one-third of NGOs employ armed guards, while Singer (2006) contends that 25 per cent of 'high end' PMSCs have humanitarian clients. The aforementioned ODI document found that 35 per cent of surveyed NGO field offices reported PMSC usage (Buchanan and Muggah 2005: 9; Singer 2006: 70; Stoddard *et al.* 2008: 9).

This PMSC utilization by NGOS reflects the broader literatures of risk transference in contemporary conflicts (Carmola 2011). For international NGOs specifically, the transfer of risk is evident in the increased reliance on indigenous staff; compared to expatriates, local personnel have increasingly borne the brunt of causalities (Glaser 2011). With PMSC protective and deterrent approaches now in the mix, risk is transferred to an even broader population such that there is a growing 'gulf between protected humanitarian workers and unprotected beneficiaries' (Speers-Mears 2009: 9). In this vein, relying on PMSCs means that security for NGOs comes not through solidarity, but through 'us-them' distinctions. Those in need are not only relatively unprotected and thus at risk, they are viewed as potentially threatening (Carmola 2013).

This transfer of risk, however, may be the quid pro quo of ameliorating NGO liability and duty of care issues. In this sense, the acceptance approach does not offer similar legalistic or technical refuge for NGOs wishing to avoid lawsuits and maintain their recruitment and retention levels. In the late 1990s, Van Brabant (1999) first raised concerns about lawsuits and insurance coverage given the violence humanitarians faced. Attention to the legal and ethical requirements NGOs confronted only increased during the 2000s (Carmola 2013; Kemp and Merkelbach 2011). Therefore, reliance on soft and hard PMSC services have become a way for NGOs to demonstrate their due regard in very exacting and documented ways. Some industry associations have advocated PMSC soft services so that NGOs can act to mitigate risk and not worry about any of the operational and image concerns linked to hard services noted earlier (Bearpark 2012). Nevertheless, as Speers-Mears describes, court cases and state law such as the United Kingdom's 2007 Corporate Manslaughter Act have entailed that duty of care be demonstrated 'through improved security policies and management, security trainings and consultancies, and contracts involving visible security services in the field' (2009: 6–7).

Initially though, there was no sustained thought and engagement about how humanitarians should go about their interactions with PMSCs. The ODI manual Operational Security Management in Violent Environments published in 2000 was the exception to the rule. Many authors noted that NGOs, collectively and individually, could and should have been doing more to manage their contractual relationships and to disseminate good practices both within and between organizations (Spearin 2005; Feinstein International Famine Center and International Alert 2001; Cockayne 2006). There were, however, several rationales for the hesitation, including naivety, competition among NGOs, and the desire for sustained flexibility.

More recently though, efforts have been made to consolidate and advise on good practices (Glaser 2011). This includes a new edition of the ODI manual released in 2010. While the issuing and potential following of guidance make NGOs, by design or default, complicit in the shifts towards multi-actor security governance and offer legitimacy to the PMSC industry (as we shall see below), they are in keeping, for better or for worse, with more technical and recognized security contracting processes followed by other actors including states and international organizations (e.g. the International Maritime Organization's various guiding documents for ship owners, ship operators, ship masters, and flag states).

PMSCs for/as humanitarians

Turning the focus to PMSCs, they have worked to legitimize themselves, if not the industry as a whole. While developments in regulation have helped to disassociate these firms from mercenaries, so-called good deeds have helped to lessen the stigma further. As an example, in the mid-1990s, the South African PMSC Executive Outcomes (EO) flew Sierra Leone's national football team to the African All Nations Cup in South Africa. More recently, PMSCs have supported local charities or developed their own to help those in need.

One can also categorize relations with humanitarians as good deeds. Hellinger (2004: 193) contends that firms 'recognize not only an opportunity to do business in humanitarian operations … they believe such operations would help legitimate their business'. Olive Group (2014), for instance, indicates how its services help multiple actors associated with the humanitarian space. The firm's aim is 'to provide comprehensive, project enabling protective services that secure the lives and ensure the welfare of NGO personnel while also guaranteeing their on-going access to beneficiaries'. Though PMSC activities are mostly technical and not synonymous with the acceptance approach, Blue Hackle (2013) implies solidarity with NGOs and the people they assist: 'NGOs need a team of committed security personnel to protect the lives of not only aid workers, but the lives of displaced families and refugees at risk in highly contentious environments'.

Moreover, while the chapter so far has emphasized contractual interactions, these commitments have not always been necessary. Firms such as EO and Sandline International during their African operations in the 1990s provided many services for free: the repatriation of child soldiers, the escorting of humanitarian convoys, and the provision of logistics, intelligence, and aerial evacuations for NGO personnel. In Iraq and Afghanistan, firms provided unsolicited protection by shadowing convoys, distributed free (in)security analyses, attended NGO security meetings, and offered reduced prices for humanitarian organizations (Spearin 2000; Glaser 2011; Speers-Mears 2009). Such is the perceived value of these relationships that a firm placed 'humanitarian consultancy' on its list of services on the basis of just one phone call (Stoddard *et al.* 2008). In fact, the relationships can even be virtual. The 2011 video game 'Blackwater', for which then Blackwater head Erik Prince offered advice, has gameplay featuring contractors protecting aid workers.

The provision of good deeds has over time led to PMSCs seemingly becoming humanitarians themselves. Back in 2003, the International Peace Operations Association (IPOA), a US-based lobby group for the military and security industry, indicated that member firms were not replacements for NGOs (Spearin 2008). Nevertheless, by mid-decade, representatives of a UK-based industry association trumpeted humanitarian possibilities for PMSCs independent of interactions with NGOs (Bearpark and Schulz 2007). Additionally, in 2010, IPOA changed its name to 'International Stability Operations Association' (ISOA) to reflect the wider array of opportunities for PMSCs. In this vein in 2011, an entire issue of ISOA's industry magazine, the *Journal of International Peace Operations*, was dedicated towards 'humanitarian response'. It dealt with issues as varied as aid, gender, children, development and governance.

Hence, Joachim and Schneiker (2012: 377) openly question whether PMSCs are 'the new humanitarians'; twenty-five per cent of the 200 firms they analysed emphasize their humanitarian credentials. For firms, adopting the humanitarian moniker reflects not only legitimacy requirements, but also the desire for financial self-preservation and enhanced remuneration.

Product diversification would potentially sustain commercial viability and/or make a company attractive for takeover. Moreover, firms could literally bank on state contractual opportunities given their lack of qualms about working for/with states in WOG efforts and increasing concerns from state officials about NGOs doing their bidding (Spearin 2008; Joachim and Schneiker 2012).

This perception of PMSCs as humanitarians underscores the increasing elasticity of the term 'humanitarian'. Not only have firms taken advantage of this flexibility, they have actively promoted it through their service provisions and their discursive techniques (Spearin 2008; Joachim and Schneiker 2012). Arguably, the industry first started its stretching when some firms initiated their 'humanitarian demining' services in the 1990s, a potentially lucrative worldwide endeavour then valued at US$33 billion (Spearin 2001). Unlike the 'breaching' of minefields simply for military force protection and mobility, humanitarian demining demands a high clearance rate – 99.6 per cent under United Nations standards – so that the local population can have confidence and freedom of movement. However, the usage of the word humanitarian here does not necessarily link with the three elements of the humanitarian ethic (i.e. neutrality, impartiality and independence). This is because humanitarian demining connects firms with larger 'mine action' agendas associated with human security promotion and very political efforts for reconciliation and social and economic development.

This example speaks to Barnett's observation that as the term humanitarian became more popular, 'humanitarianism became caught in the undertow of politics and implicated in broader activities and practices' (Barnett 2003: 415). The result is that one should view humanitarian space as an ideational arena that no one type of organization dominates and whose boundaries are in considerable flux. Put differently, the humanitarian space accordion described earlier might very well be a different instrument playing different music for different people for different reasons.

Indeed, there is a circular logic at play here. To explain, it is important to recognize that these broader practices and their political implications have come not just through PMSCs, WOG work, and the instrumentalization of assistance. NGOs are increasingly complicit too. Without doubt, many NGOs follow the humanitarian ethic. However, the 'humanitarian' NGO community does not have uniform policies among organizations. Though many NGOs cling to the humanitarian handle, they nevertheless also wish to bear witness and to advocate in the milieu in which they operate. This makes a strict adherence to the humanitarian ethic problematic. In a similar way, many NGOs are multi-mandate organizations. Whereas traditional humanitarianism was to comfort those in need, the shift towards development work and good governance efforts sees NGOs attempting to address those factors that initiated the need. In so doing, however, NGOs are engaging in activities that are contestable with an intended political effect (Spearin 2007). Not only does this make the notion of their protection as humanitarians, as traditionally understood, hollow, it might very well catalyse violence against these NGOs. The linking of development and governance activities and the changes this entails for the humanitarian space do not lend themselves well to the protection of NGO personnel and their operations. Hence, for multi-mandate organizations, the acceptance approach becomes untenable, hence the search for other security solutions, manifest particularly in greater opportunities for PMSCs.

Conclusions and future issues

With NGOs now delivering more assistance in terms of value compared to that distributed by the United Nations system, it stands to reason that appreciating the (in)security of NGOs personnel and their operations is vital (Perrin 2012). In large part, this can be done through considering the debates and issues related to PMSCs vis-à-vis the humanitarian space as this chapter has shown. On the one hand, contemporary NGO insecurity relates to the complicated, multi-actor conflict environments in which organizations have found themselves. The multiple agendas of different parties in modern conflicts – state and non-state, domestic and foreign alike – have revealed the acceptance approach's limitations. In turning to more robust and defensive postures, NGOs have engaged with PMSCs, a not overly comfortable relationship as PMSCs embody armed actor proliferation and pose challenges for organizations. On the other hand, PMSCs can seek legitimacy for the industry through working alongside humanitarians and they can increasingly present themselves as humanitarians. The result is that one cannot conceive of NGOs as being dominant in/over/towards the humanitarian space. The space is being recast by PMSCs, but also by NGOs with their multiplying agendas beyond the mere delivery of assistance according to the humanitarian ethic.

Looking to the future, NGOs as they conduct their work will continue to encounter PMSCs. In the 1990s, states frequently turned to NGOs in less strategically important areas in lieu of more robust engagement directed at military and political solutions. This approach – the antithesis of counterinsurgency and substantial WOG efforts – had several descriptions: 'humanitarian alibi' and 'mobilizing myth' to name but two (Minear 1997; Donini 1998: 81). As Paul (1999: 30) put it, 'relief organisations are increasingly being drawn into situations where assistance activities are not sufficiently supported by efforts to resolve the conflict'. In many cases in the 1990s, PMSCs worked with or alongside NGOs to facilitate their work and thus substantiate the alibi or myth. Looking at the present day, the focus is increasingly on PMSCs as a mechanism for states to follow 'liddism', that is 'keeping the lid on [international security concerns] rather than reducing the heat' (Rogers 2013: 14).

A number of questions are clearly ripe for consideration equally by policymakers and analysts. Will PMSCs be a favoured partner for state directed 'liddist' humanitarian activities given the problems encountered with state–NGO interactions? If so, this will continue to challenge notions of what a humanitarian actor is and does and what sort of actors should be responsible for providing security. Alternatively, does the change in context entail a change in approach? If so, will future engagements see NGOs returning to the humanitarian ethic in order to ensure their security? What issues will arise for multi-mandate organizations? Development work will no doubt remain inherently political and many organizations wish to address the root problems of conflicts. Will this mean greater NGO interaction with firms as intervening forces may no longer be present, at least to provide some sort of stability or top cover? What is more, are NGOs and PMSCs, by themselves or in combination, really a characteristic of liddism given that many are doing more than just helping those in immediate need? Even without significant intervening state presence, it would appear that understandings of humanitarian space will continue to be fluid and mutable.

Note

1   The views expressed in the chapter are those of the author and do not necessarily reflect those of the Canadian Department of National Defence or the Government of Canada.

Bibliography

Barnett, M. (2003) 'What is the Future of Humanitarianism?', *Global Governance*, 9(3): 401–16.

Bearpark, A. (2012) 'The Case for Humanitarian Organizations to Use Private Security Contractors', in

B. Perrin (ed.), *Modern Warfare: Armed Groups, Private Militaries, Humanitarian Organizations, and the Law*, Vancouver: University of British Columbia Press, pp. 157–67.

Bearpark, A. and Schulz, S. (2007) 'The Future of the Market', in S. Chesterman and C. Lehnardt (ed.), *From Mercenaries to Market: The Rise and Regulation of Private Military Companies*, Oxford: Oxford University Press, pp. 239–50.

Blue Hackle (2013) 'Non-Profit/NGOs', www.bluehackle.com/?page_id=165.

Boutros-Ghali, B. (1995) *Confronting New Challenges: Annual Report on the Work of the Organization*, New York: United Nations.

Bryans, M., Jones, B. D. and Gross Stein, J. (1999) 'Mean Times: Humanitarian Action in Complex Emergencies – Stark Choices, Cruel Dilemmas', *Coming to Terms* 1(3).

Buchanan, C. and Muggah, R. (2005) *No Relief: Surveying the Effects of Gun Violence on Humanitarian and Development Personnel*, Geneva: Centre for Humanitarian Dialogue and Small Arms Survey.

Carmola, K. (2011) *Private Security Contractors and New Wars: Risk, Law, and Ethics*, New York: Routledge.

Carmola, K. (2013) 'Private Security Companies: Regulation Efforts, Professional Identities, and Effects on Humanitarian NGOs, Professionals in Humanitarian Assistance and Protection', http://phap.org/articles/private-security-companies-regulation-efforts-professional-identities-effects.

Cockayne, J. (2006) *Commercial Security in Humanitarian and Post-Conflict Settings: An Exploratory Study*, New York: International Peace Academy.

Donini, A. (1998) 'Asserting Humanitarianism in Peace-Maintenance', in J. Chopra (ed.), *The Politics of Peace-Maintenance*, Boulder, CO: Lynne Rienner Publishers, pp. 81–96.

Feinstein International Famine Center and International Alert (2001) *The Politicisation of Humanitarian Action and Staff Security: The Use of Private Security Companies by Humanitarian Agencies*, international workshop summary report, Medford, MA: Feinstein International Famine Center/London: International Alert, www.securitymanagementinitiative.org/index.php?option=com_docman&task=doc_details&gid=310&lang=en&Itemid=28.

Ferreiro, M. (2012) 'Blurring of Lines in Complex Emergencies: Consequences for the Humanitarian Community', *Journal of Humanitarian Assistance* 24 December, http://sites.tufts.edu/jha/archives/1625.

Glaser, M. P. (2011) *Engaging Private Security Providers: A Guideline for Non-Governmental Organisations*, briefing paper, London: European Interagency Security Forum.

Hellinger, D. (2004) 'Humanitarian Action, NGOs and the Military', *Refugee Survey Quarterly* 23(4): 192–220.

Holmqvist, C. (2005) *Private Security Companies: The Case for Regulation*, policy paper no. 9, Stockholm: Stockholm International Peace Research Institute.

Joachim, J. and Schneiker, A. (2012) 'New Humanitarians? Frame Appropriation through Private Military and Security Companies', *Millennium* 40(2): 365–88.

Kemp, E. and Merkelbach, M. (2011) *Can You Get Sued? Legal Liability of International Humanitarian Aid Organisations towards Their Staff*, policy paper, Geneva: Security Management Initiative.

Minear, L. (1997) 'Humanitarian Action and Peacekeeping Operations', *Journal of Humanitarian Assistance* 26 February, http://sites.tufts.edu/jha/archives/110.

Minear, L. and Weiss, T. G. (1995) *Mercy Under Fire: War and the Global Humanitarian Community*, Boulder, CO: Westview Press.

Olive Group. (2014) 'Non-Governmental Organisations (NGOs)', www.olivegroup.com/sectors.php?sectid=15

Paul, D. (1999) *Protection in Practice: Field-Level Strategies for Protecting Civilians from Deliberate Harm*, relief and rehabilitation paper no. 30, London: Overseas Development Institute.

Perrin, B. (2012) 'Private Security Companies and Humanitarian Organizations: Implications for International Humanitarian Law', in B. Perrin (ed.) *Modern Warfare: Armed Groups, Private Militaries, Humanitarian Organizations, and the Law*, Vancouver: University of British Columbia Press, pp. 124–56.

Rogers, P. (2013) 'Security by "Remote Control": Can it Work?', *RUSI Journal* 158(3): 14–20.

Singer, P. W. (2006) 'Humanitarian Principles, Private Military Agents: Some Implications of the Privatised Military Industry for the Humanitarian Community', in V. Wheeler and A. Harmer (eds), *Resetting the Rules of Engagement: Trends and Issues in Military–Humanitarian Relations*, Humanitarian Policy Group report 22, London: Overseas Development Institute, pp. 67–79.

Spearin, C. (2000) 'A Private Security Panacea? A Specific Response to Mean Times', *Canadian Foreign Policy* 7(3): 67–80.

Spearin, C. (2001) *Ends and Means: Assessing the Impact of Commercialized Security on the Ottawa Convention*

Banning Anti-Personnel Mines, occasional paper 69, Toronto: Centre for International and Security Studies, York University.

Spearin, C. (2005) 'Humanitarians and Mercenaries: Partners in Security Governance?', in E. Krahmann (ed.), *New Threats and New Actors International Security*, New York: Palgrave, pp. 45–65.

Spearin, C. (2007) *Humanitarian Non-Governmental Organizations and International Private Security Companies: The 'Humanitarian' Challenges of Moulding a Marketplace*, policy paper no. 16, Geneva: Centre for the Democratic Control of Armed Forces.

Spearin, C. (2008) 'Private, Armed, and Humanitarian? States, NGOs, International Private Security Companies and Shifting Humanitarianism', *Security Dialogue* 39(4): 363–82.

Speers-Mears, E. (2009) *Private Military and Security Companies and Humanitarian Action*, professional development brief 1, Geneva: Security Management Initiative.

Stoddard, A., Harmer, A. and DiDomenico, V. (2008) *The Use of Private Security Providers and Services in Humanitarian Operations*, Humanitarian Policy Group report 27, London: Overseas Development Institute.

Van Brabant, K. (1999) 'Security Training: Where Are We Now?', *Forced Migration Review* 4: 7–10.

Van Brabant, K. (2000) *Operational Security Management in Violent Environments*, HPN good practice review 8, London: Overseas Development Institute.

12

PMSCs IN INTERNATIONAL SECURITY SECTOR REFORM

Sean McFate

In 2004, I was a member of a private military and security company (PMSC) team sent to Liberia. Our mission was deceptively simple: demobilize Liberia's old army and raise a new one. Curiously, our client was not Liberia but the US government. This was no easy task in a country that suffered 14 years of civil war under warlord-turned-president Charles Taylor in a conflict defined by child soldiers, blood diamonds, disappearances, rape and other gross human rights violations, some at the hands of the army. How exactly does one transform a military from a symbol of terror into an instrument of democracy? How can one make a policeman someone a child would run toward for safety rather than away from in fear? How does one convince a warlord to put down his gun and become an unemployed, hungry farmer? On the day that Liberia's post-Taylor government announced it would demobilize the standing army, the military band played 'Que Será Será' at the palace in front of the press and dignitaries.

Security sector reform (SSR) in conflict-affected states is a strategic imperative for international stability, since public security is the precondition of durable development. However, SSR is dangerous work because those that wield force in conflict countries are the de facto institutions of authority, and rewiring these power structures invites reprisal violence and armed conflict. However, not doing so may be worse for the people who live there. Professionalizing a fragile state's military and police promotes development, since corrupt security forces tend to devour the fruits of development. It is also the exit strategy for costly peacekeeping missions, since it creates the conditions where a state can secure itself without outside assistance. Lastly, it is critical for dealing with transnational threats, such as drug cartels or terrorist groups that require a regional approach. Building security capacity in partner nations across a region strengthens overall response, and stronger countries that ignore this face a difficult choice: deploy their troops abroad to do the job or permit minor threats to fester into major ones.

This vital task of SSR is increasingly privatized. This invites benefits and risks to employers, the country undergoing the reform, and international stability more generally. Benefits include cost effectiveness, innovation, and surge capacity. Risks involve a growing overdependence on the private sector to perform SSR, a key tool for global security. It also promotes the development of an international PMSC industry, a grave concern for some.

This chapter explains what SSR is, why is has become increasingly privatized, and some of the benefits and risks of outsourcing it. This is critical because SSR is vital to strategic victory in modern conflict. Many of today's armed conflicts are grievance based, and the solution lies not in decisive battlefield victory, like Waterloo, but in good governance, political inclusion, durable development and professional security services. Much of this rests on a professional security sector, hence the strategic importance of SSR. This chapter argues that privatizing SSR can significantly alter strategic outcomes.

Security sector reform

Security is the most fundamental service a state provides its citizens, and it is the foundation of legitimacy in social contract theory, starting with Thomas Hobbes. To guarantee this, a state must have the monopoly of force within its territorial boundaries to repel external threats and domestically enforce its rule of law. In fact, the state's exclusive claim to violence is the very essence of statehood for some, like Max Weber, who defined the state as 'a human community that (successfully) claims the monopoly of the legitimate use of physical force within a given territory' (Weber 2003). Variations of this definition remain widely used today, and states that cannot maintain a monopoly of force typically experience civil war, violent crime, trans-border incursions and threats emanating from ungoverned space. Such states are routinely described as 'weak', 'fragile' or 'failed.'

In contemporary international security practice, SSR is a tool that can help a country (re-)acquire the monopoly of force. In theory, it consolidates force within a territory and enables the authority – government or otherwise – to enforce its rule of law and defend itself against outside intrusions. SSR is the complex task of transforming the security sector into a professional, effective, legitimate, apolitical, and accountable sector that supports the rule of law and defends against foreign and domestic threats. SSR is not necessarily a programme for states however most SSR programmes to date support state governments. Lastly, SSR in conflict-affected states is deeply political, and technical approaches alone will fail. Programme failure risks coup d'état, war or worse.

Broadly speaking, the 'security sector' refers to those organizations and institutions that safeguard the state and its citizens from security threats. Examples of security actors include the police, military, border control, the judiciary, prisons, and the oversight institutions that manage them, such as the Ministry of Interior or Ministry of Defence. Not included in the security sector are non-statutory security forces that might threaten the state, such as liberation armies, armed criminal gangs, guerrilla forces, insurgents and political party militias. Such actors are usually disarmed, demobilized and reintegrated (DDR) into civil society, and occasionally they are integrated into the existing armed forces, although this is a dangerously myopic solution for warring parties, as the 2013 South Sudan civil war shows.

To date, creating truly successful SSR programmes remains a major challenge for the international community, despite the growing prevalence of peacekeeping missions and nation building around the world. There are several reasons for this. SSR is difficult to do, as Iraq, Afghanistan, East Timor, the Democratic Republic of the Congo (DRC) and other cases demonstrate. Also, there remains a significant theory to practice gap. SSR is generally conceived by academics, human rights lawyers and international development specialists without the benefit of experience, or voices from the field. They tend to produce normative SSR frameworks espousing human rights, democracy and sometimes near-utopian end states for the world's most dangerous places. To achieve this SSR vision, the United Nations (UN), donor states and a pantheon of global actors involved in SSR must work together in a holistic and seamless manner, which is an unreasonable expectation. There are many examples of this (Sedra 2010; Scheye 2010).

Consequently, there is no practicable doctrine, best practice or even common terminology.

The concept itself has no commonly accepted definition and has many names: security and justice reform, security sector governance, security sector development, security force assistance, foreign internal defence, security system transformation. Few practical models for SSR have been developed, despite many SSR programmes over the past 20 years, perpetuating cycles of violence in fragile states and prolonging costly peacekeeping missions. The Organization for Economic Co-operation and Development (OECD) Development Assistance Committee (DAC) has attempted to take a lead in SSR implementation with its *Handbook on Security System Reform: Supporting Security and Justice* (OECD DAC 2007). However, its approach is deeply flawed and consequently remains unused, in part because development theorists wrote most of the manual without the benefit of practical experience or security expertise. As a result, the Handbook makes little sense to military and police professionals, who frequently execute SSR programmes in the field. Additionally, key components of SSR are missing, such as how to conduct human rights vetting of security forces' candidates. Most would never dream of putting a cop on the streets of London or enlist a soldier in the US Army without a background check, yet this is done daily in SSR programmes around the world; the Handbook remains curiously silent on the matter. Lastly, the Handbook lacks concrete operational steps on how to conduct SSR, the purpose of any handbook. Owing to these and other problems, the OECD DAC Handbook remains largely ignored in the field.

The UN has suffered similar setbacks. In 2007, the UN established a SSR unit to bridge the theory to practice gap, but this office has yet to produce an actual handbook or field manual instructing practitioners on how to create a SSR programme. Instead of concrete advice, it offers platitudes that are difficult to operationalize in the field, such as, 'support in the area of security sector reform must be anchored on national ownership' and that the UN approach to security sector reform must be 'flexible and tailored to the country, region and/or specific environment in which reform is taking place' (UN SSR, 2008). Regrettably the SSR unit offers no guidance – concrete or otherwise – on how to achieve these laudable yet nebulous goals. Like the OECD, this failure is partly because UN bureaucrats and former academics manage the unit rather than seasoned experts who have successfully executed SSR in the field. More scholar-practitioners are needed to bridge the theory to practice divide.

Unfortunately, practitioners from the US are not much better. The US's nearly unprecedented efforts at SSR in Iraq and Afghanistan are failures, as the emergence of the Islamic State of Iraq and al-Sham (ISIS) and Afghanistan's 'hollow force' demonstrate. Despite the importance of SSR to the US's strategy of building partnership capacity (BPC) for regional stability, there is a disappointingly lack of focus on the topic. For example, the US Army devotes but a single chapter to SSR in both Field Manual 3-24, *Counterinsurgency*, and Field Manual 3-07, *Stability Operations* despite the centrality of the idea to these tasks (US Army 2007, 2009). Like the UN, these documents only discuss abstract principles of SSR rather than operationalizing the idea, which is the singular objective of military field manuals. Military personnel are routinely deployed to the conflict zones and expected to manage SSR programmes with almost no training or instruction, which is why these programmes fail.

Perhaps the widest point of disagreement among experts is what constitutes 'security.' Definitions range from traditional notions that can be described as 'hard security': protecting people, places and things through coercion and, if necessary, force. This perspective is common among military and law enforcement officers. The development and academic communities have broadened the idea of security into what might be labelled a variety of 'soft security' categories, such as food security, energy security and human security. However, these ideas remain unproven in the realm of SSR practice. While lack of food and energy may be contributing factors to armed conflict, SSR programmes do not attempt to rectify food shortages or energy blackouts: that would be an overreach of programme scope and best left to other development projects. Human security is also a contested concept in International Relations, not easy to define and difficult to operationalize within SSR. The lack of a clear distinction between security and safety makes nearly everything a SSR task, which is inappropriate in theory and infeasible in practice.

Consequently, SSR is often designed and conducted from a 'hard security' perspective, and this is indeed the approach of most PMSCs and their employers. One of the challenges of this approach is that it can devolve into a facile 'train and equip' programme, which only creates better-dressed soldiers who shoot straighter. Examples of this include US programmes in Iraq, Afghanistan and Sahel countries, like Mali – all of which have experienced SSR failure, endangering the people and the state. SSR is more comprehensive than traditional train and equip programmes, since it encompasses creating new institutions, facilitating force structure decisions,[1] formulating national security strategy and doctrine, recruiting and vetting new forces, constructing military bases and road infrastructure, selecting leadership, establishing oversight mechanisms within ministries and parliament, and many other complex tasks that go well beyond simple training and equipping troops. A 'train and equip' campaign will not transform a security sector, and such programmes alone invite failure.

Raising security forces for profit

SSR has proven a growth industry for PMSCs. This development was largely driven by the US' wars in Iraq and Afghanistan and the country's penchant for hiring these firms, but the trend actually started earlier. In the 1990s, the US licensed MPRI to work for Croatia and Bosnia, where it trained and equipped their forces for over US$150 million (Singer 2003: 128). The State Department contracted DynCorp International to provide 'peace verifiers' in Kosovo, train Haitian police and eradicate coco plants as a part of Plan Colombia (*Newsweek* 1999).It also hired DynCorp International and Pacific Architects and Engineers (PAE) to raise an army for Liberia in 2005. Today's armed forces of Liberia are entirely a private sector creation. The private sector has the power to alter SSR outcomes, hence it is an important area of study.

The term PMSC covers a broad range of companies and activities, with a surfeit of definitions. In this chapter, PMSCs are defined as expeditionary conflict entrepreneurs structured as companies that use lethal force or train others to do so. They can be further divided into two types: *mercenaries* and *military enterprisers*.

Mercenaries are private armies that operate as free agents in an open market for force. They can conduct autonomous military campaigns, offensive operations and force projection, and generally select clientele based on profit margin rather than ideology. At present, there are no large mercenary firms but they have existed in the recent past, such as Executive Outcomes. This South African company conducted independent military campaigns in Africa during the 1990s, notably in Angola and Sierra Leone (Shearer 1998: 73; Coker 1998: 106–7). Executive Outcomes provided its own combat units, air forces, global supply chain and so forth to defeat the enemy. Currently, mercenary firms are largely absent from the market for force, although some firms, like Blackwater, approach the mercenary end of the PMSC spectrum.

Distinct from mercenaries, military enterprisers raise armies rather than command them. Military enterprisers augment national militaries via a private-public partnership in a mediated market for force, rather than a free market. In the Thirty Years War, for instance, military enterprisers trained, equipped and fielded whole regiments to fight for their client. Most modern PMSCs are military enterprisers and make their money not by deploying their own armies but by making them for someone else, a SSR task. For example, the US has relied on contractors to develop the Afghan National Army and the Afghan National Police, even awarding DynCorp International a contract worth up to $1 billion to train the police (Government Accountability Office 2011, 2012). Most PMSCs that conduct SSR are military enterprisers rather than mercenary firms, although the most capable firms possess the requisite competences to work in either category, as the market demands.

The benefits of privatizing SSR

There are many benefits to using PMSCs for SSR. While the US military was busy chasing insurgents in Iraq and Afghanistan, it left substantial portions of SSR in those countries to the private sector. And the private sector rose to meet the challenge, developing new approaches that are superior to their public sector counter-parts, especially in terms of cost effectiveness, innovation, and surge capacity. To date, only the US has widely used this industry for SSR, although this is changing.

Private force is often cheaper than public force, although this is sometimes disputed (see Chapter 7, this volume). Renting forces is less expensive than owning them, unless a state is constantly at war, which is why much of military history is privatized (Lynch and Walsh 2000: 133). Examining the cost-effectiveness of PMCs in Iraq, the US Congressional Budget Office (CBO), an official government agency charged with reviewing congressional budget issues, found private military contractors to be cheaper than the US Army. According to CBO estimates, the Army's total cost of operating an infantry unit in Iraq was $110 million, while hiring the same size unit from Blackwater to perform the same tasks during the same time period was only $99 million. In peacetime, the cost differential jumps even more. The cost of maintaining an army infantry unit at home is $60 million, whereas the cost of Blackwater is nothing, since the firm's contract would be terminated (CBO 2008: 17). Moreover, lifetime costs for veterans' benefits are significant for the US government, especially following a decade of war, while they are non-existent if contractors are used. Maintaining a standing army is always more expensive than utilizing rental ones.

In addition to efficiency, the private sector is more innovative too, able to plug some of the theory to practice gap that plagues public sector SSR efforts. While some observers question the quality of innovation in public-private partnerships (Markusen 2003; Minow 2003; Verkuil 2007), the idea is an old one, dating back to former UK Prime Minister Margret Thatcher and US President Ronald Reagan, who mainstreamed the policy. Faced with ballooning federal deficits, Reagan established the Private Sector Survey on Cost Control to eradicate waste and inefficiency in the federal government. Its chairman, J. Peter Grace, concluded that 'government-run enterprises lack the driving forces of marketplace competition, which promote tight, efficient operations' (cited in Frank 2008). The solution was privatization: 'Turn government operations over to the private sector and you get innovation, efficiency, flexibility' (ibid.). This logic contributed to the rise of the PMSC industry, with some justification in the face of turgid bureaucracies. Or, in the words of Robert Komer (1972), a key figure in the US counterinsurgency campaign during the Vietnam War, the US lost the war because, 'Bureaucracy does its thing.'

Liberia is a good example of innovation in SSR, as that country's armed forces is a private sector product. Take, for example, human rights vetting of candidates for military service. Curiously, neither the OECD DAC, UN nor US address vetting in SSR, even though they would never dream of putting a cop or soldier on the streets of London or New York City without background checks. Currently, none of these actors have a systematic method for vetting security recruits in fragile states like Afghanistan or the DRC. Consequently, criminals and insurgents 'infiltrate' new military and police units, corrupting them and delegitimizing them in the public's eyes. In 2012, one in seven of all NATO deaths in Afghanistan occurred at the hands of the very Afghan troops the coalition is trying to help and train (*Economist* 2012). Claiming that security forces were 'infiltrated' by undesirables is disingenuous when rigorous vetting was not performed in the first place, yet this is the standard for public sector actors like the OECD DAC, UN and US.

By contrast, DynCorp International created an innovative vetting programme in Liberia for that country's new military which the International Crisis Group (ICG), a large NGO not typically friendly to the PMSC industry, called 'a notable success – the best, several experts said, they had witnessed anywhere in the world' (ICG 2009). It combined novel cross-cultural investigative techniques based on international best practices and human rights norms to judge a candidate's character and capacity for a position of trust, and to identify potential risks for security reasons. It also created a national public vetting system, allowing the public to identify anonymously security forces candidates who may have committed human rights violations or crimes in the past, such as acts of terrorism. Like most post-conflict countries, Liberia had few (if any) credible public records available to vet against. Accordingly, DynCorp gathered, analysed and prioritized all available public records in the region from non-traditional sources, helping investigators verify the identity and qualifications of candidates. There are more examples of private sector innovation too, such as embedding literacy classes instruction into basic training, and prioritizing civics and rule of law on par with marksmanship and tactics (McFate 2013).

Companies are also more nimble than their government counter-parts, and offer 'surge capacity' to their employers. Surge capacity is the ability to quickly marshal resources and mobilize large numbers of personnel to difficult locations. This is of special value to employers that have failed to anticipate problems, as was the case with the US in Iraq and Afghanistan. Since the Pentagon had not planned to keep large numbers of troops in these conflict zones for a long period of time, it relied on the private sector to do so. PMSCs were able to 'surge' personnel to these difficult places by tapping into networks and databases, running job fairs in the US, and contracting 'cheap' labour from developing world (Hammes 2010). Private companies managed to find people, hire them, and move them into country in a way that the US bureaucracy personnel management system would never allow for its employees.

The risks of privatizing SSR

However, there are significant risks to privatizing SSR. Outsourcing is more than a simple cost-benefit analysis, and the privatization of SSR heralds a growing dependency by governments on the private sector to conduct stability operations and win wars. During World War II, contractors accounted for only 10 per cent of the military workforce compared to 50 per cent in the Iraq war – a 1:1 ratio of contractors to military personnel (Government Accountability Office 2008; Schwartz 2010: 5). This ratio was even higher in the Afghanistan war. In 2010, the US deployed 175,000 troops and 207,000 contractors in war zones. Contractors are also paying the ultimate price, accounting for one-quarter of all US fatalities in the past decade of war. In the first two quarters of 2010 alone, contractor deaths represented more than half (53 per cent) of all fatalities (Schooner and Swan 2010). For example, most PMSC contractors killed in 2012 were training Afghan security forces, a SSR mission. Should this trend continue, countries would be strategically dependent on the whims of the marketplace.

SSR is more important to achieving 'victory' in modern warfare than simple brute force. Ambassadors signing peace treaties on battleships do not settle insurgencies, terror campaigns, civil wars and other forms or what is commonly called 'irregular warfare.' Many of these conflicts are grievance based, and the solution lies in good governance, political inclusion, durable development and professional security services. This makes programmes like SSR vital to strategic victory in modern conflict. Despite this, strong militaries like the US continue to ignore SSR – outsourcing it instead – in favour of traditional war fighting: hunting and killing the enemy. US military campaigns proceed in five phases:

- phase 0 is conflict prevention;
- phase 1 is the decision to deter or engage the enemy;
- phase 2 is seizing the initiative to outmanoeuvre the enemy;
- phase 3 is decisive operations to defeat the enemy on the field of battle; and
- phase 4 is postconflict transition and stability operations.

(Wald 2006: 72–5)

In 'regular' warfare, decisive victory occurs on the battlefield in phase 3. Accordingly, during the Iraq and Afghanistan campaigns, the US military concentrated on phase 3 combat operations to win the victory while it contracted out most of the 'lesser' phase 0 and phase 4 tasks, such as SSR.

However, in today's warfare, military success in phase 3 matters little. There is no greater metaphor of this than the image of President George W. Bush standing on the deck of the US aircraft carrier *Abraham Lincoln* and declaring 'victory' with a large 'Mission Accomplished' banner behind him after phase 3 combat operations ended in Iraq, just a few weeks after the invasion began. Few observers today would claim that the US had accomplished its mission on that brisk day in 2003, and the US remained embroiled in Iraqi internal warfare well after Bush's departure from the White House. Victory is more dependent on successful phase 0 and phase 4 operations, which often involve SSR. To this end, in 2009 President Barack Obama announced a 'civilian surge' to Afghanistan and established the Civilian Response Corps to accomplish these tasks, but this initiative fizzled, because there was already a robust civilian presence in Afghanistan conducting stability operations: contractors. Tens of thousands of contractors were directing phase 0 and phase 4 operations, while the Civilian Response Corps mustered only one hundred full-time personnel (US Department of State 2010). In fact, many of the specialized skills needed for stability operations can now only be found in the private sector and are considered the proprietary knowledge of PMSCs, and therefore protected under copyright law. If governments want to have access to these skills, they *must* hire the PMSCs that perform them, because the military no longer has an organic capability of its own to perform SSR.

The US is correspondingly vulnerable to strategic defeat when contractors fail. Nisour Square is the clearest case of this, as the tactical failure of Blackwater became a strategic liability for the US throughout the Middle East. But other examples exist, too. In 2010, the NATO-led International Security Assistance Force (ISAF) mission in Afghanistan determined that PMSCs had failed in their contracts to train and mentor the Afghan police. General Stanley McChrystal, then-commander of ISAF, stated that the police were one of the most crucial elements of his campaign plan, and a DOD Inspector General investigation into the matter concluded that PMSCs' failure 'hampers the ability of DOD to fulfil its role in the emerging national strategy' (Hammes 2010: 9; US Department of Defense 2010: 8). By outsourcing victory and defeat, the US and other countries like it are increasingly becoming vulnerable to the ebb and flow of the market place.

More importantly, out of work PMSCs and their personnel seek SSR employment elsewhere, such as Somalia. After the Nisour Square shootings, Erik Prince, founder of Blackwater, left the US for Abu Dhabi, where he has become a deal maker within the industry, connecting companies with clients and vice versa. He helped the South African PMSC Saracen International win contracts from Somalia's beleaguered government to protect its leaders and also train Somali forces to fend off pirates and Islamic militants. Saracen was created from remnants of Executive Outcomes and was managed by Lafras Luitingh, a former officer in South Africa's Civil Cooperation Bureau, a covert government-sponsored hit squad that operated during the apartheid era and is now defunct.

Saracen operated independently of all international and multilateral frameworks in Somalia, and little is known about the firm's intentions other than profit motive. Between May 2010 and February 2011, it trained and equipped fighters in an attempt to create one of 'the best-equipped indigenous military forces anywhere in Somalia,' according to a UN report (UN Security Council 2011: 276). Saracens' training camp near Bosaaso was the best-equipped military facility in Somalia after the UN bases in Mogadishu. The company planned to establish a force approximately one thousand strong, equipped with three transport aircraft, three reconnaissance aircraft, two transport helicopters, and two light helicopters. The maritime component of the force would be equipped with one command and control vessel, two logistical support vessels, and three rigid-hulled inflatable boats for rapid deployment and intervention. This illustrates how companies empowered by SSR can become mercenary and have potentially destabilizing impacts. It also shows that observers who think the PMSC industry is exclusively linked to the US are dangerously mistaken; this industry will grow, indigenize and proliferate, as clients seek security in an insecure world.

Conclusion

In summary, SSR is a critical function to global stability, and it is increasingly outsourced to PMSCs. There are many benefits of this arrangement, including cost effectiveness, innovation, and surge capacity. However, there are also risks, namely an overdependence on the private sector to perform SSR, a critical building block of regional security in the world's most dangerous places. This leaves states like the US strategically vulnerable to the behaviours of the marketplace. Additionally, a growing number of PMCSs are seeking jobs beyond the sight of the US, UN or state system in general. Perhaps the most risky aspect of PMSCs is that they can raise an army at all. The Liberian military is a private sector invention; PMSCs created it without significant assistance from governments beyond payment. Moreover, its relative success stands in stark contrast to failed SSR efforts by the US in Iraq and Afghanistan, or the UN in the DRC and East Timor. More jarring, if a firm has the capability to raise an army then it also has the skill to command it for its own interests. The line between military enterpriser and mercenary is thin, based largely on market conditions.

Note

1   In military parlance, a 'force structure' is the organization and hierarchy of units within an army, from the general staff down to the basic infantry squad. It is similar to a massive organizational chart for an army, and it outlines how military personnel, weapons and equipment are organized for the operations.

Bibliography

CBO (2008) *Contractors' Support of US Operations in Iraq*, Washington, DC: US Congressional Budget Office.
Coker, C. (1999) 'Outsourcing War', *Cambridge Review of International Affairs* 13(1): 95–113.
Economist (2012) 'Green-on-Blue Blues: Afghan Soldiers Increasingly Turn on Their NATO Colleagues', *Economist* 1 September, www.economist.com/node/21561943.

Frank, T. (2008) 'Government by Contractor Is a Disgrace: Many Jobs Are Best Left to Federal Workers', *Wall Street Journal* 26 November, http://online.wsj.com/news/articles/SB122765980278958481.

Government Accountability Office (2008) *DOD Needs to Reexamine Its Extensive Reliance on Contractors and Continue to Improve Management and Oversight*, GAO-08-572T, Washington, DC: Government Accountability Office.

Government Accountability Office (2011) *Afghanistan Security: Afghan Army Growing, but Additional Trainers Needed; Long-Term Costs Not Determined*, GAO-11-66, Washington, DC: Government Accountability Office.

Government Accountability Office (2012) *Afghanistan Security: Department of Defense Effort to Train Afghan Police Relies on Contractor Personnel to Fill Skill and Resource Gaps*, GAO-12-293R, Washington, DC: Government Accountability Office.

Hammes, T. X. (2010) *Private Contractors: The Good, the Bad, and the Strategic Impact*, Washington, DC: National Defense University Press.

ICG (2009) *Liberia: Uneven Progress in Security Sector Reform*, Africa Report 148, Dakar/Brussels: International Crisis Group.

Jackson, P. and Albrecht, P. (2011) *Reconstructing Security after Conflict: Security Sector Reform in Sierra Leone*, London: Palgrave Macmillan.

Komer, R. W. (1972) *Bureaucracy Does Its Thing*, Washington, DC: RAND Corporation.

Lynch, T. and Walsh, A. J. (2000) 'The Good Mercenary?', *Journal of Political Philosophy* 8(2): 133–53.

Markusen, A. R. (2003) 'The Case Against Privatizing National Security', *Governance: An International Journal of Policy, Administration, and Institutions* 16(4): 471–501.

McFate, S. (2013) *Building Better Armies: An Insider's Account of Liberia*, Carlisle Barracks, PA: Strategic Studies Institute, United States Army War College.

Minow, M. (2003) 'Public and Private Partnerships: Accounting for the New Religion', *Harvard Law Review* 116: 1229–70.

Newsweek (1999) 'On the Ground: DynCorp and Other US Firms Provide US Peace Verifiers to Kosovo', *Newsweek* February 15, www.highbeam.com/doc/1G1-53865787.html.

OECD DAC (2007) *The OECD DAC Handbook on Security System Reform: Supporting Security and Justice*, Paris: Development Assistance Committee, Organization for Economic Co-Operation and Development.

Scheye, E. (2010) *Realism and Pragmatism in Security Sector Development*, Paris: OECD.

Schooner, S. L. and Swan, C. (2010) *Contractors and the Ultimate Sacrifice*, Public Law and Legal Theory working paper series no. 512, Washington, DC: George Washington University Law School.

Schwartz, M. (2010) *Department of Defense Contractors in Iraq and Afghanistan: Background and Analysis*, Washington, DC: Congressional Research Service.

Sedra, M. (2006) 'Security Sector Reform in Afghanistan: The Slide towards Expediency', *International Peacekeeping* 13(1): 94–110.

Sedra, M. (ed.) (2010) *The Future of Security Sector Reform*. Waterloo, Canada: Centre for International Governance Innovation.

Shearer, D. (1998) 'Outsourcing War', *Foreign Policy* 112: 68–81.

Singer, P. W. (2003) *Corporate Warriors: The Rise of the Privatized Military Industry*, Ithaca, NY: Cornell University Press.

UN Security Council (2010) *Report of the United Nations Monitoring Group on Somalia and Eritrea Submitted in Accordance with Resolution 1916*, S/2011/433, New York: United Nations.

UN SSR (2008) 'Principles', http://unssr.unlb.org/SSR/Principles.aspx.

US Army (2007) *The US Army/Marine Corps Counterinsurgency Field Manual: US Army Field Manual No. 3-24: Marine Corps Warfighting*, publication no. 3-33.5, Chicago, IL: University of Chicago Press.

US Army (2009) *United States Army Field Manual No. 3-07: Stability Operations*, Washington, DC: Department of the Army.

US Department of Defense (2010) *DOD Obligations and Expenditures of Funds Provided to the Department of State for the Training and Mentoring of the Afghan National Police*, report no. D-2010-042, Washington, DC: United State Department of Defense.

US Department of Defense (2011) *Handbook for Military Support to Rule of Law and Security Sector Reform*, Washington, DC: US Government.

US Department of State (2010) 'Civilian Response Corps Reaches 100 Active Members', press release, 16 April, www.state.gov/r/pa/prs/ps/2010/04/140346.htm.

Verkuil, P. (2007) *Outsourcing Sovereignty: Why Privatization of Government Functions Threatens Democracy and What We Can Do about It*, Cambridge: Cambridge University Press.

Wald, C. F. (2006) 'New Thinking at USEUCOM: The Phase Zero Campaign', *Joint Forces Quarterly* 43(1): 72–5.

Weber, M. (2003) 'Politics as a Vocation' (trans. H. H. Gerth and C. W. Mills), in H. H. Gerth and C. W. Mills (eds), *From Max Weber: Essays in Sociology*, Abingdon: Routledge, pp. 77–128.

PART III

Debates about private security

13

GLOBAL SECURITY ASSEMBLAGES

Michael C. Williams

The study of security privatization and the emergence of a global private security industry is often framed in opposition to state authority and the public provision of security. As the sector has expanded and globalized, much academic debate has been about the extent to which the state is losing power and sovereignty, and thus getting weaker as the private is getting stronger. This was, and remains, a particularly strong narrative about security privatization in non-Western countries, where the rise of the private has often been treated as an indication – and sometimes also a cause – of state weakness and even failure. On occasion this argument is articulated as a downward spiral, where the state's inability to secure its territory and citizens is seen to have spurred the initial growth of private actors, with their existence in turn further undermining the strength, legitimacy and authority of the state. In Europe and North America, state sovereignty and authority has been an equally central topic of debate, but has taken a slightly different form. Rather than fears of incipient state failure, the rise of the private has here often been analysed as part of new forms of networked governance or multi-level governance. In this view, the state has outsourced some of its security functions and much as it may or may not be weakened by this, it continues to rule and regulate at a distance, in collaboration with a plethora of private non-state actors.

In both these framings, despite their differences, the nature of the state remains the unaltered – it might be weaker or stronger, it might lose or gain power, but as a basic unit or category of analysis it is unchanged and ontologically intact. This chapter suggests that such approaches cannot adequately capture what is at stake in security privatization. Both theoretically and empirically, the diverse processes of security privatization are part of a profound transformation of the state and its security functions, and there is no way of capturing these changes or their implications in a vocabulary that can speak only in terms of a stronger or weaker state. Instead what we are witnessing is a reconfiguring of the state and a re-articulation in different ways of the traditional distinctions between the public and the private and the global and the local. A powerful approach to these developments is to see them as the emergence of global security assemblages (Abrahamsen and Williams 2011). Global security assemblages are complex structures where a range of different global and local, public and private security agents and normativities interact, cooperate and compete to produce new institutions, practices and forms of security governance. These assemblages inhabit national settings but are simultaneously stretched across national boundaries in terms of actors, knowledge, technologies, norms and values. Within them, state power is certainly reconfigured, but it is not always and necessarily weakened. Instead, novel security institutions and practices that cross the traditional boundaries between public and private, global and local are assembled, and the relative power of the diverse actors within the assemblage remains to be discovered.

This chapter begins with an explanation of the concept of assemblage and the distinctiveness of assemblage thinking. Turning to global security assemblages, it explores the processes that led to their emergence. One of the key insights of an assemblage approach is that assemblages are infinitely diverse, and hence it cannot start not from the assumption that the state is at the centre of security delivery and governance. Instead, it calls for empirically grounded theory, that is, a careful analysis of how different security actors, discourse, values, technologies, and so on, are assembled and brought together in different localities. In order to give a flavour of such theorizing from the ground up, the chapter introduces the Cape Town City Improvement District in South Africa, a global security assemblage that has produced new security practices and institutions and where the politics of protection – the questions of who gets secured and how – is stretched across the boundaries of the nation-state. The chapter concludes that because an analysis centred on assemblages opens up the possibility that the state and the security field might be differently assembled in different places, it is not only more sensitive to place and specificity, it also allows for a deeper understanding of the politics of security and the forces and histories that produce different global security assemblages.

Assembling security

Assemblage thinking is driven in large part by dissatisfaction with the dominant ontologies that have characterized social theory, including political science, International Relations and Security Studies. In particular, this relates to state centrism and the reification of the Weberian state within these disciplines – a commitment to the state that defines it as an entity with a monopoly of legitimate force within a given territory. Social scientists (and other actors, whether they recognize it or not) use theory to make sense of the world, to order complex social phenomena into categories and causal mechanisms, sometimes forcing the social world to conform to preconceived definitions and categories. Such theories can become straitjackets, deprived of explanatory value and unable to capture rapid change and social transformations on a global scale. This has been the case in perceptions of security privatization, where the idea that the growth of private and global security firms must necessarily come at the expense of national public actors has often seemed self-evident. But like much that at first glance seems self-evident, the reality is considerably more complex. Analyses of global security assemblages seek to capture that complexity.

In rejecting totalities and reified units of analysis such as state, society or capitalism, assemblage thinking focuses instead on provisional and historically contingent relations between heterogeneous elements, both human and non-human (Latour 2007). As such, assemblage thinking is characterized both by a particular kind of critique and by a particular orientation towards academic enquiry (McFarlane and Anderson 2011). As a critique, it questions the taken-for-granted nature of concepts such as state, society, and agency, and instead embraces an orientation and ethos that is more receptive to difference and emergence. The attraction of assemblage thinking is accordingly a more open and agnostic approach to the social world; the area of study is not predetermined by existing theories and categories, but is instead approached as something to be discovered in the way that different elements are fitted together into contingent systems of varying durability (Deleuze and Guattari 2003). As a new way of studying the global, assemblages are particularly attractive as they draw attention to multi-scalar connections, abandoning strict dichotomies between the global and the local, the international and the domestic. It approaches the social world as one analytical field, and shows how assemblages both de-territorialize and re-territorialize (i.e. the assemblage is not wholly determined by its location within national settings but is instead indicative of the formation of new geographies of power).

That said, there is no single 'assemblage theory', nor one 'assemblage methodology' – indeed, to some assemblage thinking does not amount to a theory, but rather 'a repository of methods and ontological stances towards the social' (Acuto and Curtis 2014b: 3). This chapter approaches assemblages primarily as a methodology and as a process of formation, focusing on the concrete investigations that assemblages thinking makes possible and leaving aside the more philosophical stance implied, although the two are of course interlinked in numerous ways (see Acuto and Curtis 2014a). In particular, this chapter draws on Saskia Sassen's (2006) work on globalization to explain the emergence of global security assemblages. For Sassen, globalization is first and foremost a process of realignment inside the state, not a process of 'outside' forces eroding a territorially distinct 'inside'. As she observes in her analysis of the shifting relationship between territory, authority, and rights, it is the national state that has made today's global era possible. Many of the activities, institutions and structures now identified with globalization came into existence at the direct instigation of national governments, and continue to operate through transformed national institutions that enable and facilitate their operation. More specifically, Sassen suggests that the development of contemporary global structures involves three key elements: a process of 'disassembly' in which functions previously carried out by public actors are transferred to private actors; the development of 'capacities' by private actors that allow them to act at a global level; and a process of 'reassembly' whereby these new actors and capabilities become part of global assemblages that are embedded in national settings but operate at a global scale. In this way, the disassembly of the national becomes constitutive of the global, in that 'the territorial sovereign state, with its territorial fixity and exclusivity, represents a set of capabilities that eventually enable the formation or evolution of particular global systems' (Sassen 2006: 21).

This partial self-disassembly of the state, combined with the diverse social, economic, and political dynamics that characterize late modernity (see Introduction, this volume), have facilitated the spectacular growth and globalization of the private security market detailed throughout this Handbook. While the public security sector was perhaps initially more resistant to the privatization ethos than services such as health and education, the delivery of security is now increasingly privatized, outsourced, or delivered in various forms of public–private partnerships. It is important to emphasize, however, that this expansion of private security is not a purely functional response to state restructuring and the outsourcing of previously public services, but is also linked in important ways to social and cultural transformations, including changing attitudes toward crime and punishment, and the pervasiveness of various mentalities of risk. This permissive and accommodating ideational environment has allowed some private security companies to acquire the capacities (e.g. analytic abilities and appropriate skills; organizational scale and structure; material and technological resources) to operate at a global level – whether in military support operations or in the more everyday protection of 'life and assets'. The largest companies, such as G4S and Securitas, now span continents, their workforce dwarfing that of most national armies (see Abrahamsen and Williams 2011; Chapter 5, this volume). They utilize more or less the same security technologies and approaches across the globe, reflecting the commodification of security as a technology delinked from the politics of specific localities.

As a result, it is increasingly difficult and empirically inaccurate to describe and analyse security provision and governance as contained within the boundaries of the nation-state.

Worldwide, from isolated resources enclaves to densely populated urban centres, the production and governance of security (and insecurity) involves a plethora of actors and norms, some local, some global, some public and some private. As a descriptive term, assemblage captures these new geographies of power that are simultaneously global and national, public and private: diverse hybrid structures that inhabit national settings but are stretched across national boundaries in terms of actors, knowledges, technologies, norms and values. While this may in certain settings be an indication of state weakness or pose a threat to the state, this is not universally the case – as the extensive private security sector in the United States shows. Such interpretations overlook the many ways in which the empowerment of the private security sector is directly linked to the shifts in governance and to transformations inside the state, and often operates with the active endorsement and encouragement of state authorities. Moreover, they risk reifying the state and seeing any deviation from the state monopoly over security as necessarily marking a decline it its authority and legitimacy. Global security assemblages do not represent a mechanistic process of disassembly and reassembly with uniform impacts. Instead they are better understood as boundary fields, in that they are neither private, nor public, neither local, nor global, but mark analytical spaces that lie between these common distinctions and require their own empirical investigation.

The notion of the global assemblage has been invoked to analyse the implications of security privatization in a range of diverse settings, including airports (Lippert and O'Connor 2003; Berndtsson and Stern 2011), urban environments (Abrahamsen and Williams 2011), surveillance (Haggerty and Ericson 2000) and resource extraction (Abrahamsen and Williams 2009, 2011). While by no means uniform in their interpretation and utilization of assemblage thinking, these studies forge a new path by drawing attention to the multiple possibilities and diversities of emerging security formations and their implications for the politics of security.

Security and the global city

As a brief illustration, consider urban security in Cape Town, South Africa, a global security assemblage that has not only produced new security institutions and practices but that is also almost constantly in the process of formation as it interacts with the complex politics of South African security. Following the end of apartheid, private security expanded at a phenomenal rate in South Africa, partly as a result of widespread fear of crime and an actual rise in crime. South Africa's security policy also became increasingly influenced by global trends in policing and public management, which led to a focus on outsourcing, privatization, and contracting of specialist services. Faced with dwindling public resources and escalating crime rates, the South African Police Services (SAPS) and the government chose to accept and incorporate the private sector into their security strategies. In the words of SAPS, there was a need for 'the police, the public, elected officials, government, business and other agencies to work in partnership to address crime and community safety' (quoted in Berg 2004: 227). The Department of Community Safety (2006: 6) similarly concluded that the 'SA Police Service can no longer be seen as the sole agency responsible for fighting crime … other sectors of society with a force multiplying capacity must be called on to support the SA Police Service in their efforts'. As part of this transformation, some tasks have been specifically assigned as 'private' – police stations across South Africa are now, for example, guarded by private security companies in recognition that commercial guards are cheaper than police officers – while much day-to-day policing has been re-framed as a partnership with a multiplicity of private actors and local communities.

The Cape Town Central City Improvement District (CCID) initiative is one of the most extensive examples of such public–private policing partnerships. Like so-called Business

Improvement Districts that can be found in many major cities around the world, the CCID is a non-profit organization that seeks to make the city safe and secure, and to promote business and economic activity. It is an initiative of the Cape Town Partnership, a not-for-profit company founded by the City Council and the local business community, with an initial aim to reverse urban decay and capital flight from the city centre to surrounding suburbs and business parks. The CCID is funded through an additional tax on business property owners; its primary concern has been to increase security, and in 2006 when this fieldwork was undertaken, approximately 51 percent of the CCID's budget was allocated to security.

The CCID is in effect a large-scale partnership policing effort aimed at making central Cape Town safe and secure; an international city and a first class tourist destination. When the CCID started in 2000, Group4Securicor (G4S) was contracted as the main security provider.[1] At the start of the initiative, the CCID security force consisted of only seven officers, but it rapidly expanded to a total of six patrol vehicles, ten horse mounted officers and 60 foot patrol officers providing a 24-hour security presence in the city centre. At night, this force soon patrolled with 40 officers, supported by six vehicles. As a result, the presence of security personnel in the city increased significantly, and during daytime, with CCID vehicles and foot patrols frequently encountered throughout Cape Town's relatively compact city centre.

To a significant extent, the security of Cape Town was devolved to the largest security company in the world. The visibility of G4S's mounted, foot, and mobile patrols far exceeded the visibility of the police. Both the City Police and the SAPS concentrated their efforts in the poorer areas of town, where crime rates are highest, and the City Police dedicated only two mobile patrols to the city centre. Moreover, the police ceased to conduct foot patrols. Yet it would be incorrect to perceive the police as absent from Cape Town's security arrangement. G4S officers worked in close collaboration with the police, especially the City Police, but also the SAPS. CCID/G4S branded patrol vehicles included a City Police officer, although there were no police markings on the car. The CCID security patrols were also linked to the City Police control room by radio. Furthermore, G4S operated the Strategic Surveillance Unit (SSU), the control room that supervised Cape Town's 170 close circuit television cameras – cameras initially financed by the association 'Business Against Crime', and then donated to the city. Manned by around 50 G4S officers, reinforced by eight City Police officers, and in direct contact with the SAPS as well as the City Police, the SSU ensured mobile response to incidents. As part of the move towards community policing, G4S also participated in weekly sector policing fora to identify potential problems, share information and co-ordinate the provision of security with the SAPS and the City Police. G4S officers in the CCID also frequently provided support to police operations, for example, by providing perimeter security when police are searching a building or area. This is indicative of the breadth of change, seen also in the other CIDs around Cape Town and in other South African cities. The result was an assemblage of public and private, global and local security actors that G4S managers in interviews often referred to as a 'paradigm shift' in security provision.

At this point, the CCID was a striking example of the contemporary dissolution of the 'state, territory, authority' triptych that informs and underpins so many studies in International Relations (Barnett 2001). In Cape Town, as elsewhere on the African continent and across the globe, security governance, in the sense of the authoritative setting and enforcement of collective norms, increasingly transcends the nation state and includes private actors in extensive and influential roles. Cape Town's security arrangement was a global assemblage, made up of a multiplicity of actors, resources, discourses, norms and values. Drawing on a broad range of capacities and discourses for its empowerment, the CCID changed the landscape of policing and security in the city, giving private actors and their corporate sponsors new roles and influence – and arguably disempowering others, such as street children, peddlers and informal vendors, who also make their living in the urban environment but who are frequently perceived as vectors of insecurity by city managers, business owners and tourists alike. But this transformation did not represent the simple privatization of downtown Cape Town, or the exclusion of public authorities and police forces. Instead, it marked a new set of structures that were at once public and private, global and local, whose assembly into the CCID structure profoundly affected the security provision and politics of the city.

As emphasized earlier in this chapter, one of the benefits of assemblage thinking is its ability to capture chance and the emergent character of the social world. The Cape Town global security assemblage is instructive in this regard, as the CCID has reacted and interacted with the changing politics and security logics of South Africa and beyond. The growth of private security in the immediate aftermath of apartheid was highly controversial in South Africa, in large part because cheap black labour was employed to guard white wealth and privilege. Private security and the idea of profiting from crime was also in many ways anathema to the ANC, a political party whose ideology was in part opposed to capitalism. The arrival of foreign private security companies such as G4S was also treated with suspicion, seen both as a potential threat to national sovereignty and as unwelcome competition for domestic firms (see Abrahamsen and Williams 2011: 96–102).

Such tensions have continued to simmer, and provide part of the explanation for the CCID's announcement in 2008 that G4S has been replaced with Iliso Protection Services – a fully black female-owned South African company. Since the change of service provider, the CCID security force has expanded to 230 guards, making it the largest safety and security force on the streets of Cape Town. The officers are now branded as 'Public Safety Officers', despite their 'private' funding. The close co-operation with the public police continues. In 2014, for example, the CCID's Public Safety Officers assisted law enforcement officers with over 2000 arrests (CCID 2014). They also remain closely involved in Cape Town's extensive network of surveillance CCTV, which with some 650 cameras is one of the largest public area surveillance projects on the African continent. Named Cyclops, the surveillance system is yet another illustration of how multiple actors and technologies come together in new and constantly shifting global security assemblages. In Cape Town, the power and influence of one global private security company may have waned, showing the continuation of competition and negotiation within the assemblage – as well as the importance of local actors and capacities, not just global ones. But even then 'local' developments interact with global influences, and security is still embedded in a complex transnational security architecture that is both a reflection and a significant component of the shifting structures of global governance.

Conclusion

Situating the emergence of security privatization and global security assemblages within an analysis of state disassembly and reassembly draws attention to the inadequacy of explanatory accounts that look at it only in terms of whether or not the state is losing power and sovereignty in a zero-sum game with non-state or global security actors. As Berndtsson and Stern observe with reference to the global security assemblage at Arlanda Airport in Sweden:

> [To claim] that security is being provided or controlled by either public or private actors would be a vast oversimplification that obscures an intricate play of power extending far beyond the actors with whom we spoke. At the airport, overlapping

authorities, regulations, and activities illustrate the limits of political imaginaries based on maintaining clear-cut public–private or domestic–international distinctions.

(Berndtsson and Stern 2011: 417)

Instead, global assemblages highlight the fact that analysis should start form the actual practices of security and governance in a given setting and take account of shifting forms of power and authority involved.

Thus, rather than perceiving private security actors as existing outside the state, in the private domain, they are better understood as part of a continual negotiation of what is and is not the state. As this chapter shows, private security actors often operate in close co-operation with the state, and emerged as part of state restructuring and government policies. But this is not to say that global security assemblages are harmonious or stable structures. Instead, they are often marked by competition and struggles for power and influence. The very categories of public and private, global and local are resources in these struggles, with different actors appealing to different understandings of what should appropriately be 'public' and 'private' in order strengthen their own positions. As such, global security assemblages call for an investigation of the new modalities of power through which the very categories of public/private and global/local are reconstituted.

The African continent provides a valuable illustration of the importance of this point, not least because in the popular (but also the scholarly) imagination private security in Africa remains associated with mercenaries, private armies, and failed states. Contrary to such tendencies, thinking in terms of assemblages opens up the possibility that the state might be differently assembled in different places. Because assemblage thinking is more agnostic about the ontology of the state, it offers a way of capturing the specificity of the state in different places – without endlessly pathologizing it as some kind of aberration or deviant form of an ideal Western, Weberian model. In global security assemblages where the state has weak administrative or governing capacities, and where the state's financial, managerial and technical resources are often surpassed by private security companies, corporate capital or development organizations, the role of private security can be seen as crucial to both the continued functioning of state authority and the operations of international capital. Rather than reflecting an automatic decline of state sovereignty, security privatization can be analysed as reconfiguration of the very categories of state authority and its relationship to the public and the private, the global and the local.

Moreover, thinking in terms of assemblages allows us to connect apparently divergent dynamics of security privatization in different parts of the world, and to see their concrete links and causal connections. The dynamics of security privatization in the North, for instance, are often drastically different from the South. However, the two are often also deeply and intricately connected. Transformations in security governance in the northern countries, for instance, provided the pre-conditions for the emergence of significant private security firms that subsequently came to occupy key roles in the global industry and in places like the Cape Town Central City Improvement District. Similarly, shifts in the norms and discourses around security in the North – particularly the commodification of security and its treatment as a commodity within economic logics and free trade negotiations, rather than a matter solely of state sovereignty and public security, were crucial in creating a permissive (and even facilitating) environment for the expansion of private security firms. These developments did not 'cause' security privatization in the South, but they did have profound effects upon it, particularly in terms of the integration of global private security firms into other states and in constructing global security assemblages with important impacts within them. The notion of assemblage thus helps break down the distinction between the near and the far, showing how the global is present in the local and vice versa.

Approaching security privatization in this manner and studying its specific impacts in particular global security assemblages can also help to begin to answer the important questions of its implications for security, equality, and development. Global security assemblages are not neutral. They often follow and reinforce dominant structures of wealth and power. At the same time, they are not always wholly exclusionary. They can also contribute to the production of the public 'good' of security, or to the provision of security to wider parts of the populace when state authorities are unable or unwilling to do so, or to do so alone – though as the case of Cape Town shows, how this occurs may go hand in hand with reinforcing inequalities in ways that require careful examination. Global security assemblages are often as politically complex in their implications as they are concretely complex in their operations. Yet it is precisely this complexity that must be captured if we are to provide normative evaluations and political responses adequate to the realities of global security privatization. Thinking in terms of assemblages can help develop the critical tools and perspectives necessary for this understanding and evaluation; and given that these processes and impacts of security privatization across the globe seem likely to continue to grow in importance, so too will the importance of thinking creatively and critically about how security is being assembled. Rather than beginning with a set of philosophical assumptions about the public and the private, this creates a research agenda that begins from the ground up, examining how these categories function in practice, how different actors relate to the security field, and with what political consequences.

Note

1   At that time G4S still traded in South Africa as Securicor, reflecting the relatively recent merger of the two companies. It later became G4S, and to avoid confusion it is referred to as such throughout this chapter.

Bibliography

Abrahamsen, R. and Williams, M. C. (2009) 'Security beyond the State: Global Security Assemblages in International Politics', *International Political Sociology* 3(1): 1–17.

Abrahamsen, R. and Williams, M. C. (2011) *Security beyond the State: Private Security in International Politics*, Cambridge University Press, Cambridge.

Acuto, M. and Curtis, S. (eds) (2014a) *Reassembling International Theory: Assemblage Thinking and International Relations*, Basingstoke: Palgrave Macmillan.

Acuto, M. and Curtis, S. (2014b) 'Assemblage Thinking and International Relations', in M. Acuto and S. Curtis (eds), *Reassembling International Theory*, Basingstoke: Palgrave Macmillan, pp. 1–14.

Barnett, M. (2001) 'Authority, Intervention, and the Outer Limits of International Relations Theory', in T. Callaghy, R. Kassimir and R. Latham (eds), *Intervention and Transnationalism in Africa*, Cambridge: Cambridge University Press, pp. 47–65.

Berg, J. (2004) 'Private Policing in South Africa: The Cape Town City Improvement District – Pluralisation in Practice', *Society in Transition* 35(2): 224–50.

Berndtsson, J. and Stern, M. (2011) 'Private Security and the Public–Private Divide: Contested Lines of Distinction and Modes of Governance in the Stockholm-Arlanda Security Assemblage', *International Political Sociology* 5(4): 408–25.

CCID (2014) *Annual Report 2014*, Cape Town: Cape Town Central City Improvement District, www.capetowncid.co.za/docs/6564/CCID%20Annual%20Report%202014.pdf.

Deleuze, G. and Guattari, F. (2003) *A Thousand Plateaus*, Minneapolis, MN: University of Minneapolis Press.

Department of Community Safety (2006) *Provincial Government Western Cape: Strategic Plan 2oo3/04 to 2005/06*, Cape Town: Department of Community Safety.

Haggerty, K. D. and Ericson, R. V. (2000) 'The Surveillant Assemblage', *British Journal of Sociology* 51 (4): 605–22.

Latour, B. (2007) *Reassembling the Social*, Oxford: Oxford University Press.

Lippert, R. and O'Connor, D. (2003) 'Security Assemblages: Airport Security, Flexible Work, and Liberal Governance', *Alternatives* 28(3): 331–58.

McFarlane, C. and Anderson, B. (2011) 'Thinking with Assemblage', *Area* 43(2): 162–4.

Sassen, S. (2006) *Territory, Authority, Rights: From Medieval to Global Assemblages*, Princeton, NJ: Princeton University Press.

14

THE PRIVATIZATION OF SECURITY

Implications for democracy

Clifford Shearing and Philip Stenning

Concerns over personal and communal security are as old as human societies, but as societies have changed arrangements for achieving and maintaining security have evolved accordingly. In this chapter we consider the implications of these changes for the governance of security. We begin with evolution of the institutions of security and associated linguistic developments and the debates that underlie them. We then turn to the issues of governance that have been central to these debates. We conclude by considering the challenges that contemporary forms of security provision present for the realization of the democratic governance of security. We explain how major transformations in the provision of security, and especially the allocation between states and the private sector for doing so, have occurred across the world during the last thirty years or so. Globalization and the impact of technological change during this period have placed much security provision outside the regulatory capacities of nation states, and adequate alternative forms and institutions of transnational governance have not yet been devised, nor have recent developments in thinking about how democratic governance is to be realized been reflected so far in discussion of such possible alternatives.

Institutional developments, changing terminologies, emerging debates

In far distant times, a word that was commonly used to reference personal and communal security was 'peace'. In England in the sixteenth century, for instance, William Lambard (1581–2: 5) wrote of 'peace' in the following terms: '"peace": a withholding or abstinence from that injurious force or violence that unruly or boisterous men are in their natures prone to use towards others were they not restrained by laws and fear of punishment.' Individual citizens as well as communities were entitled to 'peace' (the consequences of 'breaches of the peace' varied with status and power). Typically, responsibility for ensuring peace and for holding to account (bringing to justice) those who 'breached the peace' was shared by all, or at least all adult males. Over time sovereigns began to claim something of a monopoly over the preservation of the peace, and the disciplining of those who breached it. This led to the emergence of the concept of a 'King's Peace', conceived of as a 'public peace' that applied across entire kingdoms.

This idea of a 'King's Peace', often attributed to King Arthur, initially only applied to certain places and people – for example, highways, markets, the king's court and its courtiers. Gradually it began, as the nineteenth-century historian William Maitland (1885) put it, to 'swallow up lesser peaces' (e.g. the peaces of local noblemen, lords of the manor, etc.). By the seventeenth century this process of consolidation of the King's Peace was pretty much complete. The King's (or later Queen's) Peace was understood to apply to everyone, everywhere, with sovereigns claiming a monopoly over its maintenance and enforcement across the land. Its effective maintenance and enforcement, however, still depended on the acceptance, by adult male citizens and communities, of responsibility for this, there being no state apparatus through which it could be achieved. To ensure that this responsibility was fulfilled, sovereigns designated prominent local citizens as two classes of 'peace officers' – constables and justices of the peace – to represent his/her interests in peace preservation. The job of these officers was to ensure that the King's peace was preserved and that those who breached it were brought to justice before the royal courts.

Up until the late eighteenth century in England, personal and communal security were maintained and enforced by local citizens who acted under the auspices of sovereign law and legal institutions, and under the supervision of local peace officers, with communal sanctions for failure to meet these civic responsibilities. That, at least, was the theory.

The combined forces of demographic urbanization and the beginning of the industrial revolution in the eighteenth century, however, led reformers to the conclusion that these essentially rural arrangements for the governance of security were now inadequate. First, they depended on 'local knowledge' that had existed in relatively static rural agricultural communities, and second, security was maintained and enforced principally by, and in the interests of, landed gentry, enforced by their designated agents. Attempts to transfer these practices to cities were resisted by an emerging entrepreneurial, mercantile and industrial bourgeoisie whose members demanded a system of security maintenance that would meet the needs of their growing commercial and industrial enterprises. By the late eighteenth century this had led to the demand for state-sponsored 'police'.

The word 'police' came into the English language in the eighteenth century from France. At that time, it referred not to an institution, as it does today, but rather to a desirable state of affairs. In 1769, in his famous *Commentaries on the Laws of England*, for instance, William Blackstone described it thus:

> The last species of offences which especially affect the commonwealth are those against the public *police* or *economy*. By the public police and economy I mean the due regulation and domestic order of the kingdom: whereby the individuals of the state, like a well-governed family, are bound to conform their general behaviour to the rules of propriety, good neighbourhood, and good manners; and to be decent, industrious, and inoffensive in their respective station.
>
> *(Blackstone 1723–80: 162)*

The original concept of 'police' thus bore some resemblance to the earlier concept of 'peace' and soon the term 'police' came to be used as a verb to refer to activities undertaken to 'preserve the peace'. It was not until the late eighteenth century with growing demands for the establishment of a state institution with responsibility for ensuring and enforcing 'police' or 'peace', that the term 'police' gradually ceased to refer to a desirable state of affairs and instead came to signify an institution that might be established to achieve this (see Chapter 2, this volume).

The author of a *New Municipal Manual* published in Canada in the mid-nineteenth century nicely explained this shift in usage. Explaining the recent introduction of 'Police Boards' to govern the new police forces in what is now the province of Ontario, the author wrote (plagiarizing Blackstone, as quoted above):

The word 'police' is generally applied to the internal regulations of Cities and Towns, whereby the individuals of any City or Town, like members of a well governed family, are bound to conform their general behaviour to the rules of propriety, good neighbourhood, and good manners, and to be decent, industrious and inoffensive in their respective situations ... but the word, as here used, has a still more restricted meaning, for it is intended to apply to those paid men who in every City and Town are appointed to execute police laws, and who in many respects correspond with Constables of Rural Municipalities.

(Harrison 1859: 158)

Not surprisingly, the legal authority of these new 'police officers' was referred to in contemporary statutes (and still is in many jurisdictions) as the 'original' authority of 'peace officers', and their work came to be referred to as 'policing'. As the American police scholar Egon Bittner (1970) famously argued in the twentieth century, the key defining characteristic of this work was the authority to use 'legitimate' force. Earlier, the German sociologist Max Weber had described a successful claim to a monopoly over the use of legitimate force as the key defining characteristic of the modern nation state.

Thus it was that by the late twentieth century domestic 'policing' – that is, the 'keeping of the peace' – had come, inaccurately, to be thought of as the exclusive preserve of the state and, in particular, the role and work of state-sponsored public police; inaccurately, because empirically most states have never realized a complete monopoly over policing. Nonetheless, policing scholarship at this time was almost exclusively preoccupied with the public police. During the latter decades of the twentieth century, however, the plausibility of the claim of a police monopoly over policing came increasingly to be challenged and this in turn had implications for democracy.

The co-existence of private and 'public' domestic security provision throughout the nineteenth and twentieth centuries came to be increasingly well documented in the literature. It was not until the latter half of the twentieth century, however, that the private (i.e. non-state-sponsored) provision of security began to receive serious attention from 'policing' scholars. This attention was a reaction to a growing body of evidence of a massive growth of private security organizations and personnel in the United States during the post-World War II decades. But it was not long before policing scholars in Canada, Europe, (later) Australia and (even later) South Africa and South America began to notice that this phenomenon was by no means unique to the United States, and a slowly emerging body of research literature on 'private security' developed.

At first, this literature focused on describing the growth, activities and auspices of private security provision, but soon questions began to be raised about what its implications might be for democracy and accountability. This included concerns about understandings of 'policing', the relationship between this growing private provision and 'public policing', the respective roles of 'private' and 'public' police, the governance of private security provision and how private providers of security were being and should be held to account. These concerns were reflected in robust debates about nomenclature – should private security provision be appropriately referred to as 'private policing', and if not, why not? Those who regarded 'policing' as the exclusive preserve of the state and its 'public police' resisted such usage. Others argued that 'policing' was simply another term for security provision.

Another term of crucial relevance to the relationship between security privatization and democracy is 'globalization'. This is a term with a longer history than most people who write about it acknowledge, but which, during the last decades of the twentieth century, became 'an all-purpose catchword of public and scholarly debate' (Lechner and Boli 2008: 1). It has been applied to refer to the way that all manner of economic, political and cultural activities, enterprises and processes have expanded beyond the confines of, and hence effective regulation by, individual nation states into a transnational and international realm of operation. This may refer to the fact that such enterprises are simultaneously operating in multiple nation states, and/or that they are operating in spaces that are outside the boundaries of any nation state, such as the high seas, international air space, 'space' or 'virtual space'. From one perspective, globalization refers to the 'flows' of goods, services, people, money, communication and information between and among states. Its significance for policing can be quite simply stated: just as domestic enterprises require secure environments in which to operate effectively – environments that nation states have assumed responsibility for securing through laws and policing – so too do transnational or 'global' enterprises. This poses two critical challenges for policing. The first relates to the fact that there is no transnational or international equivalent either of a national government or of a domestic police service. The second derives from the fact that, with some notable exceptions based on international treaties, conventions and covenants, etc., there is no transnational or international equivalent of a comprehensive domestic body of uniform, national laws or justice institutions.

Much effort has been devoted in the last hundred years to make up for these deficits, but this remains very much 'work in progress'. Transnational and international security provision is just as, if not more, 'pluralized' than domestic security provision and has proved even more difficult to co-ordinate and govern. It is only within the last twenty years or so that a handful of policing and security scholars have begun to turn their attention to understanding these developments and to consider the challenges they present with respect to democratic values.

'Democracy', too, is a concept with a very long history. While there has been broad agreement that it refers to the idea of government according to the 'will of the people', agreement about what institutions and processes are required to achieve this pretty much ends there, and debates about the concept and realization of democracy are as robust now as they ever were, especially as the world has become more 'globalized'. Recent scholarship in this area has indicated a shift in focus from 'representative' democracy to 'deliberative' democracy, and from models and institutions of democracy to processes of democracy.

The twentieth-century English historian Sir Charles Reith (1952: 253) was one of the first policing scholars to draw a distinction between 'regime' and 'democratic' policing. Since the 1960s there has been a growing emphasis on the need for policing to be democratically accountable, and since the 1990s there has been a concern with developing strategies for transforming policing in states in transition from authoritarian to democratic governments. The transitions from state-dominated security provision to plural security provision, and from state-based to global security provision during the latter years of the twentieth century, have posed new challenges for achieving effective democratic accountability for both domestic and global or transnational policing. It is to the debates about how to respond to these challenges that we now turn.

Governing privatized and globalized security provision

Clearly, the modern pluralization (and especially privatization) and globalization of security provision poses enormous challenges for effective and accountable democratic governance. There has been broad agreement, at least in theory and at least in democracies, that the role of state-sponsored public police is to undertake policing in the broad public interest – that is, in the interests of the public or community at large – rather than in the usually narrower, self-serving private, partisan or corporate interests of powerful people or organizations, be they politically powerful ruling elites or economically powerful corporations. Calls for community-based policing, democratic policing and policing by consent, as well as efforts to provide police with some defined independence from political direction, all reflect such expectations.

So long as state governments were thought to have a legitimate monopoly over policing, achieving such accountable democratic governance seemed to be, if not always easy in practice, at least theoretically possible, and there was no shortage of suggestions as to what laws, regulatory regimes and institutions were required to do so. Furthermore, establishing and maintaining appropriate regulatory mechanisms were seen to be well within the mandate, and usually the effective power, of established liberal democratic governments. With the pluralization, privatization and globalization of policing which developed in the late twentieth century, however, this assumption was increasingly questioned. In the context of today's market-driven understandings that argued for the devolution of the provision of services by governments to the private sector, established couplings of the public interest with the public sector and private interests with the private sector have become increasingly difficult to maintain.

These difficulties were aggravated by the fact that some transnational corporations have assets that exceed the GDP of states that seek, and depend upon, their investment. In such circumstances, many states are unable to dictate conditions for security provision. Instead, they find that they are 'required' to negotiate regulatory environments with corporations whose investment they want to attract. This means that they often find themselves having to trade off established ideals of democratic accountability against the political demands of promoting growth and economic development, with the latter not infrequently being given precedence.

This means that some corporations are able to negotiate effective 'immunity' from local laws, law enforcement and legal liability, as a condition of locating their businesses within a state. In extreme cases they may be able to enrol states to utilize tax resources to provide the security that they are able to command for their enterprises. Often this necessitates the purchase of private security provision when the requirements of the corporations involved cannot be met from existing state security resources, and domestic laws are frequently not flexible enough to provide for adequate accountability of such provision. The issue of accountability is significantly exacerbated when the 'host' country is not a democratic state (for examples, see Spearin 2003; Avant and Haufler 2012).

These challenges of democratic governance are difficult enough to meet with respect to providers who are operating within the territory of a nation state. Even more difficult is the challenge of devising mechanisms, institutions and processes to govern security provision beyond the boundaries of nation states. Conventional arrangements for democratic governance are simply not readily applicable in these international, extra-terrestrial and cyber-spaces, in which the public-private distinction becomes irretrievably blurred.

Scholars and policy makers have responded to these challenges in two quite different ways: some have focused on ways to adapt existing domestic governance institutions and processes and to devise international governance institutions and processes that mimic them; others have sought to rethink fundamental concepts of governance and democracy in ways that might help us to better understand these challenges, and suggest new forms of democratic governance that might generate effective responses to them.

Adaptation of existing governance structures

Since the 1960s states around the world have introduced laws and regulatory regimes to govern the activities of private security companies and personnel within their territories. Many of these regimes have included accountability mechanisms through which complaints from the public can be investigated and adjudicated, with administrative sanctions available to discipline delinquent operators. To this extent there has been a consistent attempt to bring private security provision into conformity with democratic norms. The efficacy of these regimes, however, has been persistently questioned, with accusations that regulatory agencies have been inadequately funded to perform their functions effectively and have been 'captured' by those they are supposed to be regulating, and that private security companies based in other countries have been able to avoid any effective regulation at all.

In many countries, including the United Kingdom until the 1980s, the only regulation to which private security providers were subject was self-regulation. Self-regulation was typically undertaken by industry associations whose membership was dominated by the largest companies, and their self-regulatory regimes were frequently criticized as unrepresentative of the private security industry as a whole, and as promoting the interests of these large providers at the expense of smaller market players, rather than promoting broader public interests. Furthermore, both government regulation and self-regulation have applied, in most countries, only to contract security providers and not to the activities of corporate in-house security organizations (Button 2002).

With the gradual emergence of plural security provision and partnerships between public and private security organizations, there came a recognition that the separate regulatory regimes for public (i.e. state-sponsored) and private security provision that had developed were no longer adequate to ensure that domestic security provision conformed to democratic norms. Ideas about how to govern a plural policing environment were slow in coming. Significantly, the Patten Inquiry into the reform of policing in Northern Ireland eventually stepped up to the challenge, proposing a governance regime with a central 'Policing Board' responsible for regulating all the players, public and private, in a plural policing environment (Independent Commission on Policing for Northern Ireland 1999). Although much discussed by both practitioners and scholars at the time, the proposal was not adopted for Northern Ireland or anywhere else in the United Kingdom, and has so far not been implemented in any other country.

In the international sphere, attempts to establish governance regimes for the globalized plural policing and security environment have been few in number and of questionable efficacy. As has been the case with domestic security provision, efforts to establish an international governance regime have involved proposals both for state-sponsored regimes and self-regulatory regimes. State-sponsored regimes have been sponsored by the United Nations and by regional government organizations such as the European Union (EU) and the Organization of American States (OAS), but have focused on the governance of state-sponsored international security organizations such as UN Peacekeeping Missions, Interpol and Europol, with almost no attention to the roles and activities of transnational private security providers.

Attempts to establish a governance regime for the latter have been based on self-regulation, with the establishment of an organization named the International Code of Conduct Association (ICoCA). The ICoCA was originally launched with support from the government of Switzerland in 2009, and inspired by the 'Montreux Document on pertinent international legal obligations and good practices for States related to operations of private military and security companies during armed conflict', published by the International Red Cross that same year. The ICoCA's membership currently includes six governments, 140 private contract security companies from many countries of the world, and 13 civil society organizations (see Chapter 26, this volume). In November 2010 ICoCA promulgated an international Code of Conduct for Private Security Providers (ICoC). Membership of the ICoCA is voluntary, but includes a commitment to operate in accordance with this Code of Conduct. On its website ICoCA claims that as of September 2013, 708 companies had formally committed to operate in accordance with the Code of Conduct'.[1] Despite the involvement of the 13 civil society organizations,[2] however, ICoCA and its Code of Conduct cannot be regarded as a democratic governance regime.

Rethinking governance

Innovation with respect to the governance of contemporary forms of policing has been at the conceptual rather than the practical level and has involved, in particular, the emergence of new conceptions of governance and of democracy. As a consequence of this conceptual focus, while new avenues of thinking have been identified, these remain, at a practical level, possibilities that have yet to be clearly identified, articulated and advanced.

A significant theoretical innovation within the governance of security has been the development of a 'governance' perspective that has deliberately sought to move thinking beyond its hitherto state-centred conceptual anchors. It has done so, in part, by attempting to extend the understanding of peace and peace keeping beyond its historical close coupling with police.

An influential conceptual development has been a shift to the term 'security' as opposed to 'policing' and an associated introduction of the idea of governance, understood as intentionally shaping the flow of events, as a source of peace. At the same time scholars working within this governance perspective have sought to develop a conceptual framing that is inclusive of a wide spectrum of auspices and providers of security that recognizes the plural nature of security delivery and the complexities of democratic accountability that this presents. In summary this perspective has envisaged 'security governance' as encompassing a fundamentally polycentric, or 'nodal governance', terrain. A central feature of this perspective has been its refusal to accord analytic priority to any one auspice or provider of security governance. Instead, the perspective argues that the nature of nodes and their relationship to each other has (as noted above) varied considerably across time and space.

The consequences of nodal arrangements for democracy are twofold. On the one hand, the pluralization of governance serves to shift decision making with respect to service provision downwards. This broadens participation in governance. On the other hand, nodal arrangements have reduced democratic accountability as existing accountability mechanisms have traditionally been state focused (Holley and Shearing 2015). This challenge is being responded to through the emergence of more horizontal and circular forms of accountability (Braithwaite 2006). These developments, however, remain in their infancy.

One consequence of this focus on mapping terrains of security governance has been a recognition of an expanded domain of 'peace', and associated harms and risks, that the term security has been used to encompass. In her book *Security*, Zedner (2009) picked up on, and discussed, this conceptual widening. She canvassed the intellectual terrains that have mobilized the term 'security' – criminology, international relations and development – and explored the new meanings that are emerging with the use of phrases such as 'food security', 'water security' and 'energy security'. Each of these emerging usages has drawn attention to a widening of the domain of 'peace and security' that extends beyond the terrains that the term policing has traditionally encompassed as well as the existing institutions for the democratic governance of security provision.

A nodal perspective has done much to encourage an emerging body of rigorous empirical work, across a range of different social contexts, that has explored the shifting shape of security governance within an increasingly wide variety of contexts – for example, transnational and domestic policing arrangements, the governance of security within cyberspace, and the security of flows of goods and services within ports and airports. An important consequence of this research has been that it has enabled the beginnings of innovative thinking at the normative level around questions of democracy and accountability to be applied in innovative ways to the governance of security.

An example of conceptual rethinking that could, but has not as yet, been drawn upon to respond to the challenges noted earlier is the work of political science scholars like John Dryzek (2010), who have been challenging established, means-focused, conceptions of democracy in favour of more ends-focused conceptions such as 'participatory' and 'deliberative' democracy. These emerging developments are enabling scholars to extend their thinking beyond models and institutions of representative democracy to ones that recognize other ways of creating more 'inclusive institutions' (Acemoglu and Robinson 2012) and accountable processes. Ayling *et al.* (2009), for example, explore the costs and risks, and potential safeguards, for governments as they seek to realize the 'public interest' within today's plural policing context.

Conclusion

In this chapter we have explored the way in which developments within the governance of security have been shaping, and reshaping, established policing terrains – a reshaping that has made it increasingly difficult for established political institutions to ensure that policing remains democratically accountable. As these developments have unfolded they have brought with them significant challenges with respect to the established values of accountability and democracy, and how they are to be realized within these new emerging contexts. To date the steps that have been taken to respond to the challenges have, for the most part, sought to 'exploit' existing regulatory possibilities rather than develop new ones. While new conceptual possibilities are emerging, these 'explorations' (March 1991) remain inchoate. Thus, while these emerging conceptual reframings carry with them considerable promise, much work needs to be done to explore these possibilities at practical levels.

Research and thinking is required at both the descriptive and explanatory, as well as at normative levels. In particular, more research is required to understand the features of nodal governance both with respect to its sources of authority and the nodes involved in the provision of security governance services within different settings. Within this context an important topic requiring further attention is the way in which the boundaries of policing are shifting and the impact this is having on the evolution of state police (Sparrow 2014). Equally important is the challenge of developing new forms of democratic accountability that recognize that security governance is today profoundly polycentric (Ostrom 2010).

Notes

1   See www.icoca.ch/en/history.
2   These are listed at www.icoca.ch/en/membership?civil_society_organizations=csos&op=Search&view_type=map&form_id=_search_for_members_filter_form.

Bibliography

Acemoglu, D. and Robinson, J. (2012) *Why Nations Fail: The Origins of Power, Prosperity and Poverty*, London: Profile Books.
Avant, D. and Haufler, V. (2012) 'Transnational Organisations and Security', *Global Crime* 13(4): 254–75.

Ayling, J., Grabosky, P. and Shearing, C. (2009) *Lengthening the Arm of the Law: Enhancing Police Resources in the Twenty-First Century*, Cambridge: Cambridge University Press.

Bittner, E. (1970) *The Functions of Police in Modern Society*, Washington, DC: National Institute of Mental Health.

Blackstone, W. (1723–80) *Commentaries on the Laws of England in Four Books*, Book IV: 'Of Public Wrongs', 1884 reprint, Chicago, IL: Callaghan.

Braithwaite, J. (2006) 'Accountability and Responsibility through Restorative Justice', in M. Dowdle (ed.), *Public Accountability: Designs, Dilemmas and Experiences*, Cambridge: Cambridge University Press, pp. 33–51.

Brodeur, J.-P. (2010) *The Policing Web*, Oxford: Oxford University Press.

Button, M. (2002) *Private Policing*, Cullompton: Willan.

Dryzek, J. (2010) *Foundations and Frontiers of Deliberative Governance*, Oxford: Oxford University Press.

Harrison, R. (1859) *The New Municipal Manual for Upper Canada*, Toronto: Maclear & Co.

Holley, C. and Shearing, C. (in press) 'Nodal Governance', in P. Drahos (ed.), *Regulation Institutions and Networks*, Canberra: ANU Press.

Independent Commission on Policing for Northern Ireland (1999) *A New Beginning: Policing in Northern Ireland*, London: Independent Commission on Policing for Northern Ireland.

Lambard, W. (1581–2) *Eirenarcha or the Office of Justices of the Peace*, 1972 reprint, London: Professional Books.

Lechner, F. and Boli, J. (eds) (2008) *The Globalization Reader*, Malden, MA: Blackwell Publishing.

Loader, I. and Walker, N. (2001) 'Policing as a Public Good: Reconstituting the Connections between Policing and the State', *Theoretical Criminology* 5(1): 9–35.

Maitland, F. W. (1885) *Justice and Police*, 1974 reprint, New York: AMS Press.

Manning, P. (2010) *Democratic Policing in a Changing World*, Boulder, CO: Paradigm Publishers.

March, J. (1991) 'Exploration and Exploitation in Organizational Learning', *Organization Science* 2(1): 71–87.

Ostrom, E. (2010) 'Beyond Markets and States: Polycentric Governance of Complex Economic Systems', *The American Economic Review* 100(3): 641–72.

Reith, C. (1952) *The Blind Eye of History: A Study of the Origins of the Present Police Era*, Montclair, NJ: Patterson Smith.

Sparrow, M. (2014) 'Managing the Boundary Between Public and Private Policing', *New Perspectives in Policing Bulletin*, NCJ 247182, Washington, DC: US Department of Justice, National Institute of Justice.

Spearin, C. (2003) 'Accountable to Whom? An Assessment of International Private Security Companies in South America', *Civil Wars* 6(1): 1–6.

White, A. (2010) *The Politics of Private Security: Regulation, Reform and Re-legitimation*, London: Palgrave Macmillan.

Zedner, L. (2009) *Security*, New York: Routledge.

15

MILITARY MIGRANTS AND MERCENARY MARKETS

Vron Ware

In September 2014 four civilians working for the UK-owned Group 4 Securicor (G4S) received the Queen's Gallantry Medal for their actions during an attack on the British Council compound in Kabul in 2011. The four men, all former soldiers who had served in the British Brigade of Gurkhas, were the first private security operatives to receive such an award, making this a significant step in the convergence of, and overlap between, the two sectors: private military and security companies (PMSCs) and the national armed forces. As veterans with over 50 collective years of army experience, they typify a well-established pattern whereby military-trained personnel transfer into the private sector. But there are other reasons why these hardened ex-soldiers provide a fitting introduction to this chapter on the dynamics of race and ethnicity in the private security sphere.

In this instance, the men were working for G4S Gurkha Security Services. Born in Nepal, their elite background as former Gurkhas had supplied them with a unique ethnic identification which they were able to exploit in order to sell their services as particular kinds of warriors. This marketable attribute derived from British imperial history simultaneously positioned them as distinctly 'foreign', regardless of whether they had been naturalized as UK citizens in the meantime. As both migrants and minorities, however, their status within the private security sphere would automatically entail a degree of vulnerability and 'outsiderness'. The combination of all these factors underlines the urgency of understanding the phenomenon of military migration and its growing significance within the world of private security work.

The military migrant

Military migrants are an integral feature of the contemporary military and security industry whether they are actively taking part in armed conflict or carrying out routine work involved in servicing military bases. A recent report by Al-Jazeera noted that the US military's Central Command currently employ nearly 40,000 foreign contract workers to do jobs such as cooking, housekeeping and driving in US bases in Iraq, Afghanistan and elsewhere. While these men and women are recruited to perform low-paid menial labour, their role has become indispensable to the operation of US military power, almost anywhere in the world including Guantanamo. If we include this example of service work alongside the ex-Gurkha security personnel employed by G4S, we can immediately see how hard it is to offer a concise definition of the broad category of military migration. However, within the past decade, certain strands of military-related migration have begun to attract attention from scholars who have adopted distinct but overlapping perspectives towards the study of migrant labour within the private security sector. As a result, the deep-rooted racial, ethnic and cultural hierarchies within this 'global market for force' (see Chapter 18, this volume), are gradually coming into view. This section provides an overview of this literature and its significance to understanding the wider phenomenon of military migration.

The most recent body of work considers the military migrant worker as a distinct category of person subject to governmental power without effective legal protection (Li 2015; Chapter 21, this volume). A focus on the legal aspects of military migration is essential in understanding the scale of what Darryl Li terms the 'offshoring' of military power. It is widely known, he writes, that the US military has been radically 'transformed over the past fifteen years by widespread outsourcing to private contractors, whose numbers rival or even exceed those of uniformed personnel in war zones' (Li 2015: 127). What is less well known is that the most of the overseas contractor workforce are not American citizens, but men and women known as third country nationals (TCNs). Li explains why their predicament ought to attract greater attention from policy analysts and academic researchers:

> TCNs in particular work on US bases under military authority while lacking most of the protections of American law, local regimes, or their home governments. They are often employed by non-U.S. companies subcontracted by American corporations, paid a fraction of what American contractors and soldiers make, and can be easily deported if deemed noncompliant. Many are forced to pay recruiting firms exorbitant fees to secure their jobs, leaving them highly indebted and effectively indentured.
>
> *(Li 2015: 127)*

While his analysis casts light on the hardships faced by military migrants within the US military complex, there are also broader questions to be asked about the rapid increase in privately contracted workers within a global context, whether they are trained to use lethal skills or part of the workforce maintaining military bases. Although they undoubtedly face the same problems as many other economic migrants, military migrants occupy a different status because, as Li reminds us, they are employed 'on behalf of a foreign government in the exercise of a core sovereign function: namely, the use of force' (ibid.: 127). As a result, they are frequently left in limbo in terms of employment rights, immigration regulations and access to any form of legal protection.

The second area of analysis considers what Paul Higate describes as 'the gendered and racialized contexts' of an industry made up of an increasingly 'diverse security contracting workforce' (Higate 2012: 37). Military migrants frequently endure the discriminatory terms and conditions that come with the status of being a TCN. Maya Eichler (2014) emphasizes the fact that, while there is scant data on the gender breakdown of the military migrant workforce, the vast majority of TCNs are men who come from the global South, from countries such as India, Pakistan, Bangladesh, Nepal, the Philippines, El Salvador, Chile or Uganda. However, she adds, 'the category of TCN technically includes workers from Western countries other than the USA, such as the UK, Australia, or Canada and from countries in Eastern Europe and the former Soviet Union' (ibid.: 8). This is an important point because the privatization of military work draws largely on the experience and skills provided by thousands of former soldiers eager to transfer into a more risky but lucrative job market. Yet within this market, already stratified by nationality, ethnicity, geography and reputation based on fitness for martial labour, TCNs and local nationals (LNs) are motivated 'to strike an ethnic bargain trading on assumptions around their embodied identities in return for material reward' (Higate 2012: 40). As we shall see below, the example of the former Gurkha soldiers, employed by G4S as an elite force, exemplifies this pattern.

A third dimension of the military migration phenomenon concerns the complex question of militarized citizenship and the extent to which this concept remains a key feature of post-colonial societies, especially where the legacies of imperialist history are still pending. Exploring the use of migrant labour in military and security work can help to illuminate the changing status of soldiering as an occupation that is intrinsically connected to national citizenship. As the trend towards the privatization of security and military work continues, national military institutions become less accountable to public scrutiny, less representative of national populations and increasingly detached from conventional notions of patriotism and duty.

Drawing on the valuable scholarship carried out in the areas sketched out above, this chapter suggests that the use of a racialized migrant labour force to supplement and supplant the work of state armed forces can illuminate 'the politics of market fundamentalism, militarism and disposability' (Giroux 2014) that drive modern forms of warfare. In short, the field of military migration is distorted externally by range of factors: postcolonial dynamics; geopolitical arrangements; labour trafficking; immigration controls; and deep structures of global economic inequality. Internally, the study of military migrants must also reckon with the vulnerabilities and dangers inherent in war-related work; the discrepancies between the roles and rewards entailed in being soldiers, mercenaries or unskilled service workers; the racism of military personnel which is often intensified by overseas deployment; and the changing relationship between armed security work and access to citizenship and residency rights. All these factors contribute to the market in privatized military and security work, affecting both buyers and sellers of migrant labour in a world in which the lines between state armed forces and private security and military companies are increasingly blurred. The next section addresses this convergence by examining the recent use of postcolonial migrant labour in the UK military.

Military migrants in the state sector

In his study *Corporate Warriors*, Peter Singer (2008) attributes the rapid growth of the global security industry to the break-up of the state monopoly of the military profession, a process that began to manifest itself in the 1990s. This point foregrounds the traffic of demobilized soldiers, fresh from deployment in Iraq and Afghanistan, into this emerging industry and provides one explanation for the blurring of lines between state and corporate interests. However, Eichler (2014) disagrees that the inexorable expansion of the private sector signals the weakening of the state's monopoly over legitimate force. Rather, she asserts, PMSCs have 'joined Western states as key actors in global conflict' (ibid.: 1). Focusing on the example of the US, she argues there are two reasons why the two sectors are locked in a more complex symbiosis:

> First … the neoliberal remaking of militarized citizenship through the termination of male conscription in 1973 was instrumental in paving the way for the increased privatization of military security, and second … the outsourcing of military work to private companies allows for a global rescaling of recruitment that has geographically extended the spatial and social determinants of who works for or in support of the US military.
>
> *(Eichler 2014: 1)*

With regard to her first point, the abolition of conscription within the US and North American context can be usefully compared to the situation in European national states where the practice of compulsory national service for men has been pivotal in defining the relationship between citizenship, military service, and masculinity since the late eighteenth century. Finland, Norway and Austria are in a small minority of states that have opted to retain or even extend conscription as the majority of Europe has moved to the principle of all-volunteer professional armies, particularly post-1989 (Leander and Joenniemi 2006). Despite these notable exceptions, the end of national conscription signals a radical shift towards rebranding military service as a profession that stresses individual choice, lifestyle and career enhancement. Consequently recruiting officers have to compete within a crowded employment market and therefore find it increasingly hard to attract the requisite numbers and quality of applicants even after reducing the size of the regular standing armies.

Since the UK abolished national service in 1960, the armed forces have experienced many peaks and troughs in terms of voluntary enlistment. On several occasions during the late twentieth century, the paucity (and quality) of volunteers provoked vigorous debates in parliament about how to supplement the ranks with migrant labour from former colonies. As the history of post-war Britain indicates, this unresolved imperial heritage means that successive governments have been able to draw on a vast reserve of labour to supplement the indigenous workforce, not just in the military but across the public sector. It is impossible to imagine the development of Britain's National Health Service, for example, without factoring in the historic contribution of migrant workers from the New Commonwealth and former colonies. But soldiers perform a different role from nurses, doctors and transport workers as their profession involves training in the use of lethal force. The deliberations about recruiting men (and occasionally women) from Commonwealth countries frequently alluded to the racial characteristics, reliability and martial qualities of the particular ethnicities concerned, always with an eye to the potential problems involved in compromising the national character of the armed forces.

A brief detour into the phenomenon of Britain's twenty-first-century 'Foreign and Commonwealth' soldiers (FCs) can help to throw light on the complexity of militarized citizenship in the contemporary period. In February 1998 the UK Ministry of Defence turned again to this postcolonial workforce as a way of augmenting particular sections of the armed forces that were under-recruiting. The existing five-year residency period required for Commonwealth citizens was lifted in an attempt to meet this shortfall, leading to the recruitment of thousands of young men and women from over 30 different countries throughout the Commonwealth. Fifteen years later, however, the coalition reinstated the residency rule on the grounds that they could not justify recruiting migrants at a time when so many individuals were being made redundant. Thus this particular migratory path was closed to many young men and women who had previously been eligible for this category of work, a significant proportion of whom had been actively recruited by British Army teams operating in their countries of origin (Ware 2014).

Focusing on military migrants in the state armed forces might seem a diversion from analysing the role of migrants in the private security sector, but the example provided by the UK illustrates an important point. In the current climate of populist anti-immigration politics, it is more expedient for the government to limit recruitment to UK citizens rather than continue to justify the use of migrants from outside the EU. Meanwhile, increasingly stringent measures to regulate immigration have impacted on serving migrant soldiers and their families, bringing the Ministry of Defence into direct conflict with public opinion. The ambiguous status of military migrants as they move between the public and private sectors, highlighting the changing conditions of military labour in the twenty-first century, is discussed in the next section.

The ambiguous status of military migrants

The connotations of being a 'mercenary' is relevant to the discussion of those who work in and across the private and state security spheres, not least because of its emotive force. Within the context of national military service in which employment is still rooted in notions of loyalty, citizenship and patriotism, the word 'mercenary' implies a lack of fidelity to such ideals and a readiness to perform dangerous and potentially lethal work solely for financial reward. A Fijian officer in the UK armed forces once mentioned to me that he had recently witnessed a heated discussion among his compatriots who were asking 'What are we doing in the British Army? Are we mercenaries?'. In a way this question can be interpreted as a rhetorical one, since they would have known that the constitution of the Commonwealth permits the UK government a special dispensation to recruit non-UK nationals. In addition, the oath of attestation requires individuals to pledge allegiance to the Queen who is nominally the monarch of 15 Commonwealth realms, including Fiji. In my research I heard soldiers from Fiji routinely talk about 'coming up to the UK to serve Her Majesty', implying that their postcolonial connection to Britain is understood as being more complex than a purely economic relationship.

However, the question about being mercenaries doubtless reflects the degree to which Fijian soldiers might feel like outsiders within the context of UK society. Their experience of serving in a national army, not just as ethnic and cultural minorities but also as migrants who are subject to increasingly draconian immigration regulations, can be used to expose the contradictions entailed in performing a role normally associated with what Catherine Lutz has called 'supercitizenship' within the corresponding US context (Lutz 2002: 794).

One of the outcomes of unpopular wars in Iraq and Afghanistan in the UK, particularly the high rate of fatalities and serious injuries among soldiers, has been a renewed emphasis on the soldier who is viewed as both a victim of disastrous foreign policy and a figure deserving of public support (McCartney 2010; Ware 2014). In fact the word 'soldier' has become interchangeable with the word 'hero', a label that makes the reality of migrant status all the more galling for those servicemen and women who are not UK citizens. Not surprisingly this discrepancy has often been highlighted in campaigns to stop the deportation of individuals who have served in the UK forces, often for more than a decade, and who are subsequently denied residency rights on the basis of minor infractions. In one such case, a former soldier, Isimeli Baleiwai, returned his medals in disgust at the treatment he had received. In a letter to the Prince of Wales published in the national media, he wrote: 'My service to Queen and Country has been dishonoured and I have been betrayed' (Vuibau 2013).

Although Baleiwai's case received substantial publicity, there has been relatively little public discussion of the employment of migrants in the UK armed forces. Yet aside from the fact that their presence solved major recruiting shortages in the army, their status as minority ethnic personnel also contributed to the institution's public image as a modern, multicultural employer. When recruiting began in 1998, for example, the proportion of black and minority ethnic soldiers in the army barely reached one per cent (Ware 2014: 34). According to the 2014 'diversity dashboard', a set of figures published annually by the Ministry of Defence, this figure has reached over 11 per cent. What the statistics did not reveal, however, was that migrant soldiers (who now include former Gurkhas who have transferred into the regular armed forces) outnumber UK-born minority ethnic soldiers by two to one. Nevertheless the social and political significance of these figures testifies to the symbolic role of the national military institution as a public body that is representative of society as a whole, even or especially in terms of its diversity. This has been particularly instrumental in discussions about the growing proportion of Muslims in the armed forces (Ware 2014). These examples indicate that there is a lingering value in retaining migrants in the state sector given the significance of their minority status and the politics of race and faith, especially in the context of deployments in Muslim-majority countries.

Restating the function of military institutions to fulfil their symbolic public responsibilities helps to illustrate some of the contingencies of martial labour and the restructuring of the global security industry that has taken place over the last two decades. The vulnerability of individuals such as Baleiwai and many others whose cases were picked up by the UK media, illustrate the precarious and risky nature of labour undertaken by military migrants, certainly in terms of legal status and immigration controls. They also reveal the tensions between the public perception of soldiering as a profession that is expected to confer the rights to residency, if not full citizenship, and the populist politics of immigration control. This point was driven home in the emotive campaign for the rights of ex-Gurkhas to reside in the UK which caught the national headlines in 2008–9.

Colonial constructs of difference

In his book on military orientalism, Patrick Porter (2011: 2) writes 'In and through war, people formulate what it means to be Western or non-Western ... the very idea of the "West" replenishes itself through war'. The representation of 'Gurkhas' as an exceptional group of soldiers reveals the durability of colonial constructs of ethnic difference derived from the history of racial subjugation. Although Nepalis are by no means the only ethnic group to have acquired an association with militaristic aptitude and expertise, their example underscores the value of a historical approach. For example, the concept of martial races is a crucial factor in understanding why Gurkhas were so valued within British military calculations (Chapter 18, this volume).

The Gurkha security guards who were awarded the medals for gallantry provide the perfect guide for understanding the way in which some categories of former servicemen are able to consolidate their ethnic identity as a positive asset as they transfer into a different job market that requires minimal training and preparation for jobs using lethal force. The brochure advertising G4S Gurkha Security Services explains that, 'Our workforce consists of enhanced security officers from a variety of backgrounds and former British Army Gurkha officers.' The organization is motivated by 'The Gurkha ethos', which is described as follows:

> Gurkhas have served the British Crown for almost 200 years and fought and died alongside their British comrades in nearly every major war. Displaying loyalty, energy, discipline and honour, our ex-military management team all maintain their Gurkha ethos, and this is instilled within their teams. These attributes result in very low turnover of staff and exceptional levels of professionalism, calmness and clarity – even in volatile and traumatic situations.
>
> *(G4S Gurkha Security Services brochure)*

The fluency of this advertising copy compresses an extraordinary amount of history, particularly in the first sentence. It is inevitably simplistic as well as inaccurate as it gives the impression of consistent, unquestioning loyalty to the British Crown. It also muddies the distinction between the word 'Gurkha' as a coded ethnic and gendered identification and a term that simply refers to their professional affiliation.

The notion of a 'Gurkha ethos', described in the publicity for G4S Gurkha Security Services, has been undeniably strengthened by a highly effective media discourse that stressed these qualities while also cementing the notion that military service demands particular rewards. Different representations of Gurkha heritage serve particular purposes both in Nepal and Britain, where their status as military migrants drives continuing campaigns for pensions, parity with UK troops and the right to reside in the UK with access to health services and social welfare benefits. Writing about 'Nepalese Gurkhas and their battle for equal rights', Ché Singh Kochar-George has argued that 'colonial stereotyping along racial lines' not only occupies a powerful place in the public imagination but also means that 'colonial constructs of difference' continue to influence decisions made by the courts and government (Kochar-George 2010: 44). Within this tradition, the frequent repetition of words such as 'discipline', 'loyalty', and 'honour' has also been instrumental in allowing former Gurkhas to position themselves – and to be branded – as ideal 'niche' employees within the PMSC sector as well.

However, it is important to note that following the tripartite agreement with Nepal in 1947, the Gurkha 'brand' is not confined to those who worked within the UK armed forces, even though their numbers have been drastically reduced (Ware 2011). Chisholm's valuable ethnographic work underlines the 'overall sense of exceptionalism as well as hierarchy of subclassifications' of 'Gurkha' as a label (Chisholm 2014a: 34). She discovered that most of the men she interviewed first aspired to join the British Army, then the Gurkha Contingent of the Singapore Police Force; only upon failing that would they become an Indian Gurkha. However, despite this hierarchy, she found that all of the Gurkhas 'claimed to share common traits and could easily be identified from their Nepalese civilian or police counterparts who did not share their same discipline and loyalty' (ibid.: 34). This point is worth emphasizing since Nepali nationals comprise a significant proportion of military migrants performing unskilled labour on US military bases.

The global PMSC labour market is undoubtedly a zone that is stratified by economic and political interests mirroring those of the national states, organizations and companies competing for contracts. Nationality is a surprisingly important factor as many prefer to buy security services from their co-nationals, 'often promoting this fact in their self-definitions and in the marketing of their services' (Leander 2009: 14; 2013). In the same way that armed forces routinely prefer to work with 'contractors who are either of their own nationality or at least who share a common military culture and background, private companies and individuals also find it easier to have security provided by people who share their security culture' (ibid.: 14). This fact, compounded by the reputations and aspirations of particular ethnicized and racialized groups, provides another determining element in the dynamics of military migration.

Migration journeys

Writing from a different geopolitical perspective, Brigden and Vogt make useful connections between the life choices of Salvadoran men migrating to the US and young US citizens who enlist voluntarily in the military, two groups that embody a 'neoliberal subjectivity produced through processes of violence, capital accumulation and militarization' (Brigden and Vogt 2015: 2). Arguing that the decision to join the armed forces and the decision to leave one's home may both be conceptualized 'within larger systems of social and economic uncertainty' (ibid.: 3), they suggest that:

> As archetypes in their respective societies, both migrants and soldiers embody ideals of agency: resourceful men facing violence with bravery, discipline and a sense of duty.

Migration journeys and wars can both be conceptualized as rites of passage and spaces of liminality marked by strong sense of communitas, courage and sacrifice. Migrants and soldiers search for respect, guided by notions of upward mobility, service and community, albeit in very different ways.

(Brigden and Vogt 2015: 6)

Brigden and Vogt's anthropological research provides fresh insights into these two areas – migration and military recruitment – indicating the value of a multi-disciplinary perspective. But what of the young men and women who are prepared to traverse the globe in pursuit of military work, also guided by 'notions of upward mobility, service and community'? The example of military-related migration from Fiji provides a valuable case study here. In her discussion of militarism in the Pacific region, Teresia Teaiwa (2005: 204) describes how 'the cultures of militarism that pervade contemporary Fiji life are rapidly changing in the increasing globalization of labour and rapacious consumerization of society'. Her gendered analysis illustrates the complex way in which military values and ideals both influence and reflect social, political and cultural divisions in 'the most militarized independent nation in the Pacific' (ibid.: 202).

Each year, hundreds of young people, mainly men, leave Fiji to work in PMSCs, contributing to national economies that have come to rely on their remittances. In 2006 more than 1000 Fijians were working for private corporations in Iraq and Kuwait in security, transport and training (Maclellan 2006). The following year, a journalist from Bloomberg news agency witnessed what he called a 'mercenary harvest' in the country (Copetas 2007). In 2007 the UN Human Rights Council commissioned a survey following concerns that there were large numbers of Fijian men working as private contractors in Iraq. Their report began by acknowledging that 'Fiji has an established tradition of well-trained, disciplined and highly skilled military and security personnel, who perform security functions in various capacities worldwide' (UNHRC 2008). Recognizing the different factors propelling young people to seek work in PMSCs, it warned that 'unemployment and/or underemployment, a migratory population ready to perform security work abroad, and largely unmonitored activities of private security companies in Fiji have facilitated such recruitment in Fiji for work, including in Iraq' (ibid.). However, the report warned that 'in a number of instances, the security-related functions carried out by Fijians abroad through private military and security companies (PMSCs) may qualify as mercenary-related activities' (ibid.).

Conclusion

These juridical issues affecting the employment and immigration status of military migrants clearly need to be understood within national as well as wider comparative contexts. I have expanded the category here to encompass all those drawn to work in military and security professions, regardless of whether they are classified as mercenaries, private contractors or conventional soldiers. The value of including non-nationals who work in state armed forces in this discussion is that it highlights the common dilemmas faced by governments responding to escalating costs of maintaining standing armies, falling recruitment numbers and the mounting legal, ethical and political implications of placing soldiers in situations of risk. While in many settings military service once provided a link between democratic citizenship and social welfare, the turn towards recruiting migrants, even those with strong postcolonial connections to 'the mother country', signals an underlying crisis in the relationship between citizen and state. The UK example indicates that collaboration with the private security sector is replacing the use of migrant labour as a more politically (and financially) acceptable solution to shortfalls in voluntary recruitment. This has significant implications for changing ideals of militarized citizenship.

The figure of the military migrant directs attention to the wholesale marketization of military and security work as well as to the internal hierarchies and patterns of marginalization within this market. Meanwhile the discordant representation of soldiers as selfless heroes, ready to die for their countries, and of mercenaries as self-seeking professional warriors, who sell their skills for financial gain, appears ever more stark and unconvincing.

Bibliography

Brigden, N. K. and Vogt, W. A. (2015) 'Homeland Heroes: Migrants and Soldiers in the Neoliberal Era', *Antipode* 47(2): 303–22.

Chisholm, A. (2014a) 'The Silenced and Indispensible: Gurkhas in Private Military Security Companies', *International Feminist Journal of Politics* 16(1): 26–47.

Chisholm, A. (2014b) 'Marketing the Gurkha Security Package: Colonial Histories and Neoliberal Economies of Private Security', *Security Dialogue* 45(4): 349–72.

Copetas, A. C. (2007) 'Dogs of War Unleashed by Fiji at Right Price for UN, Blackwater,' *Bloomberg* 29 October, www.bloomberg.com/apps/news?sid=aiDndsnA7.5k&pid=newsarchive.

Eichler, M. (2014) 'Citizenship and the Contracting Out of Military Work: From National Conscription to Globalized Recruitment', *Citizenship Studies* 18(6–7): 600–614.

Giroux, H. (2014) 'The Militarization of Racism and Neoliberal Violence', *Truthout* 18 August, http://truth-out.org/opinion/item/25660-the-militarization-of-racism-and-neoliberal-violence.

Higate, P. (2012) 'Martial Races and Enforcement Masculinities of the Global South: Weaponising Fijian, Chilean, and Salvadoran Postcoloniality in the Mercenary Sector', *Globalizations* 9(1): 35–52.

Kochar-George, C. S. (2010) 'Nepalese Gurkhas and Their Battle for Equal Rights', *Race and Class* 52(2): 43–61.

Leander, A. (2009) 'Contractualized Citizenship, Nationalized Contracting, Militarized Soldiering: The Market for Force and the Right to have Protection Rights', http://openarchive.cbs.dk/cbsweb/handle/10398/7962.

Leander, A. (2013) 'Marketing Security Matters: Undermining De-securitization Through Acts of Citizenship', in X. Guillaume and J. Huysmans (eds), *Security and Citizenship: The Constitution of Political Being*, New York: Routledge, pp. 97–113.

Leander, A. and Joenniemi, P. (2006) 'In Conclusion: National Lexica of Conscription', in. Joenniemi, P. (Ed), *The Changing Face of European Conscription*, London: Ashgate, pp. 151–62.

Li, D. (2015) 'Offshoring the Army: Migrant Workers and the US Military', *UCLA Law Review* 62(124): 124–74.

Lutz, C. (2002) 'Making War at Home in the United States: Militarization and the Current Crisis', *American Anthropologist* 104(3): 723–35.

MacClellan, N. (2006) 'From Fiji to Fallujah: The War in Iraq and the Privatization of Pacific security', *Pacific Journalism Review* 12(2): 47–65.

McCartney, H. (2010) 'The Military Covenant and the Civil–Military Contract in Britain', *International Affairs* 86(2): 411–28.

Porter, P. (2011) *Military Orientalism: Eastern War through Western Eyes*, New York: Columbia University Press.

Singer, P. W. (2008) *Corporate Warriors: The Rise of the Privatized Military Industry*, Ithaca, NY: Cornell University Press.

Teaiwa, T. K. (2005) 'Articulated Cultures: Militarism and Masculinities in Fiji during the Mid 1990s', *Fijian Studies* 3(2): 201–22.

UNHRC (2008) *Report of the Working Group on the Use of Mercenaries as a Means of Violating Human Rights and Impeding the Exercise of the Right of Peoples to Self-Determination*, Addendum: Mission to Fiji, 14–18 May 2007, www.ohchr.org/EN/Issues/Mercenaries/WGMercenaries/Pages/WGMercenaries Index.aspx.

Vuibau, T. (2013) 'Soldier Returns Bravery Medals', *Fiji Times* 23 January.

Ware, V. (2011) '"Johnny Gurkha Loves a Party": The Colonial Film Archive and the Racial Imaginary of the Worker-Warrior', in L. Grieveson and C. McCabe (eds), *Film and the End of Empire*, London: British Film Institute/Palgrave Macmillan, pp. 119–34.

Ware, V. (2014) *Military Migrants: Fighting for YOUR Country*, Basingstoke: Palgrave Macmillan.

16

PRIVATE SECURITY AND GENDER

Maya Eichler

In recent years, a new set of scholarship that focuses on gender and private security in global politics has emerged. This feminist and feminist-informed critical gender scholarship examines private security processes, practices, and actors through the lens of gender. It uncovers how private security shapes and is shaped by masculinities, femininities, and gendered relations of power. While gender has become established as analytical category in the study of private security, the treatment of gender in industry and policy discourses continues to be problematic. It is therefore necessary to distinguish critical from problem-solving approaches to gender and private security. A problem-solving approach frames gender issues as problems which can be solved by adding more female employees or including language on gender-based violence into regulatory frameworks. But such an approach underestimates the extent to which gender matters in private security.

The chapter outlines the central themes of the critical gender literature on private security to show that gender is fundamental to military outsourcing, the operation of the private security industry, the constitution of contractor identities, and the wide-ranging effects of private security. Critical gender scholars offer crucial empirical, theoretical, and methodological insights into private security that advance the field as a whole. They illustrate the importance of gender, but also of intersectionality, multiple scales, and the political role of PMSCs. The chapter first outlines the differences between problem-solving and critical gender approaches. Second, it identifies four key themes in the emerging field of critical gender studies in private security:

- security privatization as a gendered process;
- gendered industry practices and discourses;
- the complex gendering of contractor identities; and
- the gendered effects of private security on accountability.

In conclusion, the chapter explores potential avenues for future research and considers what it would mean for the study of private security to take gender seriously.

Problem-solving versus critical approaches

Not every scholar or practitioner neatly fits the problem-solving or critical label. However, understanding the differences between problem-solving and critical approaches allows for greater reflexivity and clarity in relation to existing conceptualizations of 'private security and gender'. The two approaches differ in their ontological, epistemological, and normative understandings. To view private security through a gender lens, as critical gender scholars do, has vastly different implications than to see gender as an incidental aspect of private security that can be 'corrected' by tweaking policies (as a problem-solving approach attempts to do). Problem-solving scholars and practitioners take as their starting point the current private security industry. The industry's existence, practices, and needs for clients, profit, and weak regulation are taken for granted. In addition to PMSCs, attention is paid to industry clients, states (as clients and regulators), and other bodies that shape the regulatory framework (e.g. United Nations, International Committee of the Red Cross, International Stability Operations Association). With this ontological starting point, gender appears only in relation to problems that may negatively affect industry reputation and revenue, be they gender-based violence committed by private contractors, negative media images of hypermasculine (i.e. excessively violent) contractors, or the marginalization of female employees within the industry. When gender is framed as a *problem* for the industry, paying attention to gender comes to be seen as potentially beneficial to industry.

A problem-solving approach is found in industry publications (such as the *Journal of Stability Operations*, previously the *International Journal of Peace Operations*), voluntary regulatory frameworks (such as the International Code of Conduct for Private Security Service Providers), as well as in the DCAF/OSCE/UN Gender and Security Sector Reform Toolkit 'Private Military and Security Companies and Gender' (Schulz and Yeung 2008). Companies' concern for their public image has spurred acknowledgement of gender-specific problems such as sexual abuse and gender-based violence through the ICOC, a voluntary regulatory document with 708 signatories as of September 2013 (see Chapter 26, this volume). Gender is seen as an issue that can be voluntarily addressed by companies, rather than as an issue that requires more robust state regulation or fundamental changes to how PMSCs operate. The DCAF/OSCE/UN Toolkit moreover argues that PMSCs can benefit from recruiting more women as it would help them improve operational effectiveness. Women are primarily seen as a 'value-added' to the industry, as they can liaise with local populations and conduct security checks on women. Writing in the *International Journal of Peace Operations*, Kristen Cordell (2012) similarly argues that enhanced revenue, reputation, and operational effectiveness are key benefits the industry will gain from including more women. In terms of its normative implications, such an approach instrumentalizes gender while legitimizing private security. The overall goal is to strengthen the functioning of the industry in the face of concerns over its impacts on women. However, an approach that focuses on industry interests underestimates the ways in which gender matters within contemporary security arrangements, including private security.

The first publication on PMSCs and gender was the DCAF/OSCE/UN Toolkit mentioned above (Schulz and Yeung 2008), which adopted an almost entirely problem-solving framework. Since 2009, however, we have seen the emergence of critical gender scholarship on private security, with a marked increase in publications in 2012. These publications have appeared in critical and feminist international relations journals as well as in numerous edited volumes. In contrast to a problem-solving approach, a critical gender approach to private security does not take the existing private security industry for granted. Instead it asks: How is gender fundamental to the emergence, functioning, and effects of private security? A critical gender approach begins from the feminist insight that the provision of security has historically been, and to this day remains, closely tied to the organization of gender. Gender refers to the socially constructed hierarchical norms of masculinities and femininities that legitimize unequal gendered relations of power. Hierarchical gender norms that privilege masculinity pervade societies across the globe, but tend to be particularly pronounced in the military and security sphere. Critical gender scholarship views the private security industry as a key site for the (re)production of gender norms. At the same time it recognizes the multiple sites at which gender norms enable and legitimize private security, be they policy and regulatory documents, company websites, media coverage and commentary, training courses, personal identities, or neoliberal discourse. Moreover, a critical gender approach looks to multiple actors to gain knowledge about private security. The state and industry are key actors, but so are ordinary women and men working in or affected by private security. Neither private security nor gender is taken for granted, but instead their co-constitution becomes the object of investigation. Such an approach broadens our understanding of gender and its relevance to private security. The normative goal of a critical gender approach is not to help legitimize the private security industry but to open up space for a reconsideration of prevailing security and gender arrangements.

The emerging field of critical gender studies in private security includes a multidisciplinary group of scholars – from political science, International Relations and Global Political Economy, sociology, and international law – working at the intersection of gender studies and private security. Key contributors to the new field of critical gender studies in private security include Amanda Chisholm, Maya Eichler, Paul Higate, Jutta Joachim, Andrea Schneiker, Saskia Stachowitsch and Ana Vrdoljak. These scholars employ a variety of perspectives, including critical, postcolonial, poststructuralist, liberal, and other feminist perspectives, as well as a wide range of methodological approaches such as ethnography, participant-observation, and discourse analysis. Critical gender scholars go beyond an analysis of masculinities and femininities in private security. Drawing on the concept of intersectionality, they emphasize the intersections between gender, class, race, nation, citizenship, and other categories of social difference, and their significance for a better understanding of the practices of PMSCs. Critical gender scholarship also highlights the importance of considering private security at multiple scales of analysis. It sees private security as a local, regional, national and global practice (as do conventional analyses of private security), but also as an embodied practice. Finally, animated by feminist concerns about gendered power relations and inequalities, critical gender scholars bring a unique political view to the study of PMSCs. They recognize PMSCs as political actors shaping not only security environments but gender norms and the gendered global order, and therefore do not treat them as neutral market actors simply filling a void in security provision.

Critical gender scholars have established gender as a key category of analysis for private security in global politics. They have done so by arguing that security privatization, industry practices and discourses, contractor identities, and problems of accountability are gendered. A discussion of each of these themes of critical gender scholarship in private security follows.

Engendering security privatization

Privatization – a key strategy of neoliberalism – has redefined the role of the state and its citizens, and opened up security provision to profit making. Critical gender scholars argue that this redrawing of the lines between state and society and state and market are fundamentally gendered. Security privatization is a gendered neoliberal economic and political project. Here critical gender scholars argue that we need to go beyond a narrow focus on the private security industry to examine how processes of security privatization shape and are shaped by gender

(Stachowitsch 2015). For example, unsettling the male citizen-soldier model is an important precondition for the large-scale outsourcing of military work to the private sector, while gendered neoliberal discourses help create legitimacy for market solutions. Furthermore, security privatization has gender-specific effects, reinforcing masculine dominance in the military and security sphere while undermining transparency and accountability in relation to gender inequalities and gender-based violence.

One key avenue for critical gender research into private security is the neoliberal transformation of militarized citizenship. Critical gender scholars conceptualize the gendered re-organization of public militaries from conscription, all-volunteer forces, to the outsourcing of military labour as an aspect of gendered neoliberal state restructuring (Eichler 2013; Stachowitsch 2013). For example, in the US the end of conscription and the decline of the male citizen-soldier model were central aspects of the neoliberal transformation of militarized citizenship, and were instrumental in paving the way for the increased outsourcing of military and security functions to the private sector. Termination of the military draft in 1973 initiated a shift in the military sphere from the logic of citizenship to the logic of the market. The neoliberal remaking of militarized citizenship also involved a transformation of gender relations in the military and security sphere. The effects of neoliberalism on the US militarized gender order included both a disruption of established gender roles through the introduction of an all-volunteer force and reinforcement of male dominance through privatization.

Women's increased participation in the public military weakens the historically strong link between masculinity, citizenship, and military security and challenges the notion of men as militarized protectors of women. However, private security reconstitutes the link between masculinity and security by only very selectively incorporating women, and thus contributes to unequal gender relations in the military and security sphere (Eichler 2013). Stachowitsch (2013) has aptly theorized military privatization as a process of remasculinization. Remasculinization refers to the remaking and reinforcement of patriarchy through clear gender boundaries and a reaffirming of masculine primacy. The gendered implications of security privatization thus reach beyond the industry and contractors – they reinforce societal understandings of masculinized security, protection, and power.

Under neoliberalism the traditionally masculinized state and public sector have become discursively feminized, while the market has become masculinized. Such gendered constructions are used to portray public militaries as weak and ineffective, in contrast to PMSCs who are assumed to be operationally and financially efficient. While public militaries today rely more heavily on a female workforce (what some disparagingly refer to as the feminization of public militaries), the private security sector largely excludes women and refrains from gender equality policies. However, as Stachowitsch points out it is not simply the case that 'the allegedly more women-friendly state is eroding at the expense of a masculinized global market for force' (Stachowitsch 2015: 19). Instead, neoliberal policies such as security privatization redraw the boundaries between public and private, state and market, and society and citizen, with particular gendered effects. Importantly, not just the market but 'gendered state structures and their transformation are central to understanding the gendered effects of private security' (ibid.: 35).

Critical gender scholars show that privatization cannot be fully grasped without an understanding of the transformation of gendered states under neoliberalism. This transformation includes shifting relations between state and male citizen-soldiers, and between newly feminized states and masculinized markets. Thus, gender lies at the heart of changes in citizenship and state-market relations that, in part, enable security privatization.

Gendered industry practices and discourses

In addition to the state, the private security industry is a crucial site for critical gender analyses of private security. Here the focus is first on gendered hiring practices and the concomitant gendered divisions of labour within the industry, and second on gendered discourses aimed at increasing the legitimacy of the industry. Both the practices and discourses found in the private security industry rely on gender, often in ways that intersect with race and citizenship.

Critical gender scholarship draws attention to the gendered hiring practices that marginalize women from newly emerging private military labour markets (Eichler 2013; Stachowitsch 2013). PMSCs often recruit their employees from the Army and Special Forces, that is, from already heavily masculinized environments, especially when recruiting employees for security-based jobs in the field. Such a recruitment strategy exacerbates the gender inequalities found in public militaries. Women have gained entry into an increasing number of militaries and military roles over the past few decades, but women are still underrepresented, especially in combat units where they usually make up only a miniscule percentage of personnel. Even as more militaries lift the combat ban on women, most militaries still exclude women from all or some combat roles and do not permit women to join the Special Forces. Therefore, few women are considered to have the necessary training to work in the area of private security and armed protection more specifically. Instead, female employees in the private military and security industry are concentrated in feminized tasks associated with support functions such as administrative and clerical work.

The gendered division of labour in the industry also includes intra-masculine hierarchies, as a result of the heavy reliance of PMSCs on (mostly) male workers from the global South, from countries such as the Philippines, Bangladesh, Nepal, El Salvador, Chile, India, Pakistan, and Uganda (see Barker 2009; Chisholm 2014a, 2014b; Eichler 2014; Higate 2012a). The global labour market in private security rests on a hierarchy that constitutes racialized men from the global South as subordinate masculinities vis-à-vis the hegemonic masculinities of white, Western contractors. These differences are evident not only in the pay and working conditions, but in the kind of work performed. The more dangerous the work, the higher is the proportion of local and migrant workers among private security employees.

Third-country and local nationals are constructed as subordinate masculinities not only through prevalent hiring practices that rely on and reproduce global gendered, racialized, and class hierarchies but also through industry discourses, as Joachim and Schneiker (2015) show. Drawing on an analysis of company websites they explore how the construction of Western contractors as the world's 'best security experts' intersects with culture, race, and class to reinforce social inequalities. The authors argue that the power of PMSCs rests not only on efficiency and cost-effectiveness, but also on a discursive hierarchy of masculinities. In earlier work, Joachim and Schneiker (2012) explored the gendered strategies that allow PMSCs to shed the hypermasculine militarized image of mercenaries for one that emphasizes humanitarianism. Also examining constructions of masculinity, Sandra Via (2010) argues that the transition from Blackwater to Xe entailed a concerted effort to distance the company from the original self-image of 'frontier or cowboy masculinity' and shift towards a softer and more legitimate image. As these examples show, gender informs industry practices and discourses, and is a key part of the industry's struggle for legitimacy and individual companies' struggles to compete. Moreover, the gendered subordination of so-called third-country and local nationals is central to the economic and political calculations that justify the outsourcing of military labour.

The gender identities of private contractors

Critical gender scholarship also contributes to our understanding of private security as a new and crucial site for the (re)production of militarized gender identities. As discussed above, security privatization is intimately linked to the weakening of the citizen soldier as a key masculine identity of the modern nation-state. But, private contractor masculinities are not simply defined in opposition to public military masculinities, nor are they monolithic. Instead, private security masculinity needs to be understood as first, a hybridized form of public and private militarized masculinities, second, fractured by class, race, and nationality, and third, not only competing with but in part reinforcing public soldier identity. It is worth noting that while important work is being done on masculine identities in private security, there is a lacuna of research into feminine identities in private security.

Higate's (2012b) work in particular brings analytical attention to the gendered identity constructions of male private contractors. He moves away from the focus on the state or industry that is often found in critical gender scholarship and instead focuses on the micro-sociological dimensions of private security. Exploring how private contractors construct their identities on the ground, that is, how male contractors understand their masculine identities and how these get constructed and performed through discourse and practice, Higate shows that masculine identities in the private security sector are not so much defined in opposition to, but in a complex interplay of continuity and discontinuity with public military masculinities. Contractors are often ex-military personnel, who have undergone socialization and training in public military institutions. These 'hybridized soldier-contractors' bring with them, but also remake, military values and culture (Higate 2012b). Thus, the binary of public-private is misleading when it comes to gendered contractor identities. This insight speaks to ongoing discussions in the field of private security about the importance of reconceptualizing the relationship between public and private security instead of assuming a strict public/private divide.

What further emerges from Higate's often ethnographically informed work on gendered contractor identity is a different and more complex picture than the stereotypical image of hypermasculine, 'trigger-happy cowboys' associated with contractors in public media and some scholarly accounts. Drawing on memoirs of private contractors and also on his participation in a close protection training course (Higate 2012c, 2015), he argues that UK and US contractors construct their identities through gendered discourses of the professional versus the hypermasculine 'other'. UK contractors seek to distance themselves from the perceived hypermasculine US contractors, constructing instead a self-identity as professionals. Chisholm (2014a, 2014b, 2015) further complicates this picture of gendered contractor identity through her analysis of Gurkhas who work in private security. She shows that gendered contractor identities not only intersect with national identity, but are racialized and shaped by colonial histories. Gurkhas seeking work in private security, as well as their agents, reproduce British colonial discourses of Gurkhas as martial men to distinguish themselves to potential clients. But Gurkhas rely on colonial narratives also to contest their subordinate status as third-country nationals within the security industry. They often view themselves as more able and fierce warriors than their Western counterparts, constructing a distinct militarized masculine identity for themselves. Barker (2009) sheds light on another aspect of gendered identity construction in the context of privatization. She argues that the outsourcing of certain forms of work associated with reproduction (cleaning, cooking, laundry etc.) to migrant men working for PMSCs on US overseas bases helps to reaffirm a masculinized image of US soldiers. With this 'unmanly' work outsourced to the private sector and performed by migrant men from the global South, the US soldier is symbolically reconstituted as masculinized 'warrior' against the backdrop of class, gender, and racialized divisions among troops. As these examples show, the masculine identities of private contractors are complexly connected to the masculine identities of public soldiers. They also need to be understood as diverse, and intersecting with national, class, racial, and colonial identities.

Despite a lacuna of scholarship on feminine identities in private security, two preliminary observations can be made. Female employees in the private security industry are primarily found in jobs associated with femininity, reinforcing dichotomous and hierarchical gender identities. At the same time, access to economic resources may allow some women to buy security services in ways that challenge conventional gendered relations of protection. More research into female contractors and clients is, however, required for a fuller picture of the construction of feminine identities in and through private security.

The gendered effects of private security

Much of the literature on security privatization is driven by the practical challenge of how to regulate the industry and hold PMSCs politically, legally, and financially accountable. Critical gender scholars make important contributions to understanding accountability and regulation of PMSCs by foregrounding women and/or gender. They show that the use of PMSCs can negatively impact women's human security, existing regulatory regimes covering PMSCs have serious limitations in regards to gender-based violence and discrimination, and finally, that security privatization allows for a de-politicization of gender equality issues. From a critical gender perspective, security privatization is problematic on several counts.

In her work on global accountability, Sperling (2009, 2015) examines the use of private contractors as part of UN peacekeeping missions that are deployed to countries with weak state capacity. The use of PMSCs in such contexts further undermines accountability and can have detrimental consequences for women's human security, creating conditions for gender-based exploitation and violence to go unchecked. In the infamous case of DynCorp contractors employed by the International Police Task Force on UN mission in Bosnia and Herzegovina, the UN failed to adequately respond to allegations of sexual exploitation and abuse of women by peacekeepers. While this incident spurred the development of US legislation and UN policy to improve accountability vis-à-vis local citizens, none of the private contractors allegedly involved in the human trafficking of girls and women for the purposes of sexual exploitation were tried. As Sperling (2009) argues, the use of transnational military force, especially when it includes private contractors, tends to undermine accountability towards local populations, with particular gendered effects.

Vrdoljak (2011, 2015) has documented the shortcomings of existing regulatory regimes covering PMSCs in regards to gender-related violence, harassment, and discrimination. The lack of a robust regulatory framework reinforces concerns about transparency and accountability in relation to PMSCs and poses serious challenges for the security of women. Gender considerations are being incorporated into non-binding good practices guidelines – through the Montreux Document, the UN Draft Convention, and in particular the International Code of Conduct. Interestingly, the International Code of Conduct is one of the weakest tools (in terms of enforcement) but has the most detailed consideration of gender. Three of its 70 paragraphs address gender-based violence directed at both civilians during deployment and female co-workers (paragraph 38), the selection and vetting of personnel (disqualifying personnel who have formerly engaged in criminal activity including rape, sexual abuse, and human trafficking, paragraph 48), and the adoption of policies that support a healthy work environment, such as policies on sexual harassment (paragraph 64). However, as Vrdoljak (2015) argues, what is needed is an international legal instrument regulating PMSCs that can hold perpetrators to account and secure reparations for victims. The current trend towards voluntary self-regulation limits the potential for true accountability when it comes to the violation of women's human rights through PMSCs, whether of female employees or local women on the ground.

Security privatization creates problems of accountability felt most immediately by women in the countries of operation, but equally, it creates problems for domestic accountability in states undertaking military outsourcing that have particular gendered effects. The privatization of military security not only enables states to circumvent citizens' democratic control over questions of war and peace, but also undermines the claims for greater inclusion in the military sphere made by women and minority groups over the past decades. The private sector is by definition based on de-regulation that allows for questions of gender equality to be sidelined. The market logic by which the private sector operates displaces gender equality principles that exist in the public sphere. Privatization depoliticizes questions of gender equality, while at the same time it reduces transparency in regards to gendered employment practices in the military and security sphere (Eichler 2013; Stachowitsch 2013).

As these examples show, privatization creates serious problems for addressing gender inequalities and gender-based violence. Critical gender scholarship underscores the need for stronger national and international regulation that is informed by feminist insights and not primarily by problem-solving concerns. It also highlights the importance of including gender in our critique of the depoliticizing effects of privatization.

Conclusion

This chapter has provided an overview of four key themes in critical gender scholarship on private security:

- security privatization as a gendered process;
- gendered industry practices and discourses;
- the complex gendering of contractor identities; and
- the gendered effects of private security on accountability.

Recent work by critical gender scholars has moreover examined gendered sacrifice, the politics of protection, heteronormativity, and feminist ethics in relation to private security (see Baggiarini 2015; Eichler 2015; Hendershot 2015; Terry 2015). There are many more aspects of private security that would benefit from the insights of critical gender scholars. Most importantly, we need to study the experiences of female employees in private security and the ways in which the private security industry reinforces gender inequalities. Similarly, we know very little about the gendering of private security clients, and how privatization reshapes protection relations. Furthermore, the gendered family dynamics of private contractors and the effects of outsourcing on often already militarized families require attention. It is essential to document allegations of gender-based violence perpetrated by private contractors beyond the case of sex trafficking in Bosnia. Finally, more feminist attention needs to be paid to ongoing regulatory developments and enforcement mechanisms, if these are to have any significant positive effect on women's security. These are just a few examples of potential avenues for future research in the field of critical gender studies in private security.

Taking gender seriously both widens and sharpens our lens onto private security. It makes us consider a broader range of actors and effects, and a broader set of scales and interactions.

Beyond the conventional focus on states, PMSCs and international organizations, we now see men and women in and around the industry as gendered beings. We think about problems of accountability, regulation, and depoliticization in ways that include gender and women in meaningful ways. We can recognize the importance of examining security privatization at global, national, regional, and local sales as well as the scale of the body. And we begin to pay attention to the interactions of gender, class, race, nationality, and other categories of difference in private security. As such, we are able to see complexly gendered bodies engaged in and affected by private security practices, gender dynamics at the heart of military outsourcing and its effects, and gendered discourses that position PMSCs in hierarchical relation to other actors. Examining private security through a critical feminist-informed gender lens allows for a richer and more accurate account of the outsourcing of military work, and a more accurate accounting of its costs (Enloe 2014).

Bibliography

Baggiarini, B. (2015) 'Military Privatization and the Gendered Politics of Sacrifice', in M. Eichler (ed.), *Gender and Private Security in Global Politics*, New York: Oxford University Press, pp. 37–54.

Barker, I. V. (2009) '(Re)producing American Soldiers in an Age of Empire', *Politics and Gender* 5(2): 211–35.

Chisholm, A. (2014a) 'The Silenced and Indispensable: Gurkhas in Private Military Security Companies', *International Feminist Journal of Politics* 16(1): 26–47.

Chisholm, A. (2014b) 'Marketing the Gurkha Security Package: Colonial Histories and Neoliberal Economies of Private Security', *Security Dialogue* 45(4): 349–72.

Chisholm, A. (2015) 'From Warriors of Empire to Martial Contractors: Reimagining Gurkhas in Private Security', in M. Eichler (ed.), *Gender and Private Security in Global Politics*, New York: Oxford University Press, pp. 95–113.

Cordell, K. (2012) 'From Remedial Action to Women's Empowerment: Implications of the US National Action Plan for PMSCs', *Journal of International Peace Operations* 7(4): 12–13.

Eichler, M. (2013) 'Gender and the Privatization of Security: Neoliberal Transformation of the Militarized Gender Order', *Critical Studies on Security* 1(3): 311–25.

Eichler, M. (2014) 'Contracting Out Military Work: From National Conscription to Globalized Recruitment', *Citizenship Studies* 18(6–7): 600–14.

Eichler, M. (2015) 'Gender, PMSCs, and the Global Rescaling of Protection: Implications for Feminist Security Studies', in M. Eichler (ed.), *Gender and Private Security in Global Politics*, New York: Oxford University Press, pp. 55–72.

Enloe, C. (2014) 'The Recruiter and the Sceptic: A Critical Feminist Approach to Military Studies', *Critical Military Studies* 1(1): 3–10.

Hendershot, C. (2015) 'Heteronormative and Penile Frustrations: The Uneasy Discourse of the ArmorGroup Hazing Scandal', in M. Eichler (ed.), *Gender and Private Security in Global Politics*, New York: Oxford University Press, pp. 146–65.

Higate, P. (2012a) 'Martial Races and Enforcement Masculinities of the Global South: Weaponising Fijian, Chilean, and Salvadoran Postcoloniality in the Mercenary Sector', *Globalizations* 9(1): 35–52.

Higate, P. (2012b) 'In the Business of (In)Security?', in A. Kronsell and E. Svedberg (eds), *Making Gender, Making War: Violence, Military and Peacekeeping Practice*, New York: Routledge, pp. 182–96.

Higate, P. (2012c) 'Cowboys and Professionals: The Politics of Identity Work in the Private and Military Security Company', *Millennium: Journal of International Studies* 40(2): 321–41.

Higate, P. (2015) 'Aversions to Masculine Excess in the Private Military and Security Company and their Effects: Don't Be a "Billy Big Bollocks" and Beware the "Ninja!"', in M. Eichler (ed.), *Gender and Private Security in Global Politics*, New York: Oxford University Press, New York: Oxford University Press, pp. 131–45.

Joachim, J. and Schneiker, A. (2012) 'Of 'True Professionals' and 'Ethical Hero Warriors': A Gender Discourse Analysis of Private Military and Security Companies', *Security Dialogue* 43(6): 495–512.

Joachim, J. and Schneiker, A. (2015) 'The License to Exploit: PMSCs, Masculinities, and Third Country Nationals', in M. Eichler (ed.), *Gender and Private Security in Global Politics*, New York: Oxford University Press, New York: Oxford University Press, pp. 114–28.

Schulz, S. and Yeung, C. (2008) 'Private Military and Security Companies and Gender', in M. Bastick and K. Valasek (eds), *Gender and Security Sector Reform Toolkit*, Geneva: DCAF, OSCE/ODIHR, UN-INSTRAW.

Sperling, V. (2009) *Altered States: The Globalization of Accountability*, Cambridge: Cambridge University Press.

Sperling, V. (2015) 'Engendering Accountability in Private Security and Public Peacekeeping', in M. Eichler (ed.), *Gender and Private Security in Global Politics*, New York: Oxford University Press, pp.169–86.

Stachowitsch, S. (2013) 'Military Privatization and the Remasculinization of the State: Making the Link between the Outsourcing of Military Security and Gendered State Transformations', *International Relations* 27(1): 74–94.

Stachowitsch, S. (2015) 'Military Privatization as a Gendered Process: A Case for Integrating Feminist International Relations and Feminist State Theories', in M. Eichler (ed.), *Gender and Private Security in Global Politics*, New York: Oxford University Press, pp. 19–36.

Terry, J. (2015) 'Responsibility, Empathy, and the Morality of Mercenaries: A Feminist Ethical Appraisal of PMSCs', in M. Eichler (ed.), *Gender and Private Security in Global Politics*, New York: Oxford University Press, pp. 208–25.

Via, S. (2010) 'Gender, Militarism, and Globalization: Soldiers for Hire and Hegemonic Masculinity', in L. Sjoberg and S. Via (eds), *Gender, War, and Militarism: Feminist Perspectives*, Santa Barbara: Praeger, pp. 42–53.

Vrdoljak, A. F. (2011) 'Women and Private Military and Security Companies', in F. Francioni and N. Ronzitti (eds), *War by Contract: Human Rights, Humanitarian Law and Private Contractors*, Oxford: Oxford University Press, pp. 151–70.

Vrdoljak, A. F. (2015) 'Women, PMSCs, and International Law', in M. Eichler (ed.), *Gender and Private Security in Global Politics*, New York: Oxford University Press, pp. 187–207.

17

PRIVATE SECURITY'S ROLE IN SHAPING US FOREIGN POLICY

Renée de Nevers

Foreign policy is the pursuit of national interest in the international arena. This was long the domain of the state, involving state-to-state interactions undertaken by diplomats. Three changes over time complicate our understanding of foreign policy today. The first is the challenge of defining the national interest in a globalized world, when states confront challenges, ranging from climate change to terrorism, that require multilateral and multisector solutions. The second is the erosion of not only the state's role in pursuing its foreign policy, but also the role of diplomats, as other actors, both government agencies and non-state actors, have entered into the arena of government-to-government interaction that was formerly the diplomatic realm.

The third, particularly in the US case, is the blurring of lines between foreign policy and national security policy. This partly reflects the perceived vulnerabilities of a dominant global power, with an expansive view of its international commitments. It is also a response to the terrorist attacks of 11 September 2001 (hereafter '9/11') on New York and Washington DC that generated a climate of insecurity and pervasive threat. This was only heightened by the expanded role of the Defense Department (DOD) in functions formerly undertaken by the State Department, in ways that have put a military face on US foreign policy to a degree that distinguishes it from most other liberal democratic states.

The private security industry is a relatively new actor in the foreign policy arena, and one whose impact has been controversial. Private military and security companies (PMSCs) have both direct and indirect effects on foreign policy. Because specialized PMSCs can be hired for specific tasks, they may effectively implement policies, potentially at reasonable costs. This can facilitate states' foreign policy goals. PMSCs may also take on tasks that enable them to shape perceptions of the national interest and foreign policy, which has raised questions about whether national and corporate interests coincide. Indirectly, PMSCs can have an impact on foreign policy if their actions colour overseas perceptions of their home state, either favourably or negatively.

State actors need to be cognizant of the potential impact of reliance on PMSCs for their broader foreign policy goals. PMSCs are likely to be part of the international environment for the foreseeable future, and governments rely on them for a broad range of tasks. It is critical to understand both how PMSCs affect foreign policy making and how their use affects the international environment in which foreign policy is conducted.

In this chapter I examine the variety of ways that private security affects foreign policy. Private actors shape foreign policy by influencing the decision-making processes guiding foreign policy, and they carry out tasks to support government actors and to implement foreign policy. I then examine the implications of PMSC involvement in the foreign policy process. Domestically, reliance on PMSCs affects both the capacity of the state to make foreign policy decisions and what those decisions look like. Their actions have international effects as well, shaping state-to-state relations in numerous different ways. I explore each of these in turn.

Shaping foreign policy decisions

One of the most critical ways in which private actors influence foreign policy decision-making is through their role as intelligence providers. To date, this is a particularly US phenomenon. A significant portion of intelligence analysis – and increasingly, collection, is done by private contractors (Chapter 8, this volume). After the 9/11 attacks, the US intelligence community was reorganized and it expanded exponentially to address a broad range of perceived threats. Much of this expansion occurred in the private sector. In 2010, 1,931 private companies were working on intelligence-related programmes; of these, 533 had been created after the 9/11 attacks (Priest 2010). By one estimate, contractors made up thirty percent of the US intelligence workforce at that time.

Within the intelligence community, contractors carry out a range of tasks with direct influence on foreign policy. Domestically, these range from analysing terrorist networks to providing advice to government officials, and staffing critical facilities in the defence and intelligence agencies. Intelligence functions are undertaken by contractors internationally as well. Contractors have been used to recruit spies, conduct interrogations, spy on foreign governments, gather information on local factions in fragile states and war zones, and to kill enemy fighters. This means that private security actors shape the intelligence on which foreign policy decisions are based.

In addition to intelligence, PMSCs provide a variety of consulting and training services that offer expertise in foreign and security policy. Private companies have contributed to strategic policy decisions, conducting reviews of government policies such as Plan Colombia, the US effort to aid the Colombian government's efforts to combat drugs (Singer 2003: 207). PMSCs provide training for intelligence analysts as well as policy-makers. Contractors have conducted classroom training and run simulation exercises for the US State Department and other agencies. This training gives PMSCs an important role in defining both the problems the government perceives in the international arena, and how it chooses to respond (Leander 2006). This has generated concern that corporate interests will distort policy because the profit motive could give companies an interest in extending their business opportunities, rather than resolving conflicts. Crises can be good for business.

Logistics and protection

PMSCs engage in a broad range of tasks related to foreign policy making, in both support and active functions. Their activities fall within three categories: logistics, protection, and reconstruction functions. I address the first two here. PMSCs provide logistical support both for state actors and for international operations supported by states such as humanitarian operations and reconstruction activities (Chapter 7, this volume). The US military has outsourced virtually all of its support functions, ranging from the supply of food and fuel, and construction of overseas bases. European militaries are following suit. Indeed, in the US case, contractors and generals have noted that the military would be hard-pressed to operate overseas without them. This includes peacekeeping operations that support foreign policy goals. This outsourcing follows the logic of liberalization and privatization that gained strength in the 1990s. The UN began formally developing recommendations regarding contracting with PMSCs to support UN operations in 2011, with the goal of establishing a comprehensive approach to UN reliance on contractors – and simply to acknowledge that this contracting takes place (Østensen 2011).

Protection functions involve activities that more directly enable diplomats and other actors to carry out their tasks. Protection services are perhaps the foreign policy function most closely associated with PMSCs today. Many UK-based PMSCs have quietly provided protection (and military training) services for governments friendly to the UK for years. In Iraq and Afghanistan, PMSCs were far more visible. PMSC employees guarded Afghan President Karzai and the head of the Coalition Provisional Authority (CPA) in Iraq in 2003, Paul Bremer. Because the need for security expanded beyond its ability to provide government security personnel, the State Department's Bureau of Diplomatic Security outsourced diplomatic protection by hiring three companies as part of its Worldwide Protective Personal Services contract to provide security for its personnel in high-risk zones, including the now-notorious company Blackwater USA. Security services also include protection of buildings and of convoys. The protection these companies provide has facilitated diplomatic activities at a time when heightened security concerns and requirements for diplomats have made it difficult for them to operate more freely. At the same time, reliance on contractors for these protection functions provoked concern that this created a 'fortress' mentality among diplomats that stymied action.

Reconstruction and security sector reform

PMSCs have also undertaken activities associated with reconstruction after conflicts and humanitarian disasters. As states have recognized that weak states and ungoverned spaces pose potential dangers, assisting in peacebuilding and reconstruction after conflict has become a critical foreign policy goal. Reconstruction can include rebuilding of the state's physical infrastructure as well as efforts to strengthen institutions by providing training and support for government employees and civil society groups, in areas ranging from rule of law to public administration and security sector reform (Avant and de Nevers 2011). Among the functions undertaken by PMSCs, for both states and the UN, are mine clearance, logistics, administration functions, and safety functions (Kinsey 2005).

PMSC activities in this area contribute to the foreign policy goals of states seeking to aid stability and reconstruction. They also illustrate gaps in government capacity to conduct these activities. In some cases, PMSCs have been hired for reconstruction efforts because civilian government employees could not or would not take on these tasks. Notably, in Afghanistan, Provincial Reconstruction Teams (PRTs) were established to enable civilian and military personnel to work jointly to provide reconstruction assistance in regions throughout the country, including development assistance. But the paucity of State Department or USAID employees able or willing to participate led to reliance on contractors to fill the civilian positions on these teams. This also illustrates the relative decline in presence and foreign policy influence of the State Department or USAID, due to the security environment and to resource disparities. USAID, whose employees initially engaged in long-term development activities, now operates primarily through contracts, many of them with PMSCs (Stanger 2009: 62–3).

PMSCs have also played a large role in security sector reform (SSR) efforts, which have been critical not only to peacebuilding after conflicts but also in promoting democratic governance of the armed forces and police. After communism's collapse in the Soviet Union and Eastern Europe, reform of the military to ensure civilian control was considered a key step for states seeking to join NATO, as proof that democratic reforms were being consolidated. SSR extended to police and law enforcement agencies as well. PMSCs were involved in some of these activities in parts of Eastern Europe, and have taken on a significant role in military and police training more broadly.

A significant amount of US foreign aid takes the form of weapons sales or military training, and the training function has largely been outsourced to PMSCs. Training activities are intended to support foreign policy goals by enhancing engagement between states, training and nurturing ties with future leaders, and generating greater understanding and sympathy for the sending country. PMSCs have long provided training in the US, and some have provided military training abroad. In some cases, companies contract with other governments with US government consent, providing military training to allies such as Saudi Arabia. In other cases, PMSCs are hired directly by US agencies. Northrop Grumman was hired by the State Department to provide peacekeeping training in Africa in 2002, for example, the first instance of direct outsourcing of this kind of training function outside the US. By the late 2000s, the scope of training missions that were contracted out had expanded dramatically (see Chapter 12, this volume), with contractors training the Iraqi and Afghan National armies and police. The State Department and DOD also rely on contractors to provide military training in Africa and in Latin America. This is not unique to the US. UK-based PMSCs have long provided military training for countries friendly to their government as well, as a way to nurture contacts with those governments. France also offers military advice and training by both government troops and more recently by a private consortium in which the government owns a stake. This training is designed to bolster French arms sales and to nurture strong ties with former colonies. PMSCs from a range of states now offer training programmes, and most of these explicitly support their home state's foreign policy goals.

Implications: hollowing or force multiplier?

Concern about PMSCs' potential negative impact on foreign policy was raised in some of the earliest studies of the private security industry. Yet the prospect that PMSCs could help generate solutions to long standing problems was also noted (Singer 2003; Avant 2005). On the positive side, outsourcing offers benefits in flexibility and cost savings. PMSCs enable states to hire contractors with specialized skills to address particular tasks or threats, and this allows the government to rely on sophisticated technology that requires specialized training. Alternately, reliance on PMSCs has been characterized as transferring government responsibilities to private hands, which can damage democratic institutions. The debate this has generated remains unresolved, and is linked with broader ideological views about privatization and outsourcing of government functions. I focus on several elements of this debate here: the impact of outsourcing on the state, transparency and accountability, and militarization and reputational effects.

Reliance on PMSCs in foreign policy could lead to a hollowing-out of the state. If the government becomes too dependent on contractors, it could lose the capacity to act without them, or to act in the ways that it wishes. This can affect foreign policy decision-making and practice. As tasks are outsourced, the government may lose the capacity to independently evaluate contracts and decisions on issues such as licensing of security exports. Indeed, the explosion of contracting in the 2000s overwhelmed the capacity of US government agencies to adequately oversee contracts. Overstretched government oversight and evaluation enables

PMSCs to influence decisions regarding their own actions on behalf of the state, giving commercial interests greater opportunity to affect public policy. This is what may have occurred when MPRI convinced the State Department to allow the company to work in Equatorial Guinea, in spite of long-standing State Department proscriptions against working with regimes suspected of human rights abuses (Avant 2005: 155).

Proponents argue that outsourcing provides flexibility because it enables governments to hire contractors with skills needed to address specific tasks that government actors may not possess. These include language skills or knowledge of specific policies or technologies. Yet, reliance on contractors could also lead to less policy flexibility. Government goals may change, but contractors may not shift their policies to adhere to modified government goals. This may have occurred at times in Iraq. The US and coalition partners revised their guidelines regarding interactions with the Iraqi population as they sought to quell the insurgency that developed after 2003, but companies were not contractually obligated to follow suit, including the companies providing protection to US diplomats. Companies are liable only to the terms of the contracts they have signed, regardless of their fit with new policies.

Finally, heavy reliance on contractors means policy decisions may well be made by these private actors. Reliance on private companies for risk assessments, reviews, and advice encourages a shift in the centre of gravity for decision making. Yet, this distances decision making from both the public and from elected officials, which may circumvent the democratic process (Singer 2003: 215). Moreover, because PMSCs are in the business of security provision, their perception of the national interest may be coloured by corporate goals or capabilities.

An alternative perspective on the potential hollowing of the state is the view that PMSCs can act as 'force multipliers' in foreign policy. The blurred lines between foreign and security policy are evident, in the US case, in the use of this military jargon by high level officials to describe the potential contribution of private actors such as contractors and NGOs to US foreign policy goals. In the US and some other states, governments operate on the assumption that trusted PMSCs will act of their own accord to further state interests. This gives the state a different kind of flexibility, in that it can rely on PMSCs to influence foreign policy while avoiding both the expense and attention that direct reliance on diplomats or troops entails. Moreover, PMSCs may be willing to undertake messy tasks that state governments and militaries would rather avoid (Shearer 1998). Many prominent PMSCs are populated by former military officers and some state department officials, who have explicitly stated their goal of working to further state goals with preferred clients; MPRI is an obvious example. Only one state, South Africa, has sought to constrain PMSCs from operating internationally. This is explained in part by South Africa's recent history and its desire to play a positive foreign policy role on the continent, which was seen as directly contradicted by the activities of mercenary companies like Executive Outcomes, an early PMSC created by demobilized South African military officers (Shearer 1998). Many African states have acceded to the 1989 African Union Convention that banned reliance on mercenaries. Yet, many of these governments allow PMSCs to operate in their territories as foreign policy proxies, either training local police and military forces or guarding multinational business activities, and indigenous mercenaries are also commonplace (Ebo 2008).

PMSCs enable states to pursue foreign policy goals with greater latitude because the state can deny involvement, and can circumvent domestic oversight and potentially international obligations as well (Singer 2003; Lehnardt 2007: 140). This use of private actors as foreign proxies is not new, or geographically limited. PMSCS have been used to support Colombia's counter-drug efforts and to strengthen its military and police capacity since 2000 as part of the US's Plan Colombia. Reliance on contractors circumvented Congress's limits on military personnel. Private contractors and US soldiers jointly analyse intelligence, conduct surveillance, and train Colombian troops in counter-guerrilla operations (de Nevers 2006: 381).

Transparency and accountability

The shift in decision making towards private actors reflects a second implication of reliance on private security; a reduction in transparency, particularly with regard to decision making. Reliance on contractors can remove policy decisions from public view because of corporate confidentiality clauses regarding contracts. On the positive side, one could argue that less transparency and public debate would help rationalize foreign policy decision making (Avant 2005: 156). Moreover, outsourcing can help avoid the bureaucratic infighting and red tape that can obstruct policy making. There are several downsides, however. In particular, lack of transparency leads to less oversight with regard to both spending and tasks. In the context of Iraq, opaque contracting made it impossible to determine how government funds were being spent by PMSCs. The fact that much PMSC activity is undertaken via subcontracts erodes transparency further. The use by the US DOD of supplemental financing to fund its overseas operations during the 2000s only exacerbated this trend, because supplemental budgets give lump sums to agencies to spend as they see fit (Stanger 2009: 87, 165).

Reliance on PMSCs in foreign policy also erodes accountability. Contracting enables governments to undertake tasks without public debate, because they need not explain to legislatures how contractors will be used in the way that they would if soldiers or diplomats were tasked to operate overseas. Governments can also deny responsibility for actions undertaken by private security actors, particularly if they go badly, although this is risky (ibid.: 8–10).

Militarization and reputation effects

Outsourcing can also contribute to the militarization of foreign policy. This is particularly evident in the US, but other countries are following their lead in reliance on PMSCs. As noted previously, the State Department's role as the government's key foreign policy representative has eroded as other government agencies have expanded their international activities, and global communications have enabled broader international information and contacts. Since the end of the Cold War, the State Department's resources have been shrinking, constraining its ability to sustain its diplomatic presence overseas. One consequence has been an increase in contracting by both State and USAID, the main US development agency. Although the State Department sought to expand its presence in stability and reconstruction after 9/11, it has struggled to get funding in this area. At the same time, the DOD has taken on additional responsibilities in the international arena, partly because it has more capacity to act in post-conflict zones. These responsibilities include functions previously carried out by the State Department or USAID, and as the DOD lacks the expertise for these tasks it has relied heavily on contractors. As part of its efforts to stabilize Iraq, for example, the DOD took on governance tasks that had previously been carried out by the State Department, and recent strategic policy reviews include 'stability operations' as a core mission, although these policies were previously characterized as development activities undertaken by USAID (Stanger 2009).

Reputationally, PMSCs can influence foreign policy by contributing to state-to-state relations, and by influencing international attitudes toward their home state. As noted previously, the sale of military services abroad generally requires government approval. When governments allow commercial sales of arms or training, this is a tacit indication of good relations with the recipient country even if the state is not directly involved in the sale. This is a way to generate good will to potential partners, while also signalling US support to arms and service recipients – and to their potential opponents. Thus, it is another form of foreign policy by proxy, which enables the state to influence events in its preferred direction without direct involvement (Avant 2005). US support for Croatia's president Franjo Tudjman in the 1990s is one such example, as are the training missions undertaken in Liberia (see Chapter 12, this volume) and in Mexico in support of the Merida Initiative in the 2000s. French and British companies have offered protective services in Libya since 2011 to support EU activities there, and to encourage economic ties with their home states (Tran 2012).

PMSCs can also influence foreign policy negatively if their actions generate discord with the host country. A significant challenge arising from reliance on PMSCs in the foreign policy realm is that the distinction between 'government' and 'private' actors may be lost on the local populations in places were PMSCs are working. This matters because if PMSCs actions have a negative impact on local communities, this can have a corrosive effect on attitudes toward the company's home state. This has been most pronounced with US reliance on PMSCs in places like Iraq, but also in Afghanistan and Pakistan.

In Iraq, for example, local populations did not distinguish between soldiers and PMSC employees working for the State Department or private interests; they were lumped together as Americans, and poor behaviour by American contractors – even if the employees were not American citizens – negatively shaped attitudes toward the US. This was particularly problematic as PMSCs gained a reputation for shooting at innocent civilians in Baghdad and elsewhere. Moreover, they appeared to do so with impunity, due to the immunity from prosecution that PMSCs were granted in Iraq in 2003-2004. Contractors were involved in multiple shooting incidents in Iraq, with allegations that contractors deliberately shot at civilian bystanders and Iraqi government employees, as well as US Marines (Krahmann 2010: 209–10). The most egregious example was an incident in Baghdad in September 2007 in which Blackwater employees that were employed as a State Department convoy killed seventeen Iraqi civilians and injured more. This was one of the few incidents that resulted in criminal prosecution, and four contractors were convicted of murder or voluntary manslaughter in October 2014, seven years after the shootings.

Similarly, US relations with Pakistan, already frayed by disagreements over Afghanistan and the Taliban during the 2000s, were deeply strained when a former Blackwater employee contracted to work under cover with the CIA in Pakistan shot and killed two Pakistanis while driving through Lahore in January 2011. This confirmed Pakistani suspicions that the CIA was operating clandestinely inside Pakistan, and incited fury against the US among a population already angered by what were perceived as indiscriminate US drone strikes in the country. This fury was exacerbated when the contractor, Raymond Davis, was allowed to leave the country without prosecution after the US government paid 'blood money' to the families of the shooting victims (Mazzetti 2013). Anti-Americanism in Pakistan rose to an 80 percent 'unfavourable' rating in Pew's Global Attitudes Survey in 2012, shortly after this incident (Pew Research Center 2014: 10).

Foreign policy scandals have been triggered by other private security actions. The British government was damaged by the 1997 Sandline affair, in which Sandline International, a UK-based private military company contracted by the Sierra Leonean government to undertake military operations on its behalf against rebel groups, was discovered to have imported weapons to Sierra Leone in violation of an international arms embargo, with the Government's knowledge and at least tacit consent (Singer 2003: 115). Then Foreign Secretary Robin Cook was almost forced to resign. Private contractors were implicated in the abuses that occurred at Abu Ghraib prison in Iraq in 2004, and the secret interrogation programme run by the CIA relied heavily on contractors. These and other actions have been termed 'diplomatic disasters' (Stanger 2009: 4). They can have deleterious effects on foreign policy by making it more difficult for a state to gain the trust and cooperation of other state actors. In conflict zones, this may also generate outright opposition in ways that make fighting the asymmetric wars of the twenty-first century more difficult, by limiting local willingness to cooperate with foreign forces, and bolstering insurgencies against them.

Conclusion

Private security actors have become integrated in multiple facets of foreign policy, even as foreign policy and security policy have become increasingly blurred in recent years. PMSCs shape foreign and security decisions through private involvement in intelligence, policy analysis, and training of government officials and troops. Increasingly, PMSCs help shape the way states see the world, through their risk and security analyses and consulting services. Private activities in support of foreign policy goals include logistics, protection, and reconstruction functions. PMSCs increasingly conduct security sector reform activities and the military training that is a major part of US foreign aid, and by acting as foreign policy proxies they enable governments to extend their foreign influence.

Debate continues about the impact that reliance on PMSCs has on the state. The privatization of security functions has generated concern by hollowing out states' capacity to act without contractors. But PMSCs may also work as force multipliers, enabling states to do more in foreign policy with less cost and official commitment. Reliance on PMSCs has had pernicious effects on transparency and accountability, two core democratic principles. Reputationally, PMSCs as proxies can extend a state's influence, but poor behaviour by PMSCs can corrode state-to-state relations and poison popular sentiment toward the countries that employ these companies.

In the US foreign and security policy context, PMSCs have become virtually indispensable; the state is no longer able to engage in many foreign policy activities without reliance on private actors. Dependence on private actors is not so pronounced in other countries, but outsourcing is increasingly common among other Western states as well. This trend is unlikely to change soon.

Private security is thus a fact of life in the foreign policy and security realm. Some scholars argue that contracting could be done in ways that enhance states' power and prestige. This would require thinking about what conditions would make outsourcing effective (Stanger 2009: 163). Ensuring that contracting states regain the capacity to oversee private actors and actions is key. This will be an uphill battle given the decline in oversight capacity that has accompanied the explosion in contracting in recent years. State regulations governing PMSCs need creation or strengthening in most countries, particularly with regard to activities conducted outside the companies' home states; the industry's reach expanded more rapidly than the regulatory framework. In the interim, reliance on voluntary codes of conduct and industry standards provides a stop-gap that can encourage companies seeking to do business with reputable states and clients to engage in responsible business practices (also Chapter 26, this volume). More broadly, states should consider their aims in pursuing foreign policy, and what this implies regarding appropriate tasks to be assigned to private actors. Corporate interests and national interests do not always align.

Bibliography

Avant, D. (2005) *The Market for Force: The Consequences of Privatizing Security*, Cambridge: Cambridge University Press.

Avant, D. and de Nevers, R. (2011) 'Military Contractors and the American Way of War', *Daedalus* 140 (3): 88–99.

Chesterman, S. and Fischer, A. (2010) *Private Security, Public Order: The Outsourcing of Public Services and its Limits*, Oxford: Oxford University Press.

de Nevers, R. (2006) 'The Geneva Conventions and New Wars', *Political Science Quarterly* 121(3): 369–96.

Dickinson, L. (2011) *Outsourcing War and Peace: Preserving Public Values in a World of Privatized Foreign Affairs*, New Haven, CT: Yale University Press.

Ebo, A. (2008). 'Private Actors and the governance of Security in West Africa', in A. Alexandra, D.-P. Baker and M. Caparini (eds), *Private Military and Security Companies: Ethics, Policies and Civil-Military Relations*, Abingdon: Routledge, pp. 143–58.

Kinsey, C. (2005) 'Examining the Organizational Structure of UK Private Security Companies', *Defense Studies* 5(2): 188–212.

Krahmann, E. (2010) *States, Citizens, and the Privatization of Security*, Cambridge: Cambridge University Press.

Leander, A. (2006) 'Privatizing the Politics of Protection', in J. Huysmans, A. Dobson and R. Prokhovnik (eds), *The Politics of Protection: Sites of Insecurity and Political Agency*, New York: Routledge, pp. 19–33.

Lehnardt, C. (2007) 'Private Military Companies and State Responsibility', in S. Chesterman and C. Lehnardt (eds), *From Mercenaries to Market: The Rise and Regulation of Private Military Companies*, Oxford: Oxford University Press, pp. 139–57.

Mazzetti, M. (2013) 'How a Single Spy helped Turn Pakistan against the US', *New York Times Magazine* 9 April, www.nytimes.com/2013/04/14/magazine/raymond-davis-pakistan.html.

Østensen, Å. (2011) *UN Use of Private Military and Security Companies: Practices and Policies*, Geneva: Geneva Centre for the Democratic Control of the Armed Forces.

Pew Research Center (2014) *A Less Gloomy Mood in Pakistan*, Washington, DC: Pew Research Center, www.pewglobal.org/files/2014/08/PG-2014-08-27_Pakistan-FINAL.pdf.

Priest, D. (2010) 'National Security, Inc.' *The Washington Post* 20 July, http://projects.washingtonpost.com/top-secret-america/articles/national-security-inc.

Shearer, D. (1998) *Private Armies and Military Intervention*, Oxford: Oxford University Press for the International Institute for Strategic Studies.

Singer, P. W. (2003) *Corporate Warriors: The Rise of the Privatized Military Industry*, Ithaca, NY: Cornell University Press.

Stanger, A. (2009) *One Nation under Contract: The Outsourcing of American Power and the Future of Foreign Policy*, New Haven, CT: Yale University Press.

Tran, P. (2012) 'Regulation, Expansion of French Private Security Firms Urged', *Defense News* 26 February, http://archive.defensenews.com/article/20120226/DEFFEAT02/302260010/Regulation-Expansion-French-Private-Security-Firms-Urged.

18

POSTCOLONIALITY AND RACE IN GLOBAL PRIVATE SECURITY MARKETS

Amanda Chisholm

The political and economic phenomena giving rise to private military and security companies (PMSCs) and broader trends of security commercialization are attracting the attention of academics from the disciplines of international relations (IR) and security studies, feminist security studies and criminology. These literatures have filled important gaps in research on PMSCs by making visible the ways commercial security is a product of larger neoliberal narratives and norms, how commercial security operations remasculinize security, how they impede women's participation, and how the security industry creates a gendered division of labour.

Importantly, emerging analyses also shows how these same practices are racialized and rest upon existing colonial relations, which result in material and social inequalities for the people who participate as security contractors. Such investigations have focused on the experiences of third country national (TCN) security contractors and have not only revealed the increasing role of labour from the global South in security operations, but also how racial logics of what constitutes good security underpins how global security is practised. Making visible TCNs' labour conditions and how these men (and sometimes women) are naturalized into particular roles highlights the vast differences in experiences among security contractors globally and illuminates the culture of whiteness that pervades the industry, privileging some men and masculinities while marginalizing others. This chapter draws upon the scholarship on TCN security labourers to demonstrate how bringing in postcolonial analysis to the study of PMSCs, shows the interconnecting colonial histories, racial and gendered practices intimately that bind security participants and security narratives across geopolitical regions and markets.

Seeing commercial security through a postcolonial lens

Much like the feminist concerns over the absence of gender in the current discussions on private security (Eichler 2015; Chapter 16, this volume), postcolonial authors argue that colonial histories and race have been largely overlooked (Chisholm 2015). As a result the current literature fails to capture how colonial geographies and histories continue to mediate the experiences of security labourers but also how securities and insecurities are articulated. Postcolonial scholars pay particular attention to how colonial histories and racial practices shape how we understand and live in the world. More accurately, they have envisioned IR as constituted through many worlds with interweaving histories and a multitude of knowledge sources (Agathangelou and Ling 2009). Drawing upon imagery of flowing water, Ling (2014) describes postcolonial IR as constituted through multiplicities of intertwining histories flowing and merging together. Like Ling, other postcolonial scholars understand knowledge production as constituted through a fluid multidirectional exchange rather than a top down or lineal process. Consequently, such an understanding of IR necessitates postcolonial inquiry to look to the margins of mainstream IR, to use these marginal experiences and positions to re-evaluate dominant understandings of history and to reveal the particularities of these global practices.

Applying a postcolonial analysis to PMSCs allows one to ask in what ways colonial histories and colonial legacies constitute private security markets and who and what knowledge is silenced in the current configurations? By focusing on the colonial relationships that inform security practices, postcolonial scholars make visible how the intersection between colonial histories and race with gender establishes white privilege in commercial security and how the value of labour from the global South is determined by how it relates to normalized 'white' security.

Postcolonial analysis speaks to the ways in which power is established by paying attention to how colonial histories and colonial legacies constitute and make intelligible gendered and racial subjectivities in contemporary political, social, and economic landscapes. Postcolonial gender scholars have employed the concept of racial masculinities to explore the intersectionality of gender and race in asking how the subjectivities of men and women remain relational, how racial logics work to value and naturalize particular masculine knowledge claims. Postcolonialism also stresses that all subjects are complicit in the production of these overarching gender-based hierarchies. Consequently, by conceptualizing private security and the marketing of military and guarding labour through a postcolonial gendered lens, we can begin to observe the ways colonialism reinvents itself in the representations and experiences of the global South labourer, referred to by the security industry as TCNs and naturalizes them into lesser valued labour roles. We can also ask how a culture of whiteness works to privilege the experiences and subjectivities of the white security contractor and how both TCN and Western security contractors are complicit in these security practices.

The remainder of this chapter focuses on the current postcolonial analyses of the industry, illustrating the argument mainly with reference to the place of Gurkha, and contains four sections. The first section below discusses how martial race remains a foundational logic underpinning the use of TCN labour in PMSCs. I then highlight how colonial histories of the British and the Gurkhas have mediated current security practices surrounding the use of Gurkhas as TCN labourers in Afghanistan. The following section draws upon the work by Joachim and Schneiker (2012, 2015), concerning how PMSCs use racial language in reproducing white and Western privilege in security practices and security knowledge production. Finally, I suggest possible future directions for postcolonial research on PMSCs that involve engaging with feminist global political economy (GPE) in order to understand PMSCs as a global industry that connects to other globalized industries.

Orientalism, martial race and white privilege

Practices of colonialism have constituted Western military recruitment of global South labour since the British Empire. They have been underpinned by a particular martial race logic that purported that some races were more suited for military service than others. Martial race communities include, for example, the Highlanders of Scotland, the Gurkhas of Nepal, the Fijians, and the Sikhs of India. The idea of martial races was used by the colonial administration to turn these indigenous communities into colonial militaries and police forces the colonizer could trust. The logics of martial race were rooted in larger Victorian ideas around race, that we could know people through their biological attributes. Establishing the 'martial' of a particular community was as much about constructing trusted indigenous soldiers as it was about reasserting colonial superiority. Such practices were not confined to the British, but appeared in French colonial administration practices as well (Womack 2006).

While not seamless, there are continuities in the colonial logics that determined global South military labourers today. The legacies of colonialism are observed in the UK/US and among other national recruitment strategies. Basham (2013: 112–37) discusses practices of race and ethnicity in the contemporary British military landscape. Through interviews with racial minorities in the military, Basham traces how their experiences are shaped by race and colonialism to produce different 'ethnic' soldiers within the British military, and how these men and women negotiate and make sense of their respective representations. Basham reveals how colonialism 'as a practice and as a set of assumptions' (ibid.: 112), is reflected in the ways in which the British military conducts its operations, and in how racism is reproduced through constructions of different ethnic soldiers. Similarly, Ware (2012; Chapter 15, this volume) details the racial and colonial logics that underpin the experiences of the British 'military migrants'.

PMSCs, independent of nationality, follow similar colonial practices when hiring 'military migrants' from the global South. Barker (2009) shows how colonial economic models underpin the gendered and racial divisions of labour among US security operations. Taking the US operations in Iraq as an example, Barker demonstrates how Indian labour is taking on the feminized administration work leaving the manly soldiering to the US soldier. Yet the marketization of military labour is not only about getting post-colonial 'martial' men to perform the feminized labour. It is also a part of a larger neoliberal restructuring of military operations whereby these individuals are characterized through a flexible work model, a model that the individual military migrant is complicit in. Men from the global South sign up to these contracts in the belief that their sacrifice and risk will result in economic gain for their families. MacLellan (2007) and I (Chisholm 2014a) both build on Barker's work. Drawing upon interviews with global South security labourers we trace how these men are seduced to participate in an industry that rests upon their marginal status. We contextualize these men's choices with reference to an overarching neoliberal promise that seduces them, a promise that claims to increase economic, political and social prosperity for those who work hard.

For the military migrants, their desperate situations not only shape their ability to freely choose to work in the commercial security industry, it also limits their ability to demand better work conditions once employed by the industry. MacLellan (2007) makes specific reference to Fijians' experiences in private security. Drawing upon interviews and local newspaper commentary, MacLellan takes the personal accounts of Fijian security labourers to illustrate the human cost in marketing migrant labour (ibid.: 53–5). Through the interviews, he gives voice to the Fijian contractors who speak of their individual navigation in choosing to take up dangerous and poorly managed work in order to support their families. Fiji, a country dependent upon foreign remittances and with a large population of underemployed military labour resulting from a downscaling in peacekeeping operations, is ripe for military recruitment. By highlighting the position of the Fijian military labourer and his family, MacLellan demonstrates how choice is severely restricted and how these workers' opportunities to demand better conditions are almost non-existent. His analysis is reinforced in my own interviews with Gurkhas and the white men who manage them in private security (Chisholm 2014a).

Taking the martial soldier to market

Postcolonial analysis of the security industry became important to me during my fieldwork in Kabul, Afghanistan. I was interested in how race and gender produced a hierarchy of global security labourers. To answer this question, I conducted participatory observations and interviews with Gurkhas and the white men who managed them. Both the observations and interviews demonstrated the many ways race is present in the representations of Gurkha security labour.

Gurkhas are men from Nepal with an over 200-year military history with the British. Their identities as military labourers are the product of British colonial enterprise. Gurkhas' 'natural' suitability for dangerous work was described to me during interviews with security company managers of TCN labour during my fieldwork in Afghanistan, because of their 'martial' raced culture and their 'heartiness' and 'sheer determination'. Their martial histories provide them access to the security industry but at the same time position them in subaltern roles; roles requiring the management of their white counterparts in order for their labour to be properly professionalized (Chisholm 2014a). Consequently, as I was repeatedly told during interviews with private security managers that Gurkhas can endure long and monotonous tasks. This made them more suitable for positions as static guard and convoy protection than their Western counterparts. This language produces the Gurkha as static. Their martial security identities are made intelligible through their intimate connections to colonial histories in which their communities are 'ethnicitized' as 'martial', making them more suitable for colonial military labour.

Security company managers' use of colonial language naturalizes the Gurkha into lower status, poorly paid and dangerous roles. Such naturalization hampers their possibilities of reaching managerial positions or achieving greater economic, political or social opportunities. For example, in my interviews, Gurkhas and their managers alike repeatedly acknowledged a paygap (Chisholm 2014b). The Gurkhas would receive $1500 a month, compared with their white counterparts receiving $8000–$10,000 per month. Some of the pay gap could be explained by different roles these men were contracted to perform (although not always). Importantly, and what appeared to concern Gurkhas the most in interviews was the difference in contractual obligations and the work environment of Gurkhas and Westerners. Some Gurkhas complained about having their passports confiscated for the duration of their contract. Others mentioned restrictions on movement through the compound and the city of Kabul, restricted access to eating times and the limited variety of foods available for them to choose from. Their ability to advance in their security career from static guards/convoy protection to management was also limited as a result of their 'martial' characteristics popularly understood to make them amenable to certain roles. Positioning Gurkhas, and other TCN workers, as 'natural' security labourers in the industry is a reflection of the growing trend to recruit global South 'martial' labourer for the lesser valued security work – such as static guards and convoy protection – at the periphery to the commercial security market in order to maximize profits and drive down security prices.

Highlighting TCN experiences does more than demonstrate how race works to naturalize these men into particular roles, it also makes visible how colonial histories and race constitute and perpetuate inequality among labourers and global economies. Private security, captured through a postcolonial gender lens that takes the intersectionality of gender, race and colonial histories seriously, raises different issues and questions that so far the literatures on commercial security has yet fully to address. Such scholarship is, for example, questioning the ways commercial security rests upon and reproduces raced and gendered logics that sustain global divisions of labour among security contractors.

The pattern of global South security labour recruitment follows colonial imaginings of these 'martial' men whereby the Western security companies see these men as the more desirable military labourers. This colonial logic is not unique to the security industry, but perhaps is foregrounded in existing military procurement practices whereby colonial histories mediate the employment of 'ethnic' soldiers such as the Gurkhas and Fijians within the British military (Ware 2012). Colonial histories and raced practices not only shape who gets recruited, they also produce a division of labour among soldiers whereby soldiers from the global South are deemed 'ethnic'.

Such realities of the global South labourer counter the 'freeness' of the market and highlight how race continues to produce a masculine hierarchy of global labourers. Emerging critical gender research offers important insights into how on the one hand the US has used neoliberal logic of freeing military labour to pave the way for marketizing the military and on the other hand, how the US draws upon colonial geographies and desperate global South economies that result in cheap, and at times unfree, labour (Stillman 2011). Higate (2012) describes how these colonial geographies are legitimized and sustained through martial race that naturalizes these men into these positions. Eichler (2014) expands this work by describing the economic desperation of many men from the global South that mediate their contract negotiations. In many cases, these men would simply put up with bullying and intimidation in their employment because they felt they had no alternative (ibid.: 608–9) or, as Higate (2012: 37, 40–41) argues, because they strike an 'ethnic bargain' with the security industry; a bargain that is understood as a necessity for short term individual gain, but which also reinforces their subaltern and marginal status within the industry. However, as I have written elsewhere (Chisholm 2014b: 38–9), these Gurkha's bargains with the industry are not just individual conscious choices mediated through a sense of economic desperation. Their decisions to take on these roles are also rooted in their own emotional attachments to these martial histories. Repeatedly in interviews, Gurkhas explained that they saw their roles as security labourers as a calling. They claimed it was their job to take on dangerous work in order to protect the white managers and their clients.

Gurkhas intellectually and emotionally drew upon the language of their martial masculine empowerment, located in their 'protector' of the white contractor subjectivity as a reason to take on the more dangerous (and less remunerated) work. Such an identity, as I was told in interviews with Gurkhas, is rooted in a long tradition of Gurkhas protecting the white men from the dangerous of war and insecurity. Yet at the same time their protector identity, situated within the larger political economy geographies of global security, is also a precarious one. This was highlighted during a focus group I had with four Gurkhas who were recently injured when an improvised explosive device (IED) was detonated beside their compound in southern Afghanistan. These men spoke about the anxiety of having to leave their employment to seek medical treatment and their inability to financially provide of their families. They expressed concern over being able to come back to work in Afghanistan given the tightened Afghan regulations towards contracting foreign labour at the time. Their financial security was in maintaining a strong and healthy body in order to maintain the employment they were contracted to perform. Unlike many Western countries where white contractors come from, in Nepal, there is little social security or health care measures offered to those who cannot pay and the men, in varying degrees, expressed worry about being a financial burden on their families. This lack of social protection from home countries place Gurkhas, and other TCN labourers, in precarious positions in the global security market(s).

Overall these analyses of the industry and the experiences of TCN labourers show how neoliberal globalization of military labour ensures that some foreign nationals will almost always be excluded from access to social and economic rights that are granted to Western labour. This is not to say that white Westerners taking on employment in private security do not face precarity in their work environment or job insecurity observed in the flexible and short-term work contracts. They certainly do. But the juxtaposition of the global South labourer labour experiences, next to the Western labourer where their skills are more financially valued and their job location is generally behind guarded walls or armoured vehicles, demonstrates how the degrees of risk and sacrifice are significantly different and how race and colonial relations underpin the degrees of sacrifice and the differences in overall labour experiences of the two contractor subjects. White privilege is also reinforced in how the market assigns value to security contractor skillsets – observed in the establishment of the white security expert.

The white security expert

Racial constitutions of the professional security contractor remain integral in shaping security labour hierarchies in private security markets. Feminist security studies scholars have argued that appeals to professional/expert status are also appeals to authority and that these appeals remain masculinized and therefore reproduce the gender dichotomies separating public/private and skilled/natural labourers (Sjoberg 2010: 4–5). The use of 'professional' is a reference to the masculine subject who acquires skills through training. Conversely women are naturalized into particular roles, such as the role of caregiver. Women are said to have a natural ability and aptitude for these particular caring roles and therefore do not require the same value assigned to the professional 'acquired' skills. Importantly, feminist scholars have reminded us that masculine privilege is formed through a variety of subject-forming intersections inclusive of race, religion, age, sexuality and class (Higate and Henry 2004: 481–98). Accordingly this same practice also has a racial dimension. As in the case of the TCN labourer, the racialization of their labour happens through forms of constructing semi-skilled, deviant and dangerous masculinities, embodied, for example, historically in the colonial native subject and contemporarily in security labour from the global South.

Within private security markets, professional versus natural labour binaries generate racial hierarchies among men. To claim to be an expert is also a claim to masculine white privilege. It allows the person to have authority and decision-making power over their particular subject-matter. When we consider global security contractors, privilege does not function in isolation but is relational to the 'subaltern' subjectivities. These relational power practices are present in PMSCs, whereby a particular masculine whiteness (embodied in the western contractor), as I have argued elsewhere (Chisholm 2014a) underpins the constitution of the expert private security contractor and legitimizes hierarchies among all security labourers because it is distinct and separate from the 'subaltern', seen as semiskilled or unskilled global South security labourer.

Joachim and Schneiker (2012, 2015) have documented a privileged white masculinity through examining how PMSC use particular language in their marketing strategies and training programmes, which they argue employ gendered and raced language of flexibility, empathy, and cultural awareness to describe their services and their contractors.

To highlight the white privilege in constituting the security expert, and the construction of the subaltern masculine other, embodied in the TCN and local national (LN) labourer, Joachim and Schneiker draw upon the language PMSCs use to describe the training of LNs and TCNs. In such cases, PMSCs use a narrative of the highly skilled western military trainers working closely with and mentoring the TCN labour. PMSCs narrate how the 'unskilled' or 'semi-skilled' TNC labourer becomes professionalized through training conducted by 'professional' western contractors; such professionalization positions the western labourer as the manager and mentor of the TCN labourer. It also works to reinforce that it is the West that has the acquired (valued) skills and necessitates them to professionalize the global South's 'natural' talents through mentoring and training – a process reminiscent of colonial encounters and martial race.

Postcolonial gender analysis in IR has demonstrated that colonialism was a gendered and racial practice, whereby the devaluing of indigenous men and women, and indigenous femininities and masculinities, was a particular strategy adopted in order to subordinate indigenous peoples and knowledge (Sinha 1995). The racialization of local men and women worked to impede them from exercising political and military power and positioned the colonizer in a place of authority, as a superior race that would mentor and develop the colonized. These colonial gendered relations were brought into existence and made intelligible through the larger colonial practices of accumulation and dispossession used in re-shaping African and Indian economies for the benefit of colonizers (ibid.). Contemporary applications of postcolonial analysis demonstrate that the practice of devaluing the colonial subject through racialization does not end with the political independence of former colonies. Scholars particularly concerned with postcolonial masculinities focus on the ways colonial histories and contemporary neo-colonial global processes rest upon and reproduce raced and gendered subaltern subjectivities locally and globally.

Seeing security through a global political economy lens

While the postcolonial analysis of the security industry has lent attention to the ways in which hierarchies among men are constructed and divisions of labour established, it says very little about security as work and in comparison to other global markets relying upon global workforce. What does it mean when we understand the security industry as one that is supported by a global workforce? Such questions direct attention to how race, gender, and colonial histories condition and discipline the global South security labour supply chains – a particular concern with feminist GPE scholars. As such, there is much to be gained by exploring these supply chains through a GPE lens.

While just emerging, research on this topic has shown that global labour is constituted through racial and gendered practices, how these practices inflate differences and hierarchies among labourers and naturalize people into particular devalued work. Postcolonial gender scholarship has thus far demonstrated how certain men were devalued in order to draw upon indigenous labour for colonial power, and how these practices have certain continuities in the postcolonial moment. Yet, there is not an explicit engagement with how these colonial conditions are also foundational to global markets and how such markets rest upon naturalizing race and racial labour. The racialization and colonial constitutions of global markets are made clearer when we apply postcolonial critiques of contemporary security and political practices to existing feminist GPE research that explores contradictions within capitalist and neoliberal discourse and the growing economic disparities between men and women of the global South and global North (Elias 2005). Such examinations connect to the ways colonial histories impact upon how Gurkhas are represented within the global political economy of private security.

By further exploring the security industry through a global political economy framing, current postcolonial and racial analysis of the industry can shift focus from PMSCs constituted through a process and marketization of security, to offer analyses that sees the security industry as composed not just of racialized security providers, understood in terms related to the state (as exploited victims, professionals or rogue mercenaries) but as workers in global markets as well. GPE can highlight how security markets relate to other globalizing markets in how they reproduce colonial geographies and dual economies to ensure a global supply of cheap and compliant labour. Taking security markets out of an exceptional security space, we can begin to further question how this security work is conditioned by both culture and neoliberal economics to explain variations of capitalist experiences among men and women from the global South. Such analysis can focus on the specific techniques applied to condition and discipline global labour chains and how military labour practices also inform other commercial industries.

Feminist GPE scholarship pays attention to the ways men and women are conditioned to perform particular labour, and how their labour is commodified. McDowell (2009) discusses how gender, race, and class intersect to produce a multitude of labourers for the market, and examines how women's work is feminized in order to offer cheap labour to the market. She further shows how masculinities and race work in tandem to produce working class, tough, men and business class (white) men. Elias (2005) complements this gender assessment of the market by exploring how the textile industry was feminized and labour in it was devalued through its association with 'women's work', in order to reduce labour costs by having women take up work in the textile industries. Cowen (2014) uses postcolonial and global political economy scholarship to demonstrate the similarities in logistical planning between the military and other expeditionary industries such as oil and gas and mining. Such explorations highlight further the blurring between military and security supply chain procurement practices and those of commercial global industries.

Emerging research and ways forward

Current postcolonial and feminist scholarship on PMSCs is moving in interesting directions. Both are engaging more with feminist GPE literatures on global labour supply chains (Chisholm and Stachowitsch 2016). This empirical and theoretical move enriches research on race, colonial histories and labour within private security in two key ways. Firstly, it allows us to compare security markets with other markets to see the ways in which these racial, colonial histories and gendered practices connect to the creation and disciplining of global workforces in other industries. It shifts our thinking towards a questions regarding how security is also found in the unexceptional, the mundane and the everyday. Such conceptualization of security allows us to re-think the ways in which militarization and neoliberalism interact within and beyond military arenas. By extension, a synthesis of feminist security studies and global political economy of private security studies also allows us to see military and private security service as racial, gendered work. By placing primacy on the concept of work, we can begin to track how this work is shaped by and shaping larger practices of militarization and neoliberalism and how individual labourers negotiate these practices in their everyday lives. Such conceptualization allows us to consider, for example, how PMSCs are constituted through affective labour, that is the emotional and supportive labour (generally done by women). We can begin to consider how security contractors draw upon emotional support from their former military colleagues and how security contractors' families use established military communities to maintain a sense of belonging once transitioned into the private security industry. By engaging with feminist GPE scholarship, more deeply, postcolonial and feminist analysis of PMSCs can ask how does/can the militarization of private security labour also operate as a space and site for resistance to neoliberalism: although military communities are not immune to neoliberalization, the military's sense of community underpinned by personal obligations to other comrades continues to offer a different subjectivity to celebrated enterprising neoliberal individual. Such engagement with security as work, and a synthesis of feminist security studies and global political economy develops understandings of how security markets are enmeshed with these neoliberal practices in other global capitalist enterprises. By moving research away from an exceptional military/security space to include issues of labour, future analysis can potentially open avenues of exploration into not only the men and women who participate in private security work (actual security contractors), but also those who support the private security industry. These emerging research trends are important as they allow us to explore the far reaching militarization within and outside traditional military and security spaces and how racial, gendered and colonial practices within PMSCs impact upon but also are informative of our everyday lives.

Conclusion

This chapter has reviewed the literatures that have contributed to discussions around postcolonial and raced practices in commercial security – specifically, PMSCs that operate globally. Much of this literature uses postcolonial insights to explain and reveal the vast differences and experiences of the TCN labourer when compared to his Western counterpart. By doing so, this scholarship has demonstrated how the security industry draws upon colonial logics and practices to sustain hierarchies among global labourers and devalue labour from the global South. While such examples are important to highlight the global divisions of labour and the racial and colonial logics that reinforce them, postcolonial analysis of the security industry has the potential to reveal much more about the security industry.

The chapter has focused on how, by engaging with postcolonial and feminist analysis within global political economies, we can begin to ask new questions surrounding the global political economy of security and security labour chains. Consequently we can see how race and gender underpin global security markets as well as demonstrate how such practices are prevalent in other global markets linking culture to capital in both particular and general ways. Overall by developing postcolonial insights into how security and insecurity are constituted, we stand to gain much more understandings of the various ways colonial pasts continue to inform our colonial present(s).

Bibliography

Agathangelou, A. and Ling, L. H. M. (2009) *Transforming World Politics: From Empire to Multiple Worlds*, Abingdon: Routledge.

Bakker, I. and Silvey, R. (2008) *Beyond States and Markets: The Challenges of Social Reproduction*, Abingdon: Routledge.

Barker, I. V. (2009) '(Re)producing American Soldiers in an Age of Empire', *Politics and Gender* 5(2): 211–35.

Basham, V. M. (2013) *War, Identity and the Liberal State*, Abingdon: Routledge.

Chisholm, A. (2014a) 'Marketing the Security Package: Colonial Histories and Neoliberal Economies of Private Security', *Security Dialogue* 45(4): 349–72.

Chisholm, A. (2014b) 'The Silenced and Indispensible: Gurkhas in Private Security', *International Feminist Journal of Politics* 16(1): 26–47.

Chisholm, A. (2015) 'From Warriors of Empire to Martial Contractors: Reimagining Gurkhas in Private Security', in M. Eichler (ed.), *Gender and Private Security in Global Politics*, Oxford: Oxford University Press, pp. 95–113.

Chisholm, A. and Stachowitsch, S. (2016) 'Globalizing Security Labour: Gendered and Racialized Patterns of Global Security Labour and Migration', *Globalizations* Special Issue: A Feminist Global Political Economy of Everyday Life.

Connell, R. (2005) *Masculinities*, vol. 2, Berkeley, CA: University of California Press.

Cowen, D. (2014) *The Deadly Life of Logistics: Mapping Violence in Global Trade*, Minnesota, MN: Minnesota University Press.

Eichler, M. (2014) 'Citizenship and the Contracting Out of Military Work: From National Conscription to Globalized Recruitment', *Citizenship Studies* 18(6–7): 600–614.

Eichler, M. (2015) *Gender and Private Security in Global Politics*, Oxford: Oxford University Press.

Elias, J. (2005) 'Stitching-up the Labour Market', *International Feminist Journal of Politics* 7(1): 90–111.

Higate, P. (2012) 'Cowboys and Professionals: The Politics of Identity Work in the Private and Military Security Industry', *Millennium: Journal of International Studies* 40(2): 321–41.

Higate, P. and Henry, M. (2009) *Insecure Spaces: Peacekeeping, Power and Performance in Haiti, Kosovo and Liberia*, New York: Zed Books.

Joachim, J. and Schneiker, A. (2012) 'Of "True Professionals" and "Ethical Hero Warriors": A Gender-Discourse Analysis of Private Military and Security Companies', *Security Dialogue* 43(6): 495–512.

Joachim, J. and Schneiker, A. (2015) 'The Licence to Exploit: PMSCs, Masculinities and the Third Country National', in M. Eichler (ed.), *Gender and Private Security in Global Politics*, Oxford: Oxford University Press, pp. 114–30.

Ling, L. H. M. (2014) *The Dao Of World Politics: Towards a post-Westphalian, Worldist International Relations*, Abingdon: Routledge.

MacLellan, N. (2007) 'Fiji, Iraq and Pacific Island Security', *Race and Class* 48(3): 129–51.

McDowell, L. (2009) *Working Bodies: Interactive Service Employment and Workplace Identities*, Chichester: Wiley-Blackwell.

Sinha, M. (1995) *Colonial Masculinity: The "manly Englishman" and the "Effeminate Bengali" in the Late Nineteenth Century*, Manchester: Manchester University Press.

Sjoberg, L. (2010) *Gender and International Security: Feminist Perspectives*, Abingdon: Routledge.

Stillman, S. (2011) 'The Invisible Army: For Foreign Workers on US Bases in Iraq and Afghanistan, War Can Be Hell', *The New Yorker* 6 June, www.newyorker.com/magazine/2011/06/06/the-invisible-army.

Ware, V. (2012) *Military Migrants: Fighting for YOUR Country*, New York: Palgrave Macmillian.

Womack, S. (2006) 'Ethnicity and Martial Races: The Garde Indigene of Cambodia in the 1880s and 1890s', in K. Hack and T. Rettig (eds), *Colonial Armies in Southeast Asia*, Abingdon: Routledge, pp. 100–118.

19

SECURITY FAIRS

Leila Stockmarr

'Now hurry to the booths. We only have three days to make the world a better place.' With these words, the annual security and defence fair ISDEF International Defense and HLS Expo in Tel Aviv was declared opened in June 2013. In contrast to governments' secretive strategies for the collection of intelligence and arms procurement, security fairs are to a large extent open-access fora where lethal and non-lethal technology for military operations, surveillance and population control are showcased to a broader audience. The fairs stand as a clear proof of the internationalization of security technologies and practices, and are visible signs that the military industry has moved from serving domestic needs to relying on exports and global demands (Sköns and Dunne 2006). While the arms trade has been the object of much scrutiny (Feinstein 2011; Gifford 2004; Stavrianakis 2010), less attention has been given to the nature, culture and rules of security fairs. In recent years commercial security fairs have grown in number and expanded in size and have come to include more companies and actors on a global scale.

Security fairs are microcosms of public and private cumulative experiences of warfare and control, distilled into commercial platforms of technological problem-solving tailor-made to fit the needs of the buyer/consumer. The fairs are crucial nodal points in connecting war experiences and national defence visions to global avenues of security commerce in the preparation for war or security governance 'somewhere else'. The marketplace is crucial for both private companies and states to dispatch their way of war and control to a global community of security entrepreneurs. In this way the security fairs are an important part of the making of truly global security practices (Introduction, this volume).

This chapter shows how the security fair is both a transmission belt for and a shaper of security practices and discourses, and examines the effects of the encounter between the micro-politics of the fair and the macro-politics of war and security. It unfolds the process through which input from manufacturers is turned into output and solutions for buyers of security technologies, and explores the security fair as a globalized platform for the transmission of security technologies and a venue where the meaning and purpose of security is negotiated. First the chapter introduces the phenomenon and development of security fairs, before showing how they are a form of translation of security and field-configuring events. The fair is then examined as a conceptual showroom for war and security, showing the role of trade fairs in advancing and altering the global economy of security. The analysis draws on observations and interviews conducted at two fairs in 2012 and 2013 in Israel, a major fair in Paris in 2012 and in London in 2014, as well as websites and PR-material from several other fairs.[1]

Setting the scene: the security fair

The term 'security fair' encompasses fairs involved in exhibiting, promoting and selling arms, defence, security and policing technology and know-how. In the broadest sense the events are both trade fairs for selling and buying and a venue for the production and negotiation of the meaning of security and its artifacts. Historically, security fairs (and previously conventional defence exhibitions) have moved from being secretive shows in the 1960s and 1970s to more open, advanced commercial exhibition circuits (Alexander 2013). This development was linked to a series of transformative events, including the end of the Cold War when excessive capacity and increased laxity in issuing export licenses led companies to combine arms production with explicit strategies of internationalization (Sköns and Dunne 2006). This was reinforced by the post-Fordism of the 1980s and the Revolution in Military Affairs (RMA), and throughout the 1990s the possibilities of dual use strengthened the production of off-the-shelf security and defence technology (Introduction, this volume; Gray 2004; Metz and Kievit 1995; Singer 2010). The internationalization of the defence trade also corresponds with the globalization of modes of violence and warfare through sharing and learning (Khalili 2010, 2013) and through a clandestine mercenary sector (Percy 2007). With this steady commercialization and privatization of defence and security arms, the fairs have become more open to outsiders.

Today security fairs vary from all-purpose fairs, covering security and defence more broadly, to more niche-based specialized fairs. The latter covers sub-fields such as homeland security (HLS), fire safety, cyber security, traffic management, individual safety, disaster management, rescue and relief, anti-terror, cyber-security, surveillance, systems of urban control, counter-insurgency, border-security and protection of critical infrastructure. The former, although broader in scope, often operate with sub-themes expressed in seminars, symposiums and live demonstrations focusing on issues such as the implications of unmanned aerial vehicles (UAVs), advancement in biometrical security, or the growing demand for securing critical infrastructure. The fairs are bound into a network of military, scientific, academic actors and institutions, and a plethora of actors are usually involved in organizing and participating: weapon manufacturing and security technology companies, police and military actors, private security companies, official national delegations consisting of politicians, military attaches of diplomatic missions in the host country as well as state officials, intelligence agencies and representatives of international organizations. The fairs provide a forum for actors to meet, interact and exchange information. The exhibitors include producers of raw materials, contractors, subcontractors, laboratories, system integrators, and research and consultancy agencies. Their activities capture the entire ecosystem from research and development to deployment. Participants come to announce new products and develop industrial standards, build networks and recognize accomplishments and interpret information and transact business. The fair is infused with these various logics and is a key meeting point for the network, providing it with a platform to perform and present their wares and a social venue where success is measured by the deals made.

Field configuring events and translation of security

Very little theoretical work has been done on the function and nature of security fairs, and there is a shortage of prescriptions of how to study the venues as a both a discursive and material field. However, the broader literarture on trade fairs provides a useful startingpoint, as it approaches fairs as nodal points in global exchanges of knowledge and capital (see Kirchgeorg *et al.* 2010; Ling-yee 2008; Seringhaus and Rosson 1998). More specifically, DiMaggio's seminal work (1991) on the museum as a modus of cultural representation and a platform for field formation has influenced the study of fairs (and venues more broadly) as producers of meaning. The role of fairs as agents of change has become a growing area of study in the literature on business management, and the notion of field-configuring events (FCEs) has proved particularly instructive (Zilber 2006; Lampel and Meyer 2008; Mcinerney 2008; Garud 2007). FCEs are temporary social organizations, such as tradeshows, that encapsulate and shape the development of professions, technologies, markets, and industries (Lampel and Meyer 2008: 1026). As a field configuring event, the fair provides as a 'loci for institutional change and convenes multifarious institutional actors' (Mcinerney 2008: 1111).

As an FCE, the security fair contributes to the shaping of the broader field of (private) security. Accordingly, from a FCE perspective the fair is both an event and a mechanism for institutionalizing the way security is negotiated – both in terms of the production of meaning (i.e. what constitutes security) and the practices of selling. Like at the event of an automobile race (Rao 1994: 2008), at the security fair products are tested and evaluated by its potential buyers and users, and the fair links performativity and the strive for successful economic output. At the fair two mechanisms are structuring the field and provides the fair with a dual function: the fair is a transmission belt for knowledge, technology and capital transfer, and simultaneously a platform and institution that produces meaning and action around security. As a field configuring event the security fair contributes to the production of a codified language of security that only those with intimate knowledge of the industry's discourses and practices can relate to. In short, the fairs are field configuring as they are shaping the emergence and developmental trajectories of security technologies and their discursive embedding. The internal and non-explicated rules of the fair define the zones of acceptability; what is fact and what is fiction is defined by self-referential hoops between objects, metrics and beliefs (Garud and Rappa 1995). The discourse, the rhetoric and the way of interacting between buyers, sellers and facilitators of the event itself construct the inwards dynamics of the fair.

At the same time, the fair and its participants are embedded in and refer to broader structures of war and security. At the fair the dominant views on security are conventionalized, in the sense that certain perspectives become 'taken for granted beliefs about why certain acts and practices are normal or right' (Biggart and Beamish 2003: 452). This in turn involves a process of translation. The route of technology from the hands of the manufacturer to the hands of its end-user is a multifaceted process of translation shaped by inter-subjective negotiations and socio-technical configurations. The procedure running from displaying technology to filling it with meaning for byers entails a process of translation of security (Stritzel 2011a, 2011b), whereby language and categories are employed by fair participants and exhibitors to give technological artifacts a security purpose or repurposing these technologies as tools to promote civilized security. As a vector of translation the fair comes to express what Stritzel calls a 'global modus of security', produced through various local 'actions of translation' (Stritzel 2011b: 2492). Security fairs provide a window on how security technologies are described and sold by producers, and then adopted by users who frequently come to endorse the producers's visions and understandings of security and risk. In this way, the fair in itself is a process of translation, and the translation process and the routines and practices that characterize the fair means that it is best understood as a FCE.

The design of the fair: between tradition and the future

In their institutional form the fairs have an air of multiplicity (Zilber 2011). They are complex sites of capital accumulation, knowledge synthesis and diffusion, and competition over the meaning of 'best practice' in security. Roughly defined, three disparate, yet overlapping sets of interests and rationality prevail at the fair:

- military and security strategy, centred on questions of future threat scenarios and ways of warfare, including new military doctrines and missions of policing;
- technology and innovation 'as science' centred on questions of the 'latest and greatest' new technology (Alexander 2013); and
- the logics of business transactions and cost-effectiveness spurred by the hope of striking a deal.

Typically the fairs are constituted through the interactions of actors with multiple often overlapping and at times conflicting point of departures. Companies participate in security fairs in order to sell their products, but they also attend to study their competitors and to boost their image in the eyes of the industry and the media. Among exhibitors and company representatives there is drive for mutual recognition – providing the event with legitimacy – and an effort to project an image of a united front dedicated to security while at the same time leaving space for competition.

Most fairs are organized around a tight programme of talks, live demonstrations, lunch breaks and cocktail hours for social networking. Architecturally the fairs are sterile settings with sales booths, sales rooms and conference venues. Often tours to sites outside the venue are offered for participants to experience the military/security facilities of the host country. For example the Second Israeli Homeland Security Conference in Tel Aviv in November 2012 hosted indoor exhibitions, talks by high-level experts, military strategists and politicians, and indoor live demonstrations. The fourth day, the organizers arranged an impressive outdoor live performance of Israeli security methods. Hundreds of foreign buyers, together with numerous members of the political and private security elite, drove in buses to the port of Ashkelon in southern Israel. There, they were feted with demonstrations of how Israel's methods can be used to fight all kinds of attacks, including terrorist infiltrations by sea utilizing rubber boats and pirate assaults on tankers. That 2012 show coincided with that start of Israel's Operation Pillar of Defense, an eight-day military offensive against the Gaza Strip. While military jets were flying in the sky, in the nearby war showroom, a groovy James Bond theme song was playing, thus promoting familiarity and harmony between Israeli practices of war and the cognitive references of observer-consumers that included potential buyers from the United States, the European Union, Nigeria, China and Italy (Stockmarr 2014).

In addition to buying, visitors use fairs to compare offers and gather information on the latest developments in the market. Both sides judge their own relative standing, negotiate their capacities and as a consequence boost the industry by getting better at internalizing and playing 'the game' of the fair (Lampel and Meyer 2008). Conversations, knowledge exchange and branding maneuvers happen in a dual mode through informal conversations and through the fairs' more organized and structured schemes such as shows, performances and ceremonial features. The physical organization of the fair is also characteristic of its nature as a world of its own. The fairs espouse an air of newness in that they seek to project a futuristic image, while at the same time seeking to establish and disseminate some sort of tradition bound to their repetitive nature. Most of the fairs are separate events but are repeated each year, with new themes reflecting the challenges 'out there' and announcing new technological breakthroughs. On many companies' websites and in the narratives presented at opening ceremonies and in promotion material, the historical build-up of the fair is often disseminated through mosaics of data and video. Past successes are documented and shown to create an image of success and to convince customers of their capacity to bolster security in the future. In the case of Europe's largest security fair, the biannual Eurosatory in France, an extremely well-developed website tells the story of the fair's expansion and includes archival material and statistics to document the fair's success and progress as an institution. Originating in the French Army Experimental Unit in the 1960s, the trajectory from a 'safe military camp' to its expansive and highly commercialized version in the enormous Paris-Villepinte Exhibition Center in 2002, the trajectory is testimony to the specific success of enterprise but also reflects the shift from national procurement of national forces to internationalization, privatization and commercialization. Thus the fairs are much more than clearinghouses for information and works as a marketplace where, as Garud notes, participants can potentially be persuaded to select the virtues of one approach over the other (Garud 2007: 1081; see also Mcinerney 2008). The exhibitors' booths reflect preparation as in a supermarket where the commodities have already been pre-arranged so as to induce customers to select certain products and brands over others (Callon *et al.* 2002). The finish and size of the booths clearly express the hierarchy of companies and in some cases the comparative level of advancement. Visual materials and live demonstrations are presented in generic sceneries of warfare or urban policing.

At the fair the actors seek to represent an improvement to the overall industry; a consolidation of the platform as an internationalized network and a forum for the sharing of experiences, which can lead to new innovation. The desire to realize these potentials creates a collective identity of the industry. For example, most fairs operate with one or more themes of defence and security such as cyber security, urban warfare or drone technology, which actors collectively promote as *the* most pressing challenge. The exchange of knowledge about these challenges, and perhaps more importantly, the identification of the right technological solutions to eliminate threats becomes drivers of improvement within the fair's own logic. At the Eurosatory in Paris in 2012, for instance, the industry convened sessions to debate how to best make use of the changes in procurement policies and trends brought about by the Arab uprisings, whereas at HLS Israel 2012 experts and practitioners debated how the broader concept of 'the smart city' could be better exploited as a promotional device for the security and defence industry.

Consequently the fairs are not isolated events. Rather they are embedded within a larger flow of field unfolding activities. Many of the larger fairs have an advisory board from the host country's academic-military-security-industrial complex. They serve to provide the event with legitimacy, professionalism – even intellectualism – and expertise as well as ensuring a degree of institutional continuity between the events. To further increase cultural capital and the ethos of collectivity (and to incite competition), many of the major fairs have ceremonial features such as award ceremonies to recognize particular companies or individuals, thus adding a sense of occasion and ritual. Most fairs also support visitors with flights and accommodation, which in turn link the 'globality' of the fair to other global systems of mobility such as tourism and infrastructure. On some of the major fairs' websites one can attain a personal profile, book business-to-business meetings, request individual consulting and 'personal shoppers'. Visitors are encouraged to follow the event's site on social media platforms such as Facebook and Twitter to get the latest updates, spread the news and make the brand of the fair visible to others in their network. At the Eurosatory, a daily paper is distributed announcing premieres of new technology, ads, and interviews with exhibitors and, not least, deals sealed the previous day.

Some of the major well-organized fairs also offer consultancy on industrial strategy, for example providing geographical expertise for companies to refine and optimize their targeting skills. The organizers have institutionalized service offers such as communication to exhibitors and visitors normalizing the fair, as were they part of any other field. In short, the organizers are providing these venues engaged in selling potentially lethal technology with a civilized gaze as were they selling any kind of commodity.

Security fairs as showrooms

The security fair functions as a bridge between the initial technologies' place of origin and its destination. The dominant narratives and visions of security are shaped in the encounters between sellers and buyers, at the intersection of supply and demand. For the supply side success hinges upon the ability to present a flexible portfolio that can meet the specific needs of a wide range of customers on the demand side. It is in the adjustment of a given device, programme or operational system that the concrete meaning of security is constituted. At the fair successful security is produced and recognized as a natural extension of documented battlefield experience and success. Previous purchases by militaries and other state agencies along with visuals illustrating its use in the field is a central aspect of the promotional routines.

The references to the real battlefield allow exhibitors to draw on both the companies' own experiences and on broader national security experiences, such as concrete wars or counterterrorism campaigns. In most presentations and demonstrations of technology and hardware the opponent is merely represented as the 'enemy force', the generic terrorist or the criminal who needs to be fought, or even eliminated through lethal measures. At HLS Israel 2012 the visual representation of the areas of intervention, the enemy's landscape and the homeland/assets in need of protection was presented as dry and Mediterranean, a refugee camp or an urban slum projecting images of a generic 'Middle Eastern setting' familiar to most end-users. In this way the fair comes to represent a selected and fabricated conceptual showroom for waging of the (ideal) war. At times the documentation and illustration takes on a generic expression mapping unspecified warzones, landscapes or urban settings, while at other times a given mission is directly tied to a specific event, intervention, attack, etc. Security is thus given meaning in the meeting between grander visions and ideas of war and security and the localized, internalized practices at the security fair.

More fundamentally the fair makes up a frame within which the discursive practices of dealing with (risky) populations and protecting the people deemed at risk are articulated, produced and reproduced. The regulation of violence and technologies of brutality are through these representations banalized into a dichotomized frame of good and bad. At the fairs part of the conventionalization of best practice rests on the idea that security concerns – despite their immense messiness and complexity – can be reduced to technical truths, where it is the responsibility of the exhibitor to provide the most efficient solution. Security is constructed as involving a process of technicalization presented as a linear process from production to application in which the messy design process is forgotten and a semblance of smoothness introduced (Alexander 2013: 1). This entails a process of depoliticization and sterilization of the battlefield hinging upon a masking of the political intent behind the technology. This process of deracination is vital to ensure companies' flexibility and promotion and to broaden their appeal and client base.

When observing exhibitor's sales strategies and presentations it is clear that the lines between war and routine security intervention are increasingly blurred. This is both in relation to the capacities of the tools presented and the risk-based calculus systems so vital to war and policing (Neocleous 2014). The dynamic emanating from the routine of security supports a flexible scheme in which war can easily be reconfigured into security and vice versa. Technologies are displayed so as to fit the broadest spectrum of deployment contexts possible ranging from settings of urban control and security of mega events to more conventional war scenarios. This flexibility is sustained in a vacillation between the demonstration of the capacities to move between spectacular violence and suspended violence – the threat of violence. The fair produces and reproduces the imagery of unlimited, yet manageable insecurity, which entails a logic that carries a promise of controlling future security risks. In this way, managing (in)security through risk control (Amoore and De Goede 2008) is a major structuring theme, and technologies and know-how are made available to alleviate insecurity but also serve the function of sustaining a culture of insecurity. As security technologies are steadily marketed as necessities required in a world of indefinite risks and threats insecurity is presented as the by default condition from which decisions must be made.

Moreover for most sellers and buyers security is deemed a form of governance to regulate violence, and this is why few ethical or moral questions are raised regarding the effects of the technologies and hardware. The broad array of technology reveals that the industry is pursuing a strategy of diversifying its products to encompass technologies for non-war scenarios (i.e. more subtle homeland security technology to accommodate changes in threat perception since 2001). While the guiding logic in more narrow defence regards have been the raison d'etre of 'saving soldiers', with the expansion to homeland security it is now 'the public' that needs saving from potential threats.

National comparative advantages: between collaboration and competition

Security fairs are excellent venues for exploring states' comparative advantages and their national defence and security visions (Dvir and Tishler 2000; see also Reppy 2000). While the fairs are global in scope, they often hinge on national agendas tied to a national defence and industrial base. National security industries export a national logic intimately linked to the defence in their home countries, drawing on and boosting a national ethos and the broader militarization of the national economy. Therefore in their organizational structure most security fairs are collaborative efforts between state agencies and private contractors. This is often realized through a joint effort between a country's ministries of defence, foreign affairs, the interior, and sometimes in cooperation with the special security agencies and occasionally relevant academic and research institutions.

In practice the marketplace is both a space of collaboration and competition, and of national interests, globalized ideas and fragmented alliances. In this way the fair comes to reflect the public–private nexus of the global security industry and provides a view of how they influence the translation of security into a universal currency. At some fairs the national layer is structured around the branding of the host nation as the prime or sole exhibitor at the fair, or through fairs organized with national subdivisions or national pavilions where companies are clustered according to their country of origin. For example India's largest security fair Expo India is organized with the support of the Ministry of Home Affairs, the Indo-Tibetan border police force and the Delhi police force. Russia's Interpolitex (2013) in Moscow was organized in a collaborative effort between the Ministry of the Interior and the Federal Security of the Russian Federation. In this way nations brand themselves through an organization in national clusters or pavilions. For the country hosting the fair the national branding can take two forms: either emphasizing the host nation as an investment opportunity and potential customer for external companies, or as platform for showing its comparative advantages and thereby seeking to boost the exports of domestic security companies. In this competitive setting actors battle to conventionalize their own accounts as legitimate and effective (Mcinerney 2008: 1091–2). The ability to actually test the technology developed on the basis of experience under the slogan 'battle proven' creates a national reputation. State actors and state owned companies often play on their comparative advantages to stand out and attract attention. Battlefield experience builds up an image of distinctiveness and authenticity that is tied to nationalized security experiences, while at the same time success is tied to the ability to translate and elevate the capacities to fit technology to universalized and generalized threat scenarios.

In sum, the security fair becomes a platform that produces local discourses, but also a mechanism that facilitates the production of cross-cultural ideas of security contributing to the conventionalization and internationalization of selected practices. The fair produces homogenizing effects, which can invoke international exchanges of security or military practice and it locates debates on security and securitizing moves in temporal and spatial sequences. But while homogenizing, there are also discursive struggles. Some trends and events (e.g. 9/11) produce convergence (Bigo 2006), while others spur fragmentation. It cannot therefore be assumed a priori that actors come to share the same perception of reality through a shared experience at the fair.

Conclusion

The study of security fairs provides an entry point into an examination of the wider spaces of security promotion. The fair is more than just a transmission belt for already existing practices and ideas; it sets the stage for a number of activities shaping the meaning and use of technology and the context within which professionals thrive. Security fairs are fields of both unified narratives and competing discourses over what constitutes best practice, and works as spaces for the production and reproduction of social relations and alliances, business and profit optimization and technological reconfiguration.

The fair promotes the utopian vision of maximum security which in turn becomes a self-referential logic; a locus for the promotion of security. Once established this logic is difficult to repel, which is why security often comes to be more a matter of routine and stabilization management rather than emergency. The dominant logic of maximum security is shaped and conventionalized at the fair, and comes to colonize not only day-to-day interactions but also the future through the prevailing discourses of risk management.

Security fairs are crucial nodal points in connecting ways of practicing violence with conflicts, political strategies and business abroad. The fairs exhibit best practice of how to conduct war, fight crime and terror, and the association between technology and the civilizing effect of security as a routine and technical maneuver is a key dynamic at the fairs. Combined with the overall prevailing security logics internalized and conventionalized at the fairs, security technologies and its applicaton thus become not only as morally defensible but also as a moral duty. This not only aestheticizes and universalizes violence and control, but the process of commodification further blurs the lines between the private and the public and between security and war.

Note

1   The fairs visited were: HLS 2012, the 2nd Israel International Homeland Security Conference, Tel Aviv, 11–14 November 2012; ISDEF, the 5th International Defense and HLS Expo, Tel Aviv, 4–6 June 2013; the Eurosatory – Land and Air and Defense and Security International Exhibition, Paris, 11–15

June 2012; and SDW2014 (Security Document World), London, 16–18 June 2014. Other fairs included were: IMDEX, the International Maritime Defense Exhibition, Interpolitex, Moscow; DefExpo Defense Expo, New Delhi; IDEAS defence expo, Pakistan; DIMDEX Defense Expo, Qatar; Counter Terror Expo, London; and IFSEC International, London.

Bibliography

Alexander, J. (2013) 'Interrogating the Security-Technology Nexus: "Security Etiquette" and the Role of Technology in the Diffussion of Risk, Threat and Fear', paper presented at the 8th Pan-European Conference on International Relations, Warsaw, September.

Amoore, L. and De Goede, M. (2008) 'Governing by Risk in the War on Terror', in L. Amoore and M. De Goede (eds), *Risk and the War on Terror*, Abingdon: Routledge, pp. 5–20.

Biggart, N., and Beamish, T. (2003) 'The Economic Sociology of Conventions: Habit, Custom, Practice, and Routine in Market Order', *Annual Review of Sociology* 29: 443–64.

Bigo, D. (2006) 'Globalized (in)Security: The Field and the Ban-opticon', in N. Sakai and J. Solomon (eds), *Translation, Biopolitics, Colonial Difference*, Hong Kong: University of Hong Kong Press, pp. 109–56.

Callon, M., Méadel, C. and Rabeharisoa, V. (2002) 'The Economy of Qualities', *Economy and Society* 31(2): 194–217.

DiMaggio, P. (1991) 'Constructing an Organizational Field as a Professional Project: US Art Museums, 1920–1940', in W. Powell and P. DiMaggio (eds), *The New Institutionalism in Organizational Analysis*, Chicago, IL: University of Chicago Press, pp. 267–92.

Dvir, D., and Tishler, A. (2000) 'The Changing Role of the Defense Industry in Israel's Industrial and Technological Development', in J. Reppy (ed.), *The Place of the Defense Industry in National Systems of Innovation*, Ithaca, NY: Cornell University Press, pp. 194–217.

Feinstein, A. (2011) *The Shadow World: Inside the Global Arms Trade*, New York: Farrar Straus and Giroux.

Garud, R. (2007) 'Institutional Entrepreneurship as Embedded Agency: An Introduction to the Special Issue', *Organization Studies* 28(7): 957–69.

Garud, R. and Rappa, M. (1995) 'A Socio-Cognitive Model of Technology Evolution: The Case of Cochlear Implants', *Organization Science* 5(3): 344–62.

Gifford, C. (2004) *The Arms Trade*, Hong Kong: Chrysalis Education.

Gray, C. (2004) *Strategy for Chaos: Revolutions in Military Affairs and the Evidence of History*, London: Frank Cass Publishers.

Khalili, L. (2010) 'The Location of Palestine in Global Counterinsurgencies', *International Journal of Middle East Studies* 42(3): 413–33.

Khalili, L. (2013) *Time in the Shadows: Confinement in Counterinsurgencies*, Stanford, CA: Stanford University Press.

Kirchgeorg, M., Springer, C. and Kastner, E. (2010) 'Objectives for Successfully Participating in Trade Shows', *Journal of Business and Industrial Marketing* 25(1): 63–72.

Lampel, J. and Meyer, A. D. (2008) 'Introduction: Field-Configuring Events as Structuring Mechanisms: How Conferences, Ceremonies, and Trade Shows Constitute New Technologies, Industries, and Markets', *Journal of Management Studies* 45(6): 1024–35.

Ling-yee, L. (2008) 'The Effects of Firm Resources on Trade Show Performance: How Do Trade Show Marketing Processes Matter?', *Journal of Business and Industrial Marketing* 23(1): 35–47.

Mcinerney, P. (2008) 'Showdown at Kykuit: Field-Configuring Events as Loci for Conventionalizing Accounts', *Journal of Management Studies* 45(6): 1089–1116.

Metz, S. and Kievit, J. (1995) *Strategy and the Revolution in Military Affairs: From Theory to Policy*, Carlisle Barracks, PA: Strategic Studies Institute, US Army War College.

Neocleous, M. (2014) *War Power, Police Power*, Edinburgh: University of Edinburgh Press.

Percy, S. (2007) *Mercenaries: The History of a Norm in International Relations*, Oxford: Oxford University Press.

Rao, H. (1994) 'The Social Construction of Reputation: Certification Contests, Legitimation, and the Survival of Organizations in the American Automobile Industry: 1895–1912', *Strategic Management Journal* 15(1): 29–44.

Reppy, J. (2000) *The Place of the Defense Industry in National Systems of Innovation*, Ithaca, NY: Cornell University Press.

Seringhaus, R. H. F and Rosson, J. P. (1998) 'Management and Performance of International Trade Fair Exhibitors: Governmet Stands vs Independent Stands', *International Marketing Review* 15(5): 398–412.

Singer, P. (2010) *Wired for War the Robotics Revolution and Conflict in the Twenty-First Century*, New York: Penguin Books.

Sköns, E. and Dunne, J. P. (2006) *Economics of Arms Production*, Stockholm: International Peace Research Institute and the University of West England.

Stavrianakis, A. (2010). *Taking Aim at the Arms Trade: NGOs, Global Civil Society and the World Military Order*, London: Zed Books.

Stockmarr, L. (2014) 'Seeing Is Striking: Selling Israeli Warfare', www.jadaliyya.com/pages/index/16044/seeing-is-striking_selling-israeli-warfare.

Stritzel, H. (2011a) 'Security as Translation: Threats, Discourse, and the Politics of Localisation', *Review of International Studies* 37(5): 2491–2517.

Stritzel, H. (2011b) 'Security: The Translation', *Security Dialogue* 42(4–5): 343–55.

Zilber, T. B. (2006) 'The Work of the Symbolic in Institutional Processes: Translations of Rational Myths in Israeli High Tech', *Academy of Management Journal* 49(2): 281–303.

Zilber, T. B. (2011) 'Institutional Multiplicity in Practice: A Tale of Two High-Tech Conferences in Israel', *Journal of Organization Science* 22(6): 1539–59.

20

THE PRIVATIZATION OF PUNISHMENT IN THE UNITED STATES

Shannon Wheatley Hartman and Roxanne Lynn Doty

The privatization of punishment exists in countries throughout the world. Although the scope is wide, for-profit prisons and detention facilities appear most entrenched in Australia, the United Kingdom, South Africa, and the United States. This chapter offers an overview of the privatization of punishment in the United States. The US imprisons more people – both per capita and in absolute terms – than any other country in the world. Over 2.2 million people are currently incarcerated in the US, and the privatization of punishment is both a response to and a contributing factor to this proliferation of jailed and detained individuals.

In this chapter we pay particular attention to the private prison and detention industries, which have become popularly known as the 'prison industrial complex'. We argue that the privatization of punishment – in its many forms – reflects the increased blurring of the public/private sectors. Drawing upon the insights of Michel Foucault we argue that the privatization of punishment serves multiple functions such as the construction of criminality, the management of marginalized populations, and the extension of sovereign power through the private sector. Contrary to neoliberal claims, the increased role of privatization does not shrink the size of government, but serves to extend its reach through governance by distributing power through for-profit corporations. Throughout this chapter we describe one component of privatized punishment that shows no immediate signs of decline – the privatization of migrant detention centres. We conclude by anticipating the growth of the industry in yet another emerging market; the incarceration of migrant children.

Privatization of prisons and detention centres

Imprisonment is one of the most severe sanctions that can be imposed. It deprives individuals of liberty and has the effect of creating vulnerable populations that exist on the margins of society. This practice in itself raises a series of moral, ethical, political, legal, psychological and social concerns, and these concerns become even more acute when for-profit corporations turn punishment into a business and inmates into a commodity. In this section we describe the role of corporations in the 'prison industrial complex' (PIC).

The term PIC is derived from the term 'military industrial complex' of the 1960s. Much like the military industry, albeit on a much smaller scale, the prison industry has been allowed to emerge to provide a service that has been traditionally considered the responsibility of the state. The PIC describes the coordination of interests between public and private sectors, and includes, but are not limited to, private companies that provide, manage, and police prisons; corporations that contract prison labour; construction companies that build prison facilities; companies that supply food, phone, laundry, cleaning, visitation and medical services within the facility; the surveillance industry; private probation companies; as well as lawyers, lobbying groups, government agencies and legislators. The PIC thrives on the belief that punishment is the solution to economic, social and political problems. In other words, it is not only a set of corporations and government agencies, but it is also a state of mind. The PIC capitalizes on the popular but arguably flawed belief that imprisonment is the solution to homelessness, unemployment, drug addiction, mental illness, immigration, illiteracy and so on. To be clear, the PIC is not a conspiracy but a confluence of special interests that creates a seemingly self-sustaining system.

Success of the privatization of punishment has been contingent on the neoliberal belief in the market. The fiscal conservatism that began in the US during the 1970s, followed by the crisis that resulted from President Ronald Reagan's monetarism in the 1980s, played significant roles in the rise of private prisons. US states were confronted with increasing budget deficits, revenue constraints, and overcrowding in existing prison facilities. Tough anti-drug abuse legislation revived federal mandatory minimum sentencing and further taxed an already stretched penal system. Private prisons appeared to be an attractive alternative to states borrowing money or using tax revenues for the construction of new facilities. It was during this period that private prison corporations emerged and won their first contracts to run immigrant detention centres.

Although private prisons encountered financial problems in the late 1990s, the 1996 Illegal Immigration Reform and Immigrant Responsibility Act (IIRIRA) and subsequent pieces of legislation offered relief in the form of increased demand for detention beds and new contracts. The industry continued to be stimulated by post-9/11 security budgets, which allowed for subcontracts with for-profit corporations in the pursuit of furthering homeland security. According to the US Department of Justice, these policies resulted in the private prison industry increasing by 1600 per cent between 1990 and 2009 (West *et al.* 2010). In 2010, the two largest private prison companies, Correction Corporation of America (CCA) and the GEO Group, reported earnings of US$1.7 billion and US$1.27 billion respectively to their shareholders (CCA 2010; Geo Group 2010).

CCA is the oldest and largest for-profit private prison corporation in the US. The company was founded in 1983 by Tom Beasley, T. Don Hutto, Doctor Crants and backed by venture capitalist Jack Massey. According to Beasley, the company was founded on the principle that you could sell prisons 'just like you were selling cars, or real estate, or hamburgers' (Selman and Leighton 2010: 58). He saw prison facilities as a product that could be packaged, marketed, and sold to impressionable consumers. This seemingly benign description of private prisons was reinforced by its achievement of real estate investment trust (REIT) status in 2013. Designed to reduce the payment of corporate federal income taxes, REITs are a special tax designation for companies that focus on real estate holdings. CCA was able to make the successful claim to the Internal Revenue Service (IRS) that the money they collect from government entities for holding prisoners is essentially the same as rent collection. In other words, the prison industry is treated as a housing service and in many ways confirms Beasley's strategy of treating it like any other industry.

Unlike other industries, however, prisons do not provide consumers with a tangible good or service. Private punishment is in the business of *depriving* individuals of liberty, which is a distinctly different type of business model. Moreover, the privatization of punishment has the effect of creating commodities out of incarcerated or even potentially punishable individuals. For this business model to work and to expand, the prison industry must not only incarcerate all criminals, it must also actively work to construct new threats that can be addressed through incarceration. This is no secret. Private prison companies admit that their business model depends on high rates of incarceration and the incarceration of individuals that commit what has been traditionally consider a minor offense. As stated in the Corrections Corporation of America 2010 Annual Letter to Shareholders:

> The demand for our facilities and services could be adversely affected by the relaxation of enforcement efforts, leniency in conviction or parole standards and sentencing practices or through the decriminalization of certain activities that are currently proscribed by our criminal laws. For instance, any changes with respect to drugs and controlled substances or illegal immigration could affect the number of persons arrested, convicted, and sentenced, thereby potentially reducing demand for correctional facilities to house them.
>
> *(CCA 2010)*

It should come as no surprise then that CCA and the Geo Group actively lobby for and even help to shape legislation that contributes to the increasing criminalization of minor offenses. Take for example CCA's membership in the American Legislative Exchange Council (ALEC), a political organization known for incubating and proliferating conservative political agendas. Although ALEC touts itself as the largest 'membership association of state legislators', almost 98 per cent of its revenue comes from sources other than legislative membership dues, such as corporations, trade associations, and corporate foundations. The organization focuses on influencing lawmakers at the state level by drafting and disseminating model legislation (Elk and Sloan 2011). To put this in context, US state legislators are empowered to pass laws within their respective states. This is often achieved without much public scrutiny or debate. Federal legislation trumps state laws, however, in the silences of federal law, individual states have a great amount of power. ALEC has focused its energy on influencing state legislation.

CCA's influence in ALEC has been widespread and well documented. The company was a member of the Public Safety Task Force which developed model legislation such as mandatory minimum sentencing for nonviolent offenses, 'three strikes laws' that require repeat offenders to be sentenced to jail for a mandatory 25 years to life, and 'truth-in-sentencing' laws that require prisoners to serve most or all of their time without a chance for parole (Elk and Sloan 2011). These types of legislation, adopted by many states, have the overall effect of expanding punishment of offenses that would otherwise be considered minor while simultaneously requiring mandatory increases in the amount of time that individuals will serve for these offenses. Both kinds of legislation, expanding what constitutes punishable offenses and extending the length of incarceration for these offenses, have the overall effect of benefiting the financial bottom line of the private prison industry.

Arguably the most direct link between private prison interests and state legislation was the passage of SB1070 in Arizona. In 2010, State Senator Russell Pearce of Arizona championed and successfully passed SB1070; legislation that requires state and local law enforcement officials to determine the immigration status of people with whom they come into 'lawful contact'. The purpose is to allow state and local law enforcement to police immigration – a job that traditionally has been in the jurisdiction of federal law enforcement. The most immediate effect of this legislation is the increased flow of undocumented immigrants into detention.

As uncovered by Laura Sullivan (2010), the model legislation for SB1070 was developed in 2009 in a Public Safety and Elections Task Force meeting, attended by both Pearce and representatives of CCA. According to Sullivan's investigative report, CCA identified immigration as a profit-centre for the growth of the private prison industry. The private prison industry operates about half of all immigrant detention facilities, and as such, SB1070 and other anti-immigration legislation are financially important to CCA. Not only was CCA present at the secretive ALEC meeting where the legislation was drafted, but Governor Brewer of Arizona, who signed the legislation into law, had close ties to the private prison industry. Her spokesman Paul Senseman and campaign manager Chuck Coughlin were both former lobbyists for private prison companies. Moreover, 30 of the 36 state representatives who voted for the passage of SB1070 received donations from lobbyists representing the private prison industry.

These and other state laws have led to a social context in which immigrants are more likely to be arrested and detained for acts that have not been traditionally viewed as illegal. As such, undocumented immigrants are now more likely to come into the criminal justice system and end up in immigration detention centres, which are proliferating to meet the increase in demand. Immigrants are now the fastest growing population in federal custody. Since 1996 immigrant detention has increased exponentially with the most recent spike occurring after 9/11. In 1994, the average daily population in custody was 6,785 detainees. By 2007 this figure had increased to over 30,000 detainees. Between 2003 and 2011 the total number of non-citizens detained by US Immigration and Customs Enforcement (ICE) per year increased from 231,500 to an all-time record high of 429,247 detainees (Meissner *et al.* 2013).

CCA and GEO Group each receive over ten per cent of their revenue directly from ICE, and for both companies ICE revenues have increased significantly over the past seven years. At a conference call with investors in June of 2009 CCA's president, Damon Hininger said, 'We believe this suggests that ICE will continue providing meaningful opportunity for the industry for the foreseeable future' (Feltz and Baksh 2009). The CEO of Geo Group echoed a similar sentiment to investors, stating that 'My personal view is that Homeland Security and the detention beds necessary to detain illegal aliens will increasingly be seen as a national imperative to protect U.S. workers and their jobs' (ibid.).

As of today, CCA manages more than 60 facilities with a capacity of more than 85,000 beds. The company has entered into contracts not just with ICE but also the Federal Bureau of Prisons, the US Marshals Service, half of the US states, and several local municipalities. The GEO group is similarly situated, operating approximately 100 facilities in several countries with an 80,000 bed capacity. Both corporations promote an interesting twist on market-based solutions to socio-political problems by claiming to be more efficient and cost effective than the government. However, both tout their partnerships with the public sector in the form of government oversight. As described by Steven Owen, Director of Public Affairs for CCA, his corporation combines the efficiency of the business model with the accountability of the government (Doty and Wheatley 2013). This sounds like a relatively straightforward model, however, the blurring of the public/private sectors is far from simple.

There are various types of contracts, arrangements, and partnerships between the government and private prison corporations. The privatization of punishment might involve the ownership of the facility where prisoners are housed, the private use of prison labour and taking of profits from their labour, or private management of the facility that includes the day-to-day supervision and care of prisoners. There are more extraordinary examples of privatization, such as CCA's longstanding desire and failed attempts to buy the entire state of Tennessee's correctional system. More modest examples include CCA's outright purchase of a state prison, the Lake Erie Correctional Institution, for $72.7 million. Instead of hiring a contractor to operate the facility or pay a company to build and run a new facility, the state of Ohio sold an already existing facility to CCA (Smyth 2011). Following the purchase of Lake Erie, CCA sent letters to 48 other states, heralding its acquisition of the facility as a shining example of the benefits of selling state run prisons to private businesses. In the letter, CCA offers to help address states' challenging corrections budget in exchange for a 20-year management contract and assurance that state prisons would remain at least 90 per cent full (Kirkham 2012).

The most popular form of privatization today is when corporations operate (and often own) secure facilities for prisoners, detainees, migrants, or juveniles and then solicit contracts with local, state, or federal agencies. It should be noted, however, that the economic incentives to privatize punishment reach well beyond the substantial task of operating and managing facilities. Additional aspects of privatization include subsidiary contracts for the internal, day-to-day operations such as providing medical and health services, transportation, food, laundry, telephone, visitation, and maintenance. Perhaps most troubling is the all too common practice of transferring inmates to empty beds around the country. This practice, which could be described as importing and exporting prisoners via interstate commerce, is commonly known as 'rent-a-cell'. When states are pressed with overcrowding, they turn to companies like Dominion Management that serve as 'bed brokers' and help transfer inmates to empty cells around the country. The bed broker will search for a facility with empty beds at the right price. The cost per prisoner per day ('man-day') can range from $25 to $60, depending on the type of facility and its level of occupancy. Bed brokers earn a commission of $2.50 to $5.50 per man-day. The county that does not operate the prison but gives it legal status can also charge a fee of as much as $1.50 per man-day (Schlosser 1998). This practice is just one of many that illustrates the growing reach, influence, and embedded nature of the privatization of punishment. Local economies also claim to benefit from the prison industry through tax revenue, employment, demand in the housing industry, and patronage to local businesses. In many states, prisoners are even counted as part of the population, which offers a set of tax and federal funding benefits for the community. The overall effect results in residents relying on the prison industry and even embracing their status as living in a 'prison town'.

A good example is the small town of Florence, Arizona. Located in desert terrain between Phoenix and Tucson, the highway leading to town is lined with private prisons, retirement villages, mobile-home parks, and fast food restaurants. The city of Florence was built around the prison industry in the early twentieth century and residents share pride in its history. These prisons are much more visible than in the neighbouring 'prison town' of Eloy, Arizona. Eloy is more of a 'pass through' town with only two major sources of revenue: the Speedco truck stop and CCA (Doty and Wheatley 2013). Although the prisons and detention facilities are deliberately located outside of Eloy, the residents of both Eloy and Florence are acutely aware of the jobs and revenue that the business of incarceration brings to their hometowns. The very existence of these towns calls into question the function of incarceration. Although the stated function of incarceration is to maintain public safety, the motivation has shifted to economic revitalization of local towns and communities. This invites a series of questions: What else does the privatization of punishment make possible? What possibilities are foreclosed because of the economic incentives to punish? How does the privatization of punishment impact our communities and shape our sense of self?

The privatization of sovereignty function and immigrant detention

In *Discipline and Punish: The Birth of the Prison* (1979), Michel Foucault describes how the prison system never really succeeded. As he explains:

One would be forced to suppose that the prison, and no doubt punishment in general, is not intended to eliminate offenses, but rather to distinguish them, to distribute them, to use them: that is not so much that they render docile those who are liable to transgress the law but that they tend to assimilate the transgression of the laws in a general tactic of subjection.

(Foucault 1979: 272)

For Foucault, the 'successful failure' of the penal system relies on the ability of the state to create, manage, and problematize anomalies of the social body. Anomalies of the social body must be identified and transformed into problems to be managed thus diverting attention from and questioning of the social body itself. In the process of management, state power proliferates and what might be seen as evidence of the failure of the entire penal system becomes a management problem. The more technical 'solutions' become embedded in the complex, the more difficult it becomes to make fundamental changes to a system that depends on newly characterized entities being regarded as an anomaly. Management of this anomaly – as an anomaly – becomes an essential aspect of statecraft. 'Solutions' to the anomaly, however flawed and ineffective in terms of the overall situation, serve the interests of segments of society, some of whom yield a tremendous amount of power and influence, and some who have little or no influence.

We refer to the inclusion of private corporations into this process as the 'privatizing sovereignty function' (Doty and Wheatley 2013). The state itself is increasingly mobile and fluid, often blurring boundaries between public and private sectors and in the process increasing the power of both, especially vis-à-vis the population of persons in prison or potentially subject to incarceration. The privatizing sovereignty function does not necessarily result in a diminishing of sovereignty or of state power. It can, however, lead to a diminishing of oversight and democratic accountability and can function to conceal the workings of sovereign power. We argue that this is precisely the case with the privatization of punishment.

Take for example the dubious and joint efforts by the state and private prisons to control information. Existing federal Freedom of Information Act (FOIA) regulations do not extend to private prisons. Advocates have for years argued that privately contracted facilities should be subject to open records law. Since 2005, legislators have introduced the Private Prison Information Act (PPIA), a federal bill that would subject private prisons to the same open record laws, but it has repeatedly died in subcommittee. CCA and other private prison corporations have lobbied against various incarnations of PPIA, with CCA alone spending millions to keep information closed. Through partnering with private corporations to dispense punishment, the state is positioned to benefit from allowances given to for-profit enterprises. Private prisons are not subject to the same legal requirements as public prisons to provide incident reports on assaults, escapes, deaths, or rape. People seeking this information can submit an FOIA to the government agency, but if releasing this information exposes 'business secrets' then the request can be denied. The blurred relationship between public and private interests makes transparency almost impossible. The state is not diminished by this relationship but instead strengthened by its cooperation with private corporations.

Market solutions are frequently perceived as shrinking the size and reach of government. As we have suggested, this is not necessarily the case. Prison privatization and private detention has increased the reach of government, expanded social control, and has encouraged an entrepreneurial spirit around the sanctioning, punishment, and social control of fellow citizens and non-citizens – all done in partnership or under contract with the state. Such management serves the neoliberal agenda, but is by no means disconnected from increased state power. The privatization of punishment reflects a deep blurring and even hybridization of the public/private sectors for the seeking of new markets and creating new commodities.

Future markets

We have illustrated how the prison industrial complex benefits from the incarceration of a greater number of people. To achieve mass incarceration, the industry has actively lobbied for the criminalization of nonviolent practices like drug abuse and migration. For the industry to expand, new markets must emerge. We anticipate certain populations of children to increasingly become such anomalies of society designed to be in need of management.

Private prisons have not shied away from the business of incarcerating children. Private corporations helped to draft the Drug-Free Schools Act, which increased drug law enforcement presence on public school campuses and tougher sentencing for drug offences in 'drug-free school zones'. CCA even participated in law enforcement actions in schools. The 'school-to-prison pipeline' is a term used to describe a widespread pattern in the US of pushing disadvantaged students out of school and into the criminal justice system. Although there are many factors that have led to this phenomenon, the private prison industry is yet once again well positioned to benefit from the increase in incarceration.

Take for example the 'kids for cash' scandal: In Wilkes-Barre, Pennsylvania, two judges, Mark Ciavarella and Michael Conohan, were found guilty of accepting $2.6 million in kickbacks from the developers of for-profit juvenile correctional facilities. The judges sent children to extended stays in private detention centres for minor offences like mocking a principal on social media, trespassing in vacant lots, and shoplifting. The judges used their discretion in sentencing to increase the overall head count in the juvenile detention facilities (Urbina 2009).

From an economic perspective, this should come as no surprise. Juveniles fit the ideal characteristics of a profitable inmate: young, healthy, and not a major security risk. According to Christopher Petrella (2014), young people of colour are overrepresented in privatized prisons. In the nine states that Petrella examined, private facilities housed higher percentages of people of colour than public facilities did. It has been well established that persons of colour are overrepresented in the US penal system in general, however, Petrella's astonishing finding is that private prisons deliberately exclude people with high medical costs. Younger, healthier inmates, he found – who've come into the system since the 'war on drugs' came into effect in the 1980s – are disproportionately people of colour. Older inmates, who generally come with a series of health problems, tend to be white. This is not to suggest that private prisons are motivated by race, but by profit. It further illustrates how inmates are seen as commodities and the desire to maximize profits can lead to incentives to incarcerate younger populations.

This insight is hardly a trade secret. Stock in both CCA and Geo Group spiked after yet another border crisis became reported in popular news outlets during the summer of 2014, resulting in an increased awareness of Central American children crossing into the US through the southern border. The number of migrant children detained by border patrol reached unprecedented levels in the summer of 2014. To manage this new anomaly, the Obama administration shifted US$405 million in funds to address the crisis and urged Congress to pass a US$3.7 billion emergency bill. Ultimately this bill failed, however, investors saw this as an opportunity. Stock in CCA climbed 8.5 per cent and Geo Group was above 7 per cent by the end of the summer. They were estimated to grow at 1.5 per cent prior to the crisis. Both companies reported better-than-expected earnings and raised their outlook for the rest of the year (Egan 2014).

In September of 2014, US officials announced plans to open a new facility, the South Texas

Family Residential Center, in Dilley, Texas to house Central American women and children. This new facility will be vastly larger than the three current family detention centres, which together have a capacity of approximately 1,300 people. These facilities are a response to the surge of migrant families crossing the southwestern border. In the last fiscal year alone, more than 66,000 family units have been detained along the southwestern border, according to US Customs and Border Protection (Department of Homeland Security 2015).

The contract for the new facility has been awarded to CCA, which has been repeatedly criticized for its treatment of migrant families. For example, The American Civil Liberties Union (ACLU) won a settlement with CCA in 2007 over prison-like conditions for migrant children at its T. Don Hutto Residential Center in Texas. The ACLU also documented sexual abuse of women in the same facility in 2011. Nonetheless, CCA will run this new centre in the city of Dilley, Texas and it is expected to open in the spring of 2015 and equipped to hold 2,4000 people. However, it is worth noting that the management contract of this facility has some unusual terms. In their rush to open the facility (originally scheduled to open in November of 2014), the Obama administration bypassed normal bidding procedures and granted management to CCA, but through its already exiting contract with the city of Eloy. That is, all federal funding for the detention centre in Dilley, Texas will pass through the small town of Eloy, Arizona – located over 1000 miles away (Hylton 2015). Serving as the intermediary, the city of Eloy will be compensated 50 cents per day per bed, regardless of whether someone is occupying the bed in Texas. That translates to $438,000 dollars annually (Harris 2015). Eloy will be paid to manage this contract, however, officials from the city of Eloy say that they do not expect to monitor, or even visit, the Dilley facility (Hylton 2015). Although this contract is unusual, it is also a clear example of the further blurring of public/private responsibilities that have the effect of creating a complicated web of interests with limited accountability.

The stated purpose of these family detention facilities is to expedite return to home countries and to deter others from migrating into the US. Prior to current trends, children would have been sent to shelters and allowed to attend school while parents were held at nearby facilities. However, due to growing concern about separating parents from children, even nursing infants, the House Appropriations Committee declared in 2005 that children should not be held in government custody unless their welfare was in question and added that the Department of Homeland Security should 'release families or use alternatives to detention' whenever possible (Talbot 2008). The report by the committee recommended a new alternative to detention known as the Intensive Supervision Appearance Program, which allows people awaiting disposition of their immigration cases to be released into the community, provided that they are closely tracked by means such as electronic monitoring bracelets, curfews, and regular contact with a caseworker. Despite congress directing ICE to stop separating families and make allowances for families to stay together in non-penal settings, ICE has increased its number of contracts with facilities that house families.

Conclusion

Criticisms of the privatization of prisons are many, ranging from the ethical to the economic. Adding profit motive to the prison system provides perverse incentives to keep incarceration rates high and operating costs low. In an effort to maximize its profit margins and bill itself as a cheaper alternative to government-run and/or owned prisons, CCA's cost-cutting measures have frequently been through practices like reducing employee benefits and salaries, operating on routinely low and dangerous staff-to-prisoner ratios, and not offering sufficient staff training. Critics also note that some inmates are denied proper services, including medical care, in attempts to keep costs low. The general criticism is that profit motives drastically change the mission of corrections from public safety to making the greatest profit.

The shrewd tactics of the prison corporations have not gone unnoticed by critics. Extensive lobbying, lavish campaign contributions, dubious effort to control information, and even working directly with legislators to craft legislation that serves the interest of the prison industry are just some of the tactics of the private prison industry. Ironically, the values that drive privatization – a general sort of conservative, anti-government, law and order orientation – are undermined by the extension of governance through corporate means. As described in this chapter, the privatization of the sovereignty function allows the state to extend its reach through private corporations but with less regulation and oversight. The overall affect is not the withering away of the state, but a new blurring of state and private sectors that make democratic accountability extremely difficult. Another function of the privatization of punishment is the increased need to create and manage anomalies in society. The industry, in partnership with the state, is able to seek out vulnerable populations, such as migrants and even migrant children that become criminalized through legislation and popular discourse.

Alternatives to privatization include decriminalizing nonviolent acts, increasing the number of community-based programmes, reducing the length of sentences, increasing the number of early release programmes, and investing in prevention programmes such as early childhood parenting and education. Advanced by the civil rights non-profit organization Color of Change, divestment campaigns have also been somewhat successful in recent years. For example, three major corporations divested from CCA and the GEO Group, collectively pulling nearly $60 million in investments in 2013. Although there is growing awareness and activism to eliminate the privatization of punishment, we do not underestimate the structural embeddedness of the prison industrial complex and predict that this industry will continue to grow.

Bibliography

CCA (2010) 'Letter to Shareholders 1', http://ir.correctionscorp.com/phoenix.zhtml?c=117983&p=irol-reportsannual.

Department of Homeland Security (2015) 'Southwest Border Unaccompanied Alien Children', www.cbp.gov/newsroom/stats/southwest-border-unaccompanied-children.

Doty, R. L. and Wheatley, E. S. (2013) 'Private Detention and the Immigration Industrial Complex', *International Political Sociology* 7(4): 426–43.

Dow, M. (2004) *American Gulag: Inside US Immigration Prisons*, Oakland, CA: University of California Press.

Egan, M. (2014) 'Wall Street Bets on Prison Growth From Border Crisis', *CNN Money* 29 August, http://money.cnn.com/2014/08/29/investing/border-crisis-prison-stocks.

Elk, M. and Sloan, B. (2011) 'The Hidden History of ALEC and Prison Labor', *The Nation* 1 August, www.thenation.com/article/162478/hidden-history-alec-and-prison-labor.

Feltz, R. and Baksh, S. (2009) 'Detention Retention', *The American Prospect* 2 June, http://prospect.org/article/detention-retention.

Fernandes, D. (2007) *Targeted: Homeland Security and the Business of Immigration*, New York: Seven Stories Press.

Foucault, M. (1979) *Discipline and Punish: The Birth of the Prison* (trans. A. Sheridan), New York: Vintage/Random House.

GEO Group (2010) *Annual Report*, Boca Raton, FL: GEO Group, www.geogroup.com/documents/2011-report.pdf.

Gilmore, R. W. (2007) *Golden Gulag-Prisons, Surplus, Crisis, and Opposition in Globalizing California*, Oakland, CA: University of California Press.

Golash-Boza, T. M. (2012) *Immigration Nation: Raid, Detention, and Deportation in Post 9/11 America*, Boulder, CO: Paradigm Publishers.

Herivel, T. and Wright, P. (2003) *Prison Nation: The Warehousing of America's Poor*, New York: Routledge.

Harris, C. (2015) 'Unique Deal to Obtain Migrants Nets Eloy $438,000', *The Republic* 18 January.

Hylton, W. S. (2015) 'The Shame of America's Family Detention Camps', *New York Times Magazine* 4

February, www.nytimes.com/2015/02/08/magazine/the-shame-of-americas-family-detention-camps.html?_r=0.

Kirkham, C. (2012) 'Private Prison Corporation Offers Cash in Exchange for State Prisons', *The Huffington Post* 14 February, www.huffingtonpost.com/2012/02/14/private-prisons-buying-state-prisons_n_1272143.html.

Meissner, D., Kerwin, D. M., Chishti, M. and Bergeron, C. (2013) *Immigration Enforcement in the United States: The Rise of a Formidable Machinery*, Washington, DC: Migration Policy Institute.

Petrella, C. (2014) 'The Color of Corporate Corrections Part II: Contractual Exemptions and the Overrepresentation of People of Color in Private Prisons', *Radical Criminology* 3: 81–100.

Schlosser, E. (1998) 'The Prison-Industrial Complex', *The Atlantic* 1 December, www.theatlantic.com/magazine/archive/1998/12/the-prison-industrial-complex/304669.

Selman D. and Leighton, P. (2010) *Punishment for Sale*, Plymouth, MA: Rowman & Littlefield Publishers.

Smyth, J. C. (2011) 'Ohio Becomes First American State to Sell Prison to Private Company', *Huffington Post* 1 September, www.huffingtonpost.com/2011/09/02/ohio-prison-sold_n_946862.html.

Sullivan, L. (2010a) 'Prison Economics Helps Drive Arizona Immigration Law', National Public Radio transcripts 28 October, www.npr.org/2010/10/28/130833741/prison-economics-help-drive-ariz-immigration-law.

Sullivan, L. (2010b) 'Shaping State Laws with Little Scrutiny', National Public Radio transcripts 29 October, www.npr.org/2010/10/29/130891396/shaping-state-laws-with-little-scrutiny.

Talbot, M. (2008) 'The Lost Children: What do Tougher Detention Policies Mean for Illegal Immigrant Families?' *The New Yorker* 3 March, www.newyorker.com/magazine/2008/03/03/the-lost-children

Urbina, I. (2009) 'Despite Red Flags about Judges, A Kickback Scheme Flourished', *New York Times* 27 March, www.nytimes.com/2009/03/28/us/28judges.html?pagewanted=all&_r=0.

West, H. *et al.* (2010) 'United States Department of Justice, Bureau of Justice Statistics, Prisoners in 2009', 33 App. Table 19.

21

PRIVATE SECURITY AND THE MIGRATION CONTROL INDUSTRY

Thomas Gammeltoft-Hansen

Border control has always been a core sovereign prerogative of the state. Yet, as unchecked immigration is increasingly perceived to challenge sovereignty, the response – paradoxically – has been a substantial outsourcing of border control itself to private security actors. The popularity of private migration management can be linked to several factors. Immigration is an area wrought with fundamental policy dilemmas; who and how many to admit and how to balance efficient immigration control and human rights principles? Private companies promise to cut the Gordian knot of separating the wanted from the unwanted in an efficient manner, often promoting technological innovations such as biometrics, digital surveillance and elaborate electronic entry–exit systems. Second, the migration control industry is part of a general commercialization of international migration, with equally profitable companies engaged in facilitating both legal and illegal migration (Gammeltoft-Hansen and Nyberg Sørensen 2013). Third, as in other sectors of public governance, privatizing migration management has been presented as cost-saving, though several studies have challenged this presumption, pointing out that if governments are not footing the bill, migrants will through the cuts on services provided (Menz 2013). Last, but not least, as immigration has come to be perceived as a security matter for many states, the move to privatization can be interpreted as part and parcel of the turn to private security more generally (Salter 2007; Guiraudon 2006; Bigo 2002).

While the growing use of contractors in migration management raises a number of questions related to private security, new public management and sovereignty that are gradually receiving increasing attention within migration studies, this chapter focuses on those related to the legal obligations of states. It argues that at least part of the explanation for the current drive towards privatization in this area is the belief that by delegating authority to private actors states are able to release themselves – *de facto* or *de jure* – from obligations otherwise owed. The migration control industry fundamentally impacts both the human rights of those subjected to control and the mechanisms to ensure democratic oversight and rule of law. At a time when asylum and immigration are highly politicized, the private migration control industry gives the appearance that migration management is, precisely, private and thus external to the state itself.

This chapter sets out by surveying the scope of the migration control industry. The subsequent sections examine the human rights implications of privatized migration management, arguing that while human rights law is in principle neutral regarding the mode of governance, privatization is nonetheless likely to raise additional barriers to ensuring state responsibility for human rights violations by non-state actors. The final section looks at the issue of transparency, pointing out that privatization also brings about procedural barriers and that a 'corporate veil' often obstructs both access to remedies and democratic oversight.

The migration control industry

In the United States, 478,000 immigrants were detained in 2012; half were held in privately run facilities (see Chapter 20, this volume). In the United Kingdom, private contractors currently run nine out of thirteen detention centres, and in Australia a single company, Serco, operates detention centres at twenty different locations. Private actor involvement in migration management is far from limited to detention, however. From airlines carrying out pre-boarding checks, to defence contractors setting up billion-dollar high-tech border surveillance systems, and to security companies ensuring deportations, the last decades have seen the emergence of a distinct 'migration control industry' (Gammeltoft-Hansen 2013) with private companies taking over a wide range of erstwhile governmental functions to screen, control, detain and return migrants.

This industry is rapidly growing and a number of defence and security contractors are currently expanding into migration management. The world's largest security company, G4S, currently operates immigration detention centres in both Australia and the United Kingdom, and passenger screening at airports in North America, Europe and the Middle East. In the United States G4S operated a fleet of custom-built fortified buses that serve as deportation transports, and until 2010 the company held the exclusive contract to carry out forced returns from the United Kingdom. Boeing's contract to set up and operate a high-tech border surveillance system along the US–Mexico border was worth US$1.3 billion and involved nearly 100 subcontractors until it was terminated in 2011. Similarly, the two largest prison companies in the United States, Corrections Corporation of America and Geo Group, have each more than doubled their revenue stemming from immigration detention in the period 2005 to 2012. Last, but not least, Serco's financial reports show that while profits in other areas have been stagnating, its immigration contracts – estimated at AU$3 billion – nonetheless ensured a 28 per cent growth in operating profits from 2009 to 2013.

However, it is important to note that at least certain parts of private actor involvement in migration management long predates the current outsourcing trend prompted by neoliberal governance. As early as 1751 Denmark levied fines from shipmasters bringing in Jewish passengers (Lausten 2012). Those found inadmissible by US immigration officers were to be transported back at the cost of the steamship company. The modern variant of such carrier sanctions emerged from the 1950s onwards in response to the increase in 'jet age' asylum seekers, which has made almost all asylum countries impose financial penalties on airlines for bringing in passengers without visas or passports. In the US, carrier liability for bringing in aliens without valid passports and visas has been part of the Immigration and Nationality Act since 1952 (the MacCarran-Walter Act, Section 273). In Canada, similar rules were introduced as part of the 1976 Immigration Act. In the European context, legislation to impose obligations and concurrent fines upon carriers was implemented by Belgium, Germany and the United Kingdom in 1987, and since 1990 required by all states party to the Schengen Convention (Cruz 1995: 5). This kind of 'indirect privatization' has made private airline companies gradually take on elaborate control functions related to document checks, forgery control and passenger profiling.

Human rights implications

The adverse effects of private involvement in migration management on migrants' rights are well documented and analysed (Gammeltoft-Hansen 2011: ch. 5). The original rationale for carrier sanctions was to physically prevent refugees from reaching the territory of prospective asylum states and thereby triggering relevant obligations under domestic and international law prohibiting return. The involvement of private actors in migration management is thus paralleled by a similar trend to 'externalize' migration control by shifting the geographical location of border control to the high seas or foreign territory (Gammeltoft-Hansen and Hathaway 2015). At the same time, the introduction of a private intermediary served to politically and legally insulate governments against wrongful rejections. Private companies such as airlines are not bound by international refugee and human rights law, nor domestic requirements to provide appeal mechanisms or to keep public records of those rejected. Given the high fines, any lack of proper documents or suspicions of document forgery are thus likely to lead to carriers rejecting passengers at the point of departure. Under EU law the amount is currently €5,000 per passenger, in addition to which airlines are liable to carry costs related to detention and return flights. As pointed out by UNHCR:

> Forcing carriers to verify visas and other travel documentation helps to shift the burden of determining the need for protection to those whose motivation is to avoid monetary penalties to their corporate employer, rather than to provide protection to individuals. In so doing, it contributes to placing this very important responsibility in the hands of those (a) unauthorized to make asylum determinations on behalf of States (b) thoroughly untrained in the nuances and procedures of refugee and asylum principles, and (c) motivated by economic rather than humanitarian considerations.
>
> *(UNHCR 1991: 3)*

Similar criticisms have been raised in connection with privately run immigration detention centres. As noted by former UN Rapporteur on Torture Nigel Rodley, 'the profit motive of privately run prisons in the United States and elsewhere has fostered a situation in which the rights and needs of prisoners and the direct responsibility of states for the treatment of those they deprive of freedom are diminished' (Rodley 2003:7). As a starting point, the very detention of asylum seekers may constitute a violation of international refugee law. Article 31 of the 1951 Refugee Convention obliges states not to penalize refugees for irregular access to their territory and was specifically inserted to recognize that refugees may occasionally have an overriding need to seek entry, even if under false pretences or not in possession of proper documentation. The coincidence of private companies running prisons and immigration detention centres has further led to situations where guards fail to recognize the difference between punitive and administrative detention, in some instances even placing asylum seekers in general prisons (Robbins 2005: 86). In 2010 an Angolan refugee died on board an aeroplane during a G4S deportation operation. Following the incident, a number of former and current G4S staff came forward, claiming that senior management had disregarded internal warnings about poor training and unsafe restraining techniques. In 2007 the Western Australian Human Rights Committee similarly ordered G4S to pay a US$500,000 fine for inhumane treatment, after G4S drivers had ignored detainees begging for water during a transport journey, leaving one to drink his own urine.

International human rights law is in principle neutral on privatization (Isa 2005: 16). Governments remain free as regards their mode of governance and nothing in the human rights treaties explicitly prohibits decisions to contract out or privatize service provision. Yet various human rights institutions have emphasized that in the process of privatization, continued respect for human rights must be ensured. As the European Court of Human Rights asserted in the *Costello-Roberts* case, a state 'cannot absolve itself from responsibility by delegating its obligations to private bodies or individuals.'[1] Certain human rights obligations are, broadly phrased, making the issue of private or public implementation irrelevant. Article 10 of the International Covenant on Civil and Political Rights thus demands that 'All persons deprived of their liberty shall be treated with humanity and with respect for the inherent dignity of the human person.' In other words, although the means and actors through which human rights obligations are realized may change in the course of privatization, states maintain ultimate responsibility under international law.

In practice, however, this view is moderated by the public–private distinction, creating a legal threshold for state responsibility in cases of privatization. As noted by the International Court of Justice, 'the fundamental principle governing the law of international responsibility [is that] a State is responsible only for its own conduct, that is to say the conduct of persons acting, on whatever basis, on its behalf'.[2] The separation between public and private spheres has been a constitutive element of liberal societies and remains a key norm of both domestic and international law. In the modern vision of the nation-state, regulatory functions and the exercise of power came to be centralized and monopolized by the state. Outside this, the market and private relations are both considered to be apolitical and thus subject to regulation under distinct legal regimes both at national and international levels (Sassen 2006: 187). As, politically speaking, the public – private distinction has become increasingly artificial, certain inroads have been made to ensure legal responsibility in cases of privatization. Yet, as a legal construction, the public–private distinction still retains importance in setting certain thresholds for establishing state responsibility and in separating the legal venues through which migrants and refugees subjected to the migration control industry may seek redress.

Under general international law, a state maintains direct responsibility for the conduct of private actors when private actors are either exercising 'governmental authority' or where it can be shown that the state is 'directing or controlling' the particular conduct.[3] Yet, the test in each instance is onerous. There is no internationally accepted definition of what constitutes governmental authority, and states have thus been seen to apply different and varying tests. According to the US Supreme Court, it is not enough that a private actor serves a 'public function', the particular task has to be one that is considered 'traditionally the exclusive prerogative of the State.'[4] While this definition ought to encompass established contractors carrying out border control and immigration detention to the extent that these functions are indeed considered traditional functions of sovereignty, it may still eclipse certain scenarios where private actors are merely considered adjunct to the immigration control performed (e.g. pre-arrival control performed by airlines). This test is not necessarily correct, however. The International Law Commission implies that under certain circumstances airlines may be exercising 'governmental authority' when carrying out security functions (Gammeltoft-Hansen 2011: 181).

Proving that a private actor acts under the direction or control of a state is no less demanding. Following the International Court of Justice, the fact that a government finances, trains and in other ways supports a private entity is not enough; it has to be shown that the particular actions in question are imputable to the state.[5] Establishing this 'real link' may become particularly problematic where privatization involves the use of subcontractors. Moreover, it may insulate the state from responsibility where private contractors act outside or in excess of their instructions. In the case of *Medina v. O'Neill*, concerning the detention of 16 stowaways by Danner Inc. mentioned above, the US Court of Appeal found that while the 'public power' test was satisfied and the government thus responsible for the detainees, the lack of knowledge of the deplorable conditions under which the immigrants were held did not constitute a violation of the stowaways' due process rights.[6]

As a matter of international human rights law, states also maintain certain positive or due diligence obligations that may provide additional avenues where the causal connection between state and private actor does not fulfil the requirements above. In *Velásquez Rodríguez v. Honduras*, the Inter-American Court of Human Rights thus found that the widespread occurrence of disappearances in Honduras, even though it could not be proved that these were directly imputable to the Honduran government, nonetheless engaged the responsibility of Honduras; not 'because of the act itself, but because of the lack of due diligence to prevent the violation or to respond to it as required by the convention.'[7] In practical terms this may require states to ensure, for example, proper regulatory frameworks for all private actors exercising migration control, relevant training and regular monitoring (Hoppe 2008: 993). Determining the exact content of due diligence obligations, however, is a matter of interpretation and depends on the factual circumstances. Consequently, what may reasonably be expected from a state is open to contestation and states have been keen to argue that they were either unknowing or incapable of taking action to prevent human rights abuses. Moreover, the application of due diligence obligations to actions overseas remains contested, possibly excluding responsibility in cases of airline control, private visa contractors and offshore detention centres (Gammeltoft-Hansen 2011: 200–204).

The legal difficulties in ensuring state responsibility for private conduct may appear paradoxical in light of the fact that privatization today constitutes a systemic feature of modern governance. Most legal responses have been characterized by ad hoc solutions with little coordination and a sometimes circular logic (Flinders 2006: 239). The very definition of the private sphere is based on its consisting of non-state actors; inter alia autonomous and independent of government funding, control, authority or direction. By defining private actors simply by what they are not, it first of all becomes difficult to discern between the very different actors in this field and their rather different relationships to the state: from bands of private vigilantes to international security or military contractors. Second, and more fundamentally, this dichotomous definition serves to reinforce the notion that private actors are prima facie removed from the sphere of public international law (Alston 2005: 3). It is in this sense that establishing state responsibility in cases of privatization becomes problematic, as it sets out by assuming a distinction that may simply not be there in the first place.

Lifting the corporate veil

Closely connected to the question of legal responsibility is the issue of institutional monitoring and public accountability. Even though norms do in principle exist to ensure state responsibility for human rights violations by private actors exercising migration control, it is quite another matter to ensure that such cases are in fact brought to public attention and prosecuted by national or international courts.

Proponents of privatization argue that governing through market mechanisms may increase accountability. Noting that control and accountability of governmental actors and institutions are often far from perfect, it has been argued that clear economic incentives and contracts may actually prove more efficient in regulating agent behaviour. Second, the distance between governments and private contractors makes it easier to carry out a critical appraisal, and private entities may be more open to reform and change. Third, the competitive environment surrounding private contractors may lead major corporations in a given market to themselves develop codes of conduct and accept accountability mechanisms in order to create a market brand vis-à-vis potential customers (Dickinson 2007: 230; McDonald 1991: 189; Logan 1990).

Several counter-arguments may, however, be raised with regard to this position, suggesting that market-based migration control is inherently difficult to govern. Even where clear contracts or other regulatory frameworks are in place, the legal barrier between states and private actors breaks the ordinary administrative chain of command (McDonald 1991: 188). Even the best of contracts may not foresee the full need for appraisal and monitoring and may thus equally become a straitjacket preventing further action and scrutiny. Second, public employees are both more visible and in many countries have explicit guarantees against repercussions for expressing opinions publicly or for whistleblowing. Third, even where legal provisions for public scrutiny are in place, the resources for governmental monitoring often lag behind the pace and scale of privatization itself (Isenberg 2007: 87–8). Lastly, private companies seldom have a direct interest in public oversight as any critique may entail negative economic consequences and be detrimental to the company's competitive position. Where such convergence of interests nonetheless exists (e.g. for reputational reasons), voluntary codes of conduct or soft law accountability mechanisms have so far not proven particularly effective (Chapters 23 and 26, this volume; Leander 2010, 2011). Studies show that codes of conduct risk being either 'ceremonialized' or used by companies to further different agendas (Leander 2012; Cockayne 2007: 207–8).

The existence of a corporate veil is perhaps most evident in regard to the use of airlines to perform de facto immigration control. Governments have been reluctant to produce and publish figures of the amount of fines imposed and seldom systematically gather data the numbers and the identities of those rejected (Guiraudon 2006; Nicholson 1997: 598). The carrier sanctions legislation is, by design, weak in terms of democratic control, accountability and judicial avenues for those rejected (Scholten and Minderhoud 2008: 131). Save for reasons of protesting against the imposition of fines mentioned above, carriers themselves have little further incentive for giving out information on these issues which may convey a negative picture of companies to customers. Thus, even where airlines are asked by governments or NGOs to provide 'denied boarding' figures, they do not always do so (Nicholson 1997: 598).

Rejection by a private company such as an airline is, moreover, not subject to national administrative regulations. It is not a public decision, and those rejected can thus be sent back without any notification of the decision and, in principle, without leaving any trace (Guiraudon 2006: 8). In addition, the extraterritorial venue of most rejections makes it even more difficult for both national institutions and civil society to access those rejected (Nicholson 1997: 598; Vedsted-Hansen 1997: 176). As a result, only a handful of cases concerning carrier controls have ever been brought before national courts, despite modern carrier legislation having been in place for more than 20 years.

Where privatization of migration control is governed by contracts, the possibilities for monitoring and visibility are somewhat improved. The higher likelihood of state responsibility for any human rights violations in these situations – as compared with the mere use of economic sanctions – may, first of all, give a greater incentive for governments to ensure accountability. Second, contracts give added possibilities for states to require vetting, adequate training of privately employed personnel, regular monitoring and performance reports. The United Kingdom has thus introduced both clear contractual limits for responsibility and a national supervisory function for the use of privately contracted immigration search officers.

Nonetheless, even where a clear contractual relationship is established, accountability and public scrutiny may still remain insufficient. This becomes clear when examining the growing number of cases of human rights abuses in privately operated detention facilities, as also mentioned in the previous section. In Australia, the conditions in some privately managed asylum and immigration detention centres have been described as gravely lacking in external accountability and monitoring.[8] Access to information about conditions in the centres has been further hampered by attempts by those managing them to prevent access from outsiders. Australasian Correctional Management (ACM), which runs four detention centres in Australia, has thus been known to require all external professionals entering their facilities (such as medical staff or teachers) to sign confidentiality agreements preventing them from disclosing any information regarding detainees or the administration of the centres.

Parallels may be found in other countries using private contractors to run asylum and immigration detention facilities. Following a BBC documentary documenting racism and physical abuse of immigrant detainees at Oakington detention centre, the UK Prisons and Probation Ombudsman issued a report pointing to several cases of misconduct by G4S in the running of the facility and their forced escort operations (Prisons and Probation Ombudsman 2005). The report further pointed to a number of problems relating to monitoring and oversight. In the United States, NGOs have pointed to the lack of oversight of privately operated immigration detention facilities and accused Corrections Corporation of America of overcrowding cells and cutting supplies and medical care to save costs.[9] An employee in charge of reviewing disciplinary cases at one of the company's Houston facilities squarely told the *New York Times*, 'I am the Supreme Court' (cited in Robbins 2005: 61).

Conclusion

This chapter has pointed to the multiple human rights issues stemming from the growing migration control industry. Of course, one should be careful not to overstate the negative human rights implications of privately run migration management. There is no shortage of examples of human rights violations by public immigration officers. Yet, as this chapter argues, by its very design the migration control industry creates certain barriers that risk further undermining the rights of migrants and refugees. Legally, privatization serves to insulate governments from liability to human rights violations following from immigration control. Institutionally, privatization works to distance control functions from the state by creating the appearance that migration control is, precisely, private and thus external to the state itself. Looking to similar cases in regard to for example military contractors and private prisons, there is much to suggest that these dynamics apply equally to other areas of private security. This is not to say that avenues for ensuring state responsibility and public accountability do not exist. Yet both legal and institutional developments are needed in order for human rights law to remain effective in the current wave of privatization.

Notes

1   *Costello-Roberts v. The United Kingdom*, European Court of Human Rights, Appl. No. 13134/87, 25 March 1993.
2   *Case Concerning the Application of the Convention on the Prevention and Punishment of the Crime of Genocide (Bosnia and Herzegovina v. Serbia and Montenegro)*, International Court of Justice, 26 February 2007, paragraph 406.
3   See Responsibility of States for Internationally Wrongful Acts, International Law Commission, annexed in UN General Assembly resolution 56/83 of 12 December 2001, articles 5 and 8.
4   *Rendell-Baker v. Kohn, United States Supreme Court*, 457 US 830 (1982), 842.
5   *Case Concerning Military and Paramilitary Activities in and against Nicaragua*, International Court of Justice, ICJ Reports 1986, 27 June 1986, paragraph 17.

6   *Medina v. B. O'Neill Garcia, United States Court of Appeal*, 5th circuit, 838 F. 2d 800 (1988), paragraph 17.

7   *Velásquez Rodríguez v. Honduras*, Inter-American Court of Human Rights, Series C, No. 4 (1988), 29 July 1988, paragraph 88.

8   Professor Richard Harding, speaking of Curtin Immigration Reception and Processing Centre in a speech delivered at International Corrections and Prisons Association on 30 October 2001. Excerpt available from www.refugeeaction.org.

9   The issue gave rise to a lawsuit, *Kiniti et al v. Myers et al*, Second Amended Complaint. United States District Court of the Southern District of California. Filed 24 January 2007. The case was settled with the Department of Homeland Security and CCA 4 June 2008.

Bibliography

Alston, P. (2005) 'The "Not-a-Cat" Syndrome: Can the International Human Rights Regime Accommodate Non-state Actors?', in P. Alston (ed.), *Non-State Actors and Human Rights*, Oxford: Oxford University Press, pp. 3–36.

Bigo, D. (2002) 'Security and Immigration: Towards a Critique of the Governmentality of Unease', *Alternatives* 27: 63–92.

Cockayne, J. (2007) 'Make or Buy? Principal–Agent Theory and the Regulation of Private Military Companies', in S. Chesterman and C. Lehnart (eds), *From Mercenaries to Markets*, Oxford: Oxford University Press, pp. 196–216.

Cruz, A. (1995) *Shifting Responsibility: Carriers' Liability in the Member States of the European Union and North America*, Stoke-on-Trent: Trentham Books.

Dickinson, L. (2007) 'Contract as a Tool for Regulating PMCs', in S. Chesterman and C. Lehnart (eds), *From Mercenaries to Markets*, Oxford: Oxford University Press, pp. 217–38.

Feyter, K. and Isa, F. G. (eds) (2005) *Privatisation and Human Rights in the Age of Globalisation*, Antwerp: Intersentia.

Flinders, M. (2006) 'The Politics of Public–Private Partnerships', *British Journal of Politics and International Relations* 7(2): 215–39.

Gammeltoft-Hansen, T. (2011) *Access to Asylum: International Refugee Law and the Globalisation of Migration Control*, Cambridge: Cambridge University Press.

Gammeltoft-Hansen, T. (2013) 'The Rise of the Private Border Guard: Accountability and Responsibility in the Migration Control Industry', in T. Gammeltoft-Hansen and N. Nyberg Sørensen (eds), *The Migration Industry and the Commercialization of International Migration*, Abingdon: Routledge, pp. 128–51.

Gammeltoft-Hansen, T. and Hathaway, J. C. (2015) 'Non-refoulement in a World of Complex Deterrence', *Columbia Journal of Transnational Law* 52(2): 235–84.

Gammeltoft-Hansen, T. and Nyberg Sørensen, N. (eds) (2013) *The Migration Industry and the Commercialization of International Migration*, Abingdon: Routledge.

Guiraudon, V. (2006) 'Enlisting Third Parties in Border Control: A Comparative Study of Its Causes and Consequences in Borders and Security Governance', in M. Caparini and O. Marenin (eds), *Borders and Security Governance: Managing Borders in a Globalized World*. Geneva: Geneva Centre for the Democratic Control of Armed Forces, pp. 79–100.

Hoppe, C. (2008) 'Passing the Buck: State Responsibility for Private Military Companies', *European Journal of International Law* 19(5): 989–1014.

Isa, F. G. (2005) 'Globalisation, Privatization and Human Rights', in K. Feyter and F. G. Isa (eds), *Privatisation and Human Rights in the Age of Globalisation*, Antwerp: Intersentia, pp. 9–32.

Isenberg, D. (2007) 'A Government in Search of Cover', in S. Chesterman and C. Lehnart (eds), *From Mercenaries to Markets*, Oxford: Oxford University Press, pp. 82–93.

Lausten, M. S. (2012) *Jøder og kristne i Danmark: Fra middelalderen til nyere tid*, Copenhagen: Anis.

Leander, A. (2010) 'The Paradoxical Impunity of Private Military Companies: Authority and the Limits to Legal Accountability', *Security Dialogue* 41(5): 467–90.

Leander, A. (2011) 'Risk and the Fabrication of Apolitical, Unaccountable Military Markets: The Case of the CIA "Killing Program"', *Review of International Studies* 37(5): 2253–68.

Leander, A. (2012) 'What Do Codes of Conduct Do? Hybrid Constitutionalization and Militarization in Military Markets', *Global Constitutionalism* 1(1): 91–119.

Logan, C. H. (1990) *Private Prisons: Cons and Pros*, Oxford: Oxford University Press.

McDonald, D. (ed.) (1991) *Private Prisons and the Public Interest*, Piscataway, NJ: Rutger's University Press.

Menz, G. (2011) 'Neoliberalism, Privatisation and the Outsourcing of Migration Management: A Five Country Comparison', *Competition and Change* 15(2): 116–35.

Menz, G. (2013) 'The Neoliberalized State and the Growth of the Migration Industry', in T. Gammeltoft-Hansen and N. Nyberg Sørensen (eds), *The Migration Industry and the Commercialization of International Migration*, Abingdon: Routledge, pp. 108–27.

Nicholson, F. (1997) 'Implementation of the Immigration (Carriers' Liability) Act 1987: Privatising Immigration Functions at the Expense of International Obligations?', *International and Comparative Law Quarterly* 46(3): 586–634.

Prisons and Probation Ombudsman (2005) *Inquiry into Allegations of Racism and Mistreatment of Detainees at Oakington Immigration Reception Centre and while Under Escort*, report, July, London: Prisons and Probation Ombudsman for England and Wales, www.statewatch.org/news/2005/jul/prison-ombs-Oakington.pdf.

Robbins, I. P. (2005) 'Privatisation of Corrections: Violation of US Domestic Law, International Human Rights, and Good Sense', in K. Feyter and F. G. Isa (eds), *Privatisation and Human Rights in the Age of Globalisation*, Antwerp: Intersentia, pp. 57–90.

Rodenhäuser, T. (2014) 'Another Brick in the Wall: Carrier Sanctions and the Privatization of Immigration Control', *International Journal of Refugee Law* 26(2): 223–47.

Rodley, N. (2003) 'Foreword', in A. Coyle, A. Campbell and R. Neufield (eds), *Capitalist Punishment: Prison Privatization and Human Rights*, Oxford: Clarity Press, p. 7.

Salter, M. (2007) 'Governmentalities of an Airport: Heterotopia and Confession', *International Political Sociology* 1(1): 49–66.

Sassen, S. (2006) *Territory, Authority, Rights: From Medieval to Global Assemblages*, Princeton, NJ: Princeton University Press.

Scholten, S. and Minderhoud, P. (2008) 'Regulating Immigration Control', *European Journal of Migration and Law* 10(2): 123–47.

UNHCR (1991) 'Position on Conventions Recently Concluded in Europe (Dublin and Schengen Conventions)', WorldWide Operations, 16 August, www.unhcr.org/43662e942.html.

Vedsted-Hansen, J. (1995) 'Privatiseret Retshåndhævelse og Kontrol', in L. Adrian (Ed.), *Ret og Privatisering*, Copenhagen: Gad Jura, pp. 159–79.

PART IV

The regulation of private security

22

NORMS AND REGULATION

Sarah Percy

The privatization of force has occurred with extraordinary speed. It is hard to imagine that in the late 1980s and early 1990s, the widespread use of private force, especially by major powers, was unthinkable. In 1989, Stephen Krasner noted that it was very difficult to explain why, even when it would seem strategically optimal, states did not use mercenaries. As he put it, the constraints against hiring mercenaries were so great that the United States could not simply 'buy a regiment or two of Gurkhas' (Krasner 1989: 91–2). Janice Thomson wrote in 1994 that 'today, real states do not use private force' (Thomson 1994). She went on to argue that since the '[anti-mercenary] norm was implemented, no state has attempted to reinstate eighteenth-century practice by reversing or even challenging' it (ibid.: 96). As the other chapters in this volume demonstrate, states today can effectively purchase large numbers of private security personnel to bolster their strategic positions. 'Real' states routinely use private force. The anti-mercenary norm appears to be under daily challenge. What is the continuing influence of this formerly powerful norm in a world where the use of private force is widespread?

The purpose of this chapter is to explain what the norm against mercenary use is, where it came from, how it has influenced the regulation of private force, and whether or not it has been challenged by the widespread use of private force today. Would Thomson still say that real states do not use private force, and if not, what does this tell us about the anti-mercenary norm? The chapter begins by defining and tracing the evolution of the anti-mercenary norm, and then discusses how the anti-mercenary norm played into debates about regulating mercenaries in the 1970s. Against this background, I explain how the rapidly evolving private security industry was met with equally rapidly changing regulation, and consider how the anti-mercenary norm played into this debate. The chapter considers how the industry's development both challenged and was shaped by the anti-mercenary norm, examining the appearance of private military companies such as Sandline in the 1990s and the proliferation of private security during the Iraq War of 2003 and afterwards. In each case I consider the impact the changing industry had on the anti-mercenary norm and the debate on regulating the industry.

The anti-mercenary norm: definitions, origins and development

What is the norm against mercenary use? We can generally define a norm as a rule or standard of behaviour. Norms can be written or unwritten. For example, there was a norm that states should declare war at the outset of hostilities, but this norm did not take the form of a written law. Norms associated with warfare have a long history, going back well before the nineteenth century. Some of these norms were transformed into formal law. For example, the idea that a white flag indicates peaceful surrender goes back to the classical era but was only recorded in law at the turn of the twentieth century, as part of the Hague Conventions. The norm against mercenary use has mainly been an unwritten norm, until the 1970s when states sought to institutionalize it by creating a Convention against the use of mercenaries.

Where did the norm against mercenary use come from, and of what does it consist? While mercenaries have always existed, so too has criticism of their use, and states and other actors have consistently attempted to control them. The anti-mercenary norm builds on the generally accepted definition of a mercenary as a financially motivated fighter who uses force outside the control of the sovereign state. The precise content of the anti-mercenary norm has shifted over the long history of mercenary use, but has generally had two components. First, mercenaries are not under the control of the sovereign state. Mercenaries can then pose a threat to the physical existence of the state but also threaten the idea that the state ought to have a legitimate monopoly on the use force. Second, mercenaries do not fight for an acceptable cause. They are financially, rather than ideologically or patriotically, motivated. While there are some foreign fighters who are widely accepted in the international system, this is usually because their cause is also widely accepted as legitimate. For example, foreign fighters in the Spanish Civil War are generally understood to be morally acceptable while foreign fighters fighting alongside Islamist groups in Syria today are not. States can have long-standing arrangements to include foreign fighters, such as the French Foreign Legion or the Gurkhas. These arrangements are usually viewed as unobjectionable, because they often include the promise of citizenship (as in the French Foreign Legion, or indeed, for foreign individuals in the American armed forces) or exist as part of a historical relationship (e.g. the Gurkhas).

It is important to note that there are many logical problems with the component parts of the anti-mercenary norm. Of course, many soldiers may be more financially motivated than any mercenary. Mercenaries may share the cause of those for whom they fight, and foreigners are not precluded from supporting someone else's cause. However, even though these concerns about mercenaries are illogical, they have deeply influenced policy towards the use of private force (Percy 2007a).

Mercenaries remained commonplace in the armies of Europe until the late nineteenth century, when they disappeared from use until the 1960s. The decision to abandon mercenaries in European armies has been extensively examined (Percy 2007a; Avant 2000; Thomson 1994) and clearly has a normative component. The decision to cast aside the mercenary system is associated with rising norms of citizen service. If citizen soldiers are being asked to fight and die for love of country, it becomes increasingly difficult to justify the use of financially motivated, foreign soldiers.

Even when mercenaries appeared again a hundred years later, in the 1960s wars of decolonization in Africa, sovereign states almost never used mercenaries. Rather, mercenaries were mostly hired by former colonial interests or insurgent groups (Percy 2007b). Mercenaries in this period 'appear to us as anomalies precisely because they are only marginally legitimate' (Thomson 1994: 97). Many states were alarmed by this reappearance of an antique, and disliked, military practice. The depth of time that had passed since mercenaries were commonplace cannot be underestimated. It would be rather like the sudden reintroduction today of execution by firing squad for deserters, a practice that disappeared approximately 100 years ago. The fact that mercenaries were used to destabilize newly decolonized states did not help their public image. It was easy to associate mercenaries with a whole host of forces that prevented national self-determination, which in turn made it easy to advocate for legal control of mercenaries in the early 1970s. Newly decolonized states entering the United Nations changed the political composition of the General Assembly, which took up issues associated with colonization and national self-determination with great vigour.

The General Assembly passed a series of resolutions criticizing mercenary use beginning in the late 1960s. There are two particularly significant resolutions. The General Assembly drafted a Definition of Aggression in 1974. This definition was meant to clarify what would constitute an act of aggression in situations where there was no declaration of war and included the sending of mercenaries alongside other acts of aggression such as the bombardment and blockade of another state's territory.[1] The General Assembly also passed a resolution on the right to self-determination in 1976,[2] stating that using mercenaries against national liberation movements is a criminal act and that mercenaries themselves are criminals.[3] An Organization for African Unity (OAU) Convention on Mercenaries, based on an earlier Luanda Draft, was signed in 1977.

The two most significant pieces of international law, both in their status as treaty law and also in the impact they have had on private force and on debates about its regulation, were developed in the 1970s and 1980s. Between 1974 and 1977, states negotiated the Protocols additional to the Geneva Convention. These Protocols were meant to extend the Geneva and Hague Conventions and regulate conduct on the battlefield. Article 47 of Protocol I deprives mercenaries of combatant status and the right to be treated as prisoners of war. It relies on a similar definition of 'mercenary' as that set out in the OAU and Luanda Conventions. This definition is extremely, and famously, problematic. It has become almost automatic when writing on Article 47 to note that 'any mercenary who cannot exclude himself from this definition deserves to be shot – and his lawyer with him'![4] Unfortunately, this problematic definition was also used in the second significant piece of international law, the International Convention against the Recruitment, Use, Financing, and Training of Mercenaries (the UN Convention). Negotiations for the UN Convention began in 1980, were complete in 1989, and the Convention entered into force in 2001.

The definition shared in both documents is cumulative, meaning that an actor would have to meet all the criteria in order to be considered a mercenary. It has two significant loopholes. First, it states that a mercenary is 'not a member of the armed forces of a Party to the conflict'.[5] Avoiding the punitive aspects of Article 47 is easy: would-be mercenaries could avoid trouble by simply enrolling in the armed forces of the state that had hired them. In fact, such avoidance techniques were commonplace in the 1990s, when private military companies like Sandline and EO insisted on this type of enrolment as part of their contracts.

The second loophole arises from Article 47's statement that a mercenary is 'motivated to take part in hostilities essentially by the desire for private gain, and in fact, is promised, by or on behalf of a Party to the conflict, material compensation substantially in excess of that promised or paid to combatants of similar ranks and functions in the armed forces of that Party'.[6] Two problems follow: first, it is probably impossible to demonstrate that a fighter is motivated to fight 'essentially by the desire for private gain'. Second, even if it is possible to do so, a clever mercenary would avoid this clause by arranging to be paid (at least on paper) the same amount as regular soldiers.

The international lawyer Antonio Cassese (1980) has argued that these loopholes reflect a deliberate attempt on the part of African states to protect themselves from mercenary attack while reserving the right to use mercenaries in the future. However, a close examination of the *travaux preparatoires* of Article 47 reveals that in the case of both loopholes states were attempting to devise law that reflected what they found to be objectionable about mercenaries. States, when devising the clause stating that enrolment in the armed forces prevented an actor from being considered a mercenary, were in fact attempting to protect non-mercenary fighters from the serious consequences of the Article. Without this clause, both regular soldiers and foreign fighters permanently enrolled in the armed forces (such as Gurkhas or the French Foreign Legion) could lose prisoner of war (POW) protection or combatant status. States clearly attempted to exclude longstanding foreign fighter arrangements such as these from the Article. Moreover, there was concern that regular soldiers who were attracted to fight by good pay (thus meeting the financial motivation aspect of the definition) would not be considered to be mercenaries. The enrolment in the armed forces clause solved both these problems.

The financial motivation loophole was included even though states were well aware it might cause problems. The Working Group drafting the article shared a clear definition of a mercenary as an individual motivated to fight 'essentially or primarily by the desire for hard cash' (Percy 2007b: 379). However, transferring this core agreement into workable law proved to be very difficult. The Working Group agreed that one solution to the problem of demonstrating whether or not an alleged mercenary was financially motivated was to require that mercenaries must be paid more than soldiers. Including the idea of financial motivation, which states felt to be essential to the idea of a mercenary, was impossible without creating loopholes. However, without it, all sense of what it meant to be a mercenary would have been lost.

The norm against mercenary use, then, can explain the faulty construction of Article 47. It is not the case that Article 47 reflected states that either did not care about mercenaries, or wanted to reserve the right to use mercenaries themselves. Instead states were very specifically and deliberately condemning mercenaries with the creation of Article 47. First, mercenaries had been generally used during intra-state wars, which was the subject of Protocol II, and not during international armed conflicts, which was the subject of Protocol I. The decision to include them in Protocol I was thus a deliberate one and excluded the situation where mercenaries had been most common. Second, the inclusion of an article meant to punish actors within the Protocols is also noteworthy. Protocol I was supposed to protect actors of all types on the battlefield regardless of their motivation. Including an article that relied at its core on the idea of motivation and also sought to punish rather than protect meant that Article 47 was significantly out of step with the humanitarian aims of the wider document. States could have opted for regulating mercenaries in line with other combatants: should a mercenary violate the laws of war, it would draw the same legal consequences as if any other actor violated the same laws. However, it is more difficult to regulate mercenaries on the basis of their status rather than the basis of their actions and states took the less efficient path (Percy 2007b). Article 47 was clearly an attempt to punish mercenaries, rather than regulate them.

The UN Convention, which followed Article 47, adopted the existing definition of a mercenary. However, it faced an additional problem. While all states agreed that mercenaries needed to be controlled, they differed significantly over what types of control were necessary. There were two points of contention. First, non-Western states wished to use the Convention to make states responsible for the actions of any citizen choosing to become a mercenary. The notion of state responsibility is very specific in international law, and the dominant view is that states cannot be held accountable for the actions of their citizens where they do not know in advance of these actions. Western states, along with some others, took the view that the importance and practicality of this approach to state responsibility meant that the mercenary threat, however serious, could not be controlled using an international convention that required national legislative and enforcement action. Second, the drafts of the Convention called for limitations on freedom of movement, which were deemed necessary to prevent would-be mercenaries from leaving home to cause trouble in the first place. Again, Western states, supported by some others, asserted that the well-established right to freedom of movement could not be superseded. Even if it could be agreed that the mercenary issue were serious enough to overturn an important right, the practical obstacles of stopping putative mercenaries from achieving their goals were also impossible to overcome.

Disagreement on these two points led a stalemate in the UN Convention, which took nearly a decade to draft. Western states indicated that if the Convention went ahead containing the clauses pertaining to state responsibility they would not sign, and they have not done so. The Convention thus made very slow progress at the negotiation stage, as states attempted to resolve these and other issues. It was completed in 1989 but only received enough signatures to enter into force in 2001, when it was quickly overcome by events.

The norm against mercenary use itself had less direct influence over the UN Convention than it had over the creation of Article 47. The decision to use the Article 47 definition further reflected that states felt quite clear about what they understood a mercenary to be, and also what they thought objectionable about mercenaries. The UN Convention process also indicates that states do have to adjudicate between competing norms. In this case, Western states took the view that the norms of freedom of movement and narrow state responsibility were more important than the anti-mercenary norm. Other states disagreed. The UN Convention does not simply reflect a lack of state interest in the mercenary question. Rather, it reflects a difference in the way states adjudicate between competing norms.

The appearance of private military companies

The appearance of private military companies (PMCs) in the 1990s provided the first test of the two (notably weak) laws regarding mercenary use. Private companies offering military services in Africa rose to prominence in the mid-1990s. The companies Executive Outcomes (EO) and Sandline International both offered a range of military and security services, including active combat. While the laws discussed above were inapplicable to PMCs, the use of private force was clearly shaped by the anti-mercenary norm. The relationship between the anti-mercenary norm and international law became more complex.

There was very little doubt that the law against mercenaries did not apply to PMCs in the 1990s (Percy 2007b; Zarate 1998). However, the fact that these PMCs were probably mercenaries was equally uncontroversial. According to the general definition of a mercenary, a person who exchanges military services in exchange for money, both companies were clearly mercenary. EO and Sandline made it perfectly clear in both their actions and in their statements that a core part of their business model was the planning and conduct of military operations. EO had a significant and still-controversial impact on the war in Sierra Leone, in large part because of the company's superior firepower and the use of combat helicopters. Tim Spicer, former head of Sandline, was explicit about his company's willingness to use force. As he put it, 'if it is going to stop the war, of course we will go and blow up those helicopters or aircraft' (Spicer 1999: 168). EO and Sandline did not like the term 'mercenary' but nor did they try and obscure the fact that they were paid to fight for money. Spicer even said he did not mind the dictionary definition of the term mercenary, but rather 'the image it conjures up in people's minds. We don't like the Rambos, the psychopaths, the killers. In the conflicts in which we become involved they actually work for the other side' (ibid.: 165). Referring to PMCs as mercenaries was also commonplace even among academic analyses during this period (Percy 2014).

The inapplicability of anti-mercenary law, coupled with the strong sense that PMCs were mercenaries and that mercenary use was problematic, led to an interesting interplay between law and norm. The UN Convention had only just come into force when PMCs came into the public eye. Angola, despite employing EO, was one of the signatories of the Convention. EO and Sandline personnel enrolled in the armed forces of the hiring state to avoid any potential legal problems. Article 47 was entirely inapplicable because it is part of Protocol I, which deals with international rather than internal armed conflicts. The law against mercenaries was never effective and the 1990s saw its death confirmed (Percy 2014; Singer 2004: 531).

While the law was ineffective, the norm remained influential. There are three particularly noteworthy examples of the considerable international disapproval of PMC activities in Africa and in Papua New Guinea during the 1990s. First, international pressure contributed to the end of PMC involvement in Angola, Sierra Leone, and Papua New Guinea. The Americans pressured Angola to end its arrangements with EO. The Sierra Leonean government, possibly under pressure from the IMF, did not renew EO's contract (Shearer 1997: 855). Australia applied direct pressure to the PNG government to cease employing Sandline (Dorney 1998: 227).

Second, the Special Rapporteur on Mercenaries, Enrique Bernales Ballesteros, provided vocal criticism of PMCs during this period. The long-serving Special Rapporteur referred to PMCs as mercenaries repeatedly. He had notably negative views of mercenaries, stating in his final report in 2003 that 'whether individually, or in the employ of contemporary multi-purpose security companies, the mercenary is generally present as a violator of human rights'[7] (see also Chapter 23, this volume).

Third, the heated criticisms of PMCs in the 1990s tended to ignore that PMCs were employed by sovereign states. States like Sierra Leone were fighting brutal civil wars against vicious adversaries. The Rebel United Front, famous for amputating arms as a terror tactic, was very close to Freetown, the capital of Sierra Leone, when the government chose to hire EO. There was no international assistance forthcoming, and yet the Sierra Leonean government was extensively criticized (Percy 2007a). PMSCs that provided combat as part of their services disappeared. Tim Spicer deliberately decided that his new company, Aegis, set up prior to the attacks of 11 September 2001, would not provide combat services because they were too controversial (Percy 2007a). When the war started in Iraq, Aegis was one of a number of companies that sought to avoid the mercenary label by avoiding combat.

The proliferation of private force, regulation, and the anti-mercenary norm

What does the commonplace use of private military and security companies (PMSCs) during the Iraq War of 2003 and afterwards tell us about the anti-mercenary norm? Do current regulatory efforts still reflect the anti-mercenary norm? I argue that despite some suggestions that the anti-mercenary norm is dead (Panke and Petersohn 2011), or at least ailing (Krahmann 2013), the anti-mercenary norm has in fact changed form. The transformation of the norm against mercenary use has occurred in part because of the events in the 1990s outlined above, and its transformation is reflected in the newest regulatory instruments devised to deal with mercenaries, the Montreux Document and the International Code of Conduct for Private Security Providers (ICoC).

It is not without logic to point out that the large number of PMSCs currently in existence, and the wide range of tasks for which they are employed, might suggest that the anti-mercenary norm is dead or dying. Petersohn and Panke are interested in explaining why the norm against mercenaries has 'disappeared' or become suddenly 'obsolete' (Petersohn 2014: 720). However, it may be more accurate to note that the norm against mercenary use has changed (ibid.; Percy 2014; Krahmann 2013). States do indeed use 'mercenaries', or actors that exchange the use of violence for money, but they do not do so in an unfettered fashion and the PMSCs of today do not resemble the mercenaries of the 1960s or the still-earlier mercenaries of the nineteenth century.

The appropriate question, then, is what about the anti-mercenary norm has changed that allows for states to use private force? The answer lies in the question of combat. Today's PMSCs are not considered to be mercenaries because they use force only in self-defence. In other words, they do not 'directly take part in hostilities' in the words of the shared definitions of Article 47 and the UN Convention. The norm against mercenary use has changed from one that prohibits mercenary use in all forms to one that allows it in restricted circumstances, specifically in 'defensive' combat.

Krahmann points out that the US has narrowed the definition of 'directly' participating in hostilities by insisting that 'private security personnel are not authorized to participate in offensive operations' and that this view is reflected in Canada and among other NATO nations (Krahmann 2013: 65). Panke and Petersohn note that the use of defensive force by private companies is now considered legitimate (Panke and Petersohn 2011: 730; Petersohn 2014).

The idea that there is a difference between offensive and defensive combat is problematic. Indeed, it is illogical, as many commentators have noted. A PMSC providing 'defensive' assistance can be required to use force vigorously, and the distinction between offense and defence may be lost on those being fired upon. How is it that this illogical distinction has allowed states to use private force legitimately?

Petersohn argues that PMSCs used a deliberate strategy of 'framing' themselves as non-combat actors. This strategy permitted them to be considered legitimate, as their defensive actions would be clearly under control of the hiring state (Petersohn 2014: 16). I have argued elsewhere that in fact the loopholes in anti-mercenary law explain how it is has been possible for the 'defensive' exception to apply. Before the anti-mercenary norm was institutionalized as law, the notion of a mercenary who did not engage in combat was nonsensical. The point of hiring mercenaries was to hire fighters. However, in the creation of the clause referring to direct participation in hostilities, the framers of Article 47 created another way for states to avoid the mercenary label and its consequences. In this case, the law itself has probably channelled the changes to the underlying norm (Percy 2014). States have interpreted 'direct' participation to mean 'offensive' operations. Defensive operations are not 'direct' participation (Krahmann 2013; Petersohn 2014: 17). The norm against mercenary use now only applies to offensive force. Private force is legitimate as long as it remains defensive.

The newest regulatory instruments dealing with private force, the Montreux Document and the ICoC, move from the starting point that PMSCs are regular actors on the battlefield (see Chapter 26, this volume). They differ substantially from the first generation of anti-mercenary law in that they no longer penalize private fighters for being private fighters. Rather, they seek to control the activities of PMSCs and ensure that they are compliant with international humanitarian law. The ICoC in particular requires PMSCs to abide by clear standards of conduct that in some cases go beyond the requirements of international humanitarian law. While both Montreux and the ICoC represent important steps forward in the regulation of the private security industry, it is important to note that they are both 'soft law'. In other words, they are non-binding agreements that do not require states to take any particular action. In the case of Montreux, states' existing obligations are merely re-stated. The ICoC lays out obligations for PMSCs but is non-binding. The failure to institutionalize the anti-mercenary norm successfully explains why these soft law instruments are the only regulatory agreements applicable to mercenaries today. They also reflect the change in the anti-mercenary norm, by no longer concentrating on the status of the mercenary but rather the type of action the mercenary undertakes. The ICoC, in its clauses on the use of force, that signatory companies will try to avoid the use of force (clause 30) and furthermore only use firearms in self-defence or in defence of an imminent threat (clause 31). The ICoC is further evidence that today, the difference between a mercenary and a private security contractor lies in the type of force used. The anti-mercenary norm has previously relied on financial motivation and the attachment to an appropriate cause in order to distinguish between mercenaries and other fighters. The interplay between international law, the activities of mercenaries and PMSCs on the ground, and the norm itself has altered the meaning of the anti-mercenary norm.

Conclusion

It is simply no longer the case that 'real states' do not use private force. As other chapters in this Handbook demonstrate, the use of private force is increasingly common. But the widespread use of private military and security companies does not indicate that the norm against mercenary use is no longer influential. In fact, the interplay of the anti-mercenary norm and regulatory efforts to deal with private force demonstrates that the norm against mercenary use has changed shape. After all, real states may use private force, but they do not use 'mercenaries'. They use private security companies. And very few states use PMSCs to replace military personnel on the battlefield, even where these activities are 'defensive'. The US is somewhat unique in having military contractors hired by the Department of Defense. In the UK, the Ministry of Defence does not use private security personnel, although the Foreign and Commonwealth Office (FCO) does. The majority of states restrict the use of private force to guarding installations such as embassies or providing security in dangerous situations that fall short of conflict.

What does the tangled evolution of the anti-mercenary norm, the participation of private fighters in conflict, and the law against mercenary use tell us about the relationship between norms and law? The anti-mercenary norm is a strong reminder that simply creating a law does not mean a practice will disappear. Rather, states and other actors will interact with that law, and interpret it differently. Both law and norms can shift as part of this process of contestation. The anti-mercenary norm has been significantly changed by the recent history of mercenary use.

What will happen to the anti-mercenary norm in the future? It may well be that use of private force on a wide scale in Iraq and Afghanistan was an anomaly. Not only are states now keen to avoid such entrenched land-based conflicts, which in turn means they will require less support from the private sector, the perceived failures of both conflicts but particularly Iraq may lead states to consider whether or not to use private force differently in the future. It may also be that an unexpected turn of events shapes the industry in a new direction. However, the recent evolution of the private military industry demonstrates that it has been shaped by the anti-mercenary norm. We can assume, whatever shape it takes, that the future industry will develop by interacting with, and possibly changing, the anti-mercenary norm.

Notes

1   GA resolution 3314 (XXIX) of 14 December 1974
2   This resolution, or a variation of it, has been reaffirmed annually up to the writing of this chapter.
3   GA resolution 31/34 of 20 November 1976.
4   Originally quoted in Best (1980).
5   Article 47(2)(e) of Protocol I Additional to the Geneva Conventions, www.icrc.org/ihl/WebART/470-750057.
6   Article 47 (2) (c).
7   UN doc. E/CN.4/2004/15 of 24 December 2003, 11.

Bibliography

Avant, D. (2000) 'From Mercenary to Citizen Armies', *International Organization* 54(1): 41–72.

Best, G. (1980) *Humanity in Warfare: The Modern History of the International Law of Armed Conflicts*, London: Weidenfeld & Nicolson.

Cassese, A. (1980) 'Mercenaries: Lawful Combatants or War Criminals?' *Zeitschrift für Ausländisches Öffentliches Recht und Völkerrecht* 40(1): 1–30.

Dorney, S. (1998) *The Sandline Affair: Politics and Mercenaries in the Bougainville Crisis*, Sydney: ABC Books.

Krahmann, E. (2013) 'The United States, PMSCs and the State Monopoly on Violence: Leading the Way Towards Norm Change', *Security Dialogue* 44(1): 53–71.

Krasner, S. (1989) 'Sovereignty: An Institutional Perspective', in J. Caporaso (ed.), *The Elusive State: International and Comparative Perspectives*, Newbury Park, PA: Sage, pp. 69–96.

Major, M.-F. (1992) 'Mercenaries and International Law', *Georgia Journal of International and Comparative Law* 22(1): 103–50.

Panke, D, and U. Petersohn. (2012) 'Why International Norms Disappear Sometimes', *European Journal of International Relations* 18(4): 719–42.

Percy, S. (2007a) *Mercenaries: The History of a Norm in International Relations*, Oxford: Oxford University Press.

Percy, S. (2007b) 'Mercenaries: Strong Norm, Weak Law', *International Organization* 61(2): 367–97.

Percy, S. (2014) 'The Unimplemented Norm: Anti-Mercenary Law and the Problems of Institutionalization', in A. Betts and P. Orchard (eds), *Implementation and World Politics: How International Norms Change Practice*. Oxford: Oxford University Press, pp. 68–84.

Petersohn, U. (2014) 'Reframing the Anti-Mercenary Norm: Private Military and Security Companies and Mercenarism', *International Journal: Canada's Journal of Global Policy Analysis* 69(4): 475–93.

Shearer, D. (1997) 'Exploring the Limits of Consent: Conflict Resolution in Sierra Leone', *Millennium* 26(3): 845–60.

Singer, P. (2004) 'War, Profits and the Vacuum of Law: Privatized Military Firms and International Law', *Colombia Journal of Transnational Law* 42(2): 521–49.

Spicer, T. (1999) 'Interview with Lt. Col. Tim Spicer', *Cambridge Review of International Affairs* 13(1): 165–71.

Thomson, J. (1994) *Mercenaries, Pirates, and Sovereigns: State-Building and Extraterritorial Violence in Early Modern Europe*, Princeton, NJ: Princeton University Press.

Zarate, J. (1998) 'The Emergence of a New Dog of War: Private International Security Companies, International Law, and the New World Disorder', *Stanford Journal of International Law* 34(1): 75–162.

23

THE EXTENSION OF INTERNATIONAL HUMAN RIGHTS LAW TO PRIVATE MILITARY AND SECURITY COMPANIES

Anton Katz with Margaret Maffai

It is with good reason that the title of this chapter refers to the *extension* of international human rights law (IHRL) to private military and security companies, or PMSCs. The use of this word, which is meant to give the impression of an on-going process, and to invoke an image of stretching something beyond its historical boundary, is intentional. For reasons this chapter will explain, PMSCs are not directly bound by international human rights law. That is, IHRL is binding only on states, which ratify treaties and show through their conduct over time which rules of law are accepted as customary international law. PMSCs, as non-state actors, do not have human rights obligations. Rather, states have human rights obligations they must uphold vis-à-vis PMSC activities. This is not to say that PMSCs operate outside the rule of law; rather those companies that violate international human rights law are subject to it only insofar as *states* hold them accountable.

The extension of international human rights law to PMSCs over the past decades has taken the form of numerous efforts by multiple stakeholders including scholars, governments, and civil society advocates. These efforts endeavour to articulate and clarify the content of states' human rights obligations vis-à-vis PMSCs. They encourage states to hold companies that violate human rights accountable and to provide effective remedies for victims. The United Nations Working Group on the use of mercenaries as a means of violating human rights and impeding the exercise of the right of self-determination (the Working Group), and its predecessor, the Special Rapporteur (SR), has been a part of this important work for the past quarter-century. Although the authors situate their analysis in the context of this work, the opinions expressed in this chapter are their own.

As the emergence of PMSCs was identified and their activities have evolved, the mandate of the Working Group and the SR also evolved to reflect the changing human rights landscape and adapt to the activities of these new actors. Since 1989, it has been a part of the mandate to 'study and identify sources and causes, emerging issues, manifestations and trends regarding mercenaries or mercenary-related activities and their impact on human rights, particularly on the right of peoples to self-determination' (UN Human Rights Council 2013: para. 19). For the past decade, this mandate has included studying the impact of the activities of private companies offering military assistance, consultancy and security services on the international market. In 2008, the UN Human Rights Council also mandated the Working Group to prepare a draft of international basic principles that encourage respect for human rights by those companies in their activities.

Beginning a discussion of private security companies with an explanation of the legal framework applicable to mercenaries often draws criticism as unfairly or inaccurately relating the two. The phenomena are historically, factually and legally linked, and have long existed side by side within the mandate of the Working Group, and the SR. The presumptions about state sovereignty, core government functions, and the state monopoly on the use of force that gave rise to international legal norms against the use and recruitment of mercenaries inform assumptions when governments debate the content of a binding international instrument regulating private security companies. This chapter situates its account of the extension of human rights law to private security companies within its historical and legal context in an effort to understand why the existing legal framework pertaining to mercenaries may be – and more importantly why it may *not* be – relevant to PMSC activities.

The chapter begins with a discussion of the emergence of modern private military and security companies in the 1990s, as reflected in the early observations and calls to action of the SR and the UN Commission on Human Rights. It transitions to the challenges faced in efforts to expand the International Convention against the Recruitment, Use, Financing and Training of Mercenaries (UN General Assembly Resolution 43/34, 1989; hereafter, the 'UN Mercenary Convention') to PMSCs. The discussion then turns to the existing human rights legal framework applicable to PMSC activities, and gaps in that framework. The chapter concludes with a description of recent efforts to extend international human rights law to PMSCs, including the Draft Convention prepared by the Working Group on the use of mercenaries and the deliberations of the open-ended intergovernmental working group on PMSCs established by the UN Human Rights Council.

The Special Rapporteur on mercenaries and the emergence of PMSCs

Beginning in the 1990s, Enrique Bernales Ballesteros, UN Special Rapporteur on the question of the use of mercenaries as a means of violating human rights and impeding the exercise of the right of peoples to self-determination, identified an emerging threat to human rights (Ballesteros 1996, 1999, 2000). In his report to the UN Commission on Human Rights on the civil war in Sierra Leone, the SR observed:

> There is clear evidence of mercenary involvement in this internal armed conflict ... the NPRC has strengthened its military capability by hiring mercenaries supplied by Executive Outcomes, a private company officially registered in Pretoria as a security company, but in this case said to have been paid in cash and, in particular, in the form of mining concessions, for supplying specially trained mercenaries and weapons.
>
> *(Ballesteros 1996: para. 64)*

As the description of the SR makes clear, Executive Outcomes was probably acting in this conflict as a mercenary group. However, it engaged in other activities as well; activities which have come to be more closely associated with modern PMSCs than the literal recruitment and training of mercenaries to engage in military operations. Company executives also supervised 'reconnaissance and aerial photography; strategic planning; training in the use of new military equipment; advising on arms purchases; devising psychological campaigns aimed at creating panic among the civilian population and discrediting the leaders of the RUF, etc.' (ibid.: para. 65). In this description, shades of the legal – although still controversial – activities PMSCs perform today for governments are clear.

In the subsequent years, the SR would continue to warn of the expansion of the role of PMSCs into traditionally governmental activities. In his January 1999 report to the Commission, he expressed his dismay at the lack of concern displayed by states for this growing phenomenon:

> This silence is alarming inasmuch as there are situations in which a country's press reports in abundant detail on the presence of companies involved in matters of national security and public safety without regard for human rights and in open contradiction with constitutional provisions that categorically state that internal order and security are the exclusive responsibility of the State.
>
> *(Ballesteros 1999: para. 65)*

He recognized as early as 2000, in his report to the General Assembly, that the existing international regulatory framework was inadequate to address the human rights impact of the activities of these 'new operational modalities for mercenary activities' and recommended greater rigour and precision in concepts and definitions, clear legal regulations, and monitoring of PMSC activities by a specialized public international institution.

The Commission on Human Rights, the predecessor to the Human Rights Council, acknowledged the seriousness of the potential danger posed to human rights by the privatization of activities traditionally performed by governments. In its Resolution 2004/5 of April 2004, the Commission noted that mercenary activities are 'taking on new forms, manifestations and modalities', and requested the Special Rapporteur to 'pay particular attention to the impact of the activities of private companies offering military assistance, consultancy and security services on the international market on the exercise of the right of peoples to self-determination'. The Commission also mandated the SR to consult with states on a new definition of mercenary, and to make proposals on possible means of regulation and international supervision of PMSC activities. In his final report to the General Assembly, the SR promulgated a new and expanded definition of mercenary, proposed as an amendment to the UN Mercenary Convention, and intended in part to bring the burgeoning private military and security industry under the umbrella of existing law.

In 2005, the Commission resolved to end the mandate of the SR and establish the Working Group. In its resolution 2005/2, the Commission mandated the Working Group to, inter alia, 'prepare draft international basic principles that encourage respect for human rights on the part of [PMSCs] in their activities', and to continue the work of the SR in strengthening the legal framework preventing and sanctioning mercenary activities and clarifying their legal definition.

Applying the UN Mercenary Convention to PMSCs: definitional challenges

By 2005, the landscape of the private military and security industry looked far different to when Executive Outcomes had recruited, trained and supervised fighters in exchange for mining concessions in Sierra Leone in the 1990s. Although there have been subsequent incidents of PMSCs involved in mercenary ventures, such as the attempted Wonga coup in Equatorial Guinea in 2006, in many contexts, they are engaged in legal business activities.

These activities have evolved and the industry has diversified. In many situations – from accompanying armed forces in the conflicts in Iraq and Afghanistan, to their expansion into the maritime security industry, to their increasing role in counter-narcotics and counter-terrorism operations – it is clear that PMSCs are a different type of actor than mercenaries. Their clients include states, non-governmental organizations, transnational corporations, and intergovernmental organizations, such as the United Nations. The Working Group encountered resistance from states to the idea of broadening the legal definition of mercenary under the UN Mercenary Convention to include PMSCs, and the definition as presently drafted is not an easy fit for most present day PMSC activities.

First, the definition of a mercenary codified in the UN Mercenary Convention applies only to individuals who are recruited to fight in an armed conflict or participate in concerted acts of violence aimed at overthrowing a government. For the majority of PMSC employees engaged in security activities outside the context of conflict areas, the UN Mercenary Convention is not applicable at all. Yet frequent contact between private security personnel and the local population poses a risk to human rights that requires adequate regulation and oversight.

Second, the UN Mercenary Convention applies only to individuals who are neither nationals nor residents of a party to the conflict. The purpose of this definitional provision was ostensibly to distinguish a foreign mercenary from nationals legitimately engaged in protest or opposition movements. However, as recently demonstrated in the Middle East, this distinction becomes problematic when local groups receive foreign funding for the purpose of engaging in hostilities and terrorism, and destabilizing governments. Although there are examples of US and British-owned companies recruiting private security company personnel from Chile, Fiji and Nepal to guard facilities in Iraq and Afghanistan (see Chapters 15 and 18, this volume), quite often PMSC employees are nationals of one of the state parties to the conflict.

Individuals who operate within the military chain of command – and are accordingly considered members of the armed forces of a party to the conflict – are also not covered by the definition of a mercenary in the UN Mercenary Convention. As in the example of one of the PMSCs implicated in the Abu Ghraib torture cases, courts may find that private military and security personnel contracted to carry out core government functions in conflict areas operate within the military chain of command. These would likely not fall within the UN Mercenary Convention's definition of a mercenary.

Finally, agreement on the present definition of a mercenary in the UN Mercenary Convention was reached after a third point was deleted in negotiations. This item would have also defined a mercenary as an individual who, whether within or without the context of conflict, is recruited for the purpose of participating in a concerted act of violence aimed at denying peoples the legitimate exercise of their right of self-determination as recognized by international law. Recent history has witnessed situations in which states have suppressed political dissent and illegitimately retained power through the use of foreign troops or locally recruited public or private forces. These suppression and recruitment activities, utilized by governments for self-preservation, are not subject to the UN Mercenary Convention.

Definitional difficulties aside, only a relatively small number of countries (33) have ratified the UN Mercenary Convention since its adoption in 1989. There appears to be a lack of political will for enforcement of international legal prohibitions against mercenarism and too often governments resort instead to the political expediency of scapegoating ethnic and racial minorities under the guise of cracking down on so-called 'mercenaries'. Although more robust state support to counter the still-critical human rights dangers of mercenaries and a new definition updated to meet contemporary challenges are needed, it became clear to the Working

Group early on that merely redefining mercenarism would be inadequate to address the human rights concerns posed by the breadth and scope of PMSC activities.

International human rights law and PMSCs

An entirely new binding international instrument is needed to fill the normative gaps in the existing legal and regulatory frameworks to adequately protect human rights in the context of PMSC activities. However, it may be inaccurate to say that PMSCs operate entirely in a human rights vacuum.

Unlike international humanitarian law, which encompasses all actors engaged in conflict areas and hostilities, international human rights law becomes binding for states through treaties and the emergence of customary international legal norms. Although PMSCs, as non-state actors, are not directly bound by international human rights law, many human rights treaties place obligations on states to exercise due diligence to identify, prevent, and mitigate human rights violations perpetrated by private actors, and provide remedies to victims.

Due diligence is the standard of care applied to measure whether a state is upholding its treaty obligations. The work of human rights treaty bodies, committees of independent experts that monitor implementation and publish their interpretation of various provisions of treaties, have elaborated on states' due diligence obligations with regard to protecting human rights from interference by private actors.

For example, according to the UN Human Rights Committee, states that outsource core activities to the private sector involving the use of force and detention of individuals retain their human rights obligations (UN Human Rights Committee 2004). Under the International Covenant on Civil and Political Rights (ICCPR), one of the core human rights treaties, states must protect individuals against torture or cruel, inhuman or degrading treatment or punishment by private persons or entities. States have a positive duty to stop ongoing violations and to provide effective remedies to victims. These obligations to ensure respect for the human rights set out in the ICCPR extend extraterritorially, to anyone within a state's power or effective control, such as international peacekeepers.

Under the UN Convention against Torture (CAT), states bear international responsibility for the acts of private contractors acting on behalf of the state, under its direction or control, or otherwise under the colour of law. This means that states have a positive obligation to prevent torture and ill-treatment by private officials and privately-run prisons, and detention centres must be monitored by the state to ensure compliance with the CAT. States' responsibility to prevent torture extends extraterritorially, including during military or peacekeeping operations, and in embassies, military bases, detention facilities, etc. (UN Committee against Torture 2008).

States that have ratified the Convention on the Elimination of All Forms of Discrimination against Women (CEDAW) undertake the obligation to eliminate discrimination against women by individuals or entities, public or private. States must exercise due diligence to prevent, investigate and punish acts of violence against women, even when perpetrated by private individuals, and States may be responsible for private acts if they fail to exercise their due diligence (UN Committee on the Elimination of Discrimination Against Women 1992).

These comments of treaty bodies that seek to elucidate the due diligence obligations of states demonstrate that although PMSCs are not directly subject to international human rights law, neither should they operate with legal impunity. It is clear from these comments that states are obligated under these international instruments to investigate and punish certain alleged incidents of human rights violations involving PMSCs. Further elaborating and clarifying state human rights obligations in the context of business activities, the Guiding Principles on Business and Human Rights do not create new international legal obligations, but rather provide guidance on how existing provisions should be implemented.

The guiding principles on business and human rights

The former Special Representative of the UN Secretary-General on transnational corporations and other business enterprises (SRSG), John Ruggie, developed guidance for states on their obligations with regard to private companies and human rights, which also addresses the obligations of companies themselves. The Guiding Principles on Business and Human Rights emphasize that states do not relinquish their human rights law obligations when they outsource core governmental functions. Rather, states must adopt legislation and contract provisions, and other necessary measures, to ensure adequate oversight of business activities. Such measures include vetting, human rights training, and mandatory reporting on the impact of business activities on human rights. Under the Guiding Principles, the obligations of states to ensure the protection of human rights in the context of business activities take on increased importance when businesses operate in conflict areas, as PMSCs often do.

The Guiding Principles also assign responsibility to businesses for human rights violations by third parties when the company contributes to or benefits from these violations. In the case of PMSCs, this is relevant to situations in which subcontractors may engage in human trafficking, forced labour, unlawful detention practices, or other human rights violations from which a parent company benefits but does not intervene.

It is important to recognize that the Guiding Principles do not create new substantive legal obligations, but rather elaborate existing norms and good practices for states and businesses. During the drafting process, the Guiding Principles faced criticism from some civil society organizations for representing a step back from the current status of international human rights law and practice with regard to states' human rights obligations and the responsibilities of non-state actors. Although the Guiding Principles themselves do not constitute a binding international instrument, the Human Rights Council voted, in June 2014, to allow a Business and Human Rights Treaty process to go ahead.

Gaps in the existing international human rights law framework

Despite these efforts to elaborate and clarify the content of states' human rights law obligations in the context of business activities, considerable gaps remain with respect to PMSCs. Although it generally cannot be said that PMSCs operate in a legal vacuum, neither can it be said that the legal framework applicable to their activities is clear, coherent, or effective.

For example, there is no prohibition in existing law on outsourcing specific core governmental activities to the private sector. There is no agreement among states on which, if any, core activities ought to be exclusive to the state and therefore inappropriate for outsourcing to PMSCs. There are also significant gaps in accountability for human rights violations in the context of PMSC operations. These operations pose serious risks to human rights and yet, due to legal gaps, jurisdictional challenges, a lack of political will and other difficulties, violations frequently go unaddressed. The case against the perpetrators of the Nisour Square shooting in Baghdad in September 2007, employees of the PMSC Blackwater, was at first rejected by US courts and many feared the case would never be heard. The perpetrators were eventually brought to justice in 2014, seven years after the incident. There are numerous examples of serious human rights violations for which no one has been held accountable.

Only a month after the Nisour Square shooting, two Iraqi women were reportedly killed by employees of Unity Resources Group, an Australian PMSC, also in Baghdad. The risks to human rights posed by presence of these companies in conflict areas were already well-reported. In 2003, photos came to light showing the torture and ill-treatment of prisoners at the Abu Ghraib prison facility in Iraq. There were no prosecutions of the interpreters and interrogators provided by the PMSCs Titan Corporation and CACI International, and the civil cases against the companies have been pre-empted by immunity claims. In 2005, a 'trophy video' posted on the internet depicted employees of the PMSC Aegis appearing to shoot randomly into civilian cars on Route Irish, the road to the Baghdad airport. These incidents serve to highlight gaps in accountability for serious human rights violations, such as torture and the arbitrary deprivation of life and liberty, involving PMSCs.

These are notorious incidents; the Working Group has reported on a wide range of other human rights violations by PMSCs. In its country reports on Chile and Fiji for example, the Working Group describes the accounts of individuals who were allegedly recruited to work as PMSC employees under false pretences, had their travel or identity documents confiscated, and were denied payment, which appear to amount to human trafficking and forced labour. In Latin America, the Working Group has reported on the adverse health effects on Ecuadorian civilians of aerial spraying by PMSCs to defoliate coca plantations in counter-narcotics operations. In these cases as well, the perpetrators have not been held to account, and the victims have not been provided access to effective remedies.

Although the states that use PMSCs may be regarded as having certain due diligence obligations under international law, the outsourcing of core state functions may lead – and indeed has led – to gaps in accountability for human rights violations. As the above examples demonstrate, it is necessary to strengthen and clarify the regulatory framework for PMSCs. Accountability mechanisms must be established and fortified, and the content of the human rights obligations of states that use PMSC services must be elaborated and enforced. Such clarification at the international level, in the form of a legally binding instrument, is needed to shore up the gaps in protection and accountability in existing international law applicable to PMSCs.

The Draft Convention for the Regulation of Private Military and Security Companies

In March of 2009, in its resolution 10/11, the Human Rights Council tasked the Working Group with consulting with intergovernmental organizations, NGOs, academic institutions and other experts on the content and scope of a possible draft convention on PMSCs, and to share elements for a possible draft convention with Member States. The Working Group developed and circulated a draft to more than 250 stakeholders and engaged in a broad consultative process, eventually receiving more than 400 responses from Member States, international organizations, civil society representatives and PMSCs.

The Human Rights Council also mandated the Working Group to hold regional consultations to discuss the regulations and other measures Member States were undertaking around the world to ensure compliance with human rights standards in the context of PMSC activities. The Working Group held these consultations in all five UN geographic regions and discussed with participants general guidelines, norms, and basic principles for the regulation and oversight of PMSCs. These conversations also informed the Draft Convention.

On the basis of this extensive collaborative process, the Working Group prepared the text of a draft convention for consideration by Member States. The Draft Convention for the

Regulation of Private Military and Security Companies was presented to the Human Rights Council in 2010. Intended as a starting off point for further discussion by Member States, the Draft Convention proposes a list of 'inherently State functions', which states may wish to consider as inappropriate for outsourcing to private actors. The list includes such activities as 'direct participation in hostilities, waging war and/or combat operations, taking prisoners, law-making, espionage, intelligence, knowledge transfer with military, security and policing application, use of and other activities related to weapons of mass destruction, and police powers, especially the powers of arrest or detention including the interrogation of detainees'.

This proposed list of core state functions inappropriate for outsourcing was based on the principle of the state monopoly on the legitimate use of force, which had been repeatedly emphasized as a guideline during expert consultations during the drafting process. The political implications of such a proposal are apparent. To endeavour to restrict the outsourcing of even a handful of these functions would dramatically impact the reach of the PMSC industry as it has come to operate, and the functioning of the states that have come to rely so heavily on it as a source of manpower and expertise. The potentiality that an internationally binding instrument would prohibit to states the ability to outsource *any* activities to PMSCs has proven as great an obstacle as any thus far in the open-ended intergovernmental working group process underway in its first phase.

In addition to a list of inherently state functions, the Draft Convention proposes a number of key provisions on the international level which states must implement through national legislation. Among these provisions are an open international registration system of PMSCs operating on the international market, standards for licensing of PMSCs and vetting of personnel, and accountability mechanisms. The draft text also requires mandatory legal and human rights training for PMSC personnel and provides for international oversight and monitoring of PMSC activities.

The Draft Convention specifically elaborates the content of state obligations to establish jurisdiction over PMSCs and their personnel to ensure adequate legal authority to carry out prosecution for human rights violations committed abroad. It addresses the legal and political problems of immunity and extradition that have thwarted accountability in past cases. The Draft Convention also sets out a grievance mechanism and inquiry procedure to address accountability gaps at the international level. To provide effective remedies for victims, the text sets out the possibility that states may consider establishing a fund for victims to provide for reparation and rehabilitation. The Draft Convention proposed by the Working Group is now under consideration by Member States participating in the open-ended intergovernmental working group to consider the possibility of elaborating an international regulatory framework on the regulation, monitoring, and oversight of the activities of PMSCs established by the Human Rights Council.

Non-binding initiatives

In addition to the work of United Nations Special Procedures mandates, such as the Mercenaries and Business and Human Rights mandates, a number of non-binding, multi-stakeholder initiatives have also endeavoured to elaborate the human rights obligations of states vis-à-vis PMSCs, and best practices for companies, in recent years. These include the Montreux Document on pertinent international legal obligations and good practices for States related to operations of private military and security companies during armed conflict of 17 September 2008, and the International Code of Conduct for Private Security Service Providers and its Association. There are also the Voluntary Principles for Security and Human Rights, and the

ANSI/ASIS PSC.1 American National Standard (Management System for Quality of Private Security Company Operations – Requirements with Guidance).

Voluntary, self-regulatory, and non-binding initiatives (see Chapter 26, this volume) are useful and welcome; they may have a real impact on the licensing, vetting, and training procedures of PMSCs that voluntarily submit to the standards and best practices set out in these documents. This is particularly true if the ventures remain multi-stakeholder; that is, if the voices of civil society organizations are valued and heard, and if states require adherence to such frameworks, or memberships in such associations as pre-requisites for government contracting. However, these initiatives cannot take the place of the role of states and intergovernmental organizations in monitoring, overseeing, and providing accountability for PMSC activities. As only states can take on legal obligations under international human rights law, only a binding international instrument can shore up the gaps in the existing legal framework applicable to PMSC activities. The governmental authority to take on and uphold international human rights obligations is at least one core state function that cannot yet be outsourced to the private sector.

Conclusion

Efforts to expand legal accountability for violations of international human rights law to private military and security companies began over two decades ago and proposals have ranged from amendments to existing international law, the promulgation of a new binding international instrument specific to PMSCs, documents clarifying existing law and setting out good practices, to multi-stakeholder associations in which members voluntarily adopt codes of conduct. Despite some advances, there is more work to be done.

Although a study is underway to collect and analyse national legislation pertaining to PMSCs (UN Working Group on the Use of Mercenaries 2013: paras. 19–59), further research can yet be undertaken to collect and analyse human rights jurisprudence at the international and regional levels, and the work of human rights treaty bodies, to support accountability for PMSCs involved in human rights violations. Human rights training curricula, and due diligence polices can be developed for governments, intergovernmental bodies, and non-governmental organizations that utilize PMSC services. Human rights due diligence policies and information-sharing platforms can be developed in relation to procurement processes for security services, and procurement data can be collected and analysed to improve transparency about industry activities. Finally, scholars may design model laws or carry out comparative analyses of existing legal and regulatory frameworks to support ongoing efforts to extend international human rights law, as well as regional and national frameworks, to PMSCs.

Due to the nature of the activities of PMSCs, in many cases taking on functions traditionally carried out by states, sometimes involving the use of force, and often undertaken in unstable situations or conflict areas, these private companies pose a serious risk to human rights. Countries that have come to rely heavily on PMSCs to perform core state functions lack the political will to adequately regulate their activities and provide accountability for human rights violations. Also, states weakened by conflict and political instability, in which many PMSCs carry out their activities, lack the necessary resources to address violations that occur on their soil and on their seas.

Although PMSCs do not directly take up the specific obligations to perform or refrain from certain activities spelled out in international human rights treaties as do states, all human beings are inherently human rights holders and PMSCs must respect the fundamental human rights of the local populations with which they come into contact in the course of their work. It is incumbent upon the states and the intergovernmental organizations that use these companies to ensure the protection of human rights in the context of PMSC activities and guarantee effective remedies for victims in the event of violations.

Bibliography

Ballesteros, E. B. (1996) *Report to the Fifty-Second Session of the Commission on Human Rights*, Special Rapporteur on the Question of the Use of Mercenaries as a Means of Violating Human Rights and Impeding the Exercise of the Right of Peoples to Self-Determination, 17 January, UN doc. E/CN.4/1996/27, New York: United Nations.

Ballesteros, E. B. (1999) *Report to the Fifty-Fifth Session of the Commission on Human Rights*, Special Rapporteur on the Question of the Use of Mercenaries as a Means of Violating Human Rights and Impeding the Exercise of the Right of Peoples to Self-Determination, 13 January, UN doc. E/CN.4/1999/11, New York: United Nations.

Ballesteros, E. B. (2000) *Report to the Fifty-Fourth Session of the General Assembly*, Special Rapporteur on the Question of the Use of Mercenaries as a Means of Violating Human Rights and Impeding the Exercise of the Right of Peoples to Self-Determination, 30 August, UN doc. A/55/334, New York: United Nations.

Chesterman, S. and Lehnardt, C. (eds) (2007) *From Mercenaries to Market: The Rise and Regulation of Private Military Companies*, Oxford: Oxford University Press.

Francioni, F. and Ronzitti, N. (eds) (2011) *War by Contract: Human Rights, Humanitarian Law, and Private Contractors*, Oxford: Oxford University Press.

UN Committee Against Torture (2008) *General Comment No. 2: Implementation of Article 2 by States Parties*, 24 January, UN doc. CAT/C/GC/2, New York: United Nations.

UN Committee on the Elimination of Discrimination Against Women (1992) *CEDAW General Recommendation No. 19: Violence against Women*, New York: United Nations.

UN Human Rights Committee. (2004) *General Comment No. 31 [80]: The Nature of the General Legal Obligation Imposed on States Parties to the Covenant*, 26 May, UN doc. CCPR/C/21/Rev.1/Add.13, New York: United Nations.

UN Human Rights Council (2013) *Resolution 24/13, The use of mercenaries as a means of impeding the exercise of the right of peoples to self-determination*, 8 October, A/HRC/RES/24/13, New York: United Nations.

UN Open-ended Intergovernmental Working Group to Consider the Possibility of Elaborating an International Regulatory Framework on the Regulation, Monitoring and Oversight of the Activities of Private Military and Security Companies (2011) *Summary of the First Session*, 5 August, UN doc. A/HRC/WG.10/1/CRP.2, New York: United Nations.

UN Open-ended Intergovernmental Working Group to Consider the Possibility of Elaborating an International Regulatory Framework on the Regulation, Monitoring and Oversight of the Activities of Private Military and Security Companies (2012) *Report to the Twenty-Second Session of the Human Rights Council on Its Second Session*, 24 December, UN doc. A/HRC/22/41, New York: United Nations.

UN Working Group on the Use of Mercenaries (2010a) *Report to the Fifteenth Session of the Human Rights Council: Draft Convention for the Regulation of Private Military and Security Companies*, 5 July, UN doc. A/HRC/15/25, New York: United Nations.

UN Working Group on the Use of Mercenaries (2010b) *Report to the Sixty-Fifth Session of the General Assembly: Elements of a Proposed Draft Convention for the Regulation of Private Military and Security Companies*, 25 August, UN doc. A/65/325, New York: United Nations.

UN Working Group on the Use of Mercenaries (2013) *Annual Report to the twenty-fourth session of the Human Rights Council*, 1 July, A/HRC/24/45, New York: UN Working Group on the Use of Mercenaries as a Means of Violating Human Rights and Impeding the Exercise of the Right of Peoples to Self-Determination.

24

THE LEGAL FRAMEWORK FOR THE ARMED FORCES AND THE REGULATION OF PRIVATE SECURITY

Mirko Sossai

The legal debate on the outsourcing of private security tasks has focused on whether contractors operate in a legal vacuum. As states increasingly contract private security providers to perform functions previously exercised by members of the regular armed forces, a fundamental question has become to what extent these commercial entities are subject to the same legal framework as the armed forces. This chapter assesses whether and how the existing legal norms regulating the armed forces, at both international and domestic level, can be effectively applied to the private security industry or whether they need to be supplemented with new norms.

In terms of international law, the unavoidable starting point is the law of armed conflict. Traditionally known as *ius in bello*, it has developed since mid-nineteenth century and has assumed citizens armies as its main model of warfare (Avant 2000), as reflected by the rules on maritime neutrality and privateering; those on foreign recruitment; as well as the principle of distinction between combatants and civilians. However, already the early codifications of international humanitarian law (IHL) recognized the existence of contractors as 'persons who accompany the armed forces without actually being members thereof'. Given that this category is also acknowledged in the 1949 III Geneva Convention, it is important to discuss if it might cover contemporary private security providers. The key question is whether IHL introduces any legal limit to privatization of certain public functions: though it explicitly assigns only few activities to the members of the states' armed forces, there is a growing consensus among states on the need to avoid the direct participation of private security actors in hostilities during an armed conflict. Other limits might derive from other branches of international law: in particular, this chapter discusses if the UN Charter regulates the employment of private security companies (PSCs) during peacekeeping operations.

At the domestic level, a ban on certain military activities by private citizens has traditionally been covered by criminal law: indeed, several states prohibit foreign enlistment as well as mercenarism. The fundamental legal framework is represented by national military law, broadly defined as the system of domestic laws and regulations for the raising, maintenance, and administration of the armed forces (Nolte and Krieger 2003). A key question is to what extent civilian contractors are subject to the military criminal jurisdiction (i.e. whether they may be tried by martial courts).

A final aspect of the legal framework covering the armed forces is the regulation of defence procurement. The final section of this chapter discusses how domestic law determines which security services may or may not be contracted. The United States have relied on the standard of 'inherently governmental functions' (Huskey and Sullivan 2012), which has also influenced the debate on the outsourcing of security function within European countries and the EU. However, criticism has been levelled against this approach, because of its vagueness, that offers little guidance to decision-makers.

Does IHL explicitly assign certain functions to the regular armed forces?

In terms of the international legal framework, the first step is to assess whether states have an obligation not to contract commercial entities to perform activities previously undertaken by their regular armed forces. In recent years, PSCs have been associated to privateers and mercenaries: the former were abolished by the Paris Declaration of 1856 (Ronzitti 2011), whereas the UN Convention of 1989 introduces a ban on the latter phenomenon. However, both categories are of limited utility for the regulation of private security during an armed conflict. In particular, PSC personnel hardly meet the cumulative requirements of the definition of mercenary set out in both Article 47 of the 1977 Additional Protocol I to the Geneva Conventions and Article 1 of the 1989 International Convention against the Recruitment, Use, Financing and Training of Mercenaries.

IHL only assigns a few tasks exclusively to state officers, including the exercise of responsible authority for prisoner-of-war camps or places of internment of civilians, under the Third and Fourth Geneva Conventions (Montreux Document 2009). There is nevertheless widespread agreement that if states intend to respect the fundamental principle of distinction between combatants and civilians, they should not contract out services which could amount to direct participation in hostilities, unless the PSCs personnel is included in their armed forces.

Given that private security providers do not generally qualify under international law as mercenaries, a core issue is whether PSC personnel belong to the armed forces of the contracting State and therefore have legitimate combatant status. Under the law of international armed conflict, private contractors are members of the armed forces of a belligerent party once they are incorporated into such forces thorough a formal procedure in accordance with domestic legislation, or because they qualify as organized armed groups under a command responsible to the contracting State (see Art. 43 Protocol I 1977; Art. 4 (A)(2) Geneva Convention III 1949). However, practice shows that security providers have rarely been integrated de jure or de facto in the armed forces. The US Department of Defence refers to the notion of 'contractors authorized to accompany the force' in contingency operations, which might include PSCs (DoD Instruction 3020.41, 2011). This qualification reflects the notion of 'civilians accompanying the armed forces without actually being members', which was already recognized in the early codification efforts to provide a legal status for civilian personnel providing auxiliary services (Art. 4(A)(4) Geneva Convention III 1949). Therefore, PSC personnel are not combatants but civilians: they do not have the right to take a direct part in the hostilities, and they would lose their protection against direct attack, if they do so (Sassoli 2013).

Private security services often entail the use of weapons. The most delicate issue is to determine under what circumstances the provision of such services during armed conflict might amount to direct participation in hostilities. This latter notion refers to specific acts carried out by individuals, but it is not defined in IHL. The Interpretive Guidance, published by the International Committee of the Red Cross, has tried to fill this gap by identifying three constitutive elements: a threshold regarding the harm likely to result from the act; a relationship of direct causation between the act and the expected harm; and a belligerent nexus between the act and the hostilities conducted between the parties to an armed conflict (Melzer 2009).

States have relied on PSCs for a variety of tasks, including the guarding of military bases, checkpoints, work sites and embassies; personal security of high ranking officials; travel security for individuals; escorts for convoys moving equipment and supplies; event security; evacuation planning and more general security advice. When PSC personnel are employed to protect high-level individuals and certain sites, the question is if use of armed force would constitute an exercise of individual self-defence or amount to a direct participation in hostilities. The legal qualification of such acts depends on two variables: whether the persons or objects to be protected constitute a military objective and whether the attacker is a criminal or belongs to a Party involved in the conflict. Since IHL does not distinguish between offensive and defensive operations, defending military targets from the enemy amounts to taking a direct part in hostilities. The opposite case would be the provision of security for civilians against crimes.

To conclude, though there is no explicit prohibition under IHL, the respect in good faith for the principle of distinction between civilians and combatants might preclude states from entrusting PSCs with tasks – including defending a military objective – amounting to a direct participation in hostilities.

Should UN peacekeepers only be members of the armed forces?

Increasing attention has recently been devoted to the involvement of PSCs in peace operations (see Chapter 11, this volume). Although they have not yet provided military troops, PSCs are extensively employed in UN peace operations performing a variety of security–related activities, particularly for the static and mobile protection of UN personnel and premises (Østensen 2011). To regulate these activities, the UN Department of Safety and Security has adopted a specific Policy on Armed Private Security Companies, which entered into force in November 2012. The policy starts from the premise that the primary responsibility for the protection of UN personnel and property rests with the host State, along with the basic obligations already contained in the 1994 Convention on the Safety of United Nations and Associated Personnel. Armed PSCs may be engaged only on an exceptional basis; that is, 'when there is no possible provision of adequate and appropriate armed security from the host Government, alternate member State(s), or internal United Nations system resources' (UN Department of Safety and Security 2012).

The security industry is also increasingly involved in provision of more sensitive services to UN peacekeeping, including data gathering, risk assessment, and training, and it is therefore important to assess whether the legal system poses a limit to outsourcing. The key question is whether PSCs should only perform activities instrumental to the competencies of the UN, or might also cover functions related to the maintenance of international peace and security.

A possible legal argument in support of a limited role of the PSCs would be that military and police contingents forming a UN peacekeeping operation need to come from regular armed forces: therefore, the Security Council, or the Secretary-General in the exercise of his delegated powers, would be prohibited from requesting personnel from commercial entities and the member states could not simply hire PSCs as part of their contribution to the troops. However, an analysis of the relevant practice does not appear conclusive: UN Security Council resolution 1327 (2000) on the implementation of the Brahimi Report recommends that member states should take 'the necessary and appropriate steps to ensure the capability of their peacekeepers to fulfil the mandates assigned to them', without any specification on the origin of the contingents (Cameron and Chetail 2013). Similarly, resolution 2086 (2013) 'encourages

Troop- and Police-Contributing Countries, in the spirit of partnership, to continue to contribute professional military and police personnel with the necessary skills and experience to implement multidimensional peacekeeping mandates'.

In one author's view, article 48 of the UN Charter would preclude the permissibility of a UN force composed of private personnel. Since that provision states that the action to carry out the Security Council decisions adopted under Chapter VII is taken by member states 'directly and through their action in the appropriate international agencies of which they are members', it has been argued that 'it would be a long stretch to argue that states could delegate this task [the maintenance of international peace and security] to private military companies' (Lehnardt 2013: 440).

It remains that the memorandum of understanding (MOU) between the United Nations and contributing states, which establishes the administrative logistics, and financial conditions of the member states' contribution in terms of personnel, equipment and services, could contain specific provisions on the possible use of private contractors, including discipline and accountability measures in case of misconduct.

Does the law of visiting armed forces apply to private security companies?

Once civilian contractors are used in support of armed forces stationed in another country, the question is whether they are covered by the rules of international law governing the legal status of such visiting armed forces (*ius in praesentia*). A status-of-forces agreement (SOFA) between the sending state and the receiving state often provides the legal framework that defines the rights and obligations of the visiting forces (Fleck 2001). The specific content of such agreements depend on various factors, including the purpose of stationing: standing or permanent SOFAs, for peacetime military cooperation, are different from SOFAs concluded for the deployment of a peace operation. Although contractor employees were initially excluded from the scope of application of SOFAs, practice shows an evolution towards a progressive recognition of certain prerogatives for private personnel.

With regard to standing SOFAs for peacetime military cooperation, there was no reference to the category of contractors in the NATO SOFA (Agreement between the Parties to the North Atlantic Treaty regarding the Status of their Forces, London, 19 June 1951). However, supplementary agreements have been concluded by the US with Germany, and subsequently Italy and Belgium, in order to grant certain prerogatives, including tax and customs exemptions, to contractor employees providing support to visiting forces, who qualify as 'technical experts/representatives' (Conderman 2013; for Germany, see Art. 73 of the NATO SOFA Supplementary Agreement).

SOFAs also regulate the delicate issue of the exercise of the criminal and civil jurisdiction over personnel of the sending state, including contractors (Frulli 2011). The US–Iraq Withdrawal/Status of Forces Agreement revoked the controversial immunity for US contractor employees from local jurisdiction provided by the Coalition Provisional Authority Order 17 in 2003: under Art. 12 of the Withdrawal Agreement, Iraq has primary right to exercise jurisdiction over US defence contractors and their personnel. In Afghanistan, a significant evolution was achieved in 2014 when the country concluded a Bilateral Security Agreement and a SOFA with the US and NATO respectively. Under this new legal framework, PSC personnel – unlike the members of the armed forces and the civilian component personnel – are subject to Afghan criminal and civil jurisdiction while operating in the country.

As for the practice of the mission-specific SOFAs, the UN model SOFA too does not include any reference to commercial entities in its provisions. In recent times, SOFAs and status-of-missions agreements (SOMAs) set forth certain facilities for contractors, as regards obtaining visas, exemption from taxes and duties on goods which are for the exclusive use of the UN operation, and freedom of movement (Mathias 2013).

Does domestic military law apply to private security companies?

There is no uniformity in the regulatory frameworks of the different countries that use PSCs extensively, and the patchwork of domestic rules covering the sector falls far short of constituting an effective regulatory framework. Regulation ranges from strict prohibitions in some states, to forms of authorizations and licensing in others, to simply laissez-faire. A comprehensive assessment of the regulatory regimes at national level is thus difficult to achieve, but needs to consider the existence of limits on outsourcing; the criteria and procedures for the authorizations, selection and contracting of PMSCs; a monitoring system for PMSCs activities; the accountability framework (Bakker and Sossai 2012).

The scope of the present analysis is narrower: to offer an insight into the application of domestic military law provisions to the phenomenon of private security. The focus will be on three different issues: the relevance of the rules criminalizing foreign enlistment for private contractors; the exercise of military jurisdiction over civilian contractors; the determination of the services suitable for privatization in the context of defence procurement.

Domestic legislation on foreign enlistment is potentially applicable to the activity of private companies in foreign territory, though it appears out-dated and practically unenforceable. As an example, the UK Enlistment Act 1870 makes it an offence for a British subject without licence from Her Majesty to enlist in the armed forces of a foreign state at war with another foreign state which is itself at peace with the UK, or for any person in Her Majesty's Dominions to recruit any person for such service.

Similar offences were introduced in many other countries. The enactment of such legislation should be assessed against the background of the state's obligations deriving from the law of neutrality: in particular, the prohibition to form and recruit corps of combatants to assist a belligerent country and the duty to prevent such activities by private individuals within its own territory (Hague Convention (V) respecting the Rights and Duties of Neutral Powers and Persons in Case of War on Land; Hague Convention (XIII) concerning the Rights and Duties of Neutral Powers in Naval War, 18 October 1907; Cameron and Chetail 2013). It remains that the relevance of neutrality legislation for PSCs is limited, since it refers to the organization and the recruitment of personnel for combat services (Tonkin 2011).

In Italy, Article 288 of the Penal Code forbids providing arms or enlisting citizens, on Italian territory and without any governmental approval, to fight on behalf of or at the service of a foreign country. In 2010, a domestic court dismissed a case against two nationals accused of unauthorized enlistment. The two had recruited three guards to provide security services in Iraq in 2004 through a PSC incorporated in the Seychelles. The Court reached its conclusion by interpreting Article 288 in light of the 1989 International Convention against mercenarism and focusing on the notion of direct participation in hostilities: it held that the guards were supposed to offer security to objects and persons 'not directly involved in the armed conflict' in Iraq; therefore, the recruitment was not aimed at providing a causal contribution to the pursuance of military objectives of the international mission therein deployed.

A different question is if domestic military law provides for employment restrictions for retired members of the armed forces. In the United States, retirees should not engage in personal or professional activities that are incompatible with the standards of conduct expected of active duty personnel. Former military officers are subject to certain restrictions on their business activities, for instance as regards the sale of services and properties to the army. Moreover, explicit approval is needed for any retiree who intends to accept civil employment with a foreign government.

Interestingly, in Italy the very fact of being a former member of the national armed forces constitutes an important prerequisite for employment as an armed private security guard (*guardie giurate*) – directly by the ship-owners or through PSCs – on board Italian commercial vessels transiting dangerous international marine areas, under the new Italian counter-piracy legislation (Law No. 130/2011). It is noteworthy that the Italian legal framework is based on a hierarchy of options: the use of armed private security guards is allowed only when protection by small teams of naval or military personnel, called vessel protection detachments (VPDs), is not available.

Are civilian contractors subject to court-martial?

The more restrictive notion of military law refers to that body of domestic law concerned with the maintenance of discipline in the armed forces. The question is under what circumstances PSC employees, as civilians, are nonetheless subject to military law and may be prosecuted by military tribunals. Again, there is no uniformity in the recent evolution of military justice in different countries. A first group of countries has suppressed military jurisdiction in peacetime (Germany, Austria, Norway, the Netherlands, Belgium, *inter alia*; Andreu-Guzman 2004). Another group of states, particularly post-authoritarian democracies, have sought to restrict the scope of military jurisdiction only to the members of the armed forces (Greece, Italy), while a third group of states has expanded the reach of military justice (Ireland, UK, USA).

For those states recognizing military jurisdiction over civilians, PSC personnel could be brought before military tribunals in two main situations; first, in case of joint commission of crimes with servicemen; second, for crimes committed by civilians accompanying the armed forces during military operations (Manacorda and Mariniello 2012).

The most relevant development in recent years has been the confirmation and even the expansion of military jurisdiction to cover civilians working overseas for the armed forces. In the UK, the Armed Forces Act 2006 has introduced a detailed discipline on the treatment of civilians subject to service discipline: it places under military jurisdiction those civilians, including PSC personnel, working on behalf of the government in designated areas outside Britain. There has been much discussion about the propriety of the application of service discipline to civilians, particularly in relation to the jurisprudence of the European Court of Human Rights. In *Martin v. UK* (no. 40426/98, 24 October 2006) the Court stated that 'the power of military criminal justice should not extend to civilians unless there are compelling reasons justifying such a situation, … since only in very exceptional circumstances could the determination of criminal charges against civilians in [military] courts be held to be compatible' with Article 6 of the European Convention on Human Rights, which codifies the right to a fair hearing by an independent and impartial tribunal.

In the US the need to respect the constitutional rights of due process has been at the basis of a number of Supreme Court decisions rejecting military jurisdiction over civilians (*Reid v. Covert*, 1957; *Solorio v. United States*, 1987). However, in 2006 the US Uniform Code of Military Justice was amended to extend military jurisdiction to civilians 'serving with or accompanying an armed force in the field' not only in times of declared war but also in the context of 'contingency operations'. This latter notion is defined as 'a military operation that is designated by the Secretary of Defense as an operation in which members of the armed forces are or may become involved in military actions, operations, or hostilities against an enemy of the United States or against an opposing military force'. A 2008 memorandum of the Secretary of Defense explained that UCMJ jurisdiction over civilian contractors would be appropriate when the 'alleged misconduct … may jeopardize good order and discipline or discredit the armed forces and thereby have a potential adverse effect on military operations' (US Secretary of Defense 2008).

In July 2012, the highest court in the US military justice system, the Court of Appeals for the Armed Forces (CAAF), upheld the constitutionality of subjecting civilians contractors to court-martial jurisdiction (*United States v. Ali*, 2012). The case involved a Canadian–Iraqi national, who was employed by a US company to provide linguistic services to US military forces in Iraq. The CAAF concluded that the due process guarantees under the US Constitution did not apply to non-citizens, therefore an alien working for a US contractor supporting a US mission overseas simply could not rely on them to challenge the jurisdiction of the court-martial (Vladeck 2015).

It is to be noted that a US federal district court convicted the former employees of Blackwater involved in the 2007 Nisour Square incident, in which 17 people were killed in Bagdad, on the basis of a different US statute, the Military Extraterritorial Jurisdiction Act (MEJA). In 2004, Congress had amended MEJA to provide jurisdiction over contractors for the Department of Defense as well as working for other agencies, 'to the extent such employment relates to supporting the mission of the Department of Defense'.

What military functions should remain inherently governmental?

The debate on the limits to the privatization of tasks previously exercised by members of the national armed forces has been very much influenced by the US policy prohibiting the outsourcing of 'inherently governmental functions'. The US Congress has defined such functions as those that are 'so intimately related to the public interest as to require performance by Federal Government employees'. Commentators have emphasized that this notion was too vague and offered little guidance for deciding whether or not to contract key activities (Huskey and Sullivan 2012), and guidance documents have sought to establish criteria to identify 'critical' functions. In particular, PSCs should not perform 'security operations in certain situations connected with combat or potential combat' (OFPP 2011). It follows that for the US Government 'inherently governmental' are those activities that are closely related to combat. However, the US Commission on Wartime Contracting observed, on the basis of the data on the use of PSCs in Afghanistan and Iraq, that '[a]fter determining whether the inherently governmental prohibition applies, decisions to contract still need a context- and risk-sensitive consideration of appropriateness for contingency operations' (COWC 2011). In this respect, the category of activities unsuitable for outsourcing should be wider in scope and include not only combat-related functions but also 'high-risk' activities in specific scenarios, such as convoy security and personal security details (i.e. providing protective security to high-ranking individuals; Tiefer 2013).

The term 'inherently governmental function' has not been part of the European political discourse until recently. Interestingly, the notion was used by the White Paper prepared by the UK Ministry of Defence (MoD) on the reform of defence equipment delivery, equipment support and logistics supply (UK MoD 2013). That document contained a proposal to replace the MoD's existing defence equipment and support agency with a 'government-owned, contractor-operated' (GoCo) body (DeWinter-Schmitt 2013). However, this plan for a privatization of defence acquisition was later abandoned, although the private sector has increased its role in providing a variety of services to the British armed forces in support of military operations worldwide. This is known as contractor support to operations (CSO), a concept which includes contractors on deployed operations (CONDO), sponsored reserves and PMSCs.

The determination of services that may not be outsourced, on the basis of the 'inherently governmental' standard, constitutes one of the main elements of the EU Concept for Contractor Support to EU-led military operations, adopted by the EU Military Committee on April 2014. The document is based on a double premise: First, the increased need for CSO on the part of reduced armed forces operating in host countries with limited capabilities, and second, the focus on logistic support functions. Nevertheless, the EU Concept clarifies that '[u]nder no circumstances EU will outsource, to private companies, inherently governmental functions, such as: direct participation in hostilities; waging war and/or combat operations; taking prisoners; law making; espionage; intelligence analysis; knowledge transfer with military; security and policing application; police powers'. This language is, perhaps surprisingly, taken from the Draft Convention on PMCSs, the controversial proposal submitted by the UN Working Group on the use of mercenaries in 2010. As for security services, the document seems to take into account the question of their possible qualification as direct participation in hostilities, stating that the EU will not outsource military contingent force protection to PSCs. It is not clear what kind of incorporation in the regular armed forces the EU Concept envisages when it states that 'Security guard services to military premises and/or to military personnel, if necessary, should only be commissioned to PSCs when integrated within military force protection, and for limited tasks such as identification, surveillance and patrolling'.

Interestingly, Article 2 of the UN Draft Convention on PMSCs uses the slightly different notion of 'inherently state functions', basing its definition on the 'classical' principle under international law of the 'state monopoly on the legitimate use of force'. However, some of the prohibited activities listed in Article 2 are not clearly derived from that principle (e.g. law-making), while the draft itself otherwise recognizes that PSC employees may carry firearms in providing security services (White 2011).

Conclusion

In evaluating the impact of the legal framework applying to the armed forces on the regulation of PSCs, the present analysis has addressed three issues: whether international and domestic norms set a limit to privatization of certain functions; to what extent the existing framework remains applicable to the conducts of PSC personnel; whether new rules need to be adopted at both international and national level. There is a clear need to develop a shared regulatory approach on state contracting of private security services. The concern is that hiring states would be able to circumvent accountability by outsourcing certain functions. At present international law mainly provides for 'implicit' limits to the privatization of tasks previously exercised by members of the regular armed forces: this is the reason why the UN Draft Convention has sought to define a standard based on the notion of 'inherent state function'. However, the chance of successfully reaching an agreement on this issue remains rather low, not only because of the diversity of constitutional traditions among the various countries, but also the criticism levelled against the US attempt to define 'inherently governmental functions'. Nonetheless, other aspects appear ripe for supplementary regulation, at both domestic and international level. In particular, the definition of specific criteria for the award of procurement contracts and the identification of clear rules of conduct for PSCs employees, including on the possession and use of firearms. Finally, the creation of an adequate oversight and accountability mechanism for any wrongdoing requires further attention. In that context, harmonized solutions are necessary as regards the exercise of criminal jurisdiction over PSC personnel, to avoid impunity and respect due process rights.

Bibliography

Andreu-Guzman, F. (2004) *Military Jurisdiction and International Law*, Geneva: International Commission of Jurists.

Avant, D. (2000) 'From Mercenary to Citizen Armies: Explaining Change in the Practice of War', *International Organization* 54(1): 41–72.

Bakker, C. and Sossai, M. (eds) (2012) *Multilevel Regulation of Military and Security Contractors*, Oxford: Hart.

Cameron, L. and Chetail, V. (2013) *Privatizing War*, Cambridge: Cambridge University Press.

Chesterman, S. and Lehnardt, C. (eds) (2007) *From Mercenaries to Market*, Oxford: Oxford University Press.

Conderman, P. (2013) 'Status of Armed Forces on Foreign Territory Agreements (SOFA)', in *Max Planck Encyclopedia of Public International Law*, vol. IX, Oxford: Oxford University Press, pp. 586–97.

COWC (2011) *Transforming Wartime Contracting: Controlling Costs, Reducing Risks*, Arlington, VA: Commission on Wartime Contracting in Iraq and Afghanistan.

DeWinter-Schmitt, R. (ed.) (2013) *Montreux Five Years On: An Analysis of State Efforts to Implement Montreux Document Legal Obligations and Good Practices*, Washington, DC: Human Rights in Business Program.

Fleck, D. (ed.) (2001) *The Handbook of the Law of Visiting Forces*, Oxford: Oxford University Press.

Francioni, F. and Ronzitti, N. (eds) (2011) *War by Contract*, Oxford: Oxford University Press.

Frulli, M. (2011) 'Immunity for Private Military Contractors: Legal Hurdles or Political Snags?', in F. Francioni and N. Ronzitti (eds), *War by Contract*, Oxford: Oxford University Press, pp. 448–69.

Huskey, K. and Sullivan, S. (2012) 'United States: Private Military Contractors and US Law After 9/11', in C. Bakker and M. Sossai (eds), *Multilevel Regulation of Military and Security Contractors*, Oxford: Hart, pp. 331–80.

Lehnardt, C. (2013) 'Private Military Companies', in N. White and C. Henderson (eds), *Research Handbook on International Conflict and Security Law*, Cheltenham: Elgar, pp. 421–43.

Manacorda, S. and Mariniello, T. (2012) 'Military Criminal Justice and Jurisdiction over Civilians: the First Lessons from Strasbourg', in C. Bakker and M. Sossai (eds), *Multilevel Regulation of Military and Security Contractors*, Oxford: Hart, pp. 559–81.

Mathias, S. (2013) 'Regulating and Monitoring Private Military and Security Companies in United Nations Peacekeeping Operations', in B. D'Aboville (ed), *Private Military and Security Companies*, Milan: Franco Angeli, pp. 121–7.

Melzer, N. (ed.) (2009) *Interpretive Guidance on the Notion of Direct Participation in Hostilities under International Humanitarian Law*, Geneva: ICRC.

Montreux Document (2009) *On Pertinent International Legal Obligations and Good Practices for States Related to Operations of Private Military and Security Companies during Armed Conflict*, Geneva: ICRC.

Nolte, G. and Krieger, H. (2003) *European Military Systems*, Berlin: De Gruyter Recht.

OFPP (2011) *Policy Letter 11-01: Performance of Inherently Governmental and Critical Functions*, Washington, DC: Office of Federal Procurement Policy.

Østensen, Å. G. (2011) *UN Use of Private Military and Security Companies: Practices and Policies*, Geneva: Geneva Centre for the Democratic Control of the Armed Forces.

Ronzitti, N. (2011) 'The Use of Private Contractors in the Fight against Piracy: Policy Options', in F. Francioni and N. Ronzitti (eds), *War by Contract*, Oxford: Oxford University Press, pp. 37–51.

Sassoli, M. (2013) *International Law and the Use and Conduct of Private Military and Security Companies in Armed Conflicts*, Barcelona: Institut Català Internacional per la Pau.

Tiefer, C. (2013) 'Restrain "Risky Business": Treat High-Risk Private Security Contractors as Inherently Governmental', *Harvard Journal on Legislation* 50(1): 209–37.

Tonkin, H. (2011) *State Control over Private Military and Security Companies in Armed Conflict*, Cambridge: Cambridge University Press.

UK MoD (2013) *Better Defence Acquisition: Improving How We Procure and Support Defence Equipment*, London: The Stationery Office.

UN Department of Safety and Security (2012) *UN Security Management System Policy on Armed Private Security Companies*, New York: United Nations.

US Secretary of Defense (2008) *UCMJ Jurisdiction Over DoD Civilian Employees, DoD Contractor Personnel, and Other Persons Serving With or Accompanying the Armed Forces Overseas During Declared War and in Contingency Operations*, Washington, DC: US Secretary of Defense.

Vladeck, S. (2015) 'Military Courts and Article III', *Georgetown Law Journal* 103: 933–1001.

White, N. (2011) 'The Privatisation of Military and Security Functions and Human Rights: Comments on the UN Working Groups Draft Convention', *Human Rights Law Review* 11(1): 133–51.

25

REGULATION THROUGH PROCUREMENT POLICIES

Elke Krahmann

Procurement decisions and policies have the potential to play a significant role in the regulation of private military and security companies (PMSCs). This is highlighted in the Montreux Document which points to the international legal responsibilities of contracting states for ensuring that their suppliers respect international humanitarian law and to take 'measures to prevent, investigate and provide effective remedies for relevant misconduct of PMSCs and their personnel' (Montreux Document 2009: 11; see also DeWinter-Schmitt 2013). The Montreux Document further includes an extensive list of 23 recommendations for contracting states, outlining in detail good practices regarding the selection, contracting and monitoring of PMSCs. Procurement decisions and practices are also critical for the effectiveness of industry self-regulation and certification schemes such as the International Code of Conduct for Private Security Service Providers (ICoC) or the management standards for Private Security Companies developed by the American National Standards Institute (ANSI) and ASIS, a US-based security industry organization. Only if the consumers of private military and security services preferentially contract certified PMSCs, will companies have a financial incentive to sign up to these schemes. Finally, the procurement policies of leading states and international organizations can set international examples of best practice, thus promoting professional standards in the absence of a global agreement on a binding regulation of the industry.

Nevertheless, the regulation of PMSCs through procurement decisions and policies has received little attention in academic research. Most studies of the potentials and pitfalls of procurement in the security and defence sectors have been confined to the specialized practitioner literature (GAO 2006, 2012). Few scholars within the political and legal sciences have considered the possible contribution of or impediments to procurement policies facilitating higher professional standards among PMSCs or the security industry as a whole. A rare exception is Laura Dickinson who has investigated possible objections to expanding contractual tools for regulatory oversight. Dickinson (2007) identifies six arguments against changing contracts to improve the regulation of PMSCs:

1   existing contracts work well;
2   it would be too costly;
3   neither governments nor industry would agree to it;
4   the structure of the market undermines contractual regulation;

5   reforms such as giving third parties rights to file grievances would be impractical; and
6   contractual terms are difficult to enforce.

Another exception is Steven Schooner (2005) who examines how US contracting enabled the contractor atrocities in Abu Ghraib. He concludes, in concurrence with many Government Accountability Office (GAO) reports, that the US government lacks the administrative capabilities to draft and oversee contracts that would enable the effective control of PMSCs in deployed operations (ibid.: 557).

Building on the above, this chapter provides an overview of the potential and impediments to regulation through procurement, focussing on the US as the largest and most sophisticated consumer of military and security services worldwide. The chapter is structured into four sections. The first identifies three procurement mechanisms theoretically available to consumers: selection, contracts and penalties/incentives. The following three sections discuss the availability and use of these mechanisms in US procurement for military and security services. The chapter observes that the potential of regulating PMSCs through procurement is considerable. However, in practice the US has failed to fully exploit this potential, despite formal policies aimed at facilitating professional standards and conduct of PMSCs. The chapter concludes that the regulation of PMSCs is likely to remain weak as long as major clients are unwilling or unable to pay more than lip service to professional standards in their actual procurement decisions.

Regulation through procurement

Procurement policies can contribute to shaping PMSC industry standards and behaviour through three sets of mechanisms. The first pertains to the selection of contractors, such as free and open competition or the specification of eligibility criteria for companies seeking a contract. These mechanisms aim to force companies that fail to meet the expected standards out of the market. The second set of mechanism includes contractual requirements, compliance monitoring and contract management. Contractual mechanisms play a major role in demanding and monitoring standards of operation among the PMSCs employed by a client. The third range of mechanisms concerns rewards or penalties, from incentive fees to contract termination and debarment from future awards. It serves to enforce standards among contractors and signals to other companies the value placed by clients in professional operations.

While these mechanisms theoretically provide clients with considerable leverage over the standards and behaviour of PMSCs, regulation through procurement faces several obstacles. The ability of consumers to choose among alternative suppliers depends on the size of the industry and the client's assessment capabilities. Competition among PMSCs can be inhibited by collusive behaviour among firms and monopolistic or oligopolistic market structures. The termination of contracts or punishment of companies that fail to meet their contractual obligations can be hindered by consumers' lack of information and expertise, the expense of changing suppliers and loyalty towards a particular supplier. The impact of contractual stipulations on professional standards relies on influential and active consumers as well as businesses that are able and willing to process and react to consumer complaints. Moreover, it requires important clients or large numbers of consumers to use procurement in order to make an impression on a particular company.

In short, the regulation of the PMSC industry standards through procurement policies and decisions depends on the structure of the market, external circumstances and client behaviour. The next sections examine how the US, which is the largest consumer of private military and security services worldwide, has utilized selection, contracts and penalties to encourage higher standards among its contractors.

Selection of companies

Due to growing international competition among PMSCs the conditions for selecting only companies with the highest professional standards for contract awards are very good. The size of the global military and security industry has expanded exponentially in only twenty years. Between 1990 and 2004, about 210 PMSCs were estimated to operate in the sector (De Nevers 2009: 485). By September 2013, already 708 international PSCs had signed up to the ICoC. However, this figure represents only a small proportion of the contemporary global PMSC industry since the ICoC excludes military support firms and is disproportionally made up of British companies. Not included are many local military and security firms such as those employed during international military operations. Over 300 local security companies were counted during the Iraq intervention and about 90 in Afghanistan (ibid.: 485). Even in non-conflict regions national private security industries have grown significantly. According to the Confederation of European Security Services there were over 52,000 private security firms in Europe in 2011 (CoESS 2011: 143). Consumers thus have a broad choice of alternative suppliers in terms of service specialization, geographical location and professional standards.

Nevertheless, the empirical practice highlights several constraints to the ability and willingness of clients to influence PMSC industry standards through selective procurement policies. Limitations to this mechanism include conditions imposed by consumers, restrictions set by countries of operation, and the influence of PMSCs on the choices of potential and existing clients. The US government's selection among competing commercial security suppliers is limited specifically with regard to company age, size and location. PMSC age and size are important concerns due to the use of open-ended and long-term contracts as means for ensuring the continuity and flexibility of military and security service provision across multiple operations (Schooner 2005: 564). In the US these awards take the form of large Indefinite Delivery, Indefinite Quantity (IDIQ) contracts, such as the Logistic Civil Augmentation Programs (LOGCAP) I–IV, the Global Contingency Services Multiple Award Contract, and the Counter-narcoterrorism Global Support contract. Size matters in IDIQ awards because contractors are required to supply a broad range of services in unspecified quantities and multiple locations worldwide. A company must be able to provide large numbers of service personnel within a short period of time either directly or by subcontracting and managing other firms. Due to the importance and duration of major IDIQ contracts, company age also plays a role. Governments want to be assured that a contractor has the experience and staying power to carry out services until the end of the award or longer (e.g. for additional 'option years').

The top US Department of Defense (DoD) contractors have thus remained stable for many years: Lockheed Martin, Boeing, Raytheon, General Dynamics, Northrop Grumman, United Technologies, L-3 Communications, SAIC, BAE Systems and KBR (FPDS 2013). The American LOGCAP contract has circulated among KBR (LOGCAP I, III, IV), DynCorp (LOGCAP II, IV) and Fluor (LOGCAP IV). The Counter-Narcoterrorism Global Support contract and the Global Contingency Services Multiple Award contract are led, respectively, by Northrop Grumman and URS. Mergers and buy-outs have contributed to reducing the choice among the largest PMSCs that are capable of managing IDIQ contracts. L-3, for instance, bought MPRI in 2000 and Titan in 2005. CSC, another top 100 DoD defence contractor, owned DynCorp between 2004 and 2005; and DynCorp merged with Cerberus Capital Management in 2010.

Other factors that induce governments to restrict their choice to the same few PMSCs include efforts to cut transaction costs, such as the expense and time for advertising and selecting among competing bidders, and a political preference for national providers. Moreover, Dickinson (2007: 231) contends that 'corruption and cronyism are rampant in the initial *award* of government contracts'. Only ten PMSCs – Blackwater, Aegis, DynCorp, Triple Canopy, EOD, Sabre, SOC-SMG, Agility Logistics, Unity Resources Group, ArmorGroup and Erinys – received 75 per cent of the US government's payments for security services in Iraq between 2003 and 2008 (SIGIR 2008: 16). Most of these companies were registered in the US, indicating a preference for national companies.

Host nation regulations and policies are other, if comparatively rare, elements which restrict consumer choice among PMSCs. Between 2010 and 2014, the Afghan President Karzai attempted to disband all armed private security companies in Afghanistan in favour of a government-controlled Afghan Public Protection Force. Although the programme was abandoned after a few years, it significantly reduced the choice among armed private security firms in the country and led to a decline in DoD security contractors from 28,686 to 5,591 armed guards (CENTCOM 2014).

Finally, PMSCs can contribute to narrowing the choice among competing suppliers through recommendations, risk advice and package deals. The influence of contractors on clients' choices of security service and suppliers has been widely noted (Leander 2005; Spearin 2003). When the US government contracted Brown & Root Services (now KBR) in 1992 to develop a worldwide plan for the provision of logistic services under LOGCAP I, the company was simultaneously asked to take over the supply if asked (GAO 1997: 2). Once Brown & Root had established itself as the DoD's prime supplier of global military logistics, it was hired again for successive contracts, including LOGCAP III and IV. Package deals are another way of committing a consumer to the same company for a range of services over many years. Today most military aircraft, unmanned aerial vehicles and ground machinery are bought with full-life cycle support, including in deployed operations. With the integration of armaments production and operations support in sole-source package deals, it is little surprising that defence manufacturers like Lockheed Martin, Boeing, Raytheon, General Dynamics and Northrop Grumman lead the DoD's top military service suppliers list.

In short, for various reasons such as path dependency, political circumstances and economic imperatives, the ability and willingness of the US to choose between alternative service suppliers has been limited, despite its privileged position as the largest global consumer of military and security services and the growing number of PMSCs. The US government has instead focussed on contracts to improve PMSC standards and operations.

Contract design and management

Following several high-profile incidents involving security contractors in Iraq, the US government has taken multiple steps to facilitate higher professional standards through new regulations, including contractual stipulations. The basis is the 2008 National Defense Authorization Act which demanded a revision of the Federal Acquisition Regulation, including 'the insertion into each covered contract (or, in the case of a task order, the contract under which the task order is issued) of a contract clause addressing the selection, training, equipping, and conduct of personnel performing private security functions' (Congress 2008: Sec. 862). Today, contractual requirements are very extensive, including prescribed standards for the vetting and training of security guards. A Statement of Work for Private Security Contractors at Camp Delaram in Afghanistan, for example, specifies the following:

Contractor shall provide individual weapons familiarization training for all personnel who shall carry weapons under this contract to include sighting on each individual's weapons. Training shall be accomplished to Army weapons qualification standards. This training shall be specified and the standard monitored by the COR [Contracting Officer Representative].

(CJSTOF 2012)

In addition, the National Defense Authorization Act of 2011 stipulated that the DoD should issue policy guidance making it a condition for contracts involving private security functions that 'each contractor receive certification from a third party that the contractor adheres to specified operational and business practice standards' (Congress 2011: Sec. 324). As part of the guidance, the DoD was asked to (1) establish criteria for defining standard practices for the performance of private security functions, (2) establish minimum requirements for weapons training and qualification of instructors, and (3) identify organizations that could carry out the certification (ibid.: Sec. 324). Presumably in order to comply with these directives, the DoD funded the development of four management standards for Private Security Companies (PSCs) by ANSI and ASIS. The PSC.1–4 Standards pertain exclusively to the management of PSCs, but they also refer to the good practices outlined in the Montreux Document and the ICoC. Since 2013, the US Defense Federal Acquisition Regulation Supplement (DFARS 2013) demands that all contracts for security services in combat, contingency or military operations must comply with the new ANSI/ASIS management standard PSC.1. Furthermore, ANSI/ASIS submitted their standards to the International Standards Organizations (ISO) as the basis for the development of a globally recognized management system standard for private security operations (ISO/DIS 18788).

Despite these developments there remain several impediments to the effectiveness of US contractual obligations for PMSC regulation. The first concerns the quality and detail of the contractual requirements for professional standards (Dickinson 2007). The second problem regards the monitoring of contractor performance and compliance (ibid.; Schooner 2005). While industry has hailed the ANSI/ASIS Standards as 'the world's first standards designed to manage risks related to security services', a closer examination reveals that they do little to raise operational standards in zones of conflict (ASIS 2013). For one, the scope of the standards is limited in two main respects. The ANSI/ASIS Standards explicitly concern only PSCs, i.e. companies which provide 'guarding; close protection; physical protection measures; security awareness; risk, security, and threat assessment; the provision of protective and defensive measures for compounds, diplomatic, and residential perimeters; escort of transport; and policy analysis' (PSC.1 2012: 86). Firms engaged in military support, military and security training, and intelligence are not included.

Second, the ANSI/ASIS Standards regard the development of a 'management system' by which PSCs can facilitate professionalism. They do not specify personnel and service standards related to training or operations for the industry. Compliance with the ANSI/ASIS Standards is achieved by companies which can demonstrate that they have put in place management processes which help them develop, implement and revise largely company specific and self-defined standards. The ANSI/ASIS Standard for the selection and vetting of personnel thus states that 'the organization shall establish, document, implement and maintain procedures for background screening and vetting of all persons working on its behalf to ensure that they are fit and proper for the tasks they will conduct' (ibid.: 19). Standard PSC.1 then proceeds to recommend that 'wherever possible' the screening shall include a number of checks such as education and employment history review, military and security services records check and evaluation for suitability to carry weapons (ibid.: 19). While Annex A of the Standard states that these management systems 'should' comply with the Montreux Document, the ICoC and international human rights law, it makes clear that the Standard merely 'provides guidance or recommendations for any PSC to identify and develop best practices' (ibid.: 33). The final pages summarize the main weakness of the Standard:

> This Standard does not establish absolute requirements for quality assurance perform-ance beyond commitments in the organization's policy to: a) Comply with applicable legal requirements and with other requirements to which the organization subscribes, b) Support prevention of undesirable and disruptive events and risk minimization; and c) Promote continual improvement.
>
> *(PSC. 1 2012: 91)*

Standard PSC.2 stipulates that there are three ways in which compliance with the ANSI/ASIS Standards can be certified:

- self-assessment and self-declaration;
- customer assessment; and
- independent third-party certification.

While the US government and ASIS would prefer third-party certification, a company can thus claim compliance with the ANSI/ASIS Standard purely by self-declaration.

The second problem for the regulation of PMSCs through contracts is the need to moni-tor whether and how contractors implement contractual requirements. Innumerable reports by the GAO, the Special Inspector General for Iraq Reconstruction (SIGIR) and the Commission on Wartime Contracting (CWC) have identified contractor monitoring in international oper-ations as a significant and long-standing problem (GAO 2006; SIGIR 2008; CWC 2011). Already during the peacekeeping mission in Bosnia, GAO (1997: 9, 20–22) reported that weak-nesses in the DoD's monitoring of Brown & Root's LOGCAP I contract contributed to cost increases in the region of $100 million, or 32 per cent. Insufficient DoD contract management in Iraq allowed contractor 'fraud, waste and abuse' (GAO 2007: 2). As late as 2012, GAO noted that further improvements were needed in contract oversight in Afghanistan. For example, not all DoD contracting officer's representatives in the operation had the necessary training to write contract statements of work or the area-specific technical expertise to evaluate contractor performance (GAO 2012: summary). DoD still lacks sufficient numbers of contracting manage-ment personnel to cope with a contractor workforce now equal in size to its military contingents in deployed operations (ibid.: 1).

In sum, although the US has significantly expanded its formal contractual requirements for PMSCs, the scope and monitoring of these requirements need strengthening. Contractor performance surveys illustrate that more effective oversight is essential as PMSC malpractices occur regularly. The next section examines how the US government deals with contractors that fail to meet the required contractual obligations and standards.

Sanctions and contract termination

Only when PMSCs can expect to be held accountable for unsatisfactory services or low standards can clients hope to influence contractor standards and operations. The US Federal Acquisition Regulation (FAR), the 2008 National Defense Authorization Act, the Defense Acquisitions

Regulation System have clear provisions for penalizing contractors, such as the removal or replacement of contractor personnel after gross violations, the withholding of a percentage of payments for services or the termination of contracts in extreme cases (Congress 2008: Sec. 862). Long term effects on the standards and operations of US military and security contractors can be achieved primarily through more drastic measures such as the temporary suspension (up to 18 months) or debarment (up to 3 years, in exceptional circumstances indefinitely) of PMSCs from future government contracts (FAR 2013: 2.101). Causes for suspension are, among others, suspicion of fraud, criminal offences and unfair trade practices. However, suspensions never exceed 18 months if no legal proceedings are entered (ibid.: 9.407-2,4). Debarment can be imposed for a conviction or civil judgement related to the above offences (ibid.: 9.406-2).

While existing regulations suggest that the US government takes a strict view on contractor mal-performance, the empirical evidence presents a different picture. In particular, contract termination and permanent debarments are rare, although they are the main means that could force PMSCs with low standards out of the market (Dickinson 2007). Many of the DoD top ten security contractors have been implicated in scandals during the military interventions in Iraq and Afghanistan. Nevertheless, they continue to be employed by the US government. Blackwater, later renamed Xe and then Academi, became infamous for its involvement in the shooting of 17 civilians in Baghdad in 2007 (Risen 2011). Regardless, Blackwater/Xe/Academi continues to work as DoD contractor, including the provision of 'security services in support of Forward Operating Base (FOB) Dwyer, and an option for FOB Delaram II' in Afghanistan until 2016 (DoD 2012). Aegis was implicated in drive-by shootings in Iraq. Yet, between 2004 and 2011, Aegis won ten US government contracts in Iraq, amounting to $1 billion (SIGIR 2011). DynCorp gained a negative image for sex-trafficking carried out during their support for the US peacekeeping operation in Bosnia in the 1990s. Irrespective of these and other incidents, DynCorp has been the third largest DoD contractor in Iraq and Afghanistan with awards totalling $7.4 billion between 2002 and 2011 (CWC 2011: 25).

The list of PMSCs that have been re-awarded US government contracts despite previous misconduct also includes many of its top defence manufacturers and support service suppliers. A DoD Report to Congress on Contracting Fraud (DoD 2011: 4) noted that, between 2006 and 2009, no less than 30 companies had been criminally convicted of fraud over $1 million, 91 had been fined in civil judgements and 120 had entered into settlement agreements. Within the same timeframe, 43 contractors had been suspended and 164 debarred from further government contracts (ibid.: 4–5). Among the 207 companies who had been suspended or debarred only 12 were excluded 'indefinitely' from future government contracts (ibid.: tables 4A, 5A). The companies implicated for fraud within the three year period included Lockheed Martin, Boeing, Raytheon, General Dynamics, Northrop Grumman, L-3 and Brown & Root/KBR (ibid.: appendix). Nevertheless, these companies continue to lead the DoD Top 100 Contractors list.

Three factors account for the US government's limited use of suspensions and debarments. The first factor has been lack of information and coordination. Until 2011 there existed no central repository for data concerning contractors which had defrauded the government, making it difficult for contracting officials to implement suspensions and debarments (ibid.: 2). Indeed, the DoD Report to Congress observed that 'in some instances, the Military Departments and the Defense Logistics Agency obligated funds to various contractors during the suspension period' and 'A similar situation was noted with regard to continued obligations to contractors who had been debarred' (ibid.: 4–5). Although the US government has made efforts to address this problem, other factors suggest that these changes may not be sufficient to exclude contractors for poor performance.

Another factor is the ability of PMSCs to change and hide their identities through mergers, name changes and the registration of companies under several Data Universal Numbering System (DUNS) identifiers in the US Federal Procurement Data System (ibid.: 2, 3). These strategies make it nearly impossible for government agents to determine whether it is the same company or another (ibid.: 2). Examples are widespread in the industry. Aegis became the successor of Sandline International, at least in terms of its leadership, after Sandline had been implicated in the 'Arms for Africa' scandal involving breaches of the United Nations arms embargo during the company's participation in the civil war in Sierra Leone in the early 1990s. MPRI was acquired by L-3 in 2000 and, together with other L-3 segments, relaunched as Engility in 2012. The most famous example of changing identities and names is indubitably Blackwater. Founded in 1997 as Blackwater USA, the company changed its name to Blackwater Worldwide in 2007. Following the shooting of 17 Iraqi civilians by some of its employees and the Iraqi government's refusal to extend the company's operating licence, Blackwater re-registered as Xe Services in 2009. After the resignation of its founder, CEO and chairman Erik Prince, Xe Services was bought by an investor group and relaunched under the name Academi. In 2014, finally, Academi, Triple Canopy and several other PMSCs were brought together as Constellis Holdings. Blackwater/Xe/Academi's acquisition of new US government awards for security services despite being charged for repeatedly and systematically violating the US Arms Export Control Act and International Trafficking in Arms Regulations has caused consternation. The US government has justified its decision to let off Blackwater/Xe/Academi with a $42 million settlement and $7.5 fine with 'the company's efforts to reform its conduct' (FBI 2012). The sale and relaunch of Blackwater/Xe as Academi had effectively and successfully wiped clear its history of misconduct.

The most important impediment to the suspension or debarment of PMSCs known for misconduct and poor performance is the dependency of the DoD on select companies in areas such as logistics, catering, maintenance and security (Schooner 2005). Without these companies US interventions have become impossible. The DoD (2011: 5) has admitted that some contracts are continued 'to ensure mission accomplishment and for safety and mission requirements' despite fraudulent behaviour. The Commission on Wartime Contracting confirms that in particular PMSCs who have won large or security relevant contracts can get away with settlements or fines. KBR, the single largest DoD contractor in Iraq and Afghanistan with awards totalling $41 billion (CWC 2011: 25), was already during the operation implicated for 'a total of 32 cases of suspected overbilling, bribery and other violations' (Nakashima 2009). Other charges against KBR included the acceptance of bribes from subcontractors, known exposure of US troops in Iraq to contaminated water, sexual harassment of employees and faulty electric work contributing to the deaths of up to 18 US soldiers (Krahmann 2010: 208; Risen 2008). Since KBR was sole provider of logistic services under LOGCAP III, it was impossible to suspend the company during the Iraq and Afghanistan interventions. When LOGCAP IV went again to KBR, although this time together with DynCorp and Fluor, it raised serious questions about the DoD's dependency on the former. 'In terms of lessons learned, how did KBR become one of the contractors on Logcap 4?' asked CWC member Linda J. Gustitus (Nakashima 2009). Even when in 2010 the Department of Justice filed a civil law suit against KBR for providing false statements to justify its unauthorized use of private security guards between 2003 and 2006, KBR was, again, not suspended from LOGCAP IV, although there were now two other companies bidding for LOGCAP task orders (Pincus 2010).

Altogether the punishment of PMSCs that have been convicted of fraud, waste and abuse has often been weak. Although the US has strict regulations for dealing with such contractors, the many instances in which they have been let off lightly signals to these firms as well as the industry as a whole that procurement decisions are usually taken on the basis of other concerns than the promotion of high professional standards.

Conclusion

Contracting states have a major responsibility for the regulation and control of PMSCs. This chapter has examined whether major clients can facilitate and enforce higher industry standards through procurement mechanisms such as selection, contracts and penalties. Focusing on the US government, it has observed that the potential for regulation through procurement is considerable. Increased competition among PMSCs, stricter procurement rules and contractual regulations, international certification and licensing schemes all support the promotion of professional standards within the PMSC industry. Nevertheless, even the largest consumer of commercial military and security services worldwide is often unable or unwilling to use procurement policies to regulate its contractors. While the global military and security service market has grown, the US government continues to contract the same few, largely national companies. Also contractual requirements for higher standards and certification are hardly effective in practice, either because they lack specificity or because of inadequate monitoring. Moreover, contractual regulation can only hope to shape industry standards in the long term if failure to comply leads to major sanctions such as suspensions or debarments from future contracts. Past experience from the interventions in Iraq and Afghanistan, however, illustrates that the US government's willingness to end established relations with its military and security contractors is very small. The repeated failure of the DoD to penalize PMSCs for non-performance and misconduct has assured the industry that it is 'business as usual' despite new demands for professionalism. In conclusion, the findings suggest that procurement policies will have little effect on the actual performance and operations of PMSCs as long as clients fail to strictly enforce them.

Bibliography

ASIS (2013) 'ASIS Completes Work on PSC Series of ANSI Standards', news release, 15 April, www.asisonline.org/About-ASIS/Who-We-Are/Whats-New/Pages/ASIS-Completes-Work-on-PSC-Series-of-ANSI-Standards.aspx

CENTCOM (2014) *Contractor Support of U.S. Operations in the USCENTCOM Area of Responsibility to Include Iraq and Afghanistan*, Washington, DC: Department of Defense, www.acq.osd.mil/log/PS/reports/CENTCOMCensusReports/5A_October_2014_Final.pdf.

CJSOTF (2012) 'A Contracting Office, Camp Vance, Afghanistan Private Security Contractor, Camp Delaram, Nimroz Province, Statement of Work', 1 August, www.fbo.gov/index?s=opportunity&mode=form&id=8a79f17d1cfe0563a2da2c04b7092b9b&tab=core&_cview=1.

CoESS (2011) *Private Security Services in Europe 2011: Facts and Figures*, Confederation of European Security Services, www.coess.eu/_Uploads/dbsAttachedFiles/Private_Security_Services_in_Europe-CoESS_Facts_and_Figures_2011%281%29.pdf.

Congress (2008) 'National Defense Authorization Act for Fiscal Year 2008', Public Law 110-181, 110th Congress, www.gpo.gov/fdsys/pkg/PLAW-110publ181/html/PLAW-110publ181.htm.

Congress (2011) 'Ike Skelton National Defense Authorization Act for Fiscal Year 2011', Public Law 111-383, 111th Congress, www.gpo.gov/fdsys/pkg/PLAW-111publ383/html/PLAW-111publ383.htm.

CWC (2011) *Transforming Wartime Contracting: Controlling Cost and Reducing Risks*, final report to Congress, August, Arlington, VA: Commission on Wartime Contracting.

De Nevers, R. (2009) '(Self)Regulating War? Voluntary Regulation and the Private Security Industry', *Security Studies* 18(3): 479–516.

DeWinter-Schmitt, R. (ed.) (2013) *Montreux Five Years On: An Analysis of State Efforts to Implement Montreux Document Legal Obligations and Good Practices*, Washington, DC: Human Rights in Business Program.

DFARS (2013) *PGI 225.74 – Defense Contractors Outside the United States*, Washington, DC: Office of the Under Secretary of Defense for Acquisition, Technology, and Logistics.

Dickinson, L. A. (2007) 'Contract as Tool for Regulating Private Military Companies', in S. Chesterman and C. Lehnhardt (eds), *From Mercenaries to Market: The Rise and Regulation of Private Military Companies*, Oxford: Oxford University Press, pp. 217–38.

DoD (2011) *Report to Congress on Contracting Fraud*, January, Washington, DC: Department of Defense, www.sanders.senate.gov/graphics/Defense_Fraud_Report1.pdf.

FAR (2013) 'Federal Acquisition Regulation', www.acquisition.gov/far.

FBI (2012) *Academi/Blackwater Charged and Enters Deferred Prosecution Agreement*, 7 August, Washington, DC: Federal Bureau of Investigation.

FPDS (2013) *Top 100 Contractors Report*, Washington, DC: Federal Procurement Data System, www.fpds.gov/fpdsng_cms/index.php/en/reports/62-top-100-contractors-report3.html

GAO (1997) *Contingency Operations: Opportunities to Improve the Logistics Civil Augmentation Program*, GAO/NSIAD 97-63, February, Washington, DC: General Accounting Office.

GAO (2006) *Military Operations: High-Level DOD Action Needed to Address Long-standing Problems with Management and Oversight of Contractors Supporting Deployed Forces*, GAO 07-145, December, Washington, DC: General Accounting Office.

GAO (2007) *Stabilizing and Rebuilding Iraq: Conditions in Iraq Are Conductive to Fraud, Waste and Abuse*, GAO 07-525T, April, Washington, DC: General Accounting Office.

GAO (2012) *Operational Contract Support: Management and Oversight Improvements Needed in Afghanistan*, GAO 12-290, March, Washington, DC: General Accounting Office.

Krahmann, E. (2010) *States, Citizens and the Privatization of Security*, Cambridge: Cambridge University Press.

Leander, A. (2005) 'The Power to Construct International Security: On the Significance of Private Military Companies', *Millennium: Journal of International Studies* 33(3): 803–25.

Montreux Document (2009) *On Pertinent International Legal Obligations and Good Practices for States Related to Operations of Private Military and Security Companies during Armed Conflict*, Geneva: ICRC.

Nakashima, E. (2009) 'KBR Connected to Alleged Fraud, Pentagon Auditor Says', *Washington Post* 5 May, www.washingtonpost.com/wp-dyn/content/article/2009/05/04/AR2009050403283.html.

Pincus, W. (2010) 'US Files Civil Suit against Defense Contractor KBR', *Washington Post* 2 April, www.washingtonpost.com/wp-dyn/content/article/2010/04/01/AR2010040103737.html.

PSC.1. (2012) *Management System for Quality of Private Security Company Operations – Requirements with Guidance*, Alexandria, VA: ASIS Commission on Standards and Guidelines.

PSC.2. (2012) *Conformity Assessment and Auditing Management Systems for Quality of Private Security Company Operations*, Alexandria, VA: ASIS Commission on Standards and Guidelines.

Risen, J. (2008) 'Pentagon Finds Company Violated Its Contract on Electrical Work in Iraq', *New York Times* 24 October, www.nytimes.com/2008/10/25/washington/25contract.html.

Risen, J. (2011) 'Ex-Blackwater Guards Face Renewed Charges', *New York Times* 22 April, www.nytimes.com/2011/04/23/us/23blackwater.html?_r=0.

Schooner, S. L. (2005) 'Contractor Atrocities at Abu Ghraib: Compromised Accountability in a Streamlined, Outsourced Government', *Stanford Law and Policy Review* 16 (2): 549–72.

SIGIR (2008) *Agencies Need Improved Financial Data Reporting for Private Security Contractors*, SIGIR 09-005, 30 October, Arlington, VA: Special Inspector General for Iraq Reconstruction.

SIGIR (2011) *Letter for Commanding General, US Army Corps of Engineers – Gulf Region District Is Adjusting its Aegis Contract Requirements for Changes in Reconstruction Activities in Iraq*, 27 April, Arlington, VA: Special Inspector General for Iraq Reconstruction, www.sigir.mil/files/audits/11-015.pdf.

Spearin, C. (2003) 'American Hegemony Incorporated: The Importance and Implications of Military Contractors in Iraq', *Contemporary Security Policy* 24 (3): 26–47.

26

TRANSNATIONAL BUSINESS GOVERNANCE THROUGH STANDARDS AND CODES OF CONDUCT

Rebecca DeWinter-Schmitt

As the private security industry (PSI) experienced unprecedented growth with the wars in Iraq and Afghanistan, a number of incidents implicating private military and security contractors in human rights violations revealed lacunae in the existing hard and soft law governance regimes. The abuses at the Abu Ghraib prison facility and the killing and wounding of civilians at Nisour Square were among the most tragic and iconic incidents of this period, and helped generate discussions at both the national and international levels about how best to regulate the PSI. When it came to addressing the human rights impacts of private security companies (PSCs), the new forms of business governance that emerged and gained relative momentum involved private actors, rather than the promulgation of hard law by states, namely an international code of conduct and management standards. The corporate social responsibility literature (e.g. Scherer and Palazzo 2011) attributes the preference for such (semi)privatized forms of governance to states being 'unable or unwilling to regulate'. However, as this chapter argues in the PSI such initiatives were the result of deliberate decisions by key contracting and home states. This is not to imply that contracting, home, and territorial states did not promulgate new national laws and regulations during this period. They did, although to varying degrees.[1] Yet the majority of regulatory efforts of key contracting and home states, including the US, UK, Switzerland, Australia and Canada, centred on voluntary initiatives that involved businesses and other stakeholders.

Transnational business governance in the private security industry

At the international level, the UN Working Group on the use of mercenaries as a means of violating human rights and impeding the exercise of the right of peoples to self-determination (UN Working Group on Mercenaries) released a draft convention in 2010 with recommendations for regulating private military and security companies. However, its efforts to gain support for a binding international instrument have failed in the face of ongoing opposition from major contracting and home states to its provisions, including those limiting the types of activities that can be outsourced. Instead these states backed an initiative led by the Swiss government and the International Committee of the Red Cross to create a non-binding declaration. The outcome was the Montreux Document on Pertinent International Legal Obligations and Good Practices for States related to Operations of Private Military and Security Companies during Armed Conflict. Released in September 2008, the so-called Montreux Document creates no new international law, but rather recalls the existing international humanitarian and human rights law obligations of states with regard to the activities of private military and security companies, and elaborates good practices to assist states in meeting those obligations. The Montreux Document set the stage for the next step of the Swiss-led initiative to develop a code of conduct for PSCs through a multi-stakeholder process. The International Code of Conduct for Private Security Service Providers (ICoC) was the culmination of those negotiations and details international human rights and humanitarian law principles for the responsible provision of security services in complex environments. The ICoC contains principles regarding the conduct of security personnel and commitments regarding the management and governance of PSCs. The multi-stakeholder ICoC Association (ICoCA), launched in September 2013, is the governance body meant to ensure implementation of, and accountability to, the ICoC. It is currently developing procedures for certification, monitoring and reporting, and grievance mechanisms as stipulated in its Articles of Association.

The other key business governance initiative examined in this chapter is a series of four national management system standards created by ASIS International with the support of the PSI and funding provided by the US Department of Defense (DoD). All four are approved as American National Standards Institute (ANSI) standards. In particular, I focus here on ANSI/ASIS PSC.1: Management System for Quality of Private Security Company Operations – Requirements with Guidance (PSC.1). PSC.1 rests on the normative foundations of the ICoC and Montreux Document, and builds on the plan–do–check–act model of management systems. It provides auditable criteria for the assurance of the quality provision of security services in a manner consistent with respect for human rights, legal obligations, and industry good practices by security providers operating in areas where governance and the rule of law have been undermined. PSC.1 is currently being developed into an International Organization for Standardization (ISO) standard, ISO 18788 Management System for Private Security Operations. I concentrate my analysis on the ICoC process and the ANSI/ASIS PSC series because they are the most developed business governance initiatives in the PSI, involve the greatest number of stakeholders, and are most similar to each other as examples of 'certification standards' that 'attempt to provide external validity to what companies say they are doing' (Gilbert *et al.* 2011: 27).

These are by no means the only governance initiatives in the PSI's regulatory institutional field, which includes company-level codes of conduct, industry trade association codes of conduct, related multi-stakeholder initiatives, regional standards, and global business and human rights standards. However, none of these governance initiatives has gained the same level of recognition and adoption, with one possible exception, the Guiding Principles on Business and Human Rights: Implementing the United Nations 'Protect, Respect, and Remedy' Framework (UNGPs). The UNGPs were drafted under the leadership of UN Special Representative John Ruggie and unanimously endorsed by the Human Rights Council in 2011. The UN backed consensus on the state obligation to protect human rights from infringement by economic actors, the corporate responsibility to engage in a due diligence process to ensure respect for human rights, and the rights of victims to access effective remedies is reflected to varying degrees in the ICoC process and the ANSI/ASIS PSC series. At this stage in the development of the ICoC process and the ANSI/ASIS PSC series it is unclear whether or not they will improve human rights protections for affected populations. Yet, this chapter suggests a preliminary assessment is possible. The effectiveness of business governance initiatives will largely depend on their institutional design. Based on interpretation of the UNGPs and studies of other industries, there is growing consensus in the transnational business governance literature and in practice about effective design for regulatory initiatives involving private actors in terms of standards setting, governance structures, and assurance frameworks. This consensus, coupled with actual experiences with the development of new forms of governance in the PSI, provides a useful starting point for a human rights-focused assessment. However, understanding the particular institutional design characteristics of the ICoC/ICoCA and the ANSI/ASIS PSC series, and their potential for positive evolution, requires an examination of the processes that account for their emergence and development and the outcomes of, at times contentious, negotiations among stakeholders situated in the PSI institutional field. The interactions among stakeholders and initiatives have created certain path dependencies that would seem to lock some outcomes in place, but have also created dynamic and open opportunities for learning and upwards convergence.

Methodological note

Three methodological matters bear mentioning. First, there has been a great deal of debate on what to call those who provide military and security related services, from encompassing terminology like private military and security companies to more derogatory terminology like mercenaries. I use the term private security companies or service providers simply because both the ICoC/ICoCA and ANSI/ASIS PSC series focus primarily on those offering armed security services, and operate from the assumption that the PSI is a legitimate industry not to be conflated with mercenarism.

Second, as Abrahamsen and Leander note in the Introduction to this volume, one feature of the multi-disciplinary and heterogeneous field of private security studies is its relationship to practice and the role of practitioners in shaping research. With this in mind, I don the hat of an academic-practitioner to discuss the potentials and limitations of emerging forms of transnational business governance for ensuring that PSCs respect human rights in their operations. The data I draw on come from a combination of being a participant–observer in the business governance initiatives discussed here, interviews with a range of stakeholders and secondary sources.[2]

Finally, speaking of voluntary or self-regulation of the PSI does not capture the complexities of the ICoC process and the ANSI/ASIS PSC series. Because these initiatives address how to regulate the legitimate use of force by private actors, state actors have played a significant role in driving and shaping them and a few states and international organizations are now requiring in laws, regulations, and procurement policies that PSCs adhere to them, thereby making any terminology invoking the idea that these are purely private, voluntary, or self-regulatory inaccurate. Therefore, I prefer to use the term transnational business governance initiative. Eberlein *et al.* (2014: 3) refer to transnational business governance (TBG) as 'systematic efforts to regulate business conduct that involve a significant degree of non-state authority in the performance of regulatory functions across national borders'. The authors contrast this with traditional notions of governance insisting on the primacy of the state in exercising regulatory authority through binding laws and regulations. Instead they examine manifestations of what they term 'regulatory governance' involving a heterogeneous array of private actors. Governance broadly understood captures 'all activities involved in conducting the affairs of a state, organization or society', and regulation is 'organized and sustained attempts to change the behavior of target actors to further a collective end, through rules or norms and means of implementation and enforcement' (ibid.: 4). Drawing on this literature allows me to capture the significant involvement of private actors – alongside state actors – in the exercise of regulatory authority over business activities that involve the use of force, a traditional matter of state control, through the promulgation of soft norms rather than just hard laws.

Effective transnational business governance

Despite differences in the nomenclature describing new forms of (semi)private governance, in the academic literature and in practice there is an emerging consensus on what constitutes effective institutional design of TBG initiatives (Dingwerth and Pattberg 2009) which can be used to examine the design of PSI-specific initiatives. The design characteristics discussed here are ideal types, as the perceived legitimacy of a particular institutional design is the result of ongoing negotiations among stakeholders and relative to the normative institutional field, and will reflect sector-specific variations (Bernstein and Cashore 2007; Fransen 2011). I understand effectiveness to mean that TBG initiatives enable companies to meet their responsibility to respect human rights as detailed in the UNGPs. The UNGPs reflect the first international consensus on the obligations of states and responsibilities of companies to ensure that people are protected from harms linked to corporate activities. According to Principle 15, the corporate responsibility to respect entails companies having in place a human rights policy commitment, a 'human rights due diligence process to identify, prevent, mitigate and account for how they address their impacts on human rights', and a remediation process to address adverse human rights impacts. Next, I discuss some of the best practices for effective design of standards, governance procedures, and assurance frameworks.

In terms of *standards-setting*, benchmarks for best practices can be divided into process and content.[3] With regard to process, standards should be developed in a transparent and inclusive multi-stakeholder fashion to ensure their 'moral legitimacy' in the eyes of 'those parties that are affected by the rules of a standard or have the ability to affect these' (Rasche 2009: 197). Requirements of standards should be grounded in international norms and have a sufficient level of specificity and clarity. According to the UNGPs (Principle 12), corporate human rights commitments should reference at a minimum internationally recognized human rights as detailed in the International Bill of Rights and the International Labour Organization's Declaration on Fundamental Principles and Rights at Work. Specificity and clarity are useful for both adopters and certifiers of a standard since they make both implementation and verification easier (Rasche 2009). Specificity and clarity also aid in preventing 'decoupling' (i.e. when companies claim to abide by a standard, or are certified as compliant with a standard, despite the fact that they may not be implementing the standard fully or not altering actual business practices; Behnam and MacLean 2011).

Governance procedures deemed to be more effective and demonstrating greater 'political legitimacy' are multi-stakeholder in nature (Bernstein and Cashore 2007). Multi-stakeholder initiatives (MSIs) tend to be viewed positively because of their inclusiveness, consensus-building, sharing of knowledge and expertise, and procedural fairness (Fransen and Kolk 2007; Fransen 2011). Typically, MSIs include companies, civil society, and at times government representatives, and seek to create a balance between participants from the Global North and South. Decision-making should be equal among stakeholders, consensus-oriented, and structured so that no significant decision can be made in the face of opposition by one of the stakeholder groups. Transparency, among stakeholders and also externally to other interested parties, is another best practice.

Assurance frameworks, borrowing language from the UNGPs, allow companies to 'know and show' that they are respecting human rights, and make them accountable to stakeholders for their actions and omissions (Rasche 2009).[4] Ideally, an assurance framework encompasses some type of ongoing auditing/monitoring and certification procedures, whereby a company can demonstrate that it has assessed its compliance with the requirements of a code or standard and may receive some type of mark for a set time period indicating as much publicly. Auditing/monitoring can be undertaken by internal and/or external parties to a company, but greater credibility is granted to audits carried out by, and certifications granted by, independent, third parties without a direct financial tie to the company (O'Rourke 2006). Auditing should not be a check-the-box exercise, and should move a company beyond mere compliance to a demonstrated commitment to respect human rights as engrained in its corporate culture, management system, and business relationships. An additional component of an effective assurance framework is some type of grievance mechanism whereby internal parties, such as whistleblowers, and external parties, such as aggrieved affected individuals and communities, can file complaints. UNGPs Principle 31 lays out effectiveness criteria for non-judicial, company grievance mechanisms, namely legitimacy, accessibility, predictability, equitability, transparency, rights compatibility, a source of continuous learning, and based on engagement and dialogue with affected stakeholders. 'Knowing and showing' respect for human rights also requires public reporting on a company's efforts to address its human rights impacts (Principle 21). Finally, an assurance framework should be accompanied by some type of graduated sanctioning regime that provides scoped responses to instances of unintended and intended non-compliance (Behnam and MacLean 2011).

Benchmarking the ICoC Process and the ANSI/ASIS PSC series

This section assesses the extent to which both initiatives meet best practices and elaborates on particular outcomes in their institutional design resulting from ongoing negotiations between stakeholders. In terms of *standards-setting*, the ICoC is itself a human rights policy commitment by signatory PSCs, and references the 'Protect, Respect and Remedy' framework (Paragraph 2). It was developed under the leadership of the Geneva Centre for the Democratic Control of Armed Forces in a transparent, inclusive, multi-stakeholder fashion; drafts were discussed at stakeholder conventions and were open for public comment. However, the ICoC, as a statement of principles, lacks specificity and calls for the creation of operational and business practice standards (Paragraph 7). The reference to business practice standards was inserted by business and government stakeholders into the draft ICoC in light of developments on the US regulatory front. At the time, major US PSCs were lobbying Congress to require in the National Defense Authorization Act (NDAA) that the DoD develop and utilize some type of third party certification to an industry generated standard when procuring security. The 2010 and 2011 NDAA contained the provisions allowing the DoD to begin funding the development of PSC.1. The DoD and PSCs had greater familiarity with management standards than multi-stakeholder processes. However, aware that a stand-alone, business generated management standard would not be viewed as credible enough, the drafters and supporters of PSC.1 had to link it to the legitimacy of the multi-stakeholder ICoC process. Hence their description of PSC.1 as the business practice standard that operationalizes the ICoC. This view is not shared by many civil society organizations (CSOs), who were largely absent in the drafting of PSC.1 and initially had envisioned that the governance and oversight mechanism for the ICoC would develop operationalized standards.

While PSC.1 requires companies seeking to demonstrate conformance with the standard to develop a 'Statement of Conformance' in line with the ICoC, the Montreux Document, and applicable international law, including human rights law (Sec. 6.3), a number of CSOs believe that there are gaps between the human rights requirements of the ICoC and PSC.1. CSOs also call into question the multi-stakeholder nature of the PSC.1 standards-setting process since ASIS International selected participants for the Technical Committee drafting the standard from three categories, users/managers, producers/service providers, and general interest, which do not reflect the more common division of stakeholders into business, government, and civil society. The DoD sought to establish the multi-stakeholder nature of PSC.1 by referencing the number and different types of organizations on the Technical Committee, their level of expert-ise, and geographical representativeness.[5] The fact that supporters of PSC.1 lay claim to this criterion indicates the widespread acceptance of the norm of multi-stakeholder participation.

One reason for the perception of gaps between the two initiatives is differences in the language of risk management standards versus multi-stakeholder codes. As noted in the Introduction to this Handbook, we have become a risk-based society, and the focus on risk management is reflected in new regulatory arrangements. For human rights CSOs, PSC.1's language is unfamiliar; human rights violations are 'undesirable and disruptive events' and respect for human rights is risk minimization. In their view, PSC.1 does not go far enough in assessing and addressing human rights impacts on affected external stakeholders. In contrast, supporters of PSC.1 believe that embedding a risk assessment requirement into a management system, based on the idea of a continual improvement process, which seeks to identify and miti-gate human rights risks to PSCs and stakeholders is largely the same thing. The latter perspective would seem to align with the Commentary to UNGPs Principle 17 which states that human rights due diligence can be part of a broader risk management system, 'provided that it goes beyond simply identifying and managing material risks to the company itself, to include risks to rights-holders'.

Reflective of Fransen and Kolk's (2007) distinction between MSIs that merely consult versus involve civil society, the nature of *governance* in both initiatives and the role of CSOs varies. With the ANSI/ASIS PSC series completed, there are limited roles for CSOs to play, other than in regularly scheduled reviews of the standards, especially when compared to civil society's full and equal integration into all functions of the ICoCA as one of three pillars, including into the governance bodies which have decision-making authority over budgetary and membership issues, the creation of assurance frameworks, and determinations over non-compliance and sanctions. All three pillars of the ICoCA have equal voting rights, and voting requirements have been set up so that no one pillar can force through significant governance or process decisions.

However, representation from the global South has been lacking, something Fransen and Kolk (2007) find to be a common shortcoming of many MSIs. CSOs made a concerted effort to bring representatives from organizations in the global South on the first board. And while PSCs headquartered in the global South are signatories to the ICoC, fewer have joined the ICoCA, and none are on the board. The make-up of the CSO pillar has been a point of contention among stakeholders, and participating CSOs have successfully excluded academics and implementing CSOs in favour of watchdog CSOs, which ideally should increase the strin-gency of the MSI (Fransen and Kolk 2007). In the membership of the government pillar, territorial states are absent, and while the contracting states are large clients of the PSI, private sector clients (such as companies in other sectors and humanitarian aid and development organizations), which account for a greater share of overall PSI revenues, are missing. These factors not only impact the multi-stakeholder nature of the ICoCA, but also influence market drivers that will affect the global reach and uptake of the ICoC by PSCs.

The ICoCA has demonstrated a high degree of operational transparency, for example making available publicly the budget and notes from Board meetings. In contrast, the disag-gregated and marketized structure of the architecture around national management system standards is very different from the centralized governance role played by the ICoCA. In broad brush strokes, organizations like ASIS International set standards which are then recognized by national standards bodies, such as ANSI, as having been created in accordance with their requirements. Accreditation bodies, like the ANSI-ASQ National Accreditation Board (ANAB), create rules and have procedures for accrediting certification bodies to audit PSCs to standards – for example, as detailed in ISO 17011 Conformity Assessment – General Requirements for Accreditation Bodies Accrediting Conformity Assessment Bodies. Certification bodies have standards by which they carry out audits, such as ISO 17021 Conformity Assessment – Requirements for Bodies Providing Audit and Certification of Management Systems, and auditors are certified after participating in accredited training programs. ANAB and ANSI are members of an international oversight body, the International Accreditation Forum. At each of these organizational levels, there are procedures to file complaints if there is a reasonable belief that standards were not adhered to; however, the degree of transparency of the complaints processes is limited.

As a core component of an *assurance framework*, certification has been a major point of contention among stakeholders, in particular because of the first mover advantage that PSC.1, and the accompanying conformity assessment and auditing standard PSC.2, enjoyed because of their completion in advance of the establishment of the ICoCA. This has shaped negotiations in the ICoCA. The ICoCA's Articles of Association sketch out in a skeletal fashion the procedures it must develop for certification, reporting, monitoring, and complaints. While the ICoCA approved a certification procedure for recognizing external standards in July 2015, the UK government in 2013 funded and completed an effort with the UK Accreditation Service and a few PSCs to test pilot certification to PSC.1, and accredit the first certification bodies. This has created certain path dependencies that governments and PSCs have been able to leverage during ICoCA negotiations. First, participating governments and PSCs stress that PSC.1 is an auditable operationalization of the ICoC's principles and thus only a few, limited gaps exist between the two. Second, they leverage the notion of 'auditing fatigue' to argue that it would be unreasonable, and a likely deterrent to participation in the ICoCA, to require companies to become certified to two different standards. Third, they call into question the resources and capabilities of the ICoCA to conduct field monitoring in complex environments relative to professional auditors, as well as expressing reticence about the possibility of having to share confidential business information.

CSOs have retorted, expressing concern that certification to a management standard is largely a desk-based exercise that captures the existence of management policies and processes, but does not identify actual and potential human rights impacts, as would be required by an adequate human rights due diligence process as laid out in the UNGPs. They also raise the issues of lack of independence and transparency, since certification bodies are paid by the PSC and any audits are confidential between the two, unless the PSC opts for disclosure. The fact that to date there has been almost no transparency of the outcomes of the UK pilot project is telling. Although it is worth noting that despite best practices to the contrary, a survey of MSIs revealed that a little more than half rely on professional audit companies, the same method of monitoring implementation typical for business standards (Fransen and Kolk 2007: 674).

The compromise solution that is emerging can be described as a 'certification plus' model. The ICoCA would accept certification to PSC.1 – or an equivalent national or international standard – but reserves the right to request additional human rights specific information. This compromise would lend legitimacy to PSC.1 certification, while enabling the ICoCA to gather information on human rights impacts and conduct spot monitoring in areas of high risk or specific instances of non-compliance. The ICoCA would thus carve out a role for itself without duplicating certification to PSC.1.

Regarding other key components of assurance frameworks, both the ICoC and PSC.1 require company-level grievance mechanisms, although the ICoCA has yet to develop grievance procedures detailing the role of the Association in that process. Its Articles of Association foresee at a minimum annual reporting on its activities, whereas in PSC.1 it is up to the company to determine whether to communicate externally about significant risks, impacts to stakeholders, and control procedures. In terms of sanctions, the ICoCA has removal of a PSC from the Association as its ultimate sanction. PSCs which do not remedy non-conformances surfaced in an audit can ultimately lose their PSC.1 certifications.

Potential human rights effects

The ICoCA is just over one year old and the Board is currently developing key procedures of its institutional design elements. Assuming these adhere closely to the provisions of the Articles of Association, one can expect that the ICoCA largely will meet best practices with regards to multi-stakeholder governance and an independent assurance framework – albeit with one exception, the specificity of the ICoC. While PSC.1 does not fully meet best practices in multi-stakeholder standards-setting, and even some of its drafters acknowledge that the quality of auditing and effectiveness of oversight of auditors and certification bodies can vary, PSC.1 does reflect an operationalized, auditable management system standard. The successful implementation of the ICoC as a statement of aspirational principles will hinge on how it is made operational. Thus the issue of effectiveness really comes down to the nature of the relationship between these two initiatives.

There are two possible outcomes. The two initiatives could go through a fitting-process, resulting in convergence and complementarity (Avant 2013). This is a likely outcome, if the ICoCA continues to develop the 'certification plus' model of accepting certification to PSC.1 in addition to some human rights related information. For example, the Board could request that a PSC share all or aspects of its audit, and provide evidence of a thorough human rights due diligence process, to include meaningful consultation with affected stakeholders, assessment of actual and potential human rights impacts, and remedying of any human rights harms. The ICoCA could also function as a watch dog, conducting field monitoring in high risk environments, responding to company-specific complaints of non-compliance, and serving as a mediator when complaints cannot be remedied at the company-level. Convergence is favoured by governments and PSCs, although much depends on the outcome of current discussions about gaps between the two initiatives. Assuming that CSOs accept in large part certification to PSC.1, the result is likely to be an effective, but somewhat less stringent, oversight and enforcement mechanism than would have been possible had PSC.1 never been created.

The second possible outcome is divergence, with the ICoCA rejecting certification to PSC.1 and opting for the creation of its own operationalized standard and more stringent certification, monitoring, and grievance mechanisms. Likely, this would result in a small subset of PSCs, already operating to high standards, remaining in the ICoCA, while others would opt out and potentially seek certification to PSC.1. Some PSCs might choose to adhere to both standards. Much would depend on the PSI's clients' expectations. In terms of effectiveness, one could presume that the PSCs participating in a more rigorous ICoCA would be able to better mitigate any human rights risks linked to their operations, while those only receiving certification to PSC.1 would display differential human rights records in part dependent upon the quality of their auditors and the extent of their internal commitment to PSC.1. It is unclear, however, if the market is big enough for two separate certification initiatives. The ICoCA would not be financially viable were it to lose more PSCs and the backing of states supporting

PSC.1, like the US and UK. Both have already committed to requiring their contractors to comply with PSC.1. It is unclear where the market pressures to adhere to the ICoC would come from if it were delinked from certification to PSC.1, since no PSI clients, other than the UN, Switzerland, and the US Department of State through the Worldwide Protective Services to solicitation, have committed explicitly their support to the ICoC.

This second outcome appears to be unlikely. As discussed, the legitimacy of the norm of multi-stakeholder governance has resulted in recognition by both governments and companies that a management system standard on its own would not be credible in the eyes of PSI critics or the broader public. By developing PSC.1 and then writing it into procurement policies, the US government leveraged its power as a client and regulator of the PSI to give PSC.1 a first mover advantage, and created a path dependency that appears to have closed the possibility of the ICoCA's Board, in particular its CSO members, completely rejecting PSC.1.

Assuming convergence is likely, the overall effect on human rights protections should be positive, in particular if the ICoCA is able to bring in non-state clients of the industry and expand participation from the global South to increase its global reach. As foreseen in the Articles of Association, the ICoCA largely is reflective of the consensus in the field of TBG on best practices in terms of design characteristics. In part based on identified shortcomings in past MSIs, such as the Voluntary Principles on Security and Human Rights, the participating CSOs, and supportive PSCs and governments, ensured that the standards-setting process and governance were transparent, open, and multi-stakeholder and that there was an upfront commitment from participating PSCs to establish an effective governance and oversight mechanism to ensure conformance to the ICoC. Although it garners less attention than MSIs and certification schemes in other industries, perhaps because of the perceived 'dirty nature' of the PSI, the ICoCA represents a transnational business governance initiative that comes very close to meeting best practice in light of the negotiated nature of MSIs.

Both of these initiatives warrant further research. Internal to them, questions arise not only about the role of specific actors and organizations in shaping outcomes of contentious negotiations, but also about how various stakeholders manifest and leverage power, in particular considering the involvement of state actors. At the level of the institutional field, more insight is needed into the influence on negotiations of other TBG initiatives, both those specific to the PSI and those making up the larger field of business and human rights. At the international level, the effects of the widespread acceptance of (semi)privatized governance of the PSI on the role of the state, as the ultimate guarantor and provider of the right to security, needs further exploration. Finally, at a more applied level, human rights impact assessment methodologies for the PSI, to include identifying criteria and metrics for measuring potential and actual human rights impacts, need to be developed and piloted.

Notes

1   For a database of national laws with regard to regulating private military and security companies, see the Private Security Monitor at http://psm.du.edu/national_regulation. See also chapters 24 and 25 in this volume.

2   For purposes of full disclosure, among the activities I have participated in either as a volunteer thematic expert at Amnesty International USA or as an academic expert are multi-stakeholder forums to revise the code of conduct of the US industry trade association, the Technical Committee responsible for developing ANSI/ASIS PSC.1, multi-stakeholder consultations on the ICoC and ICoCA, and the Project Committee that is drafting a new ISO standard for security operations.

3   See also ISEAL's Code of Good Practice for Setting Social and Environmental Standards, available at www.isealalliance.org/our-work/defining-credibility/codes-of-good-practice/standard-setting-code.

4   See also ISEAL's Code of Good Practice for Assuring Compliance with Social and Environmental Standards, available at www.isealalliance.org/sites/default/files/ISEAL-Assurance-Code-Version-1.0.pdf.
5   See Christopher Mayer's webinar briefing, Implementation of Montreux Commitments: Comparative Perspectives – USA, available at http://ihrib.org/webinar-recordings-montreux-fives-years-on-assessing-current-status-development-implementation-international-standards-private-mili tary-security-industry.

Bibliography

Avant, D. (2013) *Linking Power, Purpose and Legitimacy: The Montreux/ICoC Network and Global Governance of Private Military and Security Services*, working paper, Denver, CO: University of Denver.

Behnam, M. and MacLean, T. (2011) 'Where is the Accountability in International Accountability Standards? A Decoupling Perspective', *Business Ethics Quarterly* 21(1): 45–72.

Bernstein, S. and Cashore, B. (2007) 'Can Non-state Global Governance be Legitimate? An Analytical Framework', *Regulation and Governance* 1(4): 1–25.

De Nevers, R. (2010) 'The Effectiveness of Self-Regulation by the Private Military and Security Industry', *Journal of Public Policy* 30(2): 219–40.

DeWinter-Schmitt, R. (ed.) (2013) *Montreux Five Years On: An Analysis of State Efforts to Implement Montreux Document Legal Obligations and Good Practices*, Washington, DC: American University Washington College of Law Center for Human Rights & Humanitarian Law and NOVACT.

Dingwerth, K. and Pattberg, P. (2009) 'World Politics and Organizational Fields: The Case of Transnational Sustainability Governance', *European Journal of International Relations* 15(4): 707–44.

Eberlein, B., Abbott, K. W., Black, J., Meidinger, E. and Wood, S. (2014) 'Transnational Business Governance Interactions: Conceptualization and Framework for Analysis', *Regulation and Governance* 8(1): 1–21.

Fransen, L. (2011) 'Multi-stakeholder Governance and Voluntary Programme Interactions: Legitimation Politics in the Institutional Design of Corporate Social Responsibility', *Socio-Economic Review* 10(1):163–92.

Fransen, L. and Kolk, A. (2007) 'Global Rule-Setting for Business: A Critical Analysis of Multi-stakeholder Standards', *Organization* 14(5): 667–84.

Gilbert, D., Rasche, A. and Waddock, S. (2011) 'Accountability in a Global Economy: The Emergence of International Accountability Standards', *Business Ethics Quarterly* 21(1): 23–44.

International Committee of the Red Cross (2012) 'Special Issue: Business, Violence, and Conflict', *International Review of the Red Cross* 94(887).

Leander, A. (2012) 'What Do Codes of Conduct Do? Hybrid Constitutionalization and Militarization in Military Markets', *Global Constitutionalism* 1(1): 91–119.

O'Rourke, D. (2006) 'Multi-stakeholder Regulation: Privatizing or Socializing Global Labor Standards?', *World Development* 34(5): 899–918.

Ralby, I. (2015) 'Accountability for Armed Contractors', *Fletcher Security Review* 2(1): 1–7.

Rasche, A. (2009) 'Toward a Model to Compare and Analyze Accountability Standards – The Case of the UN Global Compact', *Corporate Social Responsibility and Environmental Management* 16(4): 192–205.

Scherer, A. G. and Palazzo, G. (2011) 'The New Political Role of Business in a Globalized World: A Review of a New Perspective on CSR and its Implications for the Firm, Governance, and Democracy', *Journal of Management Studies* 48(4): 899–931.

INDEX

Printed in Great Britain
by Amazon

19300076R00169